James II

James II

Maurice Ashley

J.M. DENT & SONS LTD

London   Toronto   Melbourne

First published 1977
© Maurice Ashley, 1977

Printed in Great Britain
by Biddles Ltd. Guildford,
Surrey and bound at
the Aldine Press Letchworth
Herts.

for
J.M. Dent & Sons Ltd
Aldine House, Albemarle Street, London

This book is set in 11 on 13pt IBM Baskerville

ISBN 0 460 12021 2

British Library Cataloguing in Publication Data

Ashley, Maurice
    James II,
    1. James, *II*, King of England
    942.06'7'0924   DA450

    ISBN 0-460-12021-2

Contents

Illustrations

A Note on Dates

During the seventeenth century there was a difference of ten days between the English method of dating (Old Style) and that used in most other European countries (New Style). Occasionally in referring to events that took place on the European mainland both styles are given; but where only one date is given it is the Old Style.

Tout comprendre c'est tout pardonner

Voltaire

I.

Introduction: the Tragedy of James II

Surprising as it must seem now to historians who know what was going to happen to him afterwards, when James Duke of York succeeded his brother Charles II as King of England, Scotland and Ireland on 6 February 1685 many of his subjects welcomed the event enthusiastically. It is true that Charles had been popular, accessible and easy-going, but his comparative laziness, his deference to France, his extravagances and open debaucheries had detracted from the respect he might have commanded as a ruler. James's reputation was different and promising. The Duke of Queensberry, about to be appointed Royal High Commissioner in Scotland, was told by a correspondent in London (the future Earl of Melfort) after James's accession: 'I assure your Grace there is the fairest hopes that ever any kingdom of England had', and the same correspondent informed the Duke four days later that 'the King is the darling of the City'.[1] The Earl of Ailesbury, who knew him intimately, was to write in his memoirs that he was 'a prince that had all the moral virtues', 'the most honest and sincere man that I ever knew', 'a great and good Englishman', in sum 'a most good and worthy prince'.[2] His financial probity was not questioned; his conscientiousness was assumed; he did not allow his pleasures to interfere with business. Looking back on his early life, his subjects saw James as a brave and resolute man, always loyal to his brother. The only doubt expressed about him was that as his religion, Roman Catholicism, was different from that of the vast majority of his subjects, if papists were too blatantly favoured by him, this might revive the pent-up emotions brought to the surface by the spurious Popish Plot seven years before and thus gravely injure his political opportunities. Yet even his open avowal of his religion was half-admired. Unlike his brother, who had not confessed to his conversion from the Anglican Church, of which he

9

was the Supreme Governor, until he lay on his death-bed, James time and again insisted that however gloomy the outlook appeared for him during Charles's reign, he had a good stock of patience and would never on any account change his religion.

The enthusiasm for the new King persisted at least until the Parliament which had assembled at the beginning of his reign was recalled in the autumn of 1685. John Evelyn, who knew James personally and had during his life seen many comings and goings, a staunch Anglican, now sixty-five years old, wrote in his diary apropos a visit by James to Portsmouth to inspect the shipyards and docks:

> What I observed in this journey: I find that infinite industry, sedulity, gravity and great understanding and experience of affairs in his Majesty, that I cannot but predict much happiness to the nation, and if he persist (as I am confident he will) there could nothing be more desired, to accomplish our prosperity, but that he were of the national religion: for certainly such a prince never had the nation since it was one.[3]

When James was young he had outshone Charles; he was thought to be handsome with excellent manners and the ability to speak French fluently.[4] He had enlisted in the French army to fight against the Spaniards when he was only eighteen. After five weeks in the field his old friend, Sir George Radcliffe wrote: 'The Duke of York hath gotten a great reputation and power in the French army; he is bold and active.' After he returned to Paris from his second campaign Edward Hyde, who was to become Earl of Clarendon and James's father-in-law, thought he had 'much grown and improved' and had earned 'extraordinary esteem with the army'. But even before he left on that campaign Hyde had asserted that he was 'a gallant gentleman and had the best reputation of any young man in Christendom'.[5] Marshal Turenne, the famous French general under whom James served, thought so well of him after only a short time that he entrusted him with real authority. Indeed Turenne is reputed to have said of him 'There was the greatest prince and like to be the best general of his time'.[6] Whether that is apocryphal or not, it is certain that Charles II was told that none had done their duty better than the Duke of York, but was advised to rebuke him for exposing himself unnecessarily to danger.[7] After peace was concluded Turenne thought so highly of James that he offered on his own responsibility to provide him with French troops to head an invasion of England in 1659. Charles II had in fact fought courageously at the battle of Worcester, but no one except his mother was told much about that. James's dutiful soldiering was contrasted with the happy-go-lucky behaviour of his brother as he moved from Court to Court in western Europe dancing, drinking and womanizing.

During Charles II's reign James had continued to distinguish himself. He had held the title of Lord High Admiral since he was a child, but now he was able to treat his duties seriously. Constantly he visited the docks and shipyards and was content to give his orders directly to Samuel Pepys, the ablest member of the Navy Board, and make sure that they were carried out. Not only was James a first-class administrator, but he fought bravely and successfully in the two wars against the Dutch. In the bloody battle of Lowestoft in 1665 he won a considerable victory, remaining on the quarterdeck while his fellow admirals and captains were being killed and wounded all around him. The Dutch recoiled, but James was not allowed to profit from his victory. In the second Dutch war the story was largely repeated. At the memorable and fiercely fought battle of Southwold Bay in 1672 James exercised the command and repulsed the Dutch even though his Admiral of the Blue, the Earl of Sandwich, drowned, and he himself was forced by chain shot and cannon ball to abandon his flagship. Once again he was forbidden to pursue the Dutch to their harbours and next year because of the passage by Parliament of the first Test Act, which prohibited Roman Catholics from occupying public offices, he felt obliged to give up his command. Nevertheless James was 'looked upon as the darling of the Nation for having so freely and so often ventured his life for the honour and interest of the King and Country'.[8] All Charles II had done as an admiral was to handle a fleet rather ineptly when he was eighteen. Without question James had earned his reputation both as a soldier and sailor as well as a man of honour and an outstanding prince.

As long as James remained by his brother's side during the trauma of the late 1670s he had continually urged Charles to be tough. The Duke was not himself directly attacked by the inventors of the Popish Plot, but his co-religionists were and because of his own faith a tremendous effort was put out to exclude him from succession to the throne. James fumed over his brother's suppleness and flexibility. 'Now or never is the time to save the monarchy', he exclaimed.[9] He urged Charles to take a firm stand to halt a republican revolution. Yet he always obeyed the King. A French ambassador in

London noted that while no one could show more zeal than the Duke for the interests of his brother, James himself was 'of a firmer spirit, had a more decisive mind, and was more conscientious in business'.[10]

When in 1679 Charles sent James away from England in the hope that the anti-papist fury would subside, first to join the Council of Scotland and then as his Royal Commissioner in Edinburgh, James continued to earn praise. 'We enjoy great peace and quietness in this country', wrote a contemporary, 'His Highness is beloved by all. His advices are mostly followed in the Council. The highlanders . . . especially the MacDonald are infinitely obliged to him.'[11] Another Scotsman, writing twenty-two months later, reported:

> His Highness doth carry himself with so great temper and diligence, is so just in his payments, so merciful in all penal matters, so impartial in giving his judgment in court, so humble and civil and obliging to all sorts of people that he hath gained the affection of all understanding and oblige-able persons, though there be a sort of Presbyterians . . . whom nothing can oblige.[12]

On his return from Scotland when the Whigs' attempts to exclude him from the throne had finally failed he was welcomed by King Charles as his right-hand man. According to the future Bishop of Salisbury, Dr Gilbert Burnet, for the last three years of Charles's reign James 'directed all our counsels with so absolute authority the King seemed to have left the whole government in his hands'.[13] His aim, it seems, was to establish a mildly authoritarian form of government not only in England but also in Ireland and Scotland where he had already made his presence felt. It was a dress rehearsal for the time when he would step into his brother's shoes. Hardly any King of England had come to the throne under such auspicious circumstances or with such a reputation for firmness and courage.

And yet by the end of a reign, which lasted for fewer than four years, what a transformation was to take place in James's character and outlook! The man who before and immediately after he became king had boasted of his determination, fearlessness and implacability showed himself to be irresolute and frightened when the dubious methods he employed to secure equality of opportunity for dissenters from the Church of England engendered a plot to overthrow him; and this in turn was followed by an invitation from revolutionaries to his nephew, William of Orange, to come over and compel him to change his ways. After Prince William of Orange landed successfully in Devon James optimistically relied upon an army numerically stronger than that of his nephew to retain his tottering hold on his kingdom. But when his commander-in-chief, Lord Feversham, went on his knees and implored the King to order the arrest of those leading men who were known or suspected to be on William's side, he was unable to make up his mind and rejected the idea of any bold stroke.[14] Instead of taking over the command of his army, strategically well placed at Salisbury, he stayed with it for only a few days during which his nose bled profusely and then hurried back to London lest its citizens should rise against him as they had done against his father. Where now was the martial figure who had been praised so highly by Turenne? James told his commander-in-chief that if he could have trusted his army he might have 'had one blow for it',[15] but instead he distrusted the weapon that he himself had forged. He said to Feversham 'though I know there were many loyal and brave men amongst you, yet you know yourself, and several of the general officers told me, it was no ways advisable to venture myself at their head.' What a rejection of leadership, what an excuse for cowardice! Already James had abandoned everything for which he had stood and had tried to achieve during his reign, making concessions right and left in the hope of placating his opponents. Pathetically he begged the bishops of the Church of England, some of whom he had accused of plotting against him and had put on trial only a few months earlier, to publish a manifesto in his support. Then he made a gesture of offering to come to terms with William, but he refused to fight him and aimed to escape in disguise to France as quickly as he could to throw himself on the mercy of the Court of Versailles.

Pressed by the King of France, who was at war with William of Orange, James landed in Ireland in 1689, where the bulk of the population were his co-religionists, and for a time played with the idea of using Ireland as a base from which to invade Scotland or England; having refused even to lead the trained and well-armed force that he had built up during his reign, he now indulged in day-dreams of regaining his thrones with a scratch army of poverty-stricken Irishmen. But in fact he did not have the courage to move out from behind his fortifications to defeat a smaller army dispatched by William to Ulster and in the following year was ignominiously defeated at the battle of the Boyne. He blamed his army and not himself for the fiasco, saying despairingly that he would lead the

Irish no longer and 'shift for himself'.[16] As the late Godfrey Davies wrote, James's efforts to save his throne in 1688 and his attempts to recover it later 'reveal a curious blend of childish folly, petty revengefulness and a moral cowardice' — strong language but on the surface at least justified.[17]

When after his abysmal adventure in Ireland James returned to France the courtiers at Paris pictured him as a tired old man whose French, once his best subject, had become poor and whose stories of his escapes grew boring. Of course he was now in his late fifties, but he was healthy enough. That was the age at which ten years later the first Duke of Marlborough won his famous victories.

Thenceforward during his exile James sank into an attitude of resignation even when his wife and Louis XIV prodded him into taking a proper part in plans for renewed operations against William, who had succeeded him as King of England. Now all he looked for was finding some excuse to press for French troops to embark first from Calais so that he might lead an army from behind. His daily prayer was 'I give Thee, O my God, most humble thanks for taking my three kingdoms from me' first because it had aroused him from the 'lethargy of sin' and secondly because such humiliation was a sure mark of eternal salvation.[18] He came to realize that everything in the world was but 'vanity and vexation of spirit' and he frequently told his wife that he wanted to die soon.[19] Such was his self-mortification and ultimate collapse.

The aim of this biography is to trace in some detail the story that has been briefly outlined. James has not had what may be called a good press, though one or two Roman Catholic writers have treated him sympathetically. Whig historians have dismissed him as a bigot of slow and narrow understanding and an obstinate, harsh and unforgiving temper. Yet one can admire, or at any rate comprehend, equally the brave and able military commander and the devoted and dedicated kind of monk. As Voltaire wrote, *'tout comprendre c'est tout pardonner.'* Other historical figures — the Emperor Charles V, for instance — have covered the same kind of journey through life. But in James's case at least the metamorphosis was tragic.

2.

Growing up

James was born on 14 October 1633 in St James's Palace London when his mother, Queen Henrietta Maria, was twenty-four. His grandfather on his mother's side was the Protestant Henry of Navarre, afterwards King of France, who had thought that Paris was well worth a Mass. (James, as it happened, was to be ironically congratulated about a century later by the Bishop of Rheims for renouncing three kingdoms for a Mass.)[1] James's mother, who was married by proxy when she was fourteen and came to England guarded and surrounded by Capuchin monks, was a devoted Roman Catholic, obedient to the Pope; her influence upon her second son, though not noticeable in her own life time, proved more profound than she could realize. Owing also to his descent from Henry IV, a veritable polygamist, James was to inherit his insatiable love for women or at any rate for sex. His father, Charles I and his paternal grandfather, James I, had rather less to offer by way of heredity. Both of them had been enthusiastic huntsmen, though James II was never to become quite such a devotee of that particular sport as his namesake had been. Like his brother, Charles II, James revered his father's memory and could never forget or forgive his execution upon the scaffold outside Whitehall in January 1649 which took place when he was a boy of fifteen. That event affected him in two ways: for while he always maintained that if his father had been tougher and more ruthless he could have avoided his fate, he himself when he became the victim of a rebellion was so fearful of suffering the same kind of capital punishment as had been meted out to his father that he fled from his capital and abandoned his kingdom.

When James was a baby he was described as a 'fair and lusty child', just as his eldest brother was called 'dark and lusty'.[2] The well-known portrait after Sir Anthony van Dyck painted when James was

15

our and which was hung over the breakfast table in Whitehall
suggests that he was a pretty boy.[3] His baptism on 24
November was a grand occasion. He was carried in by the Countess
of Denbigh, the First Lady of the Queen's Bedchamber, accompanied by his governess, the Countess of Dorset, and waited on
by the nurse, the midwife and the cradle-rocker. To his christening
came the Lord Mayor and Aldermen of London, the Judges of the
Common Law, the Barons of the Exchequer, the Judges of the
Admiralty, the two Lord Chief Justices and the Lord Chief Baron.
After the ceremony the child was brought to his father and mother
to receive their blessings in their bedchamber, to which were admitted all the lords and ladies and others of 'fitting quality'. The
Lord Mayor of London, resplendent in a scarlet gown and wearing
chains of gold, presented James with 'a fair bowl', which was at first
thought to be made of gold but turned out to be silver, filled with
500 pieces. His sponsors did not attend the baptism, but sent
deputies. Among them was James's aunt, the attractive, widowed
Queen of Bohemia, whose husband had lost two thrones, as James
was to do in the years to come; the other sponsors were her eldest
son, Charles Louis, and Prince Frederick Henry of Orange.[4]

James's birth had taken place at the happiest moment in his
parents' lives. England was then prosperous and at peace. The House
of Commons, called in 1628, which had been obstreperous and
critical of the King's policies, had been dissolved four years before
James was born and the King by being fairly economical and
avoiding foreign entanglements had not needed to summon another
parliament; he ruled without one for eleven years. Parliaments
anyway were always tiresome for the Stuarts who all felt they could
manage much better without them. Van Dyck's paintings depicted a
handsome contented-looking family, but of course Van Dyck was a
flatterer. After James had been released from the care of his nurses
he was given the same governess, the Countess of Dorset, and the
same governor, the Marquis of Hertford, as were responsible for his
brother Charles. Although Charles was three-and-a-half years his
senior, the two boys were playmates, as were also George and
Francis Villiers, sons of James I's and Charles I's favourite, the first
Duke of Buckingham, who had been assassinated five years before
James Duke of York and of Albany was born; these boys had been
virtually adopted by Charles I. They lived together at a separate
Court at Richmond in Surrey where the four boys were excellently

16

looked after. The palace, built by King Henry VII, lay between Richmond Green and the Thames, and had been presented by Charles I to his wife. Their governor, Hertford, was an elderly man who preferred indoor to outdoor entertainment; with his love of books and a secluded life he was scarcely an ideal companion for high-spirited boys. However, they were also provided with a teacher of archery, a fencing instructor and a dancing master. The background of their lives was the royal Court at Whitehall where a notable standard of good taste and good manners prevailed. For Charles was a patron of the arts while his French wife followed in the footsteps of James's paternal grandmother, Anne of Denmark, in enjoying and taking part in masques and balls set to French and English music. But by the time when James might normally have begun to profit from a full and wide education political clouds appeared over England and Scotland and these halcyon days came abruptly to an end.

Queen Henrietta Maria was not a fussy mother;[5] she had too many other occupations. By the time James was born she and her husband were immersed in one another and hated the idea of any separation. Besides sharing in the ceremonial duties of the Court, moving from palace to palace, rehearsing her parts in masques and pastorals, she took seriously the task, implicitly provided for in her marriage treaty, of being the protectress of English Roman Catholics. Cardinal Richelieu, whose influence with Henrietta Maria's mother, Marie de Médici, and her brother, King Louis XIII of France, was tremendous, had insisted that this marriage treaty should not be agreed to unless stipulations were made in it for relaxing the penal laws against Roman Catholics in England. The Queen was expected to exert her influence with her husband to see that these promises were kept. Furthermore her chapels (one was specially built for her at Somerset House) were thrown open to English Catholics, she kept up a correspondence with the Pope, and welcomed and entertained unofficial nuncios at her Court.

In an often quoted sentence Gilbert Burnet wrote of James: 'the prince was much neglected in his childhood, during the time he was under his father's care.'[6] But, after all, in those days it was unusual for kings and queens to take a close personal interest in the upbringing of their children. A queen did her part by bearing them at frequent intervals — Henrietta Maria had seven children between 1628 and 1640 — and a King's main duty after selecting his children's nursing staff, was to write letters of advice for his heirs which in practice they generally ignored.[7] Royal children were given their separate establishments, provided with their own servants, ranging from wet nurses to governors, and were not seen by their parents unless sent for. Young James was not stinted of money for food, clothes and playthings. The reason why he did not receive an entirely satisfactory education was simply that before he was nine civil war broke out in 1642. The city of Oxford, where he lived from then until he neared adolescence, was a military headquarters and not, as in normal times, abuzz with polite learning. Even so James had tutors who were College Fellows; he was taught to write legibly and spell adequately; his French was good and he learned to play the guitar. Later he became a keen student of theology though the admirable and judicious Richard Hooker failed to convince him of the apostolic authority of the Church of England.[8]

James's father was not a successful monarch.[9] He was aloof, conscientious, polite, but he was humourless and far too sure that in changing times he was only responsible to God for his actions. His own father, James I, had also believed in his divine right to govern, but he had never levied taxes without legal or parliamentary approval and he had never imprisoned members of parliament without showing cause. Charles I did both these things and also ruled the Church in a way which provoked the rising puritan movement both in England and Scotland. So, after the long interval between parliaments, the House of Commons, which was summoned in 1640, and invited to help the King deal with his recalcitrant Scottish subjects, who resented being compelled to accept religious conformity, showed itself extremely critical of the King's conduct of his affairs during the eleven years of his autocratic rule. And thus developed surprisingly quickly a headlong struggle for power between Parliament and the King which, after Charles had refused to surrender all his prerogative rights — though he voluntarily surrendered some of them — finally deteriorated into civil war.

One of Charles's defects, which was in fact common to all the Stuart rulers of England, was his inability to be loyal to his Ministers. He never cared for the capable and ruthless Earl of Strafford, who after a long delay he appointed as his Lord Lieutenant in Ireland, and he rarely accepted the advice of Archbishop William Laud, though Laud was his chosen instrument for reforming and purifying the Church. When in 1641 the Commons struck at Strafford by impeaching him as an 'evil counsellor' Charles despairingly tried to save his life by sending his eldest son, the Prince of Wales, to the House of Lords with a letter asking that his Minister should be punished with close imprisonment for life rather than by execution as a traitor. It was all in vain. And from that time onwards the Commons asked more and more by way of constitutional concessions from the King, culminating in the demand that he should hand over the control of the militia, the only armed force of any size in the country, to Parliament, together with the choice of his officers and principal servants.

These electrifying events could have meant only little to James, who was not yet eight years old when Strafford perished on the scaffold. But in the years that lay ahead he was to realize how weak and evasive his father had been and so he determined to be strong himself. The first clear consciousness of what was happening came to the young Prince in the spring of 1642, a year after the death of Strafford. By then Charles I had left London and though negotiations continued between him and Parliament, both sides had begun to prepare for civil war. The King set up his headquarters at York and ordered the Marquis of Hertford, in whose care James had been left, to bring him in the spring of 1642 from Richmond to York where he was greeted with bonfires and a guard of loyal troops and was created a Knight of the Garter.[10]

On 22 April 1642 the young Duke was sent nominally on a pleasure trip to visit Sir John Hotham, the Governor of Hull, who had been instructed to hold the town and its arsenal for Parliament.[11] Sir John was a member of parliament for the neighbouring borough of Beverley and he had no reason to love the King who sent him to prison in 1627 for refusing to collect a forced loan. But he could not very well object to receiving a friendly visit from James and his retinue, which consisted of about fifty persons including his cousin, Charles Louis Elector Palatine, two or three members of the nobility, guards and equerries. Charles hoped that once James and his party were within the town the Governor could not very well refuse to admit the King himself also. However, when next day Hotham was informed by James that his father was coming to dine with him that very afternoon with a party of Yorkshire gentlemen and a troop of horse, Hotham was pressed by one of the two local members of parliament who happened to be there to close the gates and deny Charles entry. Hotham obliged, though reluctantly, as time was to show. Apparently James was unaware of what was happening outside the town when his father arrived and went on eating a sumptuous dinner to which he and his entourage were being entertained. After abandoning his efforts to beguile the garrison, Charles perforce had to withdraw on the following day; he was followed back to York by the Duke and 'his crestfallen party of decoy ducks' who were allowed to leave one by one.[12] It was certainly a strange and memorable episode in the life of a young boy. James must have recalled it vividly, for he was to claim in his memoirs that if his father had acted quickly and boldly he could have surprised the Governor and seized the town and arsenal without difficulty; for at that time the Mayor, Aldermen and citizens of Hull had no reason to defy their King, while the Governor had simply been intimidated by his fellow member of parliament.

Negotiations having broken down at Hull and elsewhere, the King raised his standard at Nottingham to signify the opening of civil war; then he moved to Derby and finally to Shrewsbury to enlist soldiers from Wales and the west, while the commander-in-chief of the parliamentarian army, the Earl of Essex, recruited men largely in the south and then advanced from London to Worcester with the intention of challenging Charles to a decisive battle. The two forces of not unequal strength fought the first major battle of the war at Edgehill near Warwick on 23 October. Both James and his elder brother were present, but the King was determined that they should be kept away from danger. First, he asked the Duke of Richmond to look after them, but he refused; so did the Earl of Dorset, who said that 'he would not be thought a coward for the sake of any King's sons in Christendom'.[13] Finally Sir William Howard, who commanded fifty King's Pensioners, a kind of life-guard, most of whom were rather long in the tooth, was strictly ordered to take care of the young princes. While the King moved forward to inspirit his infantry, Howard carried his charges out of range of musket shot from the enemy, but was perturbed to discover a body of parliamentarian horse advancing towards them on the left of the royal foot. He then took them into a small barn, which was being used as a field dressing station, whereupon the enemy cavalry, being under the impression that they had come into contact with a sizeable reserve, hastily withdrew. After that Howard took the princes even farther away from the battlefield to the top of Edgehill.[14] It was now dusk and by the time night drew on the fighting ceased, each side claiming a victory.

After the battle James accompanied his father to Banbury and thence to Oxford where he remained throughout the first civil war. War-time Oxford was crowded and busy.[15] Not only was it the site of the Cavalier headquarters, but many strangers from all parts of England joined the inhabitants and university scholars so that the centre of the city was more like a slum than the home of gentlefolk.

James, it is clear, was left largely to his own devices in spite of the efforts of several tutors; his father was absorbed in war and politics; and his mother, who had returned after many adventures buying arms for her husband in Holland, remained there for less than a year until she fled to Exeter so as to give birth to her youngest daughter, as she hoped, in greater safety. The King took James with him when he vainly attempted to capture the city of Gloucester from the Roundheads and was defeated by the Earl of Essex at the first battle of Newbury on the way back. Next year James was summoned by writ to the House of Lords when a Cavalier parliament met in Oxford in rivalry to that at Westminster. In 1645, soon after James's eleventh birthday, the King ordered the Prince of Wales to leave Oxford for the south-west of England to act as nominal commander-in-chief of the royalist forces which at that time were still in control there.[16] By then the Queen had gone back to her birthplace, Paris, whence she animated her husband to offer every concession to regain his throne. But Charles was reluctant to give up fighting, though he wished to ensure the succession of the Stuart line, whatever fate befell him. He therefore planned that his heir apparent should join his mother in France if things grew too hot for him in England. James thus lost the company of his elder brother, while his younger brother, Henry, was a hostage of Parliament in London. The battle of Naseby, fought in June of that year, virtually brought the first civil war to an end, although it was not until over a year later that Oxford surrendered to the parliamentarians under the command of Sir Thomas Fairfax. By the terms of the treaty whereas James's cousins, Prince Rupert and Rupert's brother, Maurice, were permitted to go abroad, James was to 'be delivered into the hands of Parliament to be disposed of according to their pleasure': obviously another valuable pawn.[17] Before the city capitulated Charles I had escaped from it in disguise with the intention of seeking help from his Scottish subjects.

At some point before the King left Oxford James had been placed under the care of Sir George Radcliffe, who had been a favourite of the late Earl of Strafford and was entirely loyal to the royalist cause. Fairfax instructed Radcliffe to take the boy up to London and hand him over to the care of Algernon Percy, the tenth Earl of Northumberland. Northumberland was a wealthy magnifico, belonging to the *élite* of the English aristocracy. He was proud, able and rich and had a superb collection of Italian paintings including a Leonardo da Vinci. He had been excellently treated by the King, who in 1638 appointed him Lord High Admiral until such time as James, who had been Lord High Admiral in name since he was four years old, could actually take over the duties of the office. Northumberland was among the first to join John Pym in his attacks on the King's Government, one of the nobility who refute the notion that the civil war was a class war. He was given £7,500 a year for James's maintenance; and he provided the Duke with an embroidered coach in which he was allowed to go driving in Hyde Park. Northumberland had been previously in charge of James's sister Elizabeth and his brother Henry Duke of Gloucester. They were all housed in St James's Palace which must have seemed more of a home to James than Oxford had been. James was conveyed to the palace 'in great and fitting state', but his Oxford retinue was dismissed and new servants placed under him.[18] Nevertheless he was allowed some freedom. When later Charles I, having been handed over by the Scots to the English Parliament and then taken under the control of Fairfax's army, was placed in honourable captivity at Hampton Court, James was permitted several times to visit him there. The King instructed him to be loyal to his elder brother (who was now in Paris), never to betray the cause of the Stuart monarchy, and to escape from parliamentarian custody if he could and join his mother and brother in France.

Northumberland who treated the young princes and princess with an adequate degree of deference, had wanted to keep them not at St James's Palace but at Syon House in Isleworth, Middlesex, which had been built by his father at the cost of £9,000 and had a pretty walled garden.[19] There they might have played happily together, but it would have been so isolated as to hamper any attempts from outside to engineer their escape.

When James had been handed over by Sir George Radcliffe, he had lost the company of everyone he trusted and when he was allowed to see his father it was under a close military escort. To that extent escape was difficult. On the other hand, St James's, being in the centre of Westminster, was far from being as isolated as Syon House. The palace had several entrances and exits, one of them leading through the garden into St James's park.[20] That was clearly one way out for him. The house contained many rooms, four or five courtyards and a number of backstairs none of which was guarded. Why should they have been? It was, after all, only a houseful of children. Furthermore James was permitted to receive visitors and letters from outside.

During the winter of 1647 a plot was devised to enable him to escape with the connivance of Mrs Kilvert, a sister of the Bishop of Salisbury, and one Hill, a barber. But a letter written by James in cypher about this plan was intercepted, and the scheme was detected. James was examined by a committee of the two Houses of Parliament which threatened to send him to the Tower of London if he did not reveal the key to his cypher.[21] He had asked Mrs Kilvert to hide the key, which had been given him by his father, and at first told the committee that he had burnt it; however, under pressure, he handed it over and promised not to write nor to receive any letters in the future without informing the Earl of Northumberland and he actually refused to accept one sent to him by his mother. Northumberland was ordered to keep a closer watch over him; nevertheless James did contrive to escape.[22]

This time — it was now April 1648 — the escape was much more elaborately planned. The principal agents were Anne Murray and her lover, Colonel Joseph Bamfield.[23] These two characters were young and enterprising. Bamfield had received instructions from Charles I and a large sum of money was put at his disposal to cover the necessary expenses. Bamfield was allowed to see James and handed him a letter from his father. Then Bamfield managed to obtain the measurements of James's height and waist so as to have a girl's clothes made to fit him. The tailor, whom Bamfield employed, remarked that he had never known of a woman of so low a stature and so large a waist. Still, he produced a dress of a light colour with black stripes and an under-petticoat of scarlet. A week or two before the day chosen for his escape James had started playing games of hide-and-seek with his sister Elizabeth and his younger brother, Harry, a game singularly suited to the intricacies of St James's Palace. After they had eaten their supper on the evening of 20 April James went up to his sister's room to lock up a little dog which inconveniently was accustomed to following him everywhere. Then,

23

having somehow got hold of the requisite key, he slipped down the backstairs into the park; after he had locked the gate behind him, he carefully destroyed the gardener's own key. In the park he was met by Bamfield who threw a cloak around him and put a periwig on his head. A hackney coach stood ready for them. They drove to Salisbury House in the Strand. Then they took a boat and rowed towards London bridge, keeping to the north side of the river. Landing near the bridge, they went to a house belonging to a surgeon where Anne Murray and her maid were awaiting them. They dressed up James as a girl, and the outfit contrived by the tailor fitted perfectly; indeed they thought the boy looked very pretty in it. Thus disguised James returned with Bamfield to the river where they found a four-oared barge whose master was willing to help. Putting out his lights and with the wind behind him he quickly passed the blockhouses at Gravesend by moonlight without being challenged. At the Hope anchorage near the mouth of the Thames a small Dutch sailing vessel (or pink) was ready for them. In it James sailed across the North Sea to land without mishap in Flushing. Thence the party travelled through Middleburg to Dordrecht in Holland; James was still dressed as a girl when they reached there. Bamfield went on to The Hague to convey the news of the Duke's safe arrival to his sister Mary and her husband, Prince William II of Orange. Delightedly they sent a yacht to fetch him.

Meanwhile in London the Earl of Northumberland had discovered James's disappearance from St James's Palace and at once informed the Speaker of the House of Commons, who sent orders that all passengers embarking from ports in south-eastern England were to be held and examined. But these orders arrived too late. Nevertheless the Earl was exonerated from all blame on the ground that James had given his word of honour not to try to escape again.[24] James's allowance was of course stopped; but a larger allowance was given to Northumberland for his care of Henry Duke of Gloucester, the last of the Stuart princes left in the power of Parliament. Northumberland wisely carried him off to Syon House. After the Restoration Northumberland succeeded in making his peace with Charles and James. He must have been relieved that he had not prevented the Duke's escape.

Two months after James arrived in Holland, the cause of the royalists, although they had been comprehensively defeated in the first civil war, appeared to have brightened. Charles I, like his son, breaking his parole, fled from Hampton Court, where he was a prisoner of the Roundhead army, to the Isle of Wight. Here, although his presence was an embarrassment to the Governor of the island, he was able to live in some comfort and liberty at Carisbrooke Castle. At the end of 1647 he concluded a treaty with commissioners from Scotland, who had been admitted to see him. They engaged themselves to restore him to his throne by force in return for his promise to impose Presbyterianism on England for three years and to suppress the independent Christian sects whose influence was paramount in the Roundhead army. Before the Scots invaded England in fulfilment of this engagement risings took place in Kent and Essex; in June part of the fleet stationed in the Downs revolted against Parliament. Ten ships, followed by that of Vice-Admiral William Batten, himself a Presbyterian, arrived at Helvoetsluys ready to place themselves under the command of the nineteen-year-old Prince of Wales. As soon as James heard the news he left his sister and her husband in their house at The Hague to greet the mutineers. Although he was not yet fifteen, he still boasted the title of Lord High Admiral so he took over the temporary command of these ships and sent for his elder brother who arrived from Paris via Calais early in July.[25]

To James's disappointment the Prince of Wales then assumed the command himself, appointed Batten as his rear-admiral, and accompanied by James's cousin, Prince Rupert of the Rhine, sailed for England, leaving the Duke disconsolate behind. However, the journey was without purpose; the sailors were restless and wanted to capture prizes rather than rescue the King in the Isle of Wight or fight a battle. The parliamentarian admiral, the experienced Earl of Warwick, quickly gathered together a superior fleet; an attempt to seize Deal Castle failed; after being confronted by Warwick near the mouth of the Thames and running short of food, drink and other supplies, Prince Charles was compelled to return to Holland in September. Meanwhile the risings in the south had been suppressed and in the north Oliver Cromwell annihilated the Scottish Engagers at the battle of Preston.

While all this was happening James, an active boy on the edge of manhood, had sadly returned to the hospitality of his sister and her husband with whom he spent Christmas. The day after Twelfth Night 1649 he went to France in answer to a summons from his mother who was in the palace of St Germain near Paris. But France, like England, was in the throes of civil war. After reaching Cambrai by way of Brussels James received another letter from his mother saying that as the King of France, a boy of eight, had come to St Germain he must stay where he was until he received further orders.[26] He was entertained by the monks of St Amand — this was his first taste of Roman Catholic hospitality — until 8 February. Then he went on to St Germain where he arrived on 13 February and learned the dreadful news of his father's trial and execution in London. Thus his elder brother, who was still in Holland, assumed the title of King Charles II.

Two questions arose. The first was whom was James expected to obey: his mother or his brother? The second was how could he best help his brother to regain their father's throne? Charles arrived at St Germain during the summer, but although he did not stay there for long, he made it clear to his mother that he would no longer take her advice on matters of policy and doubtless he told James, as he certainly did later, that his brother's first duty was to himself, but that when he was away James was to defer to his mother. Secondly, Charles decided that he must try to revive the royalist cause in either Ireland or Scotland. Queen Henrietta Maria was all for the two princes going to Ireland; she informed them optimistically that they would make a better impression there if they declared themselves to be Roman Catholics. But the news soon reached France that the royalist Lord Lieutenant in Ireland, the twelfth Earl of Ormonde, who had managed to reconcile the native Irish with the royalists, had nevertheless been defeated in battle by Colonel Michael Jones (himself an Anglo-Irishman), the senior parliamentarian officer in the country. Before that Prince Rupert had been sent by Charles II with the remains of the royalist fleet to anchor off southern Ireland; he proved unable to give any material help to Ormonde, though it was hoped that when the autumn came a larger parliamentarian naval squadron, which was blockading Rupert's ships in harbour, would be compelled to withdraw and Charles would be able to land there safely. Meanwhile the King resolved to take James with him to the Channel Islands, which were still under royalist control, and to await developments there. Communications were opened up with the leaders of the Covenanting party in Scotland, which had repudiated the Engagers. The brothers decided to remain in Jersey until the situation cleared up; then it could be decided whether Charles II should make for Ireland, Scotland or even England.

Charles had already spent a couple of months not unagreeably in Jersey while he was on his way from England to France after the end of the first civil war. The royalist Governor, Sir George Carteret, was a native of the island and was able to supply his royal guests with food and drink either out of the island's resources or brought over from France. The Stuart princes were lodged in a house that had been built for Sir Edward Hyde when he was there and in which he started to write his famous *History of the Rebellion*.[27] The newcomers were accompanied by courtiers and servants including their boyhood friend, the second Duke of Buckingham, Sir Edward Nicholas, a devoted royalist who had been one of Charles I's Secretaries of State and was reappointed to that office by Charles II, by Henry Bennet, the future Earl of Arlington, who had been chosen as James's secretary at the end of 1648, and Stephen Fox (grandfather of Charles James Fox), who was employed in looking after the royal finances, such as they were. The Stuart brothers and their entourage all dressed in black while their carriages were draped in black to remind the islanders of their father's fate.[28]

Charles remained in Jersey during the winter, but by February 1650 had returned to Holland despairing of Ireland where General Oliver Cromwell with a large republican expeditionary force had landed in the early autumn of 1649 to reinforce the victory of Michael Jones. At The Hague Charles concluded an agreement with the Scottish Covenanters before sailing for his northern kingdom. James, who celebrated his sixteenth birthday in Jersey, was left behind at Elizabeth Castle after Charles had appointed him governor of the island (in place of Henry Jermyn) and lived with Sir George Carteret as his deputy governor, who no doubt did the work. There James appears to have been popular. When at St Germain he had been thought attractive at any rate by the ladies;[29] in Jersey he was described as 'tall for his age and slight in figure, but remarkably lively and pleasant in manner'.[30] Presumably he had shot up since his escape from St James's Palace two years earlier. He seized the opportunity of enforced leisure to become an expert shot and a good horseman. His closest friends were Sir John Berkeley, who had fought for Charles I in the west of England, and Lord Jermyn, who was a loyal servant of Henrietta Maria. Even so, as an energetic young man he must have found his stay in Jersey frustrating. He had vainly begged his brother to let him join Prince Rupert and his ships off Ireland;[37] so he was glad when in August 1650 after eleven months'

27

residence he was at last allowed to leave the island, where Jermyn resumed the nominal post of governor.

After departing from Jersey James went back to The Hague where he again stayed for a short time with his sister and brother-in-law, but by September he had rejoined his mother in Paris. Here he made an excellent impression. The Grande Mademoiselle (the Duchess of Montpensier), who had rejected the advances of Charles II, recorded in her memoirs how she had found the Duke of York 'a charming young prince . . . very handsome, well made and of a fair complexion. He spoke French with admirable fluency . . . the remarks he made were to the point and I enjoyed his conversation exceedingly.' Sir John Berkeley had now become his acting governor (replacing Lord Byron, his official governor) and he came under the influence of his old friend, Sir George Radcliffe and that of a clergyman, Dr Henry Killigrew. Henrietta Maria did not much care for her son's friends and tried to deflect him from them. It was against her wishes and on the advice of these friends that he decided to leave Paris for Brussels to meet Charles IV Duke of Lorraine, whose duchy had been taken away from him by the French and who now subsisted as a soldier of fortune. The idea was mooted that James should marry one of the illegitimate daughters of the Duke, who would in return put at his disposal a cavalry force with which he could fight on the side of the Spaniards, the Holy Roman Emperor and the Prince of Condé, all enemies of the French Government which during the minority of Louis XIV was being directed by the Queen Mother (Anne of Austria) and her close confidant, Cardinal Mazarin.[32] This idea was scarcely likely to meet with the approval of Henrietta Maria, who was the aunt of the boy King of France and dependent on the French Court for her home and her pension.

Although James was pleasantly received by the Duke of Lorraine, nothing came of the scheme of marrying his daughter and fighting with his regiments: so James now tried to return to The Hague out of his mother's reach; but his brother-in-law, William II, had just died of smallpox and his sister Mary was commanded by her mother not to receive him. Henrietta Maria was furious that James had left her Court without her permission and insisted that he must obey her orders. But James was now of the age when he wanted to tear himself from his mother's apron strings and resented her authority over him; having been rebuffed at The Hague, he chose instead to join his aunt, Elizabeth of Bohemia, at her home in Rhenen. Then, his mother

28

having relented, he came back to his sister at The Hague, but left there for Breda when English ambassadors arrived from London intent on concluding a firm alliance between the Commonwealth and the Dutch Republic, the influence of whose Regents was now paramount after the death of William II. Thus no opportunity opened for him. Instead he received a letter from his brother, Charles II, who was slowly enlarging his authority in Scotland (since the Covenanters had been defeated by Cromwell at the battle of Dunbar in September 1650), which ordered him to obey his mother's wishes except over questions of religion; James had no alternative but reluctantly to return to Paris where he was provided with a small pension by the French Government.

It was now the autumn of 1651 and in Paris James and his mother learned the frightening news that Charles II had been overwhelmingly defeated at the battle of Worcester, where his army of Scots which had penetrated into England had been surrounded and crushed by Oliver Cromwell, the commander-in-chief of the English Commonwealth; afterwards King Charles who had fought bravely till the very end had completely disappeared; nobody knew for certain whether he was alive or dead. However, after many adventures, Charles turned up in 'a little cock boat' at Fécamp in Normandy and was soon rapturously welcomed by his mother and brother.[33] A second French civil war — the Fronde of the Princes, as it was called — was drawing towards its climax, but all three members of the English royal family lived together somewhat uncomfortably in the Louvre, while the French Queen Mother and her son abandoned Paris and moved into the west of France out of reach of the rebel Princes, leaving Marshal Turenne to cope with the Spanish army which was fighting alongside the Frondeurs.

Under these circumstances the Stuart exiles, sandwiched as they were between two contending parties in France, faced poverty, while their outlook, with the King having been beaten both in Scotland and in England, appeared pretty hopeless. Could James obtain money by marriage? An attempt, engineered by his mother, to arrange a marriage for him to a rich heiress, the daughter of the Duc de Longueville, proved abortive. Could he then make a living and gather experience as a soldier? He himself suggested that he should join Turenne's army as a volunteer.[34] After some hesitation Charles II and his mother agreed to give him the necessary permission. He had argued convincingly that military experience would enable him to be useful to his brother when an opportunity arose for them to fight their way back to England. The Duke managed to borrow the money he needed to pay for his modest equipment and Charles provided him with six coach horses. On 24 April 1652 after visiting the peripatetic French Court, which had moved to Corbeil, twenty miles south of Paris, James, accompanied by other volunteers, and with his camp bed, his baggage, a few horses and grooms, arrived at Marshal Turenne's headquarters, stationed in a small village south of the river Marne. Thus at eighteen James became a soldier.

By the age of eighteen, it has often been said, a man's character is largely formed. He may learn from experience how to avoid obvious mistakes, but the strengths and weaknesses of his mentality, to which his heredity contributes much, will seldom change fundamentally. Two factors had affected James so far. First, his youth had been adventurous. He witnessed a battle when he was eight years old; he escaped in disguise from prison when he was fifteen; he heard of his father's trial and execution by his own subjects a year later. Secondly, he lacked regular guidance. His father was busy plotting and planning all the time he was in Oxford; his mother was only there for one year; he was separated from his brother in his early teens; his tutors and governors never stayed with him long. What he came to dislike therefore was deviousness of any sort, which had brought no rewards at all to his father. What he feared was weakness or compromises, especially with enemies; what he sought was an unchallengeable source of authority on which he could always depend. So, after his escape from St James's Palace, he was rarely again to be devious himself. Later in his life when he became King he aimed to be strong, tough and clear-cut. In between these times he recognized and accepted first the authority of a commanding officer, then that of his elder brother, and finally that of the Roman Catholic Church.

3.

In Exile

To understand the war in which James was to fight it is necessary to look back to what had been happening in France in the 1640s.

At the same time that the second civil war had been in progress in England, culminating in the trial and execution of James's father, a civil war known as the Fronde had broken out in France. The causes of the first Fronde[1] were, briefly, the resentment of proud and influential Frenchmen at the consequences of what they regarded as the absolute rule of Cardinal Richelieu, who passed away in an odour of serenity in 1642 — he is supposed to have said he did not have to forgive his enemies as they were all dead. His chosen successor, Cardinal Mazarin, an Italian by birth, who began effectively to govern the kingdom during the minority of Louis XIV, was hated even more, for he was regarded as a foreign tyrant. He was able to take over the government by means of a bloodless *coup d'état*. According to the will of Louis XIII, who died in 1643, a Regency Council, headed by his widow, Anne of Austria, who was given only limited powers, and including the Princes of the Blood and officials of the royal Court, was to rule the country. Opposition to that arrangement was to come from what was in effect a supreme law court, the Parlement de Paris, which had been reduced to being a political nonentity by Richelieu and had been obliged to register all royal decrees without even commenting upon them. Incited by Mazarin, to whom she was devoted, Anne of Austria invited the Parlement to abolish the Regency Council and recognize herself as the sole regent; delighted that it had suddenly been given a political role, the Parlement did so.

When they thus established the Regency Government the leaders of the Parlement little realized that it was setting up another though more supple cardinal to rule in the shape of Mazarin. Over the next five years grievances accumulated. The cost of the long and continuing war with Spain, which had begun in 1635, meant that taxes became numerous and oppressive while the interest on government bonds *(rentes)* was reduced or withheld. By 1648 a movement of protest had developed in the Paris Parlement, supported by other law courts, at the autocratic rule and financial incompetence of Mazarin's government. This movement French was crushed by force and two leading members of the Parlement were arrested. The barricades then went up in Paris and an armed mob defied the Regent.

The first Fronde did not last long and was mainly concentrated in Paris, which was besieged on behalf of the Regent by the Prince of Condé, a young nobleman who had distinguished himself as a general in the war against Spain. But eventually the Regent yielded to pressure and concluded a treaty with the Parlement that conceded most of its demands relating to public finance and the individual liberties of the well-to-do.

The second Fronde began in 1650 and was mainly brought about by the overweening ambitions of Condé, who after his triumphs in the field, wanted to replace Mazarin as the first Minister of the Crown. Condé was backed by his brother, the Prince of Conti, his brother-in-law, the Duke of Longueville, and (later) by Anne of Austria's own brother-in-law, Gaston Duke of Orleans, a prince of limited intelligence and unprepossessing appearance; hence the name the Fronde of the Princes. The first three of these grandees were put under arrest for treason, but so influential was the *noblesse de la cour* and its womenfolk, several of whom were rather good-looking intriguers, that Mazarin was ultimately compelled to release the princes in February 1651 and himself fled the country. In this year the Regency became almost powerless. Condé governed much of the south and south-west, Gaston of Orleans ruled Paris, while the east was faced by a Spanish army on the borders of Flanders and by Marshal Turenne, an outstanding French general;[2] at the susceptible age of forty Turenne had succumbed to the charms of Condé's sister, the wife of the Duke of Longueville, and found himself in command mainly of Spanish troops at Stenai near the north-eastern frontier, for most of the French force with which he had previously been fighting the Spaniards deserted him. Furthermore the Duke of Lorraine, whose daughter had been considered as a wife for James, had built up a mercenary army with the aid of which he hoped to draw profits from these muddied French waters by allying himself with Condé and the Spaniards.

In spite of possessing so many enemies Anne of Austria was tough. She took her son, Louis XIV, to Poitiers, some 200 miles west of Paris, while the rebel leaders, at cross-purposes with one another and with no clear aims except their own aggrandizement, were carrying on a pointless sort of warfare. Mazarin returned from exile and joined Anne at Poitiers, where he persuaded Turenne to change sides. It is not clear from Turenne's own memoirs or his official biography what induced this able general to unite with the detested Mazarin. Was he jealous of Condé, was he repelled by the anarchy in his country, was he offered a large bribe, was he ashamed of allying himself with the Spaniards or had he just grown tired of the wiles of the Duchess of Longueville, who had left him at Stenai to join her husband in Paris? The most plausible explanation is that because at this time Mazarin gave Marshal Turenne's elder brother, to whom he was devoted, two estates to compensate for the loss of the principality of Sedan, which the Cardinal had previously confiscated from him, the Marshal was placated.[3] If so, it proved to be a masterstroke by the Italian statesman.

Queen Henrietta Maria and her two sons had lived rather apprehensively in the Louvre while all this was going on. They had little money and were nervous of taking sides, for just as in England during the civil war both parties claimed to be fighting for the King, so the Frondeurs asserted that they were aiming to overthrow Mazarin and not Louis XIV, who had reached his majority at the age of thirteen in September 1651. So it was maintained at the Louvre that James was merely following his own personal inclinations in joining Turenne as a volunteer, while Charles II kept all his options open.

During the first three months of 1652 Henri de la Tour D'Auvergne, Viscount of Turenne, had accompanied the Regent and her son from Poitiers to Angers and then along the valley of the river Loire to Tours and Blois, which they reached at the end of March. In Orleans Turenne was defied by the 'Grande Mademoiselle', the fiery daughter of Gaston of Orleans. So the Marshal by-passed the city and boldly moved on in the direction of Paris. Early in April he had his first brush with Condé, who had arrived from Guienne with an army outnumbering his both in cavalry and infantry. The royal troops were stationed at two small villages south of the canal which linked the rivers Loire and Loing. Condé surprised Turenne's colleague, the Marshal of Hocquincourt, who was encamped behind the canal; a cavalry skirmish took place in which the royal troops were worsted. But Turenne turned the tables, gave Condé a bloody nose and then moved north with the aim of getting between Paris and his enemy. Condé himself went directly to the capital, leaving his men under the command of three of his subordinates in the fortified town of Etampes, about twenty miles south-west of Paris. The Queen and her son were able to move north safely from the Loire to the sizeable town of Melun just north of the Seine where they arrived on 20 April. The campaigning season proper was about to open; but until then both sides were in difficulties because of lack of forage for their horses.

On 21 April James left St Germain, west of the walls of Paris, to which his mother had moved, and skirting Paris, thus avoiding having to see his uncle, Gaston, who was supreme in the capital, arrived at Corbeil, west of the Seine, *en route* to Melun.[4] The town of Corbeil had declared itself to be neutral in the civil war. James, however, was not only able to induce the magistrates to admit him, but also to bring in some of the French King's guards whom he had met outside the city gate. Once inside, he persuaded the authorities there to declare for the Regency. It was a remarkable achievement by the young prince (who must have spoken excellent French) because it saved Turenne from having to storm the town to clear his communications with Paris. As soon as the news of his feat reached Melun Anne of Austria, accompanied by Cardinal Mazarin, moved her Court into Corbeil where, as James recorded, he was rewarded with 'a small recruit of money, another horse and two mules, all of which came very seasonably to him, for he and his poor retinue had not above twenty pistoles left amongst them at their arrival in that place'.[5] On the same evening he left Corbeil with other volunteers for the village of Châtres, some twenty miles to the east, which had become Turenne's headquarters. It must have been an exhausting day. But it meant that at the outset of his military career James was in the good books of Marshal Turenne. In due course James and Turenne became firm friends.

When James reached Châtres he discovered that from the beginning of his march from the west Turenne's intention had been to enable the King and his mother to return to Paris and thence be in a position to assert their authority. Owing to his control of Melun and, thanks to James, of Corbeil, Turenne's army had in effect inserted itself between the capital, where Condé was exerting his authority, and Etampes, where his main army was posted. Thus Anne of Austria and her son who, once he had attained his majority, thoroughly trusted Mazarin, were able to move safely to St Germain. On the night of 3 May Turenne marched to Etampes, a distance of thirty-five miles, in the hope of surprising Condé's army. Reconnaissance units reported that the enemy were drawn up on a plain outside Etampes where they were being reviewed by Anne-Marie-Louise de Montpensier, the Grande Mademoiselle. Surprise was complete; the review ended in confusion; Mademoiselle de Montpensier drove off to Paris, leaving her hosts to manage as best they could. Condé's men hastily retreated into the shelter of the suburbs. Turenne brought up his artillery, threw his cavalry against the enemy flank, and thrust such infantry as he had with him to fight hand-to-hand in the suburban streets. This was no skirmish but a genuine battle in which a thousand of the enemy were killed and many more taken prisoners. Five hundred royalists were killed while Condé's men were able to retire behind the city walls. Turenne was obliged to withdraw north along the main road to Paris before resuming the offensive.

It was not until the end of May that Turenne, on the instructions of Mazarin, who was with the Queen Mother at St Germain, began a siege of Etampes. His aim was to surround the town completely and either starve it into surrender or force the garrison to come out and fight. Just as the siege was beginning to progress Turenne learned that the Duke of Lorraine and his mercenary army had left Spanish Flanders and was coming to the aid of Condé. Obviously Turenne was in danger of being caught between the troops in Etampes and Lorraine's army marching along the valley of the Seine. But before he moved away Turenne resolved to storm Etampes. A struggle for a large *demi-lune* or outwork developed; it changed hands more than once. Turenne used not merely his infantry and grenadiers, but also cannon and squadrons of cavalry in an all-out assault. James was in the thick of the fighting and, according to Edward Hyde, 'behaved himself with extraordinary courage and gallantry'.[6] But in the end Turenne was compelled to call off his men. Thus the Duke of Lorraine could claim that he had relieved Etampes.

Turenne was an aggressive general; he had no intention of being forced on to the defensive now his army was fully blooded. He at once turned back east to confront Lorraine, whose forces were posted in the town of Villeneuve St Georges, only about ten miles south-east of Paris. The Seine was crossed at Corbeil, which had been converted into a supply base; then the river Yerre, a tributary of the Seine, was forded. Lorraine, who had been in touch with Mazarin as well as with Condé, since he sought nothing but his own advantage, offered to treat. To James's surprise he discovered that his brother, Charles II, was with Lorraine in his camp, having been appointed a mediator by the French Court. It was perfectly reasonable that the King of England should have been chosen for the task, but undoubtedly James, who had been risking his life fighting for the French King, was annoyed. He wrote in his memoirs rather unfairly that his brother was enjoying a pension from the French Court, which was 'the only visible support that he had' and that by being with the Duke of Lorraine 'he manifestly appeared in the quarrel of rebels against their lawful sovereign'.[7] When Charles asked his brother what terms Turenne would accept, James told him sharply that Lorraine must leave France within fifteen days and never again help Condé and the other insurgent princes. Turenne would stand for no shilly-shallying from Lorraine; nor would James. They were fully prepared to fight him there and then. But the Duke of Lorraine had no wish to risk his precious army. He signed the treaty and left the country for the time being. So unpopular was Charles II's mediation with the Parisians that in July he and his mother were compelled to leave the Louvre for St Germain. Meanwhile Turenne, accompanied by James, moved forward with the intention of forcing his way into Paris.

The Parisians, understandably anxious to prevent the two armies from fighting each other in the streets of the capital, refused to open the city gates. Condé with his army withdrawn from Etampes was encamped at St Cloud south of the Seine and west of the city walls; Turenne was encamped at La Chevrette north of the city and three miles west of St Denis where the French Court had established itself, having moved there to await events. Condé planned to march straight though Paris to the east where he could hope to take up a defensible position protected by the Marne and the Seine. But he was not allowed to do so; instead he skirted the city to the north making for his intended new camp.

As soon as Turenne knew of this, he planned to intercept him; James attacked Condé's rearguard as it rode past St Denis; Condé managed to get away, but was forced to turn and fight in the faubourg of Saint-Antoine. Here a desperate battle developed in which James was again to the fore. However, the Grande Mademoiselle, who had previously defied Turenne in Orleans and stimulated Condé's troops at Etampes, persuaded the Parisians to admit Condé's army into the city while she had the guns of the Bastille turned upon the French royalists fighting in the faubourg. Turenne returned to his camp, where he received the news that a Spanish army had again entered France and that the fickle Duke of Lorraine, disregarding the treaty he had signed, was joining it. That meant that the royalist army would be greatly outnumbered.

In the middle of July the King's Council met to decide what was best to do. It was originally resolved, upon the advice of Mazarin, to remove the King and his mother either to Rouen or Lyons out of reach of the invading armies. On the basis of the facts at his disposal Mazarin could hardly have given any other counsel for he could not risk the danger of Louis XIV being captured by the Frondeurs, as Charles I had been captured by the New Model Army in England. Although Turenne's elder brother was a member of the Council which reached this decision, Mazarin had omitted to consult the commander-in-chief himself. However, when Turenne, accompanied by James, arrived at St Denis later that day, he argued forcibly against what he regarded as a pusillanimous course of action. Boldness, he thought, was essential as otherwise the whole of France might capitulate to the invaders. He therefore urged the King and his mother to go to Pontoise, twenty-five miles north-west of Paris, accompanied by the royal guards, as this was a defensible town and in any case could not be reached by the King's enemies without confronting Turenne's army, which he intended to move to a camp about forty miles north-east of Pontoise, where the river Oise meets the river Aisne. To their credit the Queen and the Cardinal agreed to Turenne's proposals and Mazarin decided to leave the kingdom again, not because he was afraid for himself, but because he thought his own absence would be helpful to the royalist cause.[8]

Turenne's policy paid off. The Spanish army entered France, but after eating up the country, returned to Flanders, leaving the Duke of Lorraine with a contingent of its troops to help the Frondeurs. Once again Lorraine made for the town of Villeneuve St Georges. This time Turenne got there first. James, who must by then have been familiar with the lie of the land, reported to Turenne that the Duke of Lorraine was entrenching at Castle Ablon on the Seine north of Corbeil, which was still a royal supply depot. The royalists captured the castle and cleared their line of communications.

Lorraine withdrew north while Turennne moved forward to the north-east steadily pushing his enemy back towards the frontier. The normal campaigning season was now ending, but Turenne was determined to bring the Court back to Paris. The Parisians were tiring of their governor, Gaston of Orleans, and his amazon daughter. Overruling her other advisers, Anne of Austria agreed to leave St Germain, to which she had returned from Pontoise, and enter Paris with her son; immediately they had done so the Orleans father and daughter departed. Gaston went out of one gate while the King entered by another. The Grande Mademoiselle was thereupon ordered to follow her father.[9]

But for Turenne and James the campaign was not yet over. They were resolved to drive Condé and his mixed bag of allies out of the kingdom. By mid-December they had largely achieved their aim by retaking Bar-le-Duc and Ligny in Champagne. An Irish regiment, which had been serving with the Duke of Lorraine at Bar-le-Duc, learning that the Duke of York was with the French army, voluntarily offered to change sides. In Champagne Mazarin reappeared, his appetite improved with eating, and asked Turenne to get back other towns still garrisoned by the Spaniards, notably Rhetel and St Menehould on the Aisne. Turenne had to explain to him that in cruel winter weather no shelter was to be found for the infantry, many of whom died of the frost as they marched, and no forage for the horses. Nevertheless it was not until the end of January 1653, after the capture of Vervins, where James was nearly killed or taken prisoner by a party of enemy cavalry whom he had mistaken for his own men, that the French army was allowed to retire into winter quarters and Mazarin, the French generals and 'persons of quality', including the Duke of York, rode back to Paris where they arrived on 3 February.[10] James, who had followed Turenne everywhere and made himself useful both in reconnaissance and in fighting, recorded in his memoirs, praising his chief, how 'that long campaign ended, during which Monsieur de Turenne acquired immortal fame through saving the monarchy several times by his counsel, his conduct and his valour.'[11]

What lessons had James learnt from this remarkable apprenticeship in the art of war? First, surely, that attack is the best form of defence. At no time during the campaign of 1652 had Turenne's forces been superior in numbers to that of his enemy. Yet except when he was regrouping in preparation for a fresh advance, he was consistently aggressive. When he was repulsed, as he was at first in Etampes, Bar-le-Duc and Ligny, he did not hesitate to strike a second time. James also learned that rivers are not an insuperable barrier to an offensive.[12] Although many rivers wound their way between Paris and the Spanish frontier to the north-east they could usually be bridged or forded. Another thing that James grasped at the outset was the advantage of surprise. Twice he went with Turenne on long night marches, which only a daring commander, confident of the discipline of his troops, would have ventured to attempt. Lastly, he came to appreciate that officers must set an example to their soldiers by leading the way where the battle was at its hottest, as he did both in the suburbs of Paris and in the struggle for Etampes. One further lesson that he might have learnt, but arguably did not, was the interrelationship between war and politics. Turenne took the view that the boy King of France must stay in or near Paris if he was to enlist the loyalty of his subjects. For the same reason the Italian Mazarin, aware of his own unpopularity, twice withdrew from the kingdom so that the Queen Mother could appeal to the patriotism of Frenchmen and rally them round the throne. Perhaps, however, James was most impressed by the consideration that a king must stay in his capital or retake his capital in a way that his own father had conspicuously failed to do. That may have been why in 1688 as King of England James was so reluctant to leave London; but then of course he had no general of Turenne's capacity who was prepared to fight for him.

The campaign of 1653 began very late because that of 1652 had ended late. The French soldiers were widely scattered in their winter quarters and had to be reassembled. It was not until 4 July that James left Paris to join Turenne. As the enemy had not again crossed the frontier, Turenne first laid siege to Rethel on the Aisne; its Spanish garrison surrendered after only three days. Thence the Marshal moved north to the Oise where he received information that the enemy was marching out of Flanders to a rendezvous at Guise, which lay on the Oise. It was estimated that the Prince of Condé, the Duke of Lorraine and the Count of Fuenseldaña, who was in command of the Spaniards, had altogether 30,000 men, nearly double as many as Turenne had. It was anxiously debated what should be done. Some French officers urged that most of the infantry should be employed to garrison the frontier towns while the cavalry should harass the enemy, beat up their foragers and cut off

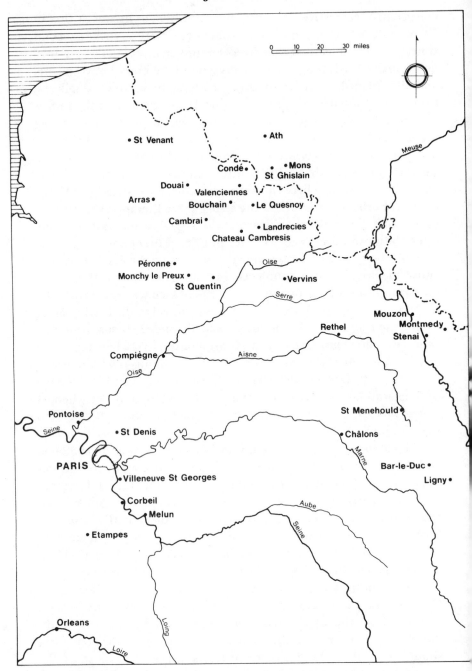

Map of north-east France

their convoys. This negative strategy was rejected by Turenne, who insisted that the army should not be divided but concentrated along the line of the Somme so as to protect Paris by denying the enemy the passage of the Somme and the Oise.[13] (Was James to remember this thirty-five years later in his life when he ordered his army to be drawn up along the line of the river Thames so as to deny London to the advancing forces of William of Orange?) For a time the sudden arrival of the Spanish army on the Somme front caused dismay among the French, but after Turenne carried out a personal reconnaissance, he drew up his army on a new line between a ravine and a high hill, a position hard to outflank. This was a gentlemanly war; the Spaniards were in no hurry. It was the month of August; the weather was hot; Fuenseldaña insisted that his men must be given the opportunity to drink river water to quench their thirsts before advancing to the attack. For two or three days the armies stared at each other; then Condé and his colleagues, perceiving the strength of the French position, marched away again. For the Spaniards there was always tomorrow.

The remainder of the campaign consisted of sieges. The French army, being reinforced because the Frondeurs in Bordeaux had been crushed, took Mouzon, a frontier town on the Meuse. At Mouzon the Spanish Governor, recognizing James by the star he wore as a Knight of the Garter, refused to let his men fire on the Duke's company, 'a respect', James remarked, 'very usual beyond sea'.[14] James asked Turenne's permission to take part in the siege of St Menehould, but he was delayed by politenesses at the French Court, which turned up at Chalons-sur-Marne, about twenty miles west of St Menehould, to follow the course of the siege; so that by the time James arrived there the town had surrendered.

The campaign of 1654 also started rather late, but before James joined Turenne he already knew that he had been given the substantive rank of lieutenant-general, one of eight lieutenant-generals who took it in turn to lead the vanguard; the rest of the time they acted simply as members of the Marshal's staff. On 19 June Hyde wrote to his friend, Nicholas: 'The Duke of York commanded this year with a large commission under Turenne, who is the best master of the trade in Christendom; the Duke is much delighted with the charge.'[15] Evidently a feeling of mutual admiration and affection had developed between the Marshal, who was in his early forties, and the young English prince, now nearing twenty-one. Turenne was an extremely modest man who certainly knew his business; he was never greedy either for offices or money; he was thoughtful about and generous to his soldiers and servants; it was largely out of his love for his brother that he had for a time been a Frondeur.[16] He married late — James had been at his wedding in 1653; once the princes were released from prison by Mazarin Turenne served the French Crown loyally for the rest of his life. James's veneration for Turenne, whom he compared favourably with other marshals taking part in these campaigns, gives a glimmer of brightness to his otherwise dull memoirs. It is understandable how pleased he was at becoming the youngest lieutenant-general in Turenne's army.

In fact, however, the situation was a little tricky from the political point of view. After the English navy had decisively defeated its enemy at sea in what is known as the first Anglo-Dutch war (1652-4) the Commonwealth of England, Scotland and Ireland, under the Protectorship of Oliver Cromwell, had become recognized throughout Europe as a Great Power. That was why Mazarin thought it was worth his while to seek an alliance with the Commonwealth in order to strengthen his hand in the interminable war with Spain. It was obvious that if such an alliance were concluded, King Charles II would be obliged to leave France. What then would happen to James? He could scarcely fight alongside Cromwell's Ironsides. In fact a compromise was reached. Charles himself departed from France to stay with his sister first at Spa and then at Cologne. Before he went, however, he gave James strict instructions,[17] among which were that 'no one was to persuade him to engage in any enterprise without first informing the King'; that he was to see that his younger brother, Henry Duke of Gloucester, who was left with his mother, did not under pressure change his religion; and that he should stand ready at any time to abandon whatever he was doing in order to wage war for the Stuart restoration. Charles added that if he himself decided to return to Scotland (where royalists were still fighting for him in the highlands), he would put James in charge of 'the business of England'.[18]

At the same time as Charles was leaving France, James joined Turenne at Peronne on 16 July 1654. Turenne now had two colleagues, Henry Duke of la Ferté-Saint-Nectaire, Governor of Lorraine, who had been appointed a marshal at the age of fifty-one, and Charles de Monchy Marquis of Hocquincourt, a brave soldier and 'a connoisseur of women and horses, especially the latter'.[19] But the French army was still outnumbered by the Spanish, who surprisingly began the campaign of 1654 early, using an army of 30,000 men and invested Arras. Arras was a strongly fortified town in open country and was at the last moment reinforced by French cavalry. The Spanish commander-in-chief, Fuensaldaña, counted on the fact that as a French force was besieging Stenai at the other end of the frontier, insufficient troops would be available to relieve Arras; but he reckoned without Turenne.

At first the French had to encamp at the village of Monchy-le-Preux, four miles from Arras, in a rough-and-ready manner standing to their arms in case the enemy decided to attack them straightaway before they had fortified their camp. James heard a story afterwards that the Prince of Condé had proposed that the French position should be assaulted at once, but the Spaniards would not agree.[20] As it was, the French army was allowed to draw up in an excellent line of defence, carefully chosen by Turenne, with a brook covering their left wing and the river Scarpe protecting their right wing; parties were sent out from there to interfere with the enemy's foragers and supply convoys. The lieutenant-generals took it in turns to lead these parties; James with a thousand cavalrymen was successful both in repulsing and then surprising small Spanish reconnaissance patrols.

By 14 August the Spaniards, having at last completed their lines of circumvallation around Arras, opened their trenches. Meanwhile Marshal d'Hocquincourt, who had been in command of the successful siege of Stenai, had joined Turenne and it was resolved to assault the Spanish lines at their weakest point where Don Fernando de Solis was in command. As James wrote, 'having served among the Spaniards', Turenne 'knew their methods of proceeding'. He felt sure that Don Fernando would have to go through the formalities of consulting everybody before actually doing anything.[21] Turenne himself consulted no one; he adopted his usual tactics of a night march before an attack at dawn. 'I remember not to have seen a finer sight of nature', wrote James, 'than was that of our foot when they were once in battle and began to march towards the lines; for then discovering their lighted matches, they made a glorious show . . .'[22] The infantry attack forced gaps in the enemy lines through which the French cavalry could penetrate. James led his squadron on Turenne's left wing; the Marshal himself was slightly wounded. By now the French soldiers had largely dispersed and given themselves over to plundering. So fearful was Turenne of a counter-attack by the infantry under his old colleague Condé that he sent urgently for James, who had four squadrons of horse all in good order, and asked for his support. Turenne had placed his artillery so carefully that, as James noted, as soon as the Spanish infantry 'came within reach of our cannon, they would not be persuaded to advance one foot farther, but shog'd off'.[23] Thus Arras was relieved, the Spaniards and their allies falling back to Cambrai and Douai. It was a considerable victory. Lord Jermyn, who took part in the battle as a volunteer, wrote to tell Charles II in Germany that at the relief of Arras 'none did their duty better than the Duke of York, if any so well'.[24]

Next the enemy were obliged to withdraw from Cambrai enabling the French to occupy and fortify Le Quesnoy in Hainault, which belonged to the King of Spain, as a base for the following year's campaign. James celebrated his twenty-first birthday at Château Cambrésis, south of Le Quesnoy, and in December returned to his mother in Paris.

Once again it was six months before James rejoined the French army in 1655. In fact by the time he reached the front the campaign had already begun with the siege of Landrecies, which lay on the Spanish side of the frontier. The Spanish unsuccessfully attempted to relieve the town by taking up a position which threatened Turenne's line of communications with Paris. Because of this James was unable to get to Landrecies before it surrendered. Its capture by Turenne meant that he had acquired an advanced supply base in which he could keep ample food and munitions for his men.

Now the war between France and Spain was at last beginning to peter out. Both sides confined themselves to leisurely sieges. Turenne's object was to expel the Spaniards completely from France. Cardinal Mazarin, who visited army headquarters after the fall of Landrecies, had recovered his nerve; he urged that it would enhance the reputation of the kingdom if Turenne could force his way across the river Scheldt, thus confronting the Spanish army with the alternatives of battle or retreat on their own soil. James was invited to attend a council of war at which Mazarin was present. Turenne argued strongly against risking his soldiers' lives in a frontal assault. His plan was to force his way across the Scheldt near Bouchain, then by-pass Valenciennes, and occupy the town of Condé. After that the army could cross the Scheldt a second time, thus outflanking the enemy along the Scheldt from the north-east.[25] Though pressed to do so by the Prince of Condé, the Spaniards failed to reinforce or hold Bouchain so Turenne's manoeuvres were successful.[26] The town of Condé surrendered on 19 August and that of St Ghislain nearby six days later. Turenne remained in Spanish Flanders for another month. His plan was to remove and carry away all the forage available on both sides of the frontier, thereby feeding his own army and hampering that of the enemy. At this time of the year the harvest was normally gathered in, so the task was a demanding one. James was put in charge of the last of these foraging expeditions. With a contingent of five battalions, forty squadrons and two cannon he penetrated nearly as far as Ath, a fortress almost eighty miles inside Spanish territory. Here, James observed, 'it was an extraordinary sight to see about ten thousand foragers, most of them with scythes in their hands, with the officers before them marching as they did, the front of them being almost half a mile in breadth.'[27]

At the close of September leaving nothing behind but straw, Turenne withdrew towards France, staying in Hainault for a fortnight. Again James was put in charge of the last foraging party there, but the frontier area had by now been so thoroughly devastated that the foragers could only bring back loads of straw. Turenne was then called away by Mazarin to the Court, which was in Compiègne, for consultation. The Marshal left James in command of the army, as by this time he was the only lieutenant-general on duty, all the others having gone home. It was nevertheless a high compliment to a young man of twenty-two even though the campaigning season was over, for it was now late November. While James awaited Turenne's return he learned that a treaty of friendship had during the previous month at last been concluded between Mazarin and Cromwell.[28] One of its secret clauses was that James was required to leave France. It appeared that his scintillating career as a French general was at an end.

4.

In the Service of Spain

The six years during which James lived in France and fought under Marshal Turenne were the happiest he ever experienced, for he knew that he was useful, that his work was appreciated, that he had mastered the art of warfare and had won many friends. He had proved himself to be bold, brave and at times resourceful. Only one dark cloud appeared in the blue: that was his strained relations with his mother.

As has already been noticed, when James returned from Jersey and Charles II went to Scotland the Duke disliked being left behind dependent upon his mother and being ordered about by her. Henrietta Maria had taken a particular dislike to Sir John Berkeley, admittedly an arrogant and self-important man, who had been involved in her husband's unfortunate escape from Hampton Court to the Isle of Wight whence he was brought to his trial and execution. Since 1650 Sir John had been in effect James's governor, that is to say he was responsible for his affairs. The Queen Mother blamed him because he had inspired James's abortive visit to the Duke of Lorraine at Brussels in October 1650, and also for reviving a scheme, which she herself had initiated, to marry James to Mademoiselle de Longueville, who was reputed to be an heiress, though Edward Nicholas claimed that she had not 5,000 pistoles a year, 'which is too little for our good Duke'.[1] Finally, Henrietta Maria had resisted, though without success, James's plea to join the French army as a volunteer.

James's reactions to his treatment by his mother were understandable. He did not like being bound by her orders in St Germain while his brother was in Scotland fighting to regain his thrones; he resented the fact that though his pension from the French Government was extremely small, his mother, who as a French princess had adequate means, refused to supplement it; he did not see why he should not be allowed to choose his own servants and advisers; finally, he disapproved of the influence that Lord Jermyn, a silky intriguer, exerted over his mother. He declared that she loved and valued Jermyn more than any of her children and fancied she was disloyal to her husband's memory.[2] For her part Henrietta Maria denigrated her second son behind his back.[3]

Thus when Charles II was engaged in the third civil war and later when he was obliged to leave Paris for Germany the Court at St Germain was a centre of intrigues and counter-intrigues. At one time James trusted his attorney-general, Sir Edward Herbert, and Sir George Radcliffe, who had brought him as a boy from Oxford to London, and two chaplains, Dr Richard Stuart, formerly Dean of the Chapel Royal, and Dr Henry Killigrew. Later Lord Jermyn managed to worm his way into James's affections. Charles II, who, perhaps on his mother's advice, was suspicious of Sir John Berkeley, had insisted that Henry Bennet (the future Earl of Arlington) was to be James's secretary and he made a point of telling his brother that he must be 'very kind' to Bennet 'and communicate freely with him, for the King will trust him more than many others who are about him'.[4] Naturally James regarded Bennet as sent to spy on his affairs.

Before he entered the French army James was involved in yet another squabble with his mother. Charles had specifically ordered him to ensure that his younger brother, Henry of Gloucester, who was also residing with his mother at St Germain, should not be encouraged to change his religion from Anglicanism to Roman Catholicism. Henry or 'Harry', as he was usually called, was a restless boy who had been permitted to see a glimpse of the fighting when he was fourteen and, like James himself, was antagonized by his mother's interference. He had been left with an ineffective Protestant tutor, Richard Lovell, and had attended Anglican services, conducted by one of Charles's chaplains in a chapel in the Louvre. The Queen insisted that Harry should be educated at an abbey in Pontoise, where a Jesuit college had been established, over which her confessor, Walter Montagu, presided. In October 1654 Lovell protested and asked Henrietta Maria for permission to write to Charles II about what was going on. Remembering his dead father's wishes, Harry also tried to resist his mother's orders, but was compelled to attend the college at Pontoise; thence he wrote not only to Charles II but also to the

Duke of York, who was still at the front, asking for their help.[5]

It is a little surprising in view of Charles's strict instructions to James that he did not immediately intervene in the matter. It is true that James did not complete his duties in the army until later in the year, but he could, on receiving his younger brother's letter, have asked Turenne for leave of absence. Charles was furious. He felt that if Harry openly declared himself to be a Roman Catholic convert, he himself would be blamed and his chances of being restored with Anglican support would be jeopardized.[6] So as soon as he learned what was happening Charles wrote firmly to his mother, to Harry and to the unhappy Mr Lovell, who had been separated from his charge, while he dispatched the Marquis of Ormonde — a twelfth earl and one of the most highly respected of all the exiled royalists — with letters and instructions to remove the boy prince from his mother's care and bring him to Cologne.[7]

How far did James obey his orders to prevent his mother from converting Harry? According to Sir Edward Nicholas, who was not in Paris but with Charles II in Cologne, James wrote 'a very good letter' to his younger brother.[8] Ormonde had been told by Charles to 'let the Duke of York know the King depends on him to stop Harry from changing his religion' and 'expects that he will care not for pleasing or displeasing anybody and that he will rather quit the French service than leave anything undone that is in his power.'[9] But when James at last returned from the front to St Germain his mother told him that he would not be allowed to see the Duke of Gloucester at all 'unless he promised not to speak to him about religion except in her presence'.[10] Ormonde was made of sterner stuff. He went to Pontoise and fetched the young prince back to Paris. Henrietta Maria sent for her youngest son, coaxed him, begged him, and threatened him with dire consequences unless he returned to the Jesuit college. Harry then fled to James for comfort. The Duke of York could do little to mollify his brother, for their mother was adamant. She commanded Harry to leave her lodgings, said she would give him no money and ordered that his bed should be stripped of sheets, that his horses were to be turned out of their stables, and that his ten-year-old sister, Henriette, must not speak to him.[11] However, the Marquis of Ormonde managed to raise enough money to pay for their journey and spirited Harry away to join Charles in Cologne.

The question that naturally arises is whether James could not have been more effective in carrying out his eldest brother's wishes. James had, as is quite commonly the case, an ambivalent relationship with his mother; he loved her, but was of an age when he resented her meddling, all the more so since as a French princess she had the whip hand over him. It may well have been, though no conclusive proof of this exists, that during the five years he had been in France and soldiered in the French army James had been impressed with the rituals of the Roman Catholic religion; it is true that Turenne himself was a Protestant, but he was later to be converted, while most of the other generals were Catholics. At any rate as early as 1651 Sir Edward Nicholas wrote to his friend and colleague, Sir Edward Hyde, of 'strange reports' that when James lived at the Louvre he had been inclined to 'the papist party'.[12] His chaplain, Richard Stuart, who had been responsible for his religious education since he was a boy, had encouraged him to attend Mass as a spectator.[13] Certainly Anglicanism can have meant little to the Duke after he left Oxford and when the Roundheads, who were Puritans not Anglicans, imprisoned him in St James's Palace. To Charles II the question was a political one. As he wrote to his mother at the end of 1654, he

> never intended to dispute with her on religion, and he knows his father never did endeavour to bring her out of love with her own . . . but I think my own safety very much in question if my brother [Harry] should change . . .[14]

James might not have thought much of that argument. Alternatively he may have been little concerned with religion — or at any rate theology — at this time of his life. He had nothing much to say about religion in the first three volumes of his memoirs. No doubt he was alive to the memory of his father, who had made him promise to be loyal to the Church of England. But, after all, he could reasonably have thought that his widowed mother knew as much about her late husband's wishes as he did.

A year later, after the desultory campaign of 1655, James had to make up his mind what he was to do with himself. Undoubtedly he would have liked to remain at St Germain with his mother who, after the quarrel over Harry was forgotten, would certainly have been pleased to keep her handsome soldier son with her. For more than one reason Cardinal Mazarin was willing that he should stay. He wrote to Oliver Cromwell after the signature of the Anglo-French treaty of October 1655, which did not embody a military alliance, asking the Lord Protector's permission to let James remain in

France, which was agreed to, provided that the Prince did not continue to fight in Flanders.[15] James appreciated Mazarin's point of view; he realized that the Cardinal needed allies to strengthen his position against Spain, which was still regarded as a mighty military power. Mazarin told James that his pension would be secured and punctually paid so long as he did not enter into active service against France. As early as November 1654 Lord Jermyn, Henrietta Maria's trusted major-domo, had written to Charles II to inform him that it was proposed if peace were made between England and France to send the Duke of York to command in Italy.[16] A year later Mazarin actually offered him the post of captain-general under the Duke of Savoy, who was fighting the Habsburgs in Piedmont. James welcomed the proposal, all the more so because his aunt, Henrietta Maria's sister, was the Duchess of Savoy, and had written to her sister expressing 'particular concern for him'.[17] But nothing came of this as the Duke of Savoy was about to take over the command of the army himself and partly because James 'was a heretic'.

Even then Mazarin did not require James to leave France. Cromwell frankly told Mazarin that he would be glad to have the Prince stay there while his brother was seeking an alliance with Spain, for it would be an advantage to the Protectorate if the two brothers were at loggerheads with each other. For his part Mazarin was aware that the Duke of York had considerable influence not only with the English volunteers serving in the French army, but also with Irish troops who were fighting under Turenne as mercenaries; thus the French forces might even be weakened if James went away and under pressure from Charles enlisted in the Spanish army.

Charles's point of view was entirely different. As soon as he learned of the French treaty with the Protectorate Government he resolved to seek assistance from the Spaniards to help him obtain his restoration to his lost thrones. The Spaniards did not believe in rushing things; so in the end Charles himself decided to leave Cologne and enter the Spanish Netherlands incognito. His enterprise was rewarded; two Spanish Ministers interviewed him at Louvain; on 12 April 1656 two treaties were signed. By one treaty the Spaniards undertook to put an invasion force at Charles II's disposal as the nucleus of a royalist army, provided that royalist sympathizers in England could capture a port at which this army could safely disembark. In return Charles promised that if he were restored with the help of Spanish arms he would assist in the long war which the

Spaniards were fighting to prevent Portuguese independence and would return Jamaica, seized by the Cromwellians in the previous year, to the King in Madrid. Before the signature of these treaties Charles instructed Ormonde, who had worked with him on the negotiations, that the Duke of York's name was not to be mentioned; 'it will be time enough', Charles said, 'when he is to quit France.'[18]

However, after the treaties were concluded, Charles had no intention of allowing James to go to Italy or anywhere else out of the reach of Spanish Flanders where an invasion force could be embarked. Although in March Edward Hyde, Charles II's Chancellor of the Exchequer, who was still in Cologne handling his debts, wrote to Ormonde that 'France seems confident of keeping the Duke of York', in early May Ormonde wrote back to Hyde to tell him that 'the Duke of York professed a readiness to come to Bruges', where Charles had set up his Court, 'whenever the King sent for him'.[19]

Turenne, with whom the Duke was now on terms of close friendship, had suggested to James that he should write to tell his brother that it would be a mistake to call him away from France, where he had established valuable contacts both with the Court and the French army, which might enable him to help the King later, whereas in Flanders 'he could do his Majesty no great service'.[20] But this idea did not work. The Spaniards insisted that the Duke must come to Bruges and sent Hyde £1,000 to pay for his expenses. In the late summer Charles II dispatched Sir Henry Bennet, who was still in name James's secretary, to tell his brother that he must set out for Flanders as quickly as possible. The Spaniards wanted him to serve in their army, to bring over whatever Irish troops he could, and in return promised to pay him a regular pension. Reluctantly the Duke made his farewells at the Court of France and on 10 September embarked on a leisurely journey to Bruges; he was met by Ormonde at Gravelines and by his two brothers at Furnes. But it was not long before, to Cromwell's delight, personal squabbles led to a breach between the Duke of York and his elder brother.

James was extremely unhappy in Bruges. Cooped up together in a small town, unimpressed by its architectural beauty or the paintings of Memling and Van Eyck which adorned its churches, the exiled Cavaliers were more concerned with cadging a decent meal or borrowing a little money of which they were perennially short. The Spaniards were proud, reserved and often gloomy. Charles II himself was not too badly off; he had an agreeable mistress in Catherine Pegge — more genteel than his first mistress, Lucy Walter, who tried to blackmail him — and made trips to Brussels and elsewhere to concert the details of military and diplomatic arrangements. James had no money after he arrived in Bruges (he had been compelled to borrow a large sum to pay for his journey), though the Spaniards did in fact grant him a pension worth about £1,000 a month as from the end of November.[21] The 'families' of the King and Duke of York quarrelled with one another, intriguing to exert influence upon the royal brothers to extract concessions from them. George Digby Earl of Bristol was at this time the King's leading courtier mainly because he could speak fluent Spanish and thus make himself useful; he could be charming enough, but he enjoyed throwing his weight about; Prince Rupert had come to hate him during the first civil war in England. James's secretary, Sir Henry Bennet, was not trusted by his master nor did he much care for Sir George Radcliffe, who was anxious to win back his favour. His closest intimates besides Sir John Berkeley were Sir John's nephew, Charles and Lord Jermyn's nephew, Henry. Sir John had a remarkable gift for getting himself disliked. Indeed Charles II had suggested to James that he could leave Berkeley behind in Paris to wind up his affairs while James himself came to Bruges, but he had insisted on bringing Berkeley with him.

For James the atmosphere was very different from that in Paris. He longed to go back there, especially as Lord Jermyn, presumably speaking for Henrietta Maria, wrote to dissuade him from entering the Spanish army 'as a thing no way proper for him to undertake, having lived so long a time in France and been treated there with so much kindness'.[22] James did not like being obliged by his brother to write letters to Irish colonels begging them to desert the French and come over to the side of Spain; and when many of the Irish did arrive in Flanders to form the basis of a royalist army, he resented the fact that they were asked to swear oaths of fidelity to King Philip IV of Spain. This question led to a quarrel between James and the Earl of Bristol, which Charles II had to smooth over. But Bristol would not leave well alone. He told James that Don John of Austria, the illegitimate son of Philip IV by an actress, had complained about the behaviour of Sir John Berkeley and that Charles wanted him to leave the country. Over that demand, however, James was extremely obstinate.

James had one consolation at this time. His sister, Princess Mary of Orange, who had been staying with her mother in Paris most of the year, arrived at Bruges just before Christmas 1656. She was troubled to see the Duke being treated as he was, 'took his part', as James related in his memoirs, 'and used all the credit she had for his assistance'.[23] Moreover she brought with her Anne Hyde, the daughter of Edward Hyde, who was one of her Maids of Honour and whom James had met for the first time in France during the previous February. She was, the Duke noted briefly, later to become his wife.[24] Under these feminine influences James decided to stand up for what he regarded as his rights. Princess Mary told him he ought to stick by his friend Berkeley and not dismiss him as Bristol had demanded. The Duke denied that the King had any right to interfere with the choice of his own servants. Although it was of course true that originally his father had selected his servants for him, he argued that the case was very different between a father and a brother and between a child 'and one arrived at man's estate'.[25]

So James resolved to abandon Bruges and return to France. In order not to arouse suspicions at Court he pretended to send Berkeley away from him, but told him to stay in Flushing until he could join him there. Then he went first to see his sister and afterwards his brother the King in effect to say goodbye, though they did not know it. Next he invited his younger brother, Harry, to come shooting with him and a few friends, including Henry Jermyn and Charles Berkeley, outside the town, though he did not invite Bennet to come to the party because he suspected his loyalty to himself. During the shoot he made an excuse to Harry for leaving him and then went via Sluys to Flushing where Sir John Berkeley awaited him. Together they continued to Middleburg and thence to Utrecht. Here he planned to go back into France, but to avoid travelling there through Spanish dominions. However, nothing came of the plan. He could have boarded a French ship to save himself a long and roundabout journey, but Charles Berkeley insisted that this would be dangerous in case they ran into a Cromwellian warship or were wrecked in the wintry seas which were becoming thick with ice. So he remained in Holland, finally being invited to stay with friends of his sister Mary in or near The Hague.

As soon as the news of James's departure became known in Bruges everybody grew agitated. Princess Mary complained that she had been left quite alone with no one to whom she could speak freely;

Don John was worried that the Duke was returning to fight in the French army; Bristol was of the opinion that he was seeking a refuge from which he could negotiate for his return to France if he were not granted reasonable terms on which he could go back into the service of his brother in the Spanish Netherlands; Charles II himself immediately sent the invaluable Marquis of Ormonde after him. Once James had been located in Holland, Ormonde was ordered to visit him carrying a message from the King that if the Duke were willing to return to Bruges, not only he himself but all his servants would be treated with kindness; and that as to Sir John Berkeley, he must stay in Holland for the time being, but within a month would be allowed to join the Court and that 'all things past should be forgotten'.[26]

This episode is fascinating. In the first place it was the only occasion in James's whole life when he directly disobeyed his brother's commands. Secondly, although he wrote a dignified letter from Holland in which he said that he sought nothing more than the glory of being the best of the King's subjects, later he wrote a longer one specifying in detail the nature of his grievances. As soon as they were met by Charles, James agreed to return. Thirdly, it shows how much Oliver Cromwell hoped he would benefit if the brothers openly quarrelled. In fact he told Mazarin

> now I shall boast to your Eminence my security in a well-builded confidence in the Lord [God]: for I distrust not but if this breach widened a little more, and this difference fomented . . . that party [the royalist] which is already forsaken of God as to the outward dispensation of mercies and noisesome to their countrymen will grow lower in the opinion of the world.[27]

This was one of the less pleasing of Oliver's pious utterances. It does look as if James's original intention had been to defy his brother and return to France, but once accidents prevented him from travelling there immediately, he reflected and changed his mind. Finally, it shows that both the King and the Spaniards really valued the services of the young prince.

Charles II was as good as his word. Not only did he allow Sir John Berkeley to return to Court, but created him a baron; James was permitted to dismiss Sir Henry Bennet from his secretaryship, although the King, who thought highly of him, dispatched him as his envoy to Madrid and hoped that later he would be reconciled to his brother. James also dismissed Dr Killigrew whom he suspected of intriguing to his disadvantage. The Earl of Bristol, whose manouevres lay at the bottom of the trouble, lost a great deal of credit. James now received his pension from the Spaniards and was appointed a lieutenant-general in their army. The King made him responsible for organizing a small royalist army consisting mainly of the Irish troops who had left the French service. Some of them came from St Ghislain, the fortified town just inside the border of the Spanish Netherlands, captured by Turenne in 1655, which they were garrisoning; persuaded by the ubiquitous Earl of Bristol, they marched out and handed it over to the Spanish army in the second week of March 1657. Thus James was thought to have performed a double service: first, because the use of his name had persuaded the Irish to desert from the French army and secondly, because as mercenaries they were ready to enlist in the Spanish forces. To begin with, only 2,000 Irish and other soldiers were available to Charles II; they were optimistically formed into six infantry regiments under the commands of James, Ormonde and other prominent royalists.

James reached Bruges after an absence of two months. Soon afterwards the whole exiled Court moved to Brussels, which James found pleasanter than Bruges. It was, after all, a capital, not a provincial town. Don John, as Governor of the Spanish Netherlands, resided there, as did the Marquis of Caracena, the new Spanish commander, a brave officer who had replaced the Count of Fuenseldaña because he failed to get on with the Prince of Condé. Condé himself was there too; he was 'very civil' to James; it is obvious from the Duke's memoirs that they swapped stories about what happened when they fought on opposite sides.[28]

James now officially joined the Spanish army. While he was in Brussels he made a good impression upon Don John, but naturally the Spaniards were somewhat worried about his loyalty to them in view of the fact that he had fought for five years on the side of the French. His recent escapade, too, must have made it known that he was contemplating a return to France. As soon as Sir Henry Bennet reached Madrid he became conscious of these doubts about James at Philip IV's Court and advised Hyde that the Duke 'should write to the King of Spain thanking him for his establishment so as to persuade the King's Ministers that he is content with his being in [Spanish] Flanders and take away any suspicion of his separating himself from the common interest of his House', that is to say, of the Stuarts.[29] James did as he was asked.

The Duke of York was put in charge of the English, or rather Irish, contingent in the Spanish army. But he was not at all pleased that his brother had allowed himself to be induced by the Earl of Bristol to appoint Lieutenant-General de Marsin, who had previously been Condé's second-in-command, to be specifically in charge of such royalist forces as existed or could be raised for service in Flanders and later, it was hoped, in England, though of course nominally he was under the Duke's orders. As Charles had little money with which to pay de Marsin he took the cheap course of appointing him a Knight of the Garter and even considered creating him an earl. James was extremely dissatisfied with the arrangement. Having the King above him 'and Monsieur de Marsin under him', he wrote, 'I might have [had] the less power and authority, or rather be made a mere cipher.'[30] Undoubtedly de Marsin was a good and experienced officer; presumably Charles felt that he would be an excellent military adviser to his brother, who was still in his early twenties.

In March 1657 the English Protectorate and the Government of France had concluded a military alliance directed against Spain, though it was not ratified until May. Cromwell had promised to dispatch 6,000 of his best infantry to France, backed by the powerful Commonwealth navy, and the French had undertaken to hand over Dunkirk, if it were captured from the Spaniards, to an English garrison. Dunkirk had long been a nest of pirates who preyed on English shipping. In the event of the neighbouring ports of Gravelines or Mardyck being taken first they were, according to the treaty, to be handed over as a pledge for the conquest of Dunkirk. Knowing of this treaty, the Spaniards concentrated a large part of their army on the Channel seaboard, weakening such inland towns as were still in their hands on either side of the frontier. Cambrai was one of these towns; Turenne, while awaiting the arrival of the English redcoats, laid siege to it as a diversion. But Condé, taking a leaf out of Turenne's own book, led a swift night march, charged the French cavalry at dawn with his own, and relieved the town.

After that James, who left Brussels late in May, went to a general rendezvous of the Spanish forces at Mons. Marshal Turenne had detached a contingent to besiege Montmédy, a small frontier town in Luxembourg, while he himself moved north to welcome the arrival of Cromwell's soldiers. The Spaniards then tried to carry out a major operation, which they had long contemplated: this was an attack on Calais. On 19 June Don John, Caracena and Condé left Mons with the cavalry, while James and de Marsin were to follow with the infantry. First, the Spanish command aimed to deceive Turenne about their intentions by marching south as if to relieve Montmédy. But after reaching Phillippeville they doubled back and the cavalry under the Prince of Ligne, the force commander, rode forward towards Calais. James followed with the infantry by way of Mons, Tournai, Armentières and Hazebrouck to Arques, twenty-five miles south-east of Calais, which he reached on 1 July. There he learned that the attempt to surprise Calais had failed. So for the rest of July, as James mournfully recalled, 'we were marching up and down to no manner of purpose'.[34]

Much of the campaign of 1657 consisted in petty frontier sieges; the French duly captured Montmédy and then Turenne laid siege to St Venant, which was in Spanish hands, while a little later the Spaniards tried to take Ardres, twenty-five miles to the north-west of St Venant; but as soon as St Venant fell they desisted and withdrew north to Dunkirk, where they impotently watched Turenne, reinforced by the English Roundheads, occupying Mardyck a few miles to the west and dismantling its fortifications.

James admired Condé, but thought very little of the Spanish commanders. He considered that if Condé had not relieved Cambrai, but left it to the Spaniards, they would have spent so much time in debating the methods of relieving it that the French would have had the leisure to finish their lines and then the place would certainly have been lost. When on one occasion James proposed to the Prince of Ligne that he should surprise a French convoy, he discovered that he would not agree without the specific orders of Don John and the Marquis of Caracena. These two gentlemen were, however, rarely available as they liked to have their regular siestas just as they did when they were in Brussels, while they never placed themselves at the head of the army unless a battle was imminent. Don John went to bed as soon as the army encamped; 'he likewise supped in bed', James noted, 'and rose not till the next morning, and those days when the army did not march, he seldom stirred abroad or got on horseback.'[32] Condé told the Duke philosophically that 'he well saw I was a stranger to the proceedings of the Spanish army' and that he must 'prepare himself to see more and grosser faults committed by them before the end of the campaign'.[33] The only time James really enjoyed himself was when under parole he chatted with friends whom he had made in the French army. He even met Sir John Reynolds, the commander of the English expeditionary force appointed by the Lord Protector; Sir John addressed James as 'your Highness' and begged him not to look upon him 'as one sent over by Cromwell, but as one serving the King of France'.[34]

It has sometimes been assumed that the six or seven years James spent in France and his attempts to return to France even after his brother signed the treaties with Spain had caused him at the most impressionable time in his life to become pro-French and that this explains why he supported his brother's francophil policies after he was restored to his throne. But James's memoirs covering this period, which he wrote and revised, do not really support the supposition. Clearly he thought that the French — particularly their commanders — were better soldiers than the Spaniards. The Spanish army, especially their pikemen, formed into *tercios*, had earned a high reputation during the reigns of Charles V and Philip II. No doubt therefore it was a surprise to James to find they were neither as efficient nor as quick-witted as the French, though he did not question their bravery. Naturally he was reluctant to leave the French army, particularly as he was on such good terms with Turenne, but he insisted that whether as a subject, whose duty it was to obey his brother the King, or as a soldier of fortune out to make a name for himself, he was entitled to change sides. At heart then he was neither pro-French nor pro-Spanish; he remained a loyal Englishman. That became crystal clear from the account he wrote of the battle of the Dunes in the coming campaign of 1658.

5.
Coming Home

Before the campaign of 1657 came to an end Turenne had captured
Mardyck, which lay five miles west of Dunkirk and in accordance
with the Anglo-French treaty handed it over to Sir John Reynolds
and his Cromwellian soldiers to garrison as a pledge for the ultimate
capture and surrender of Dunkirk itself. Mardyck commanded one
of the best harbours on the coast of Flanders. Its defences were the
fort proper and a wooden fort built on piles which defended the road
to Dunkirk. The Spanish army, encamped outside Dunkirk, watched
the troops of the English Commonwealth strengthening the defences
of Mardyck and felt annoyed. Don John decided that Spanish pride
demanded that he made at least the gesture of interfering. So during
October he organized a raid to be carried out by some 5,000 men. He
was accompanied in this operation both by the Duke of York and
King Charles II, who had come to Dunkirk to discuss with the
Spanish Governor-General the arrangements for the proposed invasion of England.

On a dark night the infantry was sent forward, the cavalry
remaining in the rear. De Marsin was in command of Condé's
infantry moving against the north of the town (Condé himself was
indisposed), the Spanish foot soldiers marched towards the western
side of the outworks while James with his miniature infantry force,
which had been decimated by medical casualties, was in the centre.
Charles was with the cavalry under Don John. The infantry succeeded in reaching the outworks and began destroying them, but the
cavalry were severely damaged by artillery fire from English frigates
moored in Mardyck harbour, known as the Splinter. James covered
the pioneers, who were engaged in slighting the outworks, by concentrating musket fire on the town fort; at break of day James
withdrew and marched his men back to Dunkirk.

The operation was a minor success, for it was hardly feasible to retake the town so late in the year, especially as Turenne had encamped within supporting distance of the English garrison during the time when the new fortifications were being completed. Few men were lost on either side, although the Marquis of Ormonde, who accompanied King Charles, had his horse killed under him. Evidently James thought very little of the whole affair; for he wrote that Don John had undertaken it

> rather out of ostentation and to make people imagine that he had a considerable design upon that fort than out of any real opinion that so inconsiderable a business was worth the exposing of the lives of so many men.[1]

The English in Mardyck, he observed, were more surprised at their departure than at their arrival. An attempt later to burn or board the frigates which rode in the Splinter was even less of a triumph. However, Spanish honour was satisfied; so all the troops retired into their winter quarters. Charles II was persuaded by his advisers that it would be foolish to risk his life on such pointless adventures and that it would be wiser to leave the fighting with the Spanish army to his younger brother so long as he did not expose himself unnecessarily to danger.[2]

In January 1658 James, after visiting Brussels, went with his brother Harry, who, like most of the Duke's officers and men had suffered from an 'ague' in the unwholesome climate of the Flemish sands, to stay with their sister Mary at Breda; then in mid-February they all joined King Charles at Antwerp.[3] The Earl of Bristol, always fruitful in expedients, some of which had injured the cause of Charles I, now propounded another bright idea, namely that James should unite his small army (which now consisted of three Irish regiments, one Scottish regiment and one English regiment, neither well armed nor adequately trained) with those under the command of Condé. The argument was that this would impress the Spaniards and compel them to fulfil the promises included in their treaties with Charles II to take part in an expedition to England. James disliked the scheme because he believed it would be more likely to antagonize than to inspire the Spaniards; as Condé made it clear that he would not consent to it, the plan quickly fell through.[4]

Charles II was rightly more concerned about Dunkirk. He had learnt through his many agents and spies that Turenne's immediate aim in the campaign in 1658 was to assault Dunkirk and hand it over to the Cromwellian army. Obviously if that could be prevented with the help of the royalists in Flanders, it would be a blow to Oliver's prestige and enhance the reputation of the Stuarts. The King therefore urgently pressed the Spaniards to reinforce Dunkirk at any rate with the men under James's command. As usual, the Spaniards procrastinated; despite the validity of Charles's intelligence, they asserted that this was a mere cover plan, that Dunkirk was in no danger, and what Turenne was really intending was to renew the siege of Cambrai, which he had earlier abandoned. They therefore strengthened the garrison of Cambrai, scattered the infantry around in other inland towns, built useless fortifications along the rivers, and left the Governor of Dunkirk, the Marquis of Lede, with a force of 3,000 men to manage as best he could with insufficient munitions and supplies. The Marquis was a competent soldier and did all he could to protect the town by breaking the dykes in the canals which led to it, thus inundating the surrounding countryside. By the time the Spanish high command agreed to let James reinforce Dunkirk, it was too late. For after successfully deceiving the Spaniards about his intentions, Turenne had managed to move an army of 25,000 men along the dyke of the canal that ran from Bergues to Dunkirk, having repaired the breaches in it, and on 25 May began building lines of circumvallation around the port. Meanwhile part of the English Commonwealth navy, consisting of twenty men-of-war under the command of Edward Montagu (the future Earl of Sandwich), an experienced admiral, made ready to support the siege from the sea by completing the blockade and assaulting the seaward defences of the encircled town.[5]

By now the Spaniards were alarmed. Turenne had thrown out forces to cover the lines of entrenchment both to the east and the west. It was clear that Dunkirk could only be relieved by the Spanish command undertaking a battle. Don John insisted upon this and the rest of his Council of War, at which James himself was accidently not present, acquiesced.[6] The Council had met on 11 June and next day James with two Spanish officers and 4,000 cavalrymen carried out a reconnaissance in force of the enemy's position; afterwards he helped select an area in the sandhills as an encampment for the entire army.[7] The next day, 13 June, the Spanish army moved into the improvised camp, its commanders optimistically believing that its mere presence there would induce Turenne to abandon the siege. But James warned his colleagues that if Turenne did not attack them that very night, he would undoubtedly do so next morning. He was told that the Spaniards desired nothing better. The Duke replied 'that I knew de Turenne so well as to assure them they should have their satisfaction'.[8]

The lay-out of the army under Don John — it was really a mongrel army rather than a Spanish army — was rather peculiar.[9] On the right were stationed four Spanish infantry regiments and no cavalry; the reason for this was that the highest sandhill was there and it was thought it would be extremely difficult to capture, while the flank was protected by the sea. Cavalry, it was believed, would be of little use because of the slippery nature of the ground; furthermore, had it been placed there, it would have been subjected to cannon fire from the English fleet. The miniature royalist infantry army was positioned in the centre of the line and, in addition, James had his own troop of horse guards. The left of the line, which was covered by the Dunkirk—Ostend canal, was held by three Flemish or Walloon regiments and five German mercenary regiments; with the exception of James's troopers all the cavalry, according to the Duke, consisting of only 4,000 men, was stationed to the rear of the infantry ready to counter-attack as soon as the opportunity arose. Don John felt pretty satisfied with these arrangements, although in fact the French army outnumbered his (even though Turenne left 6,000 men in the entrenchments around Dunkirk) while its allies, the English Protectorate's infantry contingent on the extreme left of the French, was of the finest quality; it was under the command of Sir William Lockhart, a diplomatist as well as a soldier, who had replaced Sir John Reynolds, drowned at sea when he was returning home after the campaign of 1657.

At four o'clock in the morning of 14 June, it was reported to James that French cavalry regiments had been seen by the outposts approaching the Spanish encampment. Immediately he went himself to discover exactly what was happening and rapidly came to the conclusion that Turenne's army was about to take the offensive. On his way back he met Don John, who enquired of him what were the French intentions. James answered that they were drawing out of their lines in order to give battle. The Spanish prince was incredulous; he thought that all the French were about to do was to drive in the horse guards. The Duke retorted that the foot were also on the move. Then the Prince of Condé arrived to join in the discussion. James's brother, Harry, who was now nearly eighteen, also chipped into the conversation, telling Condé that he had never seen a battle. Condé replied that in half an hour he would see one and, according to a probably apocryphal account, added that he would see one lost.[10]

The battle was begun by the English under Lockhart, who, arriving on the field ahead of the French, launched a fierce attack on the high sandhill on the Spanish right, two regiments struggling up the steep slope while covered by the muskets of their fellow soldiers.[11] Lockhart's own regiment captured the hill by push of pike and moved down to the level ground on the other side of it. The Duke of York with two troops of horse guards, one his own, the other that of Don John, which had been next to his in the right centre, led a counter-attack, but was beaten off with heavy losses. Thus the soldiers of Cromwell and Charles II confronted each other, as it were, in a fourth little civil war on the sands of Flanders.

Though James's horse carried out a second charge against the redcoats, it was again repulsed and soon the arrival of some French cavalry on the scene obliged James to retire. This outflanking of the Spanish right largely determined the result of the battle. In the centre the French infantry were too strong for the Walloons and the Germans. That meant that Condé, on the Spanish left, though he had directed his cavalry to counter-charge, was compelled to retreat, as James personally discovered before he quitted the field; the battle of the Dunes, as it was called, thus ended about midday in a French victory. In his long account of the battle James could not restrain himself from patriotically praising 'the great eagerness and courage' of the English Roundheads, who all fought on, even after their ammunition was exhausted, by butt of musket and never asked for quarter.[12] Both James and his younger brother had narrow escapes; James was saved by the thickness of his armour, Harry by the intervention of a gallant equerry.

After the battle the defeated generals withdrew first to Furnes and then to Nieuport, twenty miles east of Dunkirk on the Dunkirk–Ostend canal. It was debated what should be done once Turenne had completed his conquest of Dunkirk, which surrendered to him on 24 June after its governor had been killed. Don John proposed to defy the French along the line of the canal. James argued vehemently that such a position could not be held by a defeated and demoralized army, which, if it were beaten again in the field, might bring about the loss of all the Spanish frontier fortresses.

Eventually it was resolved to divide the remnants of the army, each section reinforcing the garrisons of threatened Flemish towns. James was left at Nieuport, Condé went to Ostend, Don John to Bruges and the Prince of Linge to Ypres. Before he departed the Prince of Condé asked James why he had had the audacity to argue with the Spanish Governor-General; James answered that he had no desire to run away again, as he had been compelled to do after the battle of the Dunes.[13]

The panic measures advocated by James did little to hamper Turenne's aggressive strategy. His original intention was to cut the Dunkirk—Ostend canal north of Nieuport, thereby imperilling the Spanish supply lines both to Nieuport and to Ypres. James discovered that Nieuport possessed ammunition only sufficient to last a fortnight so that the Marshal's strategy would have been effective. However, Cardinal Mazarin ordered Turenne to suspend his operations temporarily as the young Louis XIV was feared to be dying in Calais. Thereupon the French evacuated Dixmude, fifteen miles north of Nieuport, while the Marquis de Crequi, who had been left by Turenne to keep watch over Nieuport but not to lay siege to it, remained encamped nearby. A momentary wave of optimism swept over the Spaniards; a council of war was held at which it was arranged that a rendezvous should take place at Bruges of the main Spanish army and Condé's troops ready to attack Turenne as soon as he returned from Calais, while James was given the task of guarding not only Nieuport but also Ostend and Bruges, the principal Spanish base in Flanders. As soon as he learned that Crequi had left his camp to join Turenne, James planned an assault on the retiring French rearguard, using cavalry with supporting infantry, which was then regarded as necessary to protect the horse from a counter-attack. But the foot soldiers failed to come up quickly enough and all that happened was an indecisive skirmish.[14]

James played little part in the remainder of the campaign during which Turenne captured a number of Spanish fortresses ranging as far east as Oudenarde on the river Scheldt. After taking action to safeguard Bruges, James had returned to Nieuport where he received the news of Oliver Cromwell's death on 3/13 September 1658. The Duke at once dispatched a messenger to Don John with the information and as soon as he received the required permission he went to join King Charles in Brussels where he found the spirits of the royalists were high. The Earl of Clarendon wrote that 'all men's hearts (almost quite dead before) were of a sudden wonderfully revived to an expectation of some great change.'[15] But optimism proved premature. Richard Cromwell, a modest country gentleman, who succeeded his father as Lord Protector, did not provoke the animosities aroused by his father and for some time all was quiet in England. 'Never monarch', Clarendon added, 'after he had inherited the Crown by many descents died in more silence nor with less alteration; and there was the same or a greater calm in the kingdom than ever before.'[16] The Spaniards felt no inclination to supply the royalists with an army to invade England until first, peace had been concluded with France and secondly, royalist sympathizers had seized a port where an expedition could hope to land safely. It was therefore not until several months after Oliver's death when the Cromwellians and republicans in England began quarrelling among themselves that positive progress towards their goal was envisaged by the Stuarts in exile.

The direction of royalist affairs in England was in the hands of a body of gentlemen known as the 'Sealed Knot' or 'Secret Knot', which had been formed in the spring of 1654.[17] The members of the Knot were all extremely cautious, reasonably so since the Cromwells' Secretary of State and Chief of Intelligence, John Thurloe, was fully aware of their existence; they did not at all care for some of the younger royalists, particularly John Mordaunt, the younger son of the Earl of Peterborough, who advocated swift action instead of sitting still and doing nothing. In the spring of 1659 Charles II decided to amalgamate his two groups of supporters, calling the new body the Great Trust. But because the members of the Sealed Knot disliked Mordaunt (whom the King had created a viscount) they refused to accept the royal commission. So Mordaunt in fact founded the Trust by bringing together younger royalists of his own frame of mind including, for example, George Legge, in later years to become one of James's closest friends. Mordaunt's plan was to rally the Presbyterians to the royal cause; for they had always been monarchists, though during the reign of Charles I they had advocated the reduction of his constitutional powers, and came to dislike the republicans and religious Independents or Congregationalists. The country was divided into regions, each more or less independent, but all making ready to rise on 1 August 1659 against the Commonwealth Government, which had now, after the forced abdication of Richard Cromwell, become a republican oligarchy that was neither popular nor much trusted by Cromwell's former military officers.[18] The King was delighted with the scheme; he told Mordaunt, who came over to see him in Brussels at the end of June, that he would be ready to sail to England with an army as soon as the rising took place; he would land in one part of the country and James in another.[19] Little did Charles know at that time that one of the members of the Sealed Knot, Sir Richard Willys, was a double agent; he it was who urged the Trust to postpone the date of the insurrections and later on 29 July warned the republican authorities of what was likely to happen. Perhaps such a rebellion would have failed in any case, but fail it did.

Historians have debated about how deep, how early and how motivated were Willys's treacheries.[20] It is clear that Sir Richard was by no means solely responsible for the fiasco of August 1659, as James assumed in his memoirs.[21] The basic reason for the failure was that Mordaunt and his friends had allowed too much decentralization in their plotting of the rising. Consequently the Government's suspicions had been aroused long before Willys gave the information to Thomas Scot, who had succeeded Thurloe as the principal Commonwealth intelligence officer.[22] In any case Charles II, though enthusiastic, was cautious. He waited to hear specific news that the rising had started before he or his brother left for England. By the time that James reached Brussels, Charles had heard from Willys that the date of the insurrection had been postponed; James therefore departed from Brussels to visit his sister Mary at her home near The Hague. The very day he left Charles received the news from England that not having heard of the postponement of the general rising, Sir George Booth, a Presbyterian who had been a member of Oliver Cromwell's Parliaments, had begun a rebellion in Cheshire. Charles immediately ordered James to return to Brussels, notifying him that he himself was going to Calais to await events and that the Duke must follow him there. When James got back to Brussels, Sir Edward Nicholas told him he must go at once to Calais, leaving his brother Harry where he was.[23] James caught up Charles at Hazebrouck, a Flemish town on the route from Brussels to Calais. There it was decided that Charles should continue on his way to Calais, while James made for Boulogne in disguise (for the French were still the allies of the English republicans) where he would be sent further orders.

Accompanied by Charles Berkeley, the Duke therefore went to

Boulogne where he managed to persuade the Lieutenant-Governor in a letter dated as if it came from Brussels that he was going over to England on private business and asking permission to hire a small vessel for the purpose. A day or two later Charles arrived in Boulogne from Calais. There he explained to James that as he had not yet heard of any insurrection except that in Cheshire, neither of them ought to cross the seas until further intelligence reached them about what was happening in England. He said he was intending to go to Dieppe and Rouen and if he learned, as he hoped to do, that other risings had taken place in the west and in Wales, he would then sail there. Meanwhile James was 'to hover about these quarters' [i.e. in Boulogne] and open the King's letters.[24] After Charles's departure James went to Calais where he expected to hear most quickly the news from England. Here, however, the Lieutenant-Governor was informed that James was in the town disguised and ordered that he should be searched for. The Duke thought it wise to return to Boulogne.

At Boulogne James received letters from his mother telling him that his old friend, Marshal Turenne, whose services were no longer needed at the front because the long war with Spain was now virtually over — peace negotiations were making good progress on the Franco—Spanish frontier at Fuentarrabia — wanted to see the King of England at Amiens. James, not knowing where his brother was — he discovered that he was neither at Dieppe nor Rouen — decided to go himself to meet Turenne. It was now the third week of August. At Amiens the Marshal made James an extremely generous offer; he told him that he would put his own infantry regiment at his disposal with arms, ammunition and provisions enough to last six weeks for all the troops Charles II could collect, to arrange for their embarkation at Boulogne, and by pawning his own plate furnish sufficient money to pay the costs of an expedition to England.[25] Naturally James was grateful. The exiled royalists had recently received the news that only 250 soldiers were guarding Kent, the foot garrisoning Dover castle and the cavalry being scattered between Canterbury, Rochester, Maidstone and Sandwich. James's plan was to land at Rye with 600 or 700 men and either fortify it or use it as a base for further operations.[26]

This hopeful scheme could not be realized. One wonders what in any case would have been Mazarin's reactions when he heard about it, for Turenne admitted that the Cardinal had not been consulted.

Although Turenne's own nephew and other volunteers had agreed to accompany James to Boulogne in the first week of September, the Duke at that very time received the news that Sir George Booth had been defeated in a one-sided battle in Cheshire on 19 August and two days later had been taken prisoner and sent to the Tower of London. Furthermore, James was worried about what had happened to his brother of whose whereabouts he still knew nothing. Might he have reached Cheshire or Wales and also been captured? Turenne assured him that his brother could not have gone to England, but agreed that the expedition to Rye must be called off. So James returned disconsolate to Brussels.[27]

Charles II had in fact gone to Brittanny in the first week of September with a view to sailing from St Malo to the west of England. But by the time he reached Rennes, fifty miles south of St Malo, on his way from Normandy, he had been informed of Booth's failure. Although John Mordaunt, ever cheerful, wrote to tell Charles that 'the whole design' was 'not upset' by Booth's defeat and that Willys, whose treacheries had been exposed, would not be dangerous in the future,[28] the trusted Sir Henry Bennet was at the same time pressing the King to come to Spain in the hope of obtaining positive support from the Court of Madrid once the peace treaty with France had been signed in Fuentarrabia.[29] As Don Luis de Haro, the leading Spanish Minister (nephew of the famous Olivares) was himself on the way to Fuentarrabia, Charles decided that he had better go there to see if he could obtain help both from Spain and France. He therefore sent the Marquis of Ormonde to ask permission from Cardinal Mazarin, who was himself about to depart for Fuentarrabia, for the King to travel through France to Spain. Ormonde followed Mazarin as far as St Jean de Luz where he received a cold reception. The Cardinal said to Ormonde: 'I know that there is a king of England exiled from his kingdom. I know all his misfortunes so it is useless to tell me any more. I can do nothing for him.' He refused to grant a pass to Charles and his companions.[30]

Charles now resolved to travel to Fuentarrabia incognito, accompanied by the Earl of Bristol and Daniel O'Neill, while he instructed Ormonde to go there by another route and wait for him. The King first went to La Rochelle, where he stayed a week, hoping to get to Spain by sea. But the weather was against it, so he continued his journey by land. Bristol was a fluent linguist and Daniel O'Neill an expert at obtaining good food — they had mutton for every meal —

and other entertainment. So Charles thoroughly enjoyed himself.[31]

The royalist Court, left behind in Brussels, was far from pleased that for two or three weeks Charles disappeared into the blue; he was dubbed irresponsible. James himself was troubled about this.[32] Some of the courtiers appear even to have thought they would do better to have the Duke as their leader, as he was far more conscientious.[33] In fact Charles arrived at Fuentarrabia at an appropriate time because the main treaty, known as that of the Pyrenees, was about to be signed. There had never been any question of his affairs being included in it. As the Spaniards were still at war with the English Commonwealth, which had taken Jamaica and Dunkirk away from them, they were glad to lend their assistance to Charles. He received a warm welcome from Don Luis de Haro, who gave him comfortable lodgings and 7,000 golden pistoles, more than enough to pay for his return journey to Brussels. It was generally agreed that Charles had created an excellent impression at Fuentarrabia.

Meanwhile, back in Brussels, James was being importuned by Mordaunt, who wrote from London to say that if the King and Duke did not come to England at once 'this unequalled occasion' would be lost.[34] James, as Secretary Nicholas related, 'was very resolute to put himself into action at the first opportunity'.[35] He tried to collect the remains of his army and march it to St Omer, but the Marquis of Caracena would not permit them to move without orders from above.[36] Furthermore, he felt sure that Turenne would forbid them to enter France. And, as has been noticed, Turenne had already advised James to postpone the expedition to England until the news from there was more promising. All that the Duke could do was to assure Mordaunt that he would prepare for any real opportunity and that he hoped with Spanish help 'to have one push for England before winter is over', but he found it necessary to warn him about the difficulties of enlisting any large number of men, procuring the vessels to transport them and gather together the required arms and provisions.[37] He concluded the first (and most authentic) part of his memoirs by writing:

> This design being thus blasted, and no hopes left of attempting anything in England at that time, the Duke passed the remaining part of this year in Brussels, expecting the King his brother, who arrived thither from the conference at Fuentarrabia a little before Christmas [1659] [38]

Although James had been able to tell Mordaunt before his brother's return that the King had given him full authority to act as he thought fit, if an opportunity presented itself for an expedition to England, it is clear that he relied on two principal means of effecting a Stuart restoration: one was that Charles would 'procure such assistance and declaration from the two Crowns [of France and Spain] as may make the work at least less difficult';[39] the other was the hope of profiting from the known differences between John Lambert, who was in effective command of the army in England, and George Monck, who was in charge of the English army garrisoning Scotland: these had come to a head at the end of October after Lambert and his nominal superior, General Fleetwood, had forcibly dissolved what was known as the Rump Parliament because it had rejected petitions from the army demanding reforms. James thought it was possible that either Lambert or Monck might adhere to the King — neither had been involved in Charles I's trial and execution — and a plan was even mooted for James to marry Lambert's daughter, Mary.[40] James, though thinking that Lambert was a more likely bet than Monck, argued

> it will surely be best for the King's friends to sit still and look on till they are thoroughly engaged in blood, and then one or both will be induced easily to a conjunction with his Majesty.[41]

Thus James might reasonably have claimed that he prophesied that what was ultimately to happen.

Nevertheless royalist aspirations were badly shaken when it was learnt that George Monck, who led his army into England at the beginning of 1660, had declared that he did so simply in order to protect the republican regime at Westminster from Fleetwood, Lambert and the army in England; for five weeks before Monck reached London the Rump Parliament had reassembled and resumed full charge of the government. It certainly appeared on the surface as if the Rump, once forcibly purged by Oliver Cromwell's son-in-law, Henry Ireton, and once ousted by John Lambert, now buttressed by Monck's army, was stronger than it ever had been. The hopes of an insurrection in England in favour of the King, James wrote, were 'now reduced to their lowest ebb'.[42] In the third week of March 1660, however, Monck, who had long tired of the growing anarchy, accepted a letter sent from Charles II and given to him by his cousin, Sir John Grenville, and Monck soon replied advising the King how he should behave. He must leave Brussels and enter the United Netherlands, a Protestant realm; he must promise a general amnesty; he must guarantee liberty of conscience in religious matters; and the sale of lands made during the Interregnum must be confirmed. Charles duly left Brussels for Breda, whence he dispatched five letters to England, of which the most important was known as the Declaration of Breda, dated 4/14 April 1660, drawn up by Edward Hyde and embodying with certain qualifications Monck's ideas for a Restoration settlement. A new parliament was elected after the Rump had dissolved itself; it met on 25 April and the members invited the King to return to London.

A fleet, commanded by Edward Montagu, anchored off Schevingen, the port for The Hague; James was acclaimed Lord High Admiral and busied himself inspecting the warships, some of which were renamed to obliterate the memories of Oliver Cromwell's victories. On 21 May the Duke of York 'in yellow trimming' came aboard the fleet, accompanied by the Duke of Gloucester.[43] After allotting to every ship 'their service in relation to England' with the help of William Coventry and Samuel Pepys, James had dinner and was entertained by a harpist. The fleet set sail on 23 May, the Duke of York aboard the *London* and the King aboard the *Royal Charles* (previously the *Naseby*). Early on 25 May James and his younger brother joined the King for breakfast, eating the ship's normal diet — pease and pork and boiled beef.[44] After landing at Dover that day the royal party made for London by way of Canterbury; accompanied by James, King Charles II entered his capital on his thirtieth birthday, 29 May 1660.

Two questions arise about James's last years in exile. First, were his relations with his elder brother happy? Second, did he at that time become a Roman Catholic? Undoubtedly many at the royal Court including Edward Hyde, who had in January 1660 been appointed Lord Chancellor, thought more highly of James's behaviour that that of the King. They condemned Charles for his frivolity in Cologne and on the journey from France to Spain, while his love life in Brussels was notorious. James was annoyed over his brother's complete disappearance when Charles left him in Brussels to handle his affairs without any detailed instructions as best he could. Even after the business about Sir John Berkeley had been settled, Charles interferred with James's staff and ordered him to cut down its numbers. James also had other differences with his brother for example over his attempted mediation in 1652, over his appointment of de Marsin in 1657, over the Irish troops being made to swear oaths of allegiance to the King of Spain. Though there is no reason to suppose that James intrigued against the King — he was never an intriguer — certainly some of his friends did so. Writing from Brussels on 11 October 1659 Hyde told Ormonde that Father Peter Talbot, a Jesuit, had said 'there was a great party in the kingdom well-affected to the Duke . . . who would serve the Duke with all their power, though they would have nothing to do with the King.'[45] Other royalist agents in England confirmed this, though the adjective 'great' must have been an exaggeration. But James himself, whatever criticisms he felt about Charles's conduct and policies, recognized his duty to obey him and would never have stooped to any disloyalty.

As to James's religion, unquestionably both Charles and James attended Mass in the Spanish Netherlands. The evidence that Charles became convinced of the truth of the Roman Catholic religion about 1659, though scattered, is pretty conclusive.[46] For a long time he did not have a Protestant chaplain and he did not protest about the closure of a Protestant chapel in the Louvre which had been opened for the benefit of the English exiles. James and Anne Hyde also attended Catholic services; one of James's chaplains had actually advised him to do so to see what went on. As early as 1651 Sir George Radcliffe took James to several Masses in Brussels including a service at the cathedral; according to Lord Byron this was done 'upon pretence of hearing good music'. At this time, too, towards the end of the second Fronde, when Queen Henrietta Maria was living in the Louvre, Sir Edward Nicholas was writing anxiously to his friends about rumours that the Duke of York was being induced to become a papist.[47] But clearly James did not ask to be officially received into the Catholic Church until many years after he first went abroad. Unlike Charles, who paid lip-service to Anglicanism purely for political reasons, James was no dissembler. The fact that he did not seriously exert himself to prevent the conversion of his younger brother and sister may have been significant. By the spring of 1659 a general suspicion of his 'inclination to Popery' prevailed. The Duke nevertheless said that he would continue in profession and practice a Protestant but that 'he would not discharge servants who were Papists'.[48] One of James's biographers has insisted that those in England who would have preferred his rule to that of Charles were mostly Catholics.[49] In any case, James himself was staunch in his support of his brother, did not then seek the throne for himself, and concealed his religious opinions. It may have been out of gratitude to his brother in these days of exile that twenty years later Charles used all his resources to prevent James, by then an avowed Roman Catholic, from being excluded from succession to the throne.

6.
Lord High Admiral

Ever since he was a child James had borne the title of Lord High Admiral, but he had never been engaged in any fighting at sea. His elder brother had refused to let him sail with him when he led a royalist fleet from Holland to England in 1648. But on the eve of his restoration, when it was clear that the Commonwealth navy was about to fall into his hands like a ripe fruit, Charles II bestowed the title on him once again — on 16 May 1660 — though he did not receive his official commission until eight months later after the King was safely installed in his palace of Whitehall.

During the Interregnum the navy had been strong and successful. The Commonwealth inherited a fleet that had been built up by Charles I, and paid for out of the unpopular tax known as ship money. The office of Lord High Admiral and the old Navy Board had then been replaced by a naval commander-in-chief, the Earl of Warwick, who had warded off the threat from the makeshift royalist fleet in 1648, while a variety of committees, appointed by Parliament, undertook the administration of the navy. The leading spirits in the Commonwealth navy committee were first Giles Greene, a knowledgeable Weymouth merchant, and then Sir Henry Vane the Younger, who held the post of Treasurer of the Navy for eleven years and was to be described by another republican, Algernon Sidney, as 'an absolute Master of Naval affairs' and — though this was hardly exact — the inventor of the frigate.[1] So effective was Vane's administration that the Dutch were defeated in the first Anglo-Dutch war (1652-4) and subsequently trounced the French, the Spaniards and Algerian pirates under commanders as distinguished as Robert Blake and George Monck.

However, as anarchy loomed up after the fall of Richard Cromwell, the quality of the navy began to deteriorate, resources were depleted and a large debt for supplies and sailors' pay was accumulated. Samuel Pepys, secretary to Edward Montagu, who sailed with him when the admiral went to collect the King and the Duke of York from Holland, was of the opinion that the navy was in a deplorable state.[2] This was rather an exaggeration, for it consisted of 156 warships carrying 4,642 guns, of which only twenty-one were ketches, pinks and other small vessels.[3] The debt was about £750,000 and Charles, who in fact knew a good deal more about naval affairs than his brother, immediately allocated sufficient money to pay it off and replenish supplies.[4]

The first thing that James did as Lord High Admiral was to draw up a paper setting out how the business of the Admiralty and the navy should be regulated. This paper was referred to a committee, which reported its decisions to the Privy Council meeting under the chairmanship of the King on 2 July 1660; the Duke's recommendations were accepted and from then on he became the ruler of the King's navy much in the same way as the First Lord of the Admiralty in Gilbert and Sullivan's comic opera, *H.M.S. Pinafore.* Understandably James reverted to the idea of a small Navy Board as it had existed before the civil wars and the days of large parliamentary committees, consisting simply of a treasurer, a surveyor, a comptroller and a clerk of the acts. To these were added three commissioners without specific duties who were required to occupy themselves in general supervision of naval questions.[5] The members of the Board were all extremely experienced men. Sir George Carteret, who had been Governor of Jersey when Charles and James were there during the Interregnum, and had begun life as a sea-boy, was appointed treasurer, Sir William Batten, who had served both the Commonwealth and Charles when he was Prince of Wales as an admiral, became surveyor, Sir Robert Slyngesbie, who was selected comptroller had been a sea captain (he was soon to be replaced by Sir John Mennes, another former captain and friend of Prince Rupert) and Samuel Pepys, on the recommendation of his relative Montagu, became clerk of the acts, which meant in effect that he was secretary and accountant to the Board.

In considering James's career as Lord High Admiral it must be remembered that the indefatigable writings of Pepys as a diarist, as a compiler of minutes and as the author of innumerable other official documents and papers (still extant) are overwhelmingly the principal historical source for James's record as a naval administrator. The three commissioners were James's old friend, John Lord Berkeley, Sir William Penn, an admiral who had both fought for and been criticized by Oliver Cromwell, and Peter Pett, the leading member of an established family of ship-builders. Pett was required to reside in and look after the Chatham dockyard; later, similar resident Board members were appointed on the direction of the Duke in Harwich and Portsmouth. According to the Earl of Clarendon, the creation of the commissioners at large was on the suggestion of William Coventry, the Duke's secretary since 1660 who was later to be appointed as a commissioner himself. The Navy Board, thus constituted, was of course subject to the overall decisions of the Lord High Admiral and the King. It was in fact James's advisory council and the organ through which his commands were carried out. To start with, the Board met weekly and its members were expected to keep in close touch with one another in London, Deptford and Chatham. In his diary Pepys paid tribute to James's devotion to his work as Lord High Admiral, observing in 1664 that he 'do give himself up to his business' and that he was 'concerned to mend things in the navy himself and not leave it to other people';[6] he also noted that Admiral Montagu, who was created Earl of Sandwich by Charles II, greatly admired James's discretion and application in his work.[7]

During the early years of Charles II's reign James published three sets of instructions. The first dated 28 January 1662 was addressed to the members of the Navy Board.[8] It dealt with the duties of its various officers in a detailed and elaborate manner and added specific instructions that no member of the Board was to take advantage of his position to trade in commodities used by the navy, which had been in the past a highly profitable occupation. The members were paid salaries and not fees, ranging from £2,000 a year for the treasurer to £350 a year for Pepys and Pett. Unquestionably most of them found ways to gain other financial benefits from their positions.

Secondly, James issued 'general instructions' to the captains of warships plus a set of additional orders.[9] The first instruction was that they were 'to take care that Almighty God be duly served on board your ship twice every day by the whole ship's company, according to the liturgy of the Church of England.' Among the additional orders was the instruction that any sailor who was heard to swear, curse or blaspheme was to forfeit a day's pay for each offence; and another order was that 'those who pisseth on the decks'

were to be lashed though not more than twelve times. Finally, before
the outbreak of the second Anglo-Dutch war, James published a set
of instructions 'for the better ordering of the fleet in sailing'.[10] These
consisted mainly of how ships were to signal to one another, for
example by firing cannon or hanging out flags; they forbade commanders to take possession of disabled ships until the battle was
over; and they were told to see that fireships kept the wind if
possible.

These orders were in fact largely a repetition of the instructions
given by Monck and his fellow generals-at-sea in 1653 during the first
Anglo-Dutch war. There was, however, one striking exception. The
third article of the earlier instructions had been of a revolutionary
kind. It stated that 'the ships of every squadron shall endeavour to
keep in a line with the chief and if the chief be maimed or otherwise
disabled (which God forbid!) then every ship of the said squadron
shall still endeavour to keep in a line with the admiral or he that
commands in chief next to him and nearest the enemy.' The tactics
thus described were those of close-hauled line ahead. In James's
instructions all that is said is that 'each squadron shall take the best
advantage they can to engage with the enemy according to the order
prescribed.' In James's additional instructions of April 1665 a close
line is prescribed not in offence but in defence when the enemy
obtained the advantage of the wind 'and come to fight us'.[11]

Naturally it is impossible to be certain whether James altered or
improved upon the drafts provided for him by his subordinates,
although it does appear likely that the attempt to prevent speculation was due to him personally, and probably also the setting up of
the additional resident commissioners at the principal naval depots.
Furthermore, realizing the debts with which the navy was encum-
bered the Duke pressed the Navy Board to make all possible econo-
mies in peace time by reducing the number of pilots, cutting down
the shooting off of salutes by cannonades, and discharging superfluous workmen from the shipyards; at the beginning of 1662 James
made a speech to all the principal officers of the navy and naval
commanders in this sense.[12] He also tried to provide for the future by
encouraging the selection of gentlemen volunteers to serve in the
Royal Navy with a view to their becoming available as officers when
needed in war time.

Before James took an active part in the navy, his experience as a
soldier was invoked. An extreme puritan sect known as the Fifth

Monarchy Men, who believed that the second coming of Jesus to earth was imminent regarded it as their Christian duty to prepare the way for His return if necessary by force.[13] As a political party they had reached their apogee in 1653 when Cromwell and his officers summoned an Assembly of Saints, several of whose members were deeply influenced by Fifth Monarchy preachers outside the House. Oliver with his usual tolerance had interviewed two of their leaders, who had been arrested and imprisoned, assuring them that they had been taken into custody because of their violence and as stirrers up of sedition, not as witnesses of Christ. In fact after he became Lord Protector the Fifth Monarchists claimed that he was aiming at a secular monarchy, and they wanted no king but Jesus. When the Restoration took place they were provoked by the execution of Major-General Thomas Harrison, himself a Fifth Monarchist, as one of the regicides chosen for royalist revenge.

In January 1661 while King Charles was away from London seeing off his mother and youngest sister, who were returning from Portsmouth to France, a Fifth Monarchy rising took place in the city of London headed by Thomas Venner, a wine-bottler. A manifesto was published entitled *The Door of Hope* in which it was stated that 'they would not make any league with monarchists, but would rise against the carnal, to possess the gate of the world, to bind their kings in chains and their nobles in fetters of iron.' After killing several men in the City, Venner and his group went out to Ken Wood where George Monck, Duke of Albemarle, dispatched his own troopers to round them up. But this he was unable to do because of the enclosed nature of the country, the insurgents successfully hiding among the trees.[14] Since James had been indisposed, he had not gone with Charles to Portsmouth, but remained in Whitehall. Here George Monck, Duke of Albemarle, woke him up to tell him what was happening. The rising was in fact soon put down. When Venner and his fellow fanatics returned to the City the trained bands surrounded and killed most of them, Venner receiving nineteen wounds before surgeons patched him together so that he might be hanged. James and Monck were so agitated that they collected 1,500 cavalrymen before riding to St Paul's only to learn from the Lord Mayor that the crisis was over.[15]

This incident had a profound effect on Stuart policy. The original intention at the Restoration was to pay off Monck's army as soon as possible for two reasons: first, because of the expense of keeping it in being, secondly because Charles had doubts about its loyalty to the Crown. Only a few horse guards and life guards had been retained chiefly for ceremonial purposes. After Venner's rising James proposed to the Privy Council that it should write to the King asking his permission to stop the disbanding of Monck's troops of horse guards and regiment of foot (the Coldstreamers) and to enlist more soldiers for the security of the Government. The many nonconformists, who only wanted to practise their religion in peace, were confounded with the tiny group of Fifth Monarchists and their meetings were thought to be centres of sedition and conspiracy that needed to be watched and suppressed. The Lord Treasurer, the Earl of Southampton, and the Lord Chancellor, the Earl of Clarendon, were opposed to the proposal for obvious reasons — not only the cost but also the fears likely to be engendered by a standing army. However, they were overruled. Besides the King's, the Duke's and Monck's troops of horse guards a new infantry regiment and a new cavalry regiment were raised; thus in effect a standing army of a few thousand was created.[16] It was to form the nucleus of a large army constituted by James almost as soon as he became king. Its unpopularity with both people and Parliament contributed in no small degree to James's ultimate downfall.

Besides his duties as Lord High Admiral, as a leading member of the Privy Council and as the King's deputy when he was away from London, James was also concerned with trade and colonial affairs. One of the most profitable forms of commerce was the seizure of Negroes from the west coast of Africa and their sale at £18 a head to planters in the West Indies. James also envisaged the finding of gold ore in West Africa, as in fact it was to be. In 1663 the Royal African or Guinea Company was founded as a joint stock company; James was appointed Governor and his cousin, Prince Rupert (who had visited West Africa during the Interregnum) was a member of the Council. In 1664 the King permitted the Company to hire two warships, which were sent under the command of Sir Robert Holmes, a friend of Prince Rupert's, to Guinea where he occupied stations claimed by the Dutch along the coast. The Dutch retorted by dispatching a strong squadron under Admiral de Ruyter to the west coast of Africa to recover the lost stations and take over English factories (trading centres) there.[17]

In 1664, too, King Charles granted to James a strip of territory lying between what was to become Maryland and New England, then known as the New Netherlands because it was partly inhabited by Dutch colonists, although English settlers were to be found in Long Island. James promptly sent out an expedition under Captain Robert Nicholls again with warships allocated to him by the King; Nicholls was more successful than Holmes for he captured New Amsterdam (which was to be renamed New York after James) in August, overcoming the resistance of Peter Stuyvesant, the Dutch Governor. Finally in the same year, on 8 April, the Duke of York was appointed Governor of the Royal Fishery Company which aimed to give encouragement to English fishermen, especially those engaged in the catching of herrings, and to stimulate the consumption of fish and the building of herring boats. The overall objective of the Company was to compete successfully with the Dutch, who were much more efficient fishermen and built better boats (ultimately fishing boats had to be bought from them).[18]

All these activities presided over by James resulted in clashes with the Dutch, although the King acquiesced in their claims to the extent of sending Sir Robert Holmes to the Tower of London for seizing their stations in west Africa, while the Dutch interests in New England and New York were too small to be of much importance to them and the competition from English fishermen was too ineffective to cause them much worry. Nevertheless colonial and commercial rivalries contributed largely to the causes of the second Anglo—Dutch war which was soon to break out. One of its protagonists was William Coventry, who had been James's secretary since 1660, and the Duke himself was eager for war in which he might hope to distinguish himself as Lord High Admiral. Neither the King nor the Earl of Clarendon wanted war, but when the House of Commons showed that it did so and was willing to vote money to pay for it, Charles yielded to his brother's wishes.

The Duke of York threw himself energetically into preparations for war. As early as June 1664 he paid a visit of inspection to the Chatham dockyards and in November he went aboard the *Swiftsure*, a second-rate warship with forty-six guns, after carrying out a similar inspection at Portsmouth. He was convinced that he had under his command the best possible fleet and after cruising with it for four days in the English Channel, accompanied by Prince Rupert, who was a much more experienced seaman than his royal cousin, James felt sure that the Dutch would yield to English demands rather than go to war.[19] Except for greeting Charles's bride off Portsmouth when she arrived from Portugal in 1661 this was the first time that James had any direct experience of service at sea.

War was declared on 4 March 1665. The English fleet assembled at the Gunfleet, an anchorage south of Harwich, where James joined it at the end of the month. The fleet was divided into the Red squadron commanded by James, who had the foresight to select as his vice-admiral the highly experienced Sir John Lawson, even though he had been a republican stalwart from the outbreak of the civil wars. Rupert was in command of the White or van squadron and the Earl of Sandwich led the Blue or rear squadron. So there was no lack of skill and knowledge at James's disposal. Since he could discover no signs of any Dutch movements he boldly took his fleet across to the Dutch coast, cruising between Schevingen, the port of The Hague, which he knew so well, and the Texel farther north, the principal Dutch naval base. Within a fortnight he was back at the Gunfleet because his ships needed water and victuals, but above all beer. James was not at all pleased about this, for, as he wrote to a friend at the time:

> You will see what a great disappointment I have had, for had he [the victualler] kept touch I had not been forced to come back . . . I believe never had any great fleet ever ventured to go so far from home and upon an enemy's coast with so small a proportion of drink . . .[20]

While still at the Gunfleet James learned on 28 May that the Dutch had now put to sea with a fleet numerically larger than his own carrying more men and guns under the supreme command of Jacob Wassenaer Baron of Obdam, 'a man of quality and personal courage',[21] but as an admiral not in the same class as de Ruyter, who was still on his return voyage from Africa. Since the wind was unfavourable, blowing from the east, James resolved to move out from the Gunfleet and sail north towards Southwold Bay, where he anchored on 1 June. There the Dutch were sighted some leagues away; each side manoeuvred for position, but as the wind dropped little happened then or on the following day. By the evening of 2 June the rival fleets were two leagues apart off Lowestoft. When night came on the Dutch were seen lighting their matches, which meant that they were preparing for battle at dawn the next day.

Now James had a stroke of luck. The wind veered first to the south-west and then to the south-south-west so that the English gained the weather gauge. At three in the morning both fleets were sailing to the east, but then the Dutch put about and moving west poured broadsides into each English ship in succession. At nine o'clock James ordered his whole fleet also to tack and three times the two lines of warships sailed past one another, the fighting growing extremely ferocious. The reason why six hours elapsed between the start of the battle and its climax was that James's orders for his fleet to tack were delayed and caused confusion, almost chaos. But by ten in the morning, as James's earliest biographer wrote:

> Never was seen a more proper day to dispute the mastery of the sea; for it was very smooth, a fine steady gale at the south-west, not a cloud in the sky, nor the least appearance of any alteration of wind or weather.[22]

The first blow to the English was that Lawson, James's vice-admiral of the Red, aboard a second-rate, the *Royal Oak*, was mortally wounded while Sandwich's heavy flagship the *Prince,* which once the fleet had tacked should have been leading the van, was outsailed by James aboard the *Royal Charles*.[23] The next blow was that the *Old James*, one of the second-rate ships in James's squadron, sprang a leak and its commander, the Earl of Marl-borough, together with his nephew, the Earl of Portland, was drowned. These misfortunes caused the *Royal Charles* to be exposed to a cannonade from Obdam's flagship; a single gunshot from it killed James's great friend, Charles Berkeley, who had been created Earl of Falmouth by Charles II, Lord Muskerry, one of James's Gentlemen of the Bedchamber, and a younger son of the Earl of Burlington. James himself was splashed by their noble blood as he stood upon his quarterdeck. The tragedy occurred at midday, at which time James's squadron was in the van, Sandwich's rear squadron was in the centre, and Rupert's, the van squadron, was in the rear. Thus everything was in disorder and whatever intention James may have had of fighting in line had foundered.

By two o'clock in the afternoon the fire from the Dutch ships began to slacken and Obdam's broadsides directed at the *Royal Charles* were replaced by only two or three cannon firing at a time. Half an hour later James was able to turn the tables on his opposite number. A lucky shot from the *Royal Charles* struck the magazine on Obdam's flagship which blew up killing the Dutch commander-in-chief and 400 of his men. By four o'clock the battle had degenerated into a confused rout. James ordered his fireships to be clapped onto the Dutch warships as they became entangled with one another. As Cornelis van Tromp, who was with the Dutch fleet, reported, it 'got into such confusion that they all ran away from the enemy before the wind', losing a dozen of their ships captured or burnt. James gave instructions for a chase, which was not abandoned until about nine in the evening when it was growing dark. Thus the battle lasted for the best part of eighteen hours. It was a definite victory for the English as the Dutch losses were heavier than was normal in seventeenth-century warfare. At eleven o'clock at night James, exhausted by the bloody battle, retired to bed, fully dressed with a quilt thrown over him. He slept the sleep of a conqueror.

After the Duke went to bed an extraordinary episode occurred, which has often been related but never explained. James's Groom of the Bedchamber on duty was a certain Henry Brouncker M.P. who was supposed to watch over his master while he slept. Satisfied that the Duke was asleep, Brouncker took it upon himself to ask the master of the ship, Captain Cox, to shorten sail on the ground that since the *Royal Charles* was such a good sailer it would by its speed outdistance the rest of the fleet and when he awoke James might find himself trapped in the middle of the enemy or at least liable to become the victim of a Dutch fireship (fireships being used in those days as weapons directed by the wind against large warships, much as torpedoes were later to be employed against cruisers). Before he retired James had given Cox orders to make all the sail he could and so the master naturally told Brouncker that he could not disobey them unless they were countermanded by a higher authority. Brouncker then referred the matter to Captain John Harman, the master's superior officer. Harman was at first unmoved by Brouncker's rhetoric. Brouncker then pretended to go down to the Duke's cabin and returned to tell Harman that he had spoken to James who had asked him to convey to the captain his personal command to shorten sail without further argument. Thinking it impossible that Brouncker could be lying, Harman then acquiesced; so that when the Duke awoke next morning he found himself well astern of the Dutch and out of touch with the rest of his fleet. Vainly he pursued the enemy warships as far as the Texel, but, fearful of running onto sandbanks, allowed them to escape into safety with minor losses.

It has been claimed that no plausible explanation exists for Brouncker's behaviour. In the first place, it was odd that Sir William Penn, James's Captain of the Fleet (in effect Chief of Staff), who was aboard the *Royal Charles* was not consulted by Harman. Is it possible that Harman himself had second thoughts? After all, the argument that the life of the heir presumptive to the English throne should not be put at peril in the dark was a fairly convincing one. It was in fact for that very reason that, after James returned to England, Charles II forbade him to take any further active part in the war. A rather improbable suggestion was that after such a bloody battle Brouncker was afraid for his own life. A possibly better suggestion has been put forward that James's wife, the Duchess Anne, whom he had married in 1660 and was a powerful personality, had strictly enjoined Brouncker and other members of James's household or 'family' that it was their paramount duty to preserve her husband's life when at sea — certainly a pretty tall order. The evidence for this is a poem written by Sir John Denham. James was far from being a perfect husband nor is Anne known to have been notably uxorious; indeed she had to wink uneasily at the Duke's numerous affairs, as we shall see later. If Brouncker was persuaded by anyone to do what he did, perhaps it was not James's wife at all but his current mistress, the beautiful Margaret Brooke, who happened to be the poet Denham's own wife and was nearly thirty years younger than he was.[24] Sexual explanations of political and military events seldom find favour with historians and are usually dismissed as tittle-tattle. It may be so.

After the Dutch fleet got safely into the Texel, James returned to the Buoy of the Nore, an anchorage at the mouth of the Thames; his intention was to refit and take on supplies before going to sea again. The Queen Mother has just been paying a visit to England and when she was there she pressed Charles II not to allow James to take part in any more fighting; it was obvious enough that he had been risking his life, as not only were his friends struck down at his side, but two hundred of the crew had been killed aboard his flagship.

Accompanied by Prince Rupert, James left the Buoy of the Nore for Whitehall where Charles announced his resolve that neither James nor Rupert was to return to the sea during that campaigning season. It appears that William Coventry did not think highly of Rupert as a naval commander; at any rate the Earl of Sandwich was put in command of the fleet. James, disappointed, tried hard to induce the King to change his mind. Charles attempted to console him by pointing out that another major battle with the Dutch during the summer was unlikely; that Sandwich's duty would be chiefly to intercept Dutch merchantmen arriving from the East or West Indies;

and that, in view of the defeat inflicted on the Dutch at Lowestoft they would do all they could to avoid another confrontation.[25] By way of compensating him with other important duties the King asked James to go north where, according to spies' reports, a rising against the Government was being plotted by Cromwellians and republicans in conjunction with the Dutch. Undoubtedly many nonconformists in the West Riding of Yorkshire were unhappy about the restrictions imposed on the exercise of their religion; in 1663 the High Sheriff claimed to have unravelled a number of plots there while the second Duke of Buckingham, who was Lord Lieutenant of the West Riding, led an armed force north as a precaution against insurrection. During 1664 sixteen men were executed for treason. In 1665 wild rumours of republican conspiracies were circulating; after all, the Dutch were republicans and might light the torch of rebellion. In fact in York all was reported to be quiet; Coventry, James's secretary, was able to assure the Secretary of State, Lord Arlington, that 'there was no great danger of risings since most dangerous men were secured'. James was accompanied to York by his Duchess; he stayed there from 5 August to 23 September, spending most of his time in shooting and outdoor exercises.[26] It must all have seemed extremely peaceful after the fiercely fought battles at sea.

Before James left London the epidemic known as the Great Plague had reached the English capital from the Levant. By July thousands of deaths were counted; the Court therefore moved for safety first to Salisbury and then to Oxford where James joined his brother in September. Here Parliament met in a good-natured mood. It voted a further £1,250,000 for the continuation of the naval war and gave James £120,000 'in token of the great sense they had of his conduct and bravery' at Lowestoft. But the Great Plague, which spread to some of the sailors, and the Great Fire of London which followed in the next year, destroying Admiralty records, were handicaps to naval efficiency. The Earl of Sandwich, who had not made the most of his opportunities in the autumn of 1665, was dismissed by James for sharing the proceeds of an intercepted convoy from the East Indies with his officers without permission. Charles, remembering the services that Sandwich had performed before the Restoration, gave him the consolatory post of ambassador to Spain, while the two famous veterans, Prince Rupert and George Monck, Duke of Albemarle, took command at sea. They had a gratifying campaign in 1666 overcoming the Dutch fleet, now assisted by a French squadron, and setting fire to thousands of Dutch merchantmen and stores lying insufficiently protected in a North Sea anchorage. This operation, which took place in August, was known as Sir Robert Holmes's Bonfire; it marked the highest point reached by the English navy during the war.

As the King assumed that the war was virtually won he opened negotiations for peace with the Dutch. He was aware that the money voted by Parliament was nearly exhausted; the decision was therefore taken at the outset of 1667 to lay up the larger warships at Chatham and elsewhere, depending upon frigates to continue harassing the widespread Dutch commerce. Precisely who was responsible for persuading Charles to adopt this policy is not altogether clear. But its main cause was that when Parliament met in the autumn of 1666 the Commons, which was suspicious about how its previous grants of money for the war had been used refused to vote any more funds for it. At any rate on 24 May the King ordered James to maintain at sea only sufficient ships to distract the Dutch and disturb their trade. According to James's earliest biographer:

> The Duke opposed all he could the taking of these measures, urging, that our having no fleet at sea would raise again the spirits of our enemies, which now were very low, and give them time as well courage to set out their fleet again, having a prospect of little or no resistance.[27]

Was this an example of historical hindsight or not? It is curious that Sir William Coventry, who was still James's secretary and was a member of the Privy Council, was one of the keenest advocates, together with Lord Arlington, the Secretary of State for the South, of laying up the larger vessels of the fleet. Furthermore Coventry assured Samuel Pepys, the Clerk of the Acts at the Navy Board, whom James trusted, that the money was just not available for sending the whole fleet to sea and therefore peace was essential.[28]

The result of this decision was that in the early summer of 1667 the Dutch undertook an operation of extreme daring. A squadron assigned for the purpose bombarded Sheerness, landed a force on the Isle of Sheppey, and forced its way up the Medway to near where the English warships were docked at Chatham. The Dutch captured the *Royal Charles* and towed it across the North Sea to the intense humiliation of English patriots. This expedited the conclusion of peace; a treaty was signed at Breda on 21 July 1667.

James learned several lessons from the war. He does not appear to have been very active as Lord High Admiral except that he kept watch on the supplies of victuals to the fleet, for he realized how inadequate they had been while he was at sea; he had also ordered at the end of 1666 a platform firm enough to bear twelve guns to be erected at Sheerness and he increased the number of guardships on the Medway, which at least showed that he was aware of the danger of a surprise coup by the Dutch.[29] But lack of ready money meant that the fulfilling of these orders was delayed until it was too late. An alert Lord High Admiral would have made sure that they were carried out.

In September 1666 James and his brother took an energetic part in preventing the spread of the great fire of London by ensuring the destruction of buildings standing between the City and Whitehall. During 1667 he was involved in defending the Government against the recriminations of members of the House of Commons about the mismanagement of the war and the expenditure of the money granted to the navy. In the autumn of that year he was struck down by smallpox (or at any rate some infectious illness) from which he did not recover until the end of the year. We are fortunate in having preserved for us one of James's prayers which he must have made in the winter of 1667-8:

> I thank God for protecting me in all the battles, sieges and fights I have been in at sea as well as on land and for delivering me from other dangers . . . and for restoring his Majesty in this his kingdom; for recovering me from the smallpox, which had swept away some years before some of our family; for preserving me hitherto from the snares and plots of my enemies. I have justly deserved all the inflictions and mortifications Almighty God has pleased to lay on me.[30]

During 1668 and 1669 James set about the reform of the Admiralty. In January 1668 he complained to the Navy Board about the want of discipline in the fleet. He was informed that some of the captains appointed by Rupert and Monck were responsible for defects and disorders. Realizing, however, that the trouble was due chiefly to the slackness of the Navy Board itself, he asked Pepys, who was of course a member of the Board and had access to all its records, to draw up a paper about it, which he accepted and signed in August 1668. This paper was entitled 'Reflections on the Instructions of 1662' and was caustic about the books being badly kept and orders ignored. The other members of the Board concocted an elaborate reply, but virtually admitted the justice of the criticisms.

James then reprimanded the Board and insisted that in future his instructions must be carried out to the letter. It was at this time, too, that James instituted resident commissioners at Portsmouth and Harwich as well as at Chatham and gave them leave to act in an emergency without consulting the rest of the Board. This was clearly motivated by the Dutch raid on the Medway so it meant shutting the stable door after the horse had bolted. In September 1671 the Duke was to issue revised instructions about the control of the navy's finances, making the naval treasurer responsible directly to the rest of the Board instead of being responsible solely to the Lord High Admiral. James also tried to stimulate other reforms. For example, though sailors were relatively well paid they invariably had to wait a long time before their tickets were honoured after they returned to land; James tried to accelerate the payment of these tickets. He also gave orders about the sale of clothing, insisting that such sales should take place only in the presence of the ships' captains.

As a whole the impression is that James was a good and conscientious Lord High Admiral. We are of course largely dependent on Pepys for our picture of the Duke in this capacity and Pepys was inclined to take most of the credit for the naval administration and its reforms to himself. What is certain is that James usually followed the best advice given to him both by his admirals and his civil servants and that he reposed the utmost confidence in Pepys. He tried to get him elected member of parliament for Aldburgh at a by-election and he promoted him to being secretary to the Lord High Admiral, a key post. This confidence was reciprocated, for Pepys remained loyal to James to the very last, even as he was going into exile in 1688.

7.

Attitudes to Men, Women and God

Charles II's refusal to let James go to sea again in the latter half of 1665 or in 1666 is easy to understand. Their other brother, Henry, Duke of Gloucester, 'a prince of extraordinary hopes', had died of smallpox in September 1660 at the age of twenty. Moreover Catherine of Braganza, of whom James said after he first met her and greeted her on her arrival in England in May 1662,[1] that he had no doubt the King would be happy with such a queen, had not been able to give him any children, though she had had two miscarriages. So it hardly needed the Queen Mother to point out that to allow the Duke of York to risk his life at sea again might imperil the survival of the Stuart monarchy; for Charles himself was anxious to ensure the succession and wanted to safeguard his heir presumptive. Though as a handsome young officer at the Court of France James was said to have eclipsed his elder brother,[2] especially with the ladies, they were at no time jealous of each other. James appreciated that his hopes of future power and happiness lay in Charles's patronage; he was unflinchingly loyal to him even when his advice was rejected, as over naval policy. The Earl of Clarendon, who knew them both extremely well, recorded that the King 'had in truth a just affection for his brother, without thinking better of his natural parts than there was cause for',[3] while of James he wrote 'never any prince had a more humble and dutiful condescension and submission to an elder brother than the Duke towards the King.'[4]

Unlike Charles, James was neither supple nor devious. His conversation was limited and rarely gracious and he was handicapped, as his father had been, by a slight stutter. He was a stickler for Court etiquette, had no sense of humour and prided himself on being hard and tough; even his laudatory biographer admitted 'his outward carriage was a little stiff and constrained'. He had a hot temper.

Altogether he needed to be carefully managed. A woman or a priest or both could do it, and one or two politicians learned to handle him with tact. The contrast between the good-looking and gallant young officer and the rather disagreeable, long-faced, middle-aged prince as disclosed by his later portraits is most marked. He became haughty and unbending as a monarch until events forced him to make belated concessions to his critics. Charles II, on the other hand, knew instinctively when to yield and when to be firm, a gift always to be envied. He judged rightly that James would behave foolishly once he obtained full power. It is one of the paradoxes of Charles's character that he worked so hard for the succession to his throne of a brother whose ability to rule cleverly he clearly mistrusted.

Two characteristics the brothers had in common. One was that in taking decisions they were more influenced by men than ideas. It has been noticed how devoted James was to Sir John Berkeley in his younger days, while Charles was guided by Sir Henry Bennet. According to Clarendon, writing later in exile, they were 'too much inclined to like men at first sight and did not love the conversation of men of many more years than themselves'.[5] Clearly that was an example of sour grapes, for Clarendon himself, while he was James's principal Minister, was overruled more than once by the King, for example about going to war with the Dutch. When James became king himself he was certainly influenced by advisers like the second Earl of Sunderland and Father Petre. Clarendon added, however, that the Duke stuck to his resolutions better than King Charles, though he stressed that this was owing rather to 'an obstinacy of will' which in turn was due to 'an aversion from debate' than for 'the constancy of his judgment which was more subject to persons than arguments'.

The fact is that it is never easy to judge how a man in authority reaches his decisions, that is to say whether he studies all the arguments available to him before making up his mind or whether he simply trusts his expert advisers because he knows from experience that he can rely upon them. As was observed in the last chapter, James reposed full confidence in Pepys and thanked the Earl of Sandwich for bringing him into the service of the navy, as he once told the busy Clerk of the Acts, much to his delight.[6] Charles for his part may have given the appearance of being lazy, though in times of crisis he was always resolute. Clarendon claims that Charles 'did very often depart in matters of the highest moment to comply with his brother'.[7] 'Very often' is surely an exaggeration. For if that were so, would not Charles have taken his brother's advice about keeping the fleet in being during the spring of 1667?

The second characteristic that the brothers had in common was their obsessive love of women. Charles's remark that his brother loved women even more than he did himself has often been quoted, coupled with the generalization that James preferred plain women to beautiful ones so that he (Charles) believed 'his brother had his mistresses given him by his priests for penance'. Charles had a large number of casual affairs while he was in exile abroad and a bachelor, starting with Lucy Walter, who gave birth to his favourite son, James Crofts, Duke of Monmouth. For his part James does not seem to have had any notable affairs in France and Flanders; indeed he made his first known mistress his wife. It was not until after his first marriage that his love life became notorious.

James met Anne Hyde, who was then a Maid of Honour to his sister Mary, for the first time in 1656 and they went through a form of marriage on 24 November 1659 when she was twenty-two. It is usually asserted that she was rather a plain woman, though intelligent and witty. Her portraits do not prove her to have been plain, and one by Lely, even if he was unquestionably a flatterer of royalty, may be used as evidence to the contrary. The Count of Gramont, whose recollections are entertaining, if not always dependable, said that 'though she was not an absolute beauty, there was nobody at the Court of Holland capable of putting her in the shade'.[8] Sir John Reresby, who met Anne when she was in York with her husband and had reached the age of twenty-eight, thought her 'a very handsome woman'; as this sentence occurs in a volume of family reminiscences, it can hardly have been written with the intent of earning credit by adulation.[9] As the daughter of Edward Hyde, Earl of Clarendon, Charles II's Chancellor of the Exchequer and later Lord Chancellor, a statesman of intelligence, Anne was obviously a young woman of distinction. But it is by no means clear why James decided to make her his wife in days when princes were expected to marry princesses or at any rate rich members of the aristocracy. Maids of Honour were usually rewarded for their services, but not wedded.

The tale told by the author of James's *Life* — that part of the *Life* which was not based on the Duke's own memoirs — is that Anne 'showed both her wit and her virtue in managing the affair so dexterously that the Duke, overmastered by his passion, at last gave her a promise of marriage some time before the Restoration' and that afterwards the Duke asked the King's permission to do what he had promised.[10] The King, he continued, at first refused and 'used many arguments to dissuade the Duke from that resolution', but eventually Charles acquiesced; James and Anne were then married privately in her father's house on 3 September 1660: their first child, a boy, was born on 22 October 1660, but died in infancy. Later she was to give birth to Princess Mary and Princess Anne, to both of whom James was an excellent father.

However, the story was certainly not as simple as James's biographer pretended. In 1660, learning that Anne was with child, Charles Berkeley, egged on by his friends, insisted that he had lain with her, that she was a whore, but that he was willing to marry her. Pressed by his mother and his sister Mary not to marry Anne and believing Berkeley's falsehoods, James determined to retract his promise and 'resolved to deny that he was married and never see the woman again, who had been so false to him'.[11] That is what Anne's father wrote in his own autobiography and it is confirmed from other sources. But Charles II refused to allow the daughter of his Lord Chancellor to be treated in this disgraceful way. He insisted on the marriage and afterwards created Hyde a baron with the title of Lord Clarendon and gave him £20,000. Hyde had been dreadfully upset by the knowledge that his daughter had been James's mistress and was about to give birth to his child. For a time he shut her up in a bedroom and threatened to turn her out of his house as a strumpet. Although James was annoyed about this, he kept quiet and when he sat by the side of Clarendon as Lord Chancellor on the woolsack in the House of Lords he did not say a word about the matter and Clarendon believed that the Duke 'was resolved to think no more of it' especially as the Queen Mother had told the King that 'she would prevent with her authority so great a stain and dishonour to the Crown'.[12] Charles, however, adopted a very different attitude. He was utterly determined that James should marry Anne Hyde and told her father so. Berkeley admitted that he had lied; and although Henrietta Maria came over to England in order to prevent the marriage, she was eventually reconciled to James and his wife before she returned to Paris.

Like her father Anne was a strong character. She helped to look after her husband's financial business; he had an income of some £30,000 a year, spent about £11,000 a year on food and drink and kept out of debt.[13] To the despair of her father, who tried to reason her out of it, Anne was converted to Roman Catholicism not long after her marriage, having read all the arguments and having been convinced, above all, by that of the apostolic succession. It can hardly be doubted that she, more than anyone else, was responsible for James's own reception into the Roman Catholic Church. For she wrote a paper in which she explained for her husband's benefit why she was persuaded that the Church of England was not a true church; James published the paper in 1686.[14] In it Anne wrote that she could find 'no reasons why we left the Church of Rome except for three abominable ones': first, because of Henry VIII's urge to get rid of his wife; secondly, because King Edward VI was governed by an uncle who built his estate out of forfeited Church lands; and, lastly, because Queen Elizabeth I, not being in the opinion of the Church the lawful heiress to the Crown, could only keep it by renouncing the Roman Catholic Church which would not permit an unlawful succession. On her death-bed Anne asked James to stay by her to the end to prevent Anglican bishops attending her and to enable her to take the last sacraments of the Roman Catholic Church. Charles instructed his brother to keep her conversion 'a great secret', which he did.

Anne was fully conscious of her status as the wife of the heir presumptive to the throne and might, indeed, have shone as a queen consort. The author of James's *Life* wrote somewhat condescendingly:

> It must be confessed that what she wanted in birth, was so well made up by her other endowments, that her carriage afterwards did not misbecome her acquired dignity.[15]

In return for her publicly avowed position (the marriage was offici-ally announced at the end of 1660) Anne tolerated her husband's sexual adventures. According to Gramont, 'the Duke of York, having laid his conscience to rest by the declaration of his marriage, thought that generous effort entitled him to give his inconstancy a little scope.'[16] James pretended that his wife's own conduct was not without reproach. In 1666 Pepys, an assiduous collector of scandal, was told that there was 'a great difference . . . between the Duke and Duchess' because James suspected her of having an affair with Henry Sidney, a courtier.[17] But Sir John Reresby, writing at about the same date, observed that though Sidney, 'the handsomest youth of his time', was much in love with the Duchess, and that she was 'not unkind to him', it was all very innocent.[18] At any rate it was an excuse for James to adopt a defensive mechanism.

During his life at Charles II's Court James had five principal mistresses, though not all at the same time: these were Goditha Price, Margaret Brooke (Lady Denham), Arabella Churchill, Anne Hamilton (Countess of Southesk) and Catherine Sedley. Goditha Price was one of the Queen's Maids of Honour and the liaison was kept secret, though Pepys at least knew of it. Lady Denham was more particular. She was only eighteen when she married Sir John Denham, a poet and courtier, who was nearly three times her age. Within a year of her marriage she was acknowledged as James's mistress, who was said to follow her about like a dog, and according to Pepys, writing in June 1666, she insisted that 'she would not be his mistress as Mrs Price was to go up and down the Privy-stairs, but will be owned publicly and so she is'.[19] She died at the beginning of 1667 and James declared that he would never have another mistress. In fact he had already found himself another mistress while staying with his wife in York. This was Arabella Churchill, who was one of his Duchess's Maids of Honour. The story is that when accompanying the Duke and Duchess on a hunting party she fell off her horse and James was so struck by her graceful figure that he made her his mistress and set up an establishment for her. She was to bear him two daughters and two sons, including the future Duke of Berwick, who was to serve his father as a soldier both in England and Ireland.

Another of James's mistresses came right out of the top drawer: Anne Hamilton, the daughter of the second Duke of Hamilton, who had been killed at the battle of Worcester, was a duchess in her own right. She had married Robert Carnegie, Earl of Southesk, who on her petition was created Duke of Hamilton for life in 1660. But she soon left him and was said to have passed through the hands of several gentlemen as well as those of James. The Duke of York did not take up with Catherine Sedley until after he had severed his connection with Arabella, who was respectably married to a member of parliament, Colonel Charles Godfrey, and gave him two daughters. Catherine Sedley was Maid of Honour to James's second wife. Wealthy and witty, Catherine was James's mistress for about seven years. She could not understand how she managed to attract him; 'it cannot be my beauty', she wrote, 'for I have none; and it cannot be my wit, for he had not enough to know that I have any.'

Among other ladies to whom James was attracted were Frances Jennings, sister of Sarah, the future Duchess of Marlborough; Letitia Smith, who married Lord Robartes in 1657; Elizabeth Butler, the second wife of the second Earl of Stanhope, whom she married in 1660; Susan Lady Bellasyse, widow of Sir Henry Bellasyse, the son of Lord Bellasyse, a prominent Roman Catholic statesman; Mary Bagot, widow of the Earl of Falmouth, who was killed at the battle of Lowestoft; Frances Stewart; and Mary Kirke, one of the Queen's Maids of Honour. Of these only Mary Kirke was believed to have given him sexual satisfaction; she was also to be a mistress of James's nephew, the Duke of Monmouth.

James would have liked the young Susan Bellasyse as his second wife, but Charles II said he had made a fool of himself once and must not do so again.[20] Like Catherine Sedley, Susan was vivacious rather than beautiful. James gave her a promise of marriage and tried to convert her to Roman Catholicism. Because of his commitment he settled £2,000 a year on her out of his lands in Ireland.[21] In 1674 Charles created her Baroness Bellasyse of Osgodby in her own right. There is a copy of a letter from James to her (though it is obviously misdated) in which he said:

> The reason I have not written to you is if people had heard that I corresponded with you it would put me out of the way of doing small services. I hope that I shall soon be able to throw myself at your feet.[22]

A fragment of a letter she is supposed to have written to him (also conceivably misdated by the copyist) has also survived in which she observed:

> Your behaviour last night was very extraordinary and if you had then the excuse of having your head heated with wine, to use your own words, that was so once before when you wrote your fine threatening letter to me . . .[23]

Susan was to become a Maid of Honour and a close friend of James's second wife who wrote intimate letters to her when she and her husband were in exile. Later Susan married as her second husband James Fortrey, who had been a page of the backstairs to James, and by whom she had one son. It was from a descendant of his family that the curious letters quoted above found their way into the Bodleian library at Oxford.

Elizabeth Butler, daughter of the first Duke of Ormonde and Countess of Chesterfield in her own right, was a virtuous lady. According to Pepys, James was 'smitten in love' with her and complained to the King when her husband ordered her to retire to their country house, 150 miles from London, to avoid the Duke's advances.[24] Frances Stewart, though admired by James, was most famous because Charles II was desperately in love with her after she had unwisely been introduced to him by his *maîtresse-en-titre,* Lady Castlemaine; Charles, however, failed to persuade her to become his mistress. In November 1665 the Earl of Sandwich told Pepys 'as an infinite secret' that 'factions were high between the King and the Duke, and all the Court of Whitehall was in an uproar over their loose amours', the Duke also being so deeply in love with the delectable Miss Stewart.[25] The lady married as quickly as she could the elderly Duke of Richmond, and gave herself to no one else.

Clearly James liked his ladies to be young or very young. Susan Bellasyse was only seventeen when he offered her marriage and his second wife was fifteen when he married her. His sexual tastes were a little odd; according to Gramont, he said that no woman's leg 'was worth anything without green stockings'.[26] But the assertion that has been repeated *ad nauseam* that he preferred plain women can easily be disproved. Not a sparkling conversationalist himself, James certainly enjoyed the company of witty women, as were his first wife and Catherine Sedley. It is also true that one his first mistresses, Goditha Price, was described as 'small and stumpy and consequently no good dancer'. But, again according to Gramont, Lady Denham was 'young and handsome' and Lady Robartes was 'a striking beauty'. Of Frances Stewart he said 'it was hardly possible for a woman to have less wit or more beauty' and Pepys thought her lovelier than his favourite Lady Castlemaine; Lady Carnegie was 'tolerably handsome'; and the Countess of Stanhope was 'the prettiest woman in England'.[27] So if Gramont's recollections are to be trusted, the legend that James had no liking for beautiful women is nonsense.

Apart from his obsession with women, which, like that of Napoleon, came, or so the Earl of Ailesbury thought, 'more out of natural temper than for the genteel part of making love which he was a stranger to',[28] James had few self-indulgences. As a rule he neither ate nor drank to excess. When the question arose which were the best taxes to raise in order to pay for the upkeep of the navy, he told Ailesbury that they should be levied 'on luxury, as chocolate, tea, coffee, East Indian commodities as not necessary for the life of man' — and added, with warmth, 'on wine'; for he was 'a most sober prince'. 'Who obliges people to make themselves drunk?' he asked, 'but if they will drink, let them pay for it.'[29] He also disapproved of the reading of novels. For outdoor sport James liked fox hunting, of which he was a pioneer as well as stag hunting and greyhound coursing. Like his elder brother he enjoyed walking. In Scotland he played golf. Indoors he sometimes strummed on the guitar, which he is said to have done tolerably well, but he liked to listen to better performers playing it.

In regard to religion, it is clear that he and his first wife attended Mass when in the Spanish Netherlands and were attracted by its ceremonies and ritual. Dr Burnet wrote of a conversation he had with James in 1683 when the Duke told him that he had been converted by a nun in Flanders. Burnet asked if he was in love with the nun, but the Duke told him she was 'no tempting object'.[30] Even before he met Anne Hyde, when he was living at the French Court or serving in the French army, he must have learned that the exaggerated opposition to 'popery' in the Church of England was absurd. He made it plain then that he was ready to employ Catholic servants. As early as February 1661 Pepys had confided to his diary that he hoped James and his family would not come to the Crown, 'he being a professed friend to Catholics'.[31]

Nobody knows precisely when James was finally reconciled to the Roman Church, but it must have been before the death of his first wife in March 1671; for, as already noticed, it was she who drew his attention to what she regarded as irrefutable arguments in favour of Roman Catholicism. According to his official biographer, at the beginning of 1669 the Duke was 'more sensibly touched in conscience and began to think seriously of his salvation'.[32] It was at this time, again according to his biographer, that Charles II held a meeting with the Duke at which Lord Arundel, Lord Arlington and Lord Clifford — all Roman Catholics then or to become so later — were present when a discussion took place on how to promote the Catholic religion in the King's dominions. At that meeting Charles himself was described as having avowed with tears in his eyes his own faith in Roman Catholicism.[33] Though it might seem odd to say so in view of Charles's profligacy and laxity, it is possible that, apart from what James had been taught by his mother and first wife, he was influenced by his brother in the direction of his faith. He also read books and talked to bishops. Once he had been convinced, being less flexible than Charles, he refused to conceal his new beliefs. Yet for

97

political reasons he had hesitated before committing himself. About the end of 1668 he had sent for a Jesuit who told the Duke that he could not be received into the Catholic Church unless he ceased taking Communion in the Church of England; he also informed the Prince that he could not obtain dispensation from the Pope to appear outwardly as a Protestant. Like Charles II and Anne Hyde, James was persuaded that Christ had left behind him an infallible Church and that this infallibility was lodged in the Roman Catholic Church; he was also convinced that the Scriptures were canonical and that the Roman Church was better able to interpret them than any private individuals. Once he felt certain about all this he could never again be shaken from his beliefs.

Although, as has been noted already, it is not known exactly when James was finally converted the fragmentary evidence suggests it was between 1660 and 1671. In 1672 he ceased to attend Communion, as the King continued to do; in 1673 he resigned his office of Lord High Admiral after Parliament passed the first Test Act which laid it down that only members of the Church of England could hold public offices. In that same year he married an Italian Roman Catholic, Princess Mary Beatrice of Modena, his second wife. By 1676 he was refusing to appear at any Anglican services whatsoever.

The Duke of York's second marriage proved in the long run to be a success.[34] He and Mary lived together for nearly thirty years, although James was not always faithful to her and she found him a little tiresome in his querulous old age. After James's request to marry Susan Bellasyse was rejected by the King, Henry Mordaunt Earl of Peterborough had been dispatched on a roving mission round Europe to discover a suitable second wife for James, evidently with instructions to find a lady who was young and physically attractive. After deep research Peterborough had no hesitation in recommending the daughter of the Duke of Modena; Princess Mary Beatrice d'Este, who was then fourteen years old, was tall with an admirable figure, a fair complexion, black hair and eyes 'full of sweetness and light'. Not unnaturally she was less than enthusiastic about marrying a middle-aged *roué*, but personal inclinations had to yield to political needs. James himself was delighted; he ordered Peterborough to offer the Princess £15,000 a year as a jointure and presented her with part of his jewels.[35] A proxy wedding took place on 20 September 1673; she left for England on her fifteenth birthday. On 21 November James greeted his bride at Dover; they were married and

bedded the same night. The Princess was accompanied by her
mother as far as London, and before she left Mary was so unhappy
that she cried every time she saw her husband. But it was not long
before she became fond of him especially as (she said) he was 'so firm
and steady in our holy religion (which he professed as a good
Catholic) that he would not part from it for anything in the world'.
She also took a liking to Charles II. In later life she was to confess
that she only knew happiness from the age of fifteen to twenty;
'but', she added, 'during those years I was always having children, so
judge that happiness.' Slowly she came to realize that James was
constantly unfaithful to her and that while she had successive
miscarriages, his mistresses bore him healthy children. It is probably
right to say that it was not until after June 1688 when Mary gave
birth to a healthy son that her hold on her husband became firm. Up
to that time she was to admit that she suffered intolerable pain.
When her husband lost his throne and became more dependent on
her, she grew more assertive and sometimes lost her patience with
him.

Can it honestly be said that princes and kings and other rulers of
mankind have 'private' lives? Occasionally they can be successfully
concealed except from a few intimates, but usually they are open
secrets. The Court of Charles II was a hot-bed of gossip; although
scandal mongers like Pepys and Gramont must often have exaggerated, what they wrote was a fair representation of what went on.
From the beginning of the reign Pepys suspected that James's
favouritism for Roman Catholics might mean that at heart he was a
Catholic himself. Two aspects of James's private life — his religion
and his second marriage to a young and pretty Italian princess — had
their repercussions on his public career. When the House of
Commons, full of enthusiastic Anglicans, passed a resolution on 20
October 1673 demanding that James's second marriage should not
be consummated, the King prorogued Parliament for a week. As
soon as it met again the Commons repeated their address against the
marriage, they were then informed that it had already been completed so that the King was unable to agree to what the House asked.
That was not strictly true. By then of course it had become common
knowledge in Parliament that James was himself a Catholic since he
had not only laid down his offices after the passage of the first Test
Act, but had ceased to attend meetings of the Privy Council. The fact
that he had not yet made an open confession of his faith is irrelevant,

for the evidence that he had ceased to be an Anglican was overwhelming. These protests were the seeds of a movement to exclude James and his legitimate children, should he have any, from the succession to the throne. Anthony Ashley Cooper, an experienced statesman, who was to become the spearhead of the Exclusionist movement, tried to persuade the King to divorce his Portuguese wife (who by 1670 was known to be barren) and to marry a fertile Protestant princess, for, after all, Charles had produced several sons by his mistresses. The King would not do so. The last barrier to James's claim to become the heir apparent to the throne having thus been overcome, Shaftesbury and a majority in the House of Commons opened a campaign to exclude him from the succession by legislation. But before then James as Lord High Admiral had put to sea again.

8.

At Sea Again

After he learned that the Pope would not allow him to be received into the Roman Catholic Church unless he ceased attending the services of the Church of England, James was struck by a brilliant idea. He knew that the King, his brother, was a Catholic at heart; indeed such historical evidence as exists suggests that Charles, who always had a sharper and quicker brain than his brother, was convinced of the truth of the Catholic religion before his restoration to his throne; and it was about ten years after his return to England that he wrote: 'I thank God I have found no difficulty in making my choice.'[1] So, 'well knowing that the King was of the same mind as himself', as was stated in his official biography, he arranged for the conference (which was mentioned in the previous chapter) with Charles and some of his Catholic advisers in his own private rooms to discuss ways and means of promoting the Catholic religion throughout the royal dominions since he was resolved 'not to live any longer in the constraint he was under'. The meeting took place on 25 January 1669, the day on which the Christian Church celebrated the conversion of St Paul.[2]

Charles then was reported to have said that although he realized that if he declared his religious beliefs openly, he would be confronted with many difficulties, 'he chose rather to undertake it now, when he and his brother were in their full strength and able to undergo any fatigue than to delay it until they were grown older and less fit to go through with so great a design.' It was therefore resolved by those present that it was essential to invoke the help of Louis XIV, 'his most Christian Majesty', if they were to achieve their aims. Furthermore, it was decided to send Lord Arundel, one of the Catholic nobility who was present at the meeting, to open negotiations with the French Government because, as he was the Queen

101

Mother's Master of the Horse, a visit by him to Paris would not arouse any suspicions; for it was fully recognized that such a mission and such a plan needed to be shrouded in the deepest secrecy.

Whatever James had in mind, it is extremely doubtful if Charles was seeking a French alliance for purely religious motives. For that reason some modern historians have cast doubt on the authenticity of the conference as described by James's biographer. However, ever since the spring of 1667 Charles is known to have been looking for closer ties with France. It may well have been that he took advantage of the meeting in 1669 to rally his brother and his Catholic counsellors to his side. Certainly he was no fool; he had only to look back on the last hundred years or so of English history to realize the enormous obstacles that were bound to get in the way of leading his kingdom back to allegiance to the papacy. What Charles wanted was to break the alliance between the French and the Dutch, which had contributed to the defeat of his country in the war of 1665-7;[3] as he frankly wrote in one of his earliest letters to his sister Henriette, who was Louis XIV's sister-in-law, since she had married his only brother Philippe of Orleans (commonly known as Monsieur), he would 'never be satisfied till he has had his revenge' on the Dutch and that he was 'very willing to enter into an agreement upon that matter whensoever Louis XIV pleased'.[4]

The negotiations were elaborately camouflaged. Charles at first insisted that neither the English ambassador in Paris nor the French ambassador in London should be informed about 'the Grand Design'. The correspondence was carried on through Henriette, largely in cypher.[5] Convinced of Charles's earnestness and honesty by his confession of Catholicism, Louis responded warmly to the English approaches. By September 1669 the discussions began to crystallize into a plan for an offensive alliance against the Dutch, both the English and the French monarchs being determined to crush the upstart burghers. In November it was decided to let the French ambassador in London, Colbert de Croissy, who was the brother of Louis XIV's chief Minister, into the secret of 'the Grand Design'; James, along with four other Roman Catholic noblemen, was empowered to treat with Colbert de Croissy on the King's behalf. Realizing that the English Parliament was unlikely to vote supplies as generously as they had done during the previous war against the Dutch, Charles and James opened their mouths very widely indeed: in fact they asked the French King for a subsidy of

£2,000,000 sterling. That, however, was merely a *ballon d'essai*. But one point emphasized by James was that the English must have the command and the preponderance at sea; the allied fleet must be led by an Englishman (no doubt he had himself in mind). The French were only to provide an auxiliary squadron obedient to the orders of the English admiral.[6] In return the English would furnish a contingent of 6,000 soldiers to fight under a French general on land. The naval clause in the treaty constituted a stumbling block, but eventually Louis XIV gave way and in May 1670 James's sister Henriette came to Dover as the intermediary through whom the secret Anglo-French treaty had originally been broached, to meet her brothers and finalize the agreement.

Henriette's husband, a homosexual, had not wanted her to go to Dover at all and when overruled by his brother, the French King, had demanded to come with her. But Charles II did not fancy that; he said that if 'Monsieur' came, the Duke of York, to balance things out, would have to go over to see Louis XIV in Calais, but added that unfortunately he could not spare the time.[7] So on 16 May 1670 Charles and James aboard the royal barge greeted 'Madame' off the cliffs of Dover and then made her as comfortable as they could in the castle. James was not present at the signing of the secret treaty because his brother sent him back to London to take command of the troops there in case of a rising or demonstration by dissenters against whom another restrictive act had just been passed by Parliament. It proved a false alarm; James was able to come back to Dover in time to say farewell to his sister, who was still in her early twenties, and whom he loved. Not long after her return to France she suddenly died. As was common in the seventeenth century her husband was suspected of poisoning her.

As Lord High Admiral James was principally concerned with the naval clauses of the treaty. He was afraid that his brother would not have sufficient money to maintain a fleet at sea capable of defeating the Dutch. In February Charles had appealed to the House of Commons for funds to strengthen the navy; reluctantly they had agreed to introduce a new kind of subsidy calculated to yield £350,000 towards the cost of the navy; there was also a plan for increased import duties on sugar and tobacco, but the Commons were determined to prohibit the import of French wines and spirits altogether. In the end Charles, irritated by their behaviour, adjourned the House, which did not meet again before the outbreak of the war. So he was given little or no financial help. Furthermore the French had scaled down the subsidies that Charles had asked for. He was promised only about £230,000 a year towards the cost of waging the war. In the end he had to cease paying interest on money borrowed from bankers, a step known as the Stop of the Exchequer, a temporary expedient that could not be repeated, for it amounted almost to a declaration of bankruptcy.

James had foreseen this as soon as the secret treaty was signed. When he was at Dover he had warned the King that once the war began he would run into debt; that would place him at the mercy of Parliament which would not be likely to give him adequate supplies for a war undertaken without its advice.[8] Charles had a much more optimistic view. He thought that fifty of his own ships with a squadron of a further thirty from France would be enough to ensure victory at sea; £600,000 out of the customs' revenue would help pay for the navy, at any rate for one year. The Duke believed that fifty ships would cost a good deal more than £600,000. Moreover he did not consider that they could look the Dutch in the face with a force of eighty warships (plus fireships) as well as providing sufficient escorts for convoys of merchant vessels, while other ships would be necessary to protect the English colonies in the West Indies and North America.[9] However, he was overruled. By the seventh clause of the treaty Charles undertook to furnish fifty warships and ten fireships, while the French promised to provide thirty ships of the line carrying at least forty cannon each plus up to ten fireships. The two Kings agreed to appoint James as commander-in-chief; if he had to retire, an English admiral would take his place. The war was not to start until the French squadron was ready to join the English fleet.

According to the ninth article of the secret treaty of Dover, the war against the United Netherlands was not to begin on land or sea until after Charles II had publicly declared himself to be a Roman Catholic.[10] The French King and his Ministers were far from enthusiastic about this clause. They wanted to open the campaign against the Dutch as soon as possible and they feared, understandably enough, that once Charles announced his conversion disturbances might take place all over England and Scotland nullifying the value of any support from these two kingdoms as active allies. But Charles was in no hurry whatsoever; he procrastinated; he said that he was unable to find a suitable envoy to send to the Pope; in any case Pope Clement IX was old and frail and in fact died at the end of 1669;

after four months the College of Cardinals elected as his successor
Pope Clement X, who was ten years older than Clement IX and
reputedly just as frail; so it was all very delicate and difficult. Vainly
James, now an enthusiastic convert, begged his brother to implement his Grand Design at once; he was seconded by another recent
convert, Lord Clifford, who became Lord Treasurer in 1672. The
French ambassador told his master, Louis XIV, that the Duke of
York and Clifford were strongly urging the King to come into the
open about his religion, but Lord Arlington, Secretary of State for
the South, who knew all about the secret treaty, told Colbert de
Croissy that nothing would be more likely to prevent the King his
master from 'executing good designs' than 'the too pressing instances of the Duke'.[11] Almost certainly Charles never had any
intention of making a public declaration about his religion; he was
far too astute to jeopardize the success of the projected war against
the Dutch. In the end he compromised. On 28 February 1672 a
'simulated treaty', which disclosed the offensive alliance with
France, but omitted the religious clause and also another clause that
required the King to provide soldiers to serve with the French army,
was revealed to the Privy Council and ratified; on 15 March the King
published a Declaration of Indulgence suspending the penal laws
against Catholics and nonconformists; and on 17 March he declared
war on the United Netherlands, using as an excuse the fact that
Dutch warships had attacked an English squadron attempting to
intercept the merchant fleet arriving from Smyrna. That forced the
French King's hand. But it was not until May that he was ready to
invade the Dutch Republic.

Upon James was conferred the principal responsibility for carrying on the war against the Dutch. His aim was to defeat the Dutch
fleet and thus gain the command of the sea and then to land a party
of marines in Holland so that while the French army was advancing
upon Amsterdam the Dutch would be distracted from the rear.
James himself took charge of the Red or centre squadron and the
highly experienced Earl of Sandwich was recalled to command the
Blue or rear squadron. When the French squadron with the Count
D'Estrées as its admiral joined up with the English fleet, it was to
have the honour of becoming the White or van squadron, subject to
James's orders as the supreme commander in accordance with the
terms of the treaty. James went aboard his flagship, the *Prince,* a
brand-new first-rate with 100 guns, at the Buoy of the Nore on 19

April; the arrangement was that the French squadron would sail from Brest to St Helen's roadstead in the Isle of Wight where the two fleets would rendezvous.

The Dutch fleet was under the command of Admiral Michael de Ruyter, whom James's biographer described as 'justly esteemed the greatest sea commander of his time'.[12] He put to sea first; as soon as James learned of this, he left the Buoy of the Nore with such of his warships as were ready to sail and made for the Channel where he hoped to meet the French. In fact a thick fog came up so that the English and Dutch warships passed by without being able to see each other. So the Dutch returned home and the Duke went to St Helen's. On 2 May King Charles wrote to his brother ordering him not to fight the Dutch fleet before the French squadron had joined him, a letter that reads like a reproof.[13] On the following day Charles went to Spithead to inspect the French squadron, which had arrived there en route for St Helen's. It has been suggested that the King might have noticed that the French lacked fast frigates and smaller craft fitted to face the storms of the North Sea.[14] Certainly in his letter to his brother Charles had stressed the need for frigates to protect the trade off Ireland, for while the main fleet was confronting the Dutch it was necessary to take care that English commerce was not interrupted. In a meeting of the King's Council, attended by James before he left for the Buoy of the Nore, he had vehemently and successfully resisted a proposal that an embargo should be imposed on all outward bound ships as it would damage the receipt of Customs out of which the navy had chiefly to be paid.

Once arrangements had been adjusted with the French admiral at St Helen's and the remainder of James's own ships had joined him from the Thames, he put to sea on 8 May with a powerful fleet totalling some ninety-eight warships with the intention of bringing the Dutch to battle off their own coasts. De Ruyter was off the coast of the Spanish Netherlands near Ostend where he hoped to entice the allied fleet on to a little known sandbank called the Rumble. But James was warned of the danger by the Earl of Sandwich; he had the sandbank reconnoitred by his frigates; thus it was not until ten at night on 19 May that the two fleets sighted one another. James then had the advantage of the wind and kept his ships close-hauled to retain it. But once again a thick fog blew up and the wind veered to the north-west. So, early in the morning of 20 May the Duke tacked and stood away from Southwold Bay where he hoped the Dutch would follow him.

Against the advice of his own officers Admiral de Ruyter made up his mind to attack the Anglo-French fleet off their own coast even though his ships and guns were fewer than those of the allies and a decisive defeat might have meant the loss of the war, for by then the French armies were already lined up on the borders of Holland. His belief was that the battle was worth risking since a victory would raise the spirits of his fellow countrymen on land.

Early in the morning of 20 May the wind had shifted west, an advantage to the English.[15] Next day the Dutch were sighted by the English warships a long way to leeward; they made no attempt to close with the Dutch, but steered for Southwold Bay where they remained anchored for a week. By then the wind had become eastward so that a Dutch attack was to be expected. The Earl of Sandwich therefore urged James to put out to sea from Southwold Bay with a view to surprising the Dutch who were still taking on provisions as they lay off Goree. But Sir John Cox, an able though cantankerous sailor, who commanded James's flagship and was to be killed on it, insisted that his squadron should also take on supplies as it was unlikely that the Dutch would attack that day. Thereupon James ignored Sandwich's advice and stayed in port.

It was three o'clock in the morning of 28 May when James received positive news of the Dutch approach. In effect he was surprised, for at the time the Dutch first attacked the Duke's flagship was still being cleaned and only some forty ships belonging to the Red and Blue squadrons were in a position to meet the assault from de Ruyter and his second-in-command, Admiral van Ghent; in any case the sandbanks off Lowestoft made manoeuvring hard. Fighting began at eight in the morning, the Dutch enjoying the windward gauge. James ordered D'Estrées to keep close to the wind if possible. In attempting to do so he sailed south-east by south, thus becoming the rear squadron and was attacked by the Dutch rear squadron from Zeeland under Admiral Bankert, a much better qualified seaman than he was, even though the Dutchman had fewer vessels under his command. De Ruyter concentrated his fire on James's flagship, the *Prince* while Van Ghent picked out Sandwich's flagship, the *Royal Charles* as his main target. The battle went on all through the day. James was first obliged to shift from the *Prince,* the riggings of which were damaged by Dutch gunfire, to another first-rate, the *St Michael* and by the late afternoon he had to move once again to the *London.*

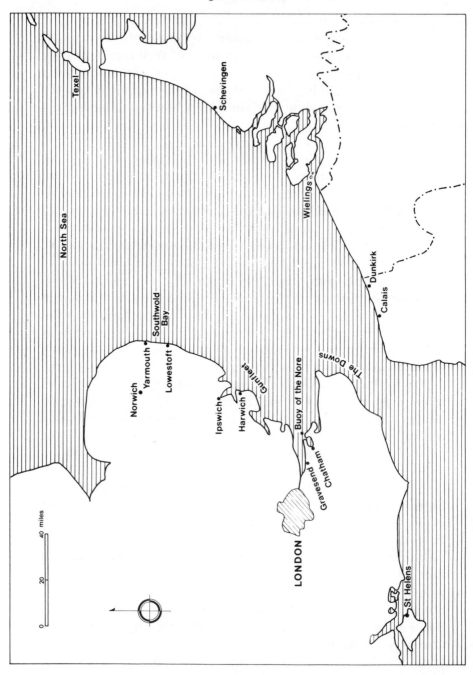

Map of the North Sea

The Duke was three-quarters of an hour in a boat before he reached his third flagship. Meanwhile the *Royal James* had been blown up and Sandwich was drowned. By dusk both sides were exhausted and drew off, the Dutch returning to their own coasts and the English into Southwold Bay. It had been a tremendous battle in which the weather gauge for once was unimportant as the sea was calm. Both sides suffered about 2,500 casualities. The Dutch lost three ships of the line; the English only lost the *Royal James*, but it took weeks for a number of severely damaged ships to be repaired. The important thing from the Dutch point of view — and that was why they were able to claim a victory — was that they had fought the battle off the English coasts, thus postponing indefinitely the danger of a landing on their own coast. It is true that James pursued the Dutch across the North Sea, but first another fog and then a gale prevented his engaging de Ruyter again. He was obliged to return to the Buoy of the Nore to refit.

Towards the end of June Charles II came to the Buoy of the Nore, accompanied by the Queen, the Earl of Shaftesbury, his Chancellor of the Exchequer, and other members of his Council. James now proposed to sail to the Wielings (south of the Texel), where de Ruyter and his fleet were lying at anchor, in the hope of fighting another battle, but Charles was persuaded it would be wiser if his brother were to intercept a Dutch mercantile fleet which was expected to arrive from the East Indies hugging the Scottish coast. Shaftesbury argued that a battle was never decisive, but the dislocation of Dutch trade might well be. James expostulated, pointing out that it would be far better to defeat de Ruyter, for then the East India fleet would be at their mercy. That appeared to be common sense; yet James was overruled by the King.[16] In July James cruised north, but bad weather prevented his doing any serious damage to the Dutch merchant fleet coming from the East Indies. He was obliged to return south, putting off 3,000 of his men, mostly sick of scurvy, at Bridlington in Yorkshire and afterwards sailing by way of Yarmouth and Lowestoft back to the Buoy of the Nore where he arrived on 23 July.

Here again James was visited at the beginning of September by his brother, accompanied by Prince Rupert, Shaftesbury and other members of his Council.[17] This time the King and his advisers favoured the idea of James's sailing across the North Sea to attack the Dutch in their own harbours, but the Duke and his leading officers insisted that it was now too late in the season to venture towards Holland in face of the autumn gales with any prospect of success, especially as they were of the opinion that the fleet was in no condition to stay at sea, 'as they had been harassed by the tempestuous seasons ever since they were abroad'.[18] In the end Charles was convinced that this was right and he ordered the big ships to be laid up in Chatham and Sheerness ready for the next year's campaign.

During the winter of 1672-3 the King made several changes in his Ministry. Shaftesbury, though he had no legal training, was appointed Lord Chancellor; Lord Clifford, who had demonstrated his financial ability as one of the Commissioners of the Treasury, became on James's advice sole Lord Treasurer, a post coveted by Lord Arlington, who remained Secretary of State. Neither Shaftesbury nor Arlington was on friendly terms with the Duke of York (James, it may be remembered, took a dislike to Arlington when he had been his secretary in exile), but Clifford, who was himself a Roman Catholic, or crypto-Catholic, was grateful to the Duke for his patronage. Charles asked Clifford and Lord Arundel, another Catholic, to persuade James to attend Holy Communion with him over Christmas. But the Duke had now acquired a conscience which prohibited him from joining in any Anglican services.

In the first week of February 1673 Parliament again met and at once demanded that Charles should withdraw his Declaration of Indulgence, claiming that penal statutes on ecclesiastical matters could only be suspended by Parliament; after a month's deliberation the King gave way. He did so because he wanted the Commons to vote supplies to carry on the war against the Dutch.[19] But the Commons were now rabidly anti-papist. They furthermore insisted that the King should publish a proclamation against Roman Catholic priests and Jesuits. In return for all this they granted the King an assessment of £70,000 a month for eighteen months. They then turned to tightening the screw even more firmly upon James's fellow religionists.

The attitude of the Commons made no difference whatever to James's loyalty to his faith. At Easter 1673 he once more refused to take Communion with the King. According to John Evelyn, this time everyone was amazed and it gave 'exceeding grief and scandal to the whole nation that the heir to the throne and the son of a martyr for the Protestant religion should apostazize'.[20] The very day before

Easter what was known as the first Test Act was passed by Parliament which excluded Catholics from holding any public office. 'What the consequences of James's apostacy will be', Evelyn concluded in his diary on Easter Day, 'God only knows and wise men dread.' What in fact happened was that on 15 June James laid down his post as Lord High Admiral and soon after his friend, Lord Clifford, resigned his place as Lord Treasurer. Prince Rupert then assumed the command of the fleet, and James's career at sea thus came to an end.

9.
The Threat of Exclusion

During the six years from 1673 to 1678 Charles II's Government was largely concerned with foreign affairs. The money, which the King with the aid of Clifford had scraped together to pay for the first year of the war against the Dutch, having been exhausted, Charles bowed to the wishes of the House of Commons in order to obtain a vote of supplies to keep the navy afloat. That was why he withdrew his Declaration of Indulgence and assented to the first Test Act. The Earl of Shaftesbury had delivered an impressive speech in which he compared the war between the English and the Dutch to that between the Romans and Carthaginians and argued that the war was merely a continuation of that of 1665-7 about which the Commons had been so enthusiastic. But although, as has been noticed, a sum of £1,260,000 was voted to the Government to support the war, Prince Rupert was unable to win the command of the North Sea. Consequently the expeditionary force that was intended to attack the Dutch from the rear was not able to land. Moreover the heroic Dutch had acquired allies. It was clear that the war was going to be a long one and that the French armies were not likely to have it all their own way. Meanwhile the Commons were becoming more and more anti-French with the result that Charles II was, as it were, awkwardly placed between his Parliament and his friend, Louis XIV.

Failure in the war at sea meant that Charles's Ministers would have to bear the blame. Gradually the group of statesmen, who had worked for the King since the Earl of Clarendon had gone into exile and with whom Charles had been well satisfied, began to break up. After Clifford's resignation in June 1673 Sir Thomas Osborne (afterwards Viscount Latimer, Earl of Danby and Duke of Leeds), who had distinguished himself as Treasurer of the Navy from 1667 to 1673, was appointed Lord Treasurer with the full approval of James who set about trying to convert him to Roman Catholicism.[1] Although he was unsuccessful in this, for five years he was one of Osborne's strongest supporters. After James had resigned as Lord High Admiral, an event which made it plain to everyone that he had been converted, he still remained at the centre of government business, attended meetings of the Privy Council and foreign committee and gave his brother the benefit of his advice. But he had made an enemy.

Because of the Duke's conversion and second marriage to a Catholic princess the Earl of Shaftesbury, who began 'beating the No Popery drum as loud as he could', turned against James.[2] The antagonism grew so sharp that it was difficult for the two men to sit in the same Council; on one occasion James was reported to have called Shaftesbury a madman and he pressed Charles to dismiss the Lord Chancellor.[3] Charles, who suspected Shaftesbury of elaborate intrigues, followed James's advice. The Earl was obliged to resign his office in November 1673 and in May 1674 was excluded from the Privy Council. The second Duke of Buckingham, a lightweight who had been a patron of Osborne, was attacked in the House of Commons, which petitioned for his dismissal too. The King relieved him of his honorific title of Master of the Horse in April 1674 and put his illegitimate son, the Duke of Monmouth, in Buckingham's place. The Earl of Arlington, who had also been attacked in the House of Commons and whom James disliked, resigned from his post of Secretary of State in September but was appointed Lord Chamberlain, being retained in office because of his deep knowledge of foreign affairs. Another of Charles's Ministers, the Duke of Lauderdale, who was extremely unpopular with the House of Commons, withdrew to Scotland. Thus James and his friend Osborne, who was created Earl of Danby in May 1674, became the King's chief advisers. But they did not agree about religion. James still hoped that his brother would revive the Declaration of Indulgence, embracing all nonconformists, while Danby tried to rally members of the House of Commons with the cry of 'Church and King' in the expectation that they would then be persuaded to vote the King more money to repair his shattered finances. However, when Parliament met in January 1674, it refused to grant any further supplies even for the navy. Thereupon the King, with the tacit approval of the Commons, concluded peace with the Dutch (by the treaty of Westminster 28 February 1674). Thus all Charles's elaborate schemes, dating from 1669, to obtain and draw profit from a French alliance, came to nothing. He told the French ambassador that if it had not been for James's folly (*la sottise de mon frère*) he would have got out of all his difficulties.[4] As it was, he prorogued Parliament and, according to Dr Gilbert Burnet, 'the King and his brother were now at their ease'.[5].

From then on Charles II's policy was directed to becoming a mediator between the French and Dutch, thus enhancing his reputation abroad, and to relying on Danby, who was an adept at bribery, to secure a majority in the House of Commons which would help him to pay off his debts amounting, it has been estimated, to over £600,000. The King dispatched a diplomatic mission, headed by the Earl of Arlington, to Holland to explore the ground and take soundings. A suggestion was put forward that James's elder daughter, Mary, who was then twelve years old, might make a suitable bride for Prince William of Orange. James was not at all pleased with that idea; he considered that Arlington (who had a Dutch wife) would be too pro-Dutch and that the mission would only annoy Louis XIV. Furthermore, the last thing he wanted was for his daughter to marry a leading European Protestant champion. He would have preferred her to have become a Roman Catholic. When two years later the Bishop of London proposed to him that he should confirm her in order that she might receive the sacrament in the Church of England James refused his consent, though he had to acquiesce when the King ordered him to do so.[6]

During 1675 and 1676 James became more and more perturbed by Danby's policy, which was to secure the maximum help for the King from Parliament, particularly by flattering the prejudices of most of the members of the House of Commons who were both anti-French and profoundly Anglican. He also tried to push through a Bill which required the members of both Houses of Parliament and all privy councillors and Justices of the Peace to swear on oath that they would never take up arms against the King and would not 'endeavour to alter the Protestant religion or the government of either Church or State'. James disliked the idea of the non-resisting oath on the ground that it would strengthen the rule of the bishops, and wanted the King to dissolve the Parliament which had already sat for fifteen years. He thought that if Parliament could be got rid of, Charles could govern autocratically with the financial and moral support of the French King. To carry out his policy he and his former secretary, Edward Coleman, accepted money from the French ambassador to bribe members of parliament into being less vehemently anti-French,[7] while he urged his brother to dissolve Parliament and to publish yet another Declaration of Indulgence. Nevertheless James sided with Danby when a premature attempt was made to impeach him for treasonable activities and by arguing that their religion could be secured by mildness and moderation he persuaded his fellow Catholics in Parliament to lend their support to the Lord Treasurer.[8]

King Charles did not accept his brother's advice about dissolving Parliament — James hoped that a newly elected House of Commons would prove itself to be less violently anti-Catholic[9] — but in November 1675 he prorogued it for eighteen months during which he enjoyed himself with two French mistresses and did what he could to bring about a peace that would satisfy Louis XIV. For his part James became more and more obsessed with the importance of his religion. He ceased to attend any Anglican services; he was annoyed when the Bishop of London complained of his allowing Coleman to write and publish a book in defence of the Pope's supremacy and later advised him to dismiss Coleman from the Duchess's service; and he was furious when Danby persuaded the King to issue an order in council prohibiting his English subjects from worshipping in the Queen's chapel or other chapels in the houses of ambassadors from Catholic countries.[10] He went on pressing the King to dissolve Parliament or, if not, to continue proroguing it. The gap between his policy and that of Danby widened and both of them knew it. In April 1677 after Parliament had been recalled Danby observed that though the King denied almost nothing to the Duke, he did not really love him.[11] He asserted that James was now 'the chief carrier of the French interest'; that he made it his business to court 'sectaries and fanatics' hoping thereby to strengthen the popish interests and that he was unhappy in his servants — no doubt he had Coleman in mind. But suspecting that Shaftesbury, Danby's leading critic, was at heart the enemy both of his brother and himself James would not side with him against Danby. Indeed he actually agreed to Danby introducing a Bill which would have limited the powers of a Catholic sovereign in Church matters. Yet James protested against the Bill when it came before the House of Lords and was relieved when it was rejected by the House of Commons.[12]

By 1677 the war between the French monarchy and the Dutch Republic had been going on for six years with neither side winning a decisive advantage. The Dutch had acquired allies, but the French army under able generals was still fighting victoriously in the Spanish Netherlands near the Dutch frontiers. William wanted the English to intervene with armed mediation. That was also Danby's plan while, when the House of Commons met again in February 1677 after its long adjournment members urged the King to conclude an offensive and defensive alliance with the United Netherlands. The King objected to his foreign policy being dictated to him and pointed out, justly enough, that he would need a lot of money to make war on France. During the summer William of Orange, James's nephew, sent over his most trusted adviser, William Bentinck, to urge armed mediation upon the King. When Bentinck brought James a personal message from the Prince, the Duke told him that

> he must not look upon his Majesty's unwillingness to enter into a war as proceeding from any other reason but self-preservation; for he foresaw the absolute ruin of the royal family if he should embark himself in a war in the condition he was now in, his magazines being empty, his fleet not in a good condition, and above all the Parliament being in such a temper that all he could do at present was to keep things quiet at home.[13]

Although the Commons asked the King four times to go to war with France, Charles told the House and Danby that this was impossible without large additional revenues. Instead he attempted to mediate peacefully, although neither side took much notice of his diplomatic efforts. The French, however, were sufficiently concerned about the pressure from his Parliament to become the active ally of the Dutch that they resolved to bribe him again in order to secure Parliament's adjournment.

As soon as the campaigning season was over William himself came to England and announced that he wanted to marry Princess Mary, who was now fifteen, and he refused to enter into any diplomatic negotiations until that was agreed to.[14] When William saw his uncle he told him that he desired 'to be yet nearer related to him by marrying the Lady Mary'.[15] James answered that he thought he should wait until the end of the war before the marriage was discussed. The Duke was surprised and annoyed when he discovered later that the King had given William permission to raise the matter with him. Furthermore a day or two afterwards Charles told James firmly that he must give his consent to the marriage. James then assured the Privy Council that he would never make any attempt to alter the established government in Church or State and as proof of his wish to preserve the peace and unity of the kingdom he told his fellow councillors that he had agreed to his daughter's marriage to a Protestant prince.[16] On 4 November William and Mary were wedded; a fortnight later after the Prince had discussed with the King the terms on which the Dutch were willing to conclude peace, his wife accompanied her unwelcome husband back to Holland. The marriage was made upon the altar of Charles II's diplomacy. The teenage princess came to love her formidable husband while James, obedient to his brother's wishes, became fully reconciled. Being an indefatigable letter writer, he then opened a regular correspondence with his son-in-law which throws much light on his character.

Louis XIV was furious about the marriage, for which he largely blamed James, and ordered the latest subsidy to Charles to be stopped. The English King explained that he was the unfortunate victim of circumstances, being pushed against his will on all sides to plunge into war, though this carried little conviction with the French; at any rate he did all he could to avoid the plunge by first negotiating and then rejecting treaties of alliance with the Dutch. To gratify his own subjects he recalled Parliament in January 1678; the Commons thereupon promised to vote him £1,000,000 provided it was spent on waging war against France. Charles wriggled and then instructed Danby to write a dispatch to the English ambassador in France, Ralph Montagu, telling him to ask the French King to supply him with 6,000,000 livres a year (about £500,000) for three years 'since it will probably be two or three years before Parliament will be in a humour to give him any supplies after making peace with France'.[17] This was diplomatic juggling of a high order.

James's mind was not attuned to such subtleties. He now differed from his brother, for his martial spirit had been aroused. He turned a volte-face. He pictured himself as commanding an expeditionary force which would join with the Dutch and their other allies into compelling the French to make peace. He first wrote to William to excuse Charles's delay in concluding a treaty of alliance. This he blamed on Parliament. He told him at the beginning of February 1678 that 'those most zealous for a war with France are those who obstruct giving of a supply'; a month later he wrote to say that he was sensible of his difficulties — for the French had begun their campaign extremely early and had captured the important Flemish town of Ghent — and again blamed Parliament and also the Spaniards for obstructing preparations for war. A week later he was able to tell his son-in-law that several regiments had been raised and would soon be ready to sail from Harwich; ten days after this he wrote that he was 'absolutely of the opinion, knowing the French, that we must have a war' and that more ships were setting out every day. But in May he had to confess that owing to the obstruction of the House of Commons in making financial grants great disorders were to be expected and therefore he urged him not to appear to be against peace.[18] In fact although the Commons had voted in favour of an immediate war on France both James and Danby had resigned themselves to its impossibility and that no doubt was a factor in the decision taken by the Dutch to agree to a truce. The Dutch and the French were soon busily negotiating a peace at Nijmegen. There was, however, a last-minute hitch which enabled James to assure his son-in-law in July that if the French did not behave themselves he would take care personally of the embarkation of English troops 'and would be ready to go with them myself if occasion be'.[19] In fact before the end of the month the French and Dutch concluded a separate treaty which purchased peace at the expense of the Spaniards. So military glory was denied to the Duke, glory that might have offset the handicap of his acknowledged popery. Parliament hastily demanded the disbandment of the newly raised forces for fear that King Charles would use them as a means to rule without it; and in the late summer of 1678 a train of events occurred which obliged James to go into exile and threatened to exclude him from succession to the throne if his brother predeceased him. It was to be a prolonged episode that was to constitute a turning point in his life.

The background of what was to be known as the Popish Plot may be traced back to the reign of the last Roman Catholic monarch known as 'Bloody Mary'.[20] Since then a series of acts against English Roman Catholic priests and laity had been passed, which were sometimes enforced and sometimes not according to the mood of the day. In fact a significant Roman Catholic minority remained in England, estimated to amount to about 50,000 out of a population of 5,000,000 in the reign of Charles II. The reasons why an anti-popery movement waxed hot in the late 1670s were twofold. First, because of fears of the overweening ambitions of the Most Christian King of France, who had set out with the initial alliance of the English King to crush the Dutch Protestant republicans; secondly, because Charles's brother and heir presumptive to the throne had revealed himself to be a Roman Catholic convert. In February 1678 the poet, Andrew Marvell, friend of John Milton and servant of Oliver Cromwell, published an influential pamphlet, *The Growth of Popery and Arbitrary Government in England* which described a design 'to change the lawful government of England into an absolute tyranny and to convert the established Protestant religion into downright Popery'; Marvell, however, did not attack James personally — indeed he praised him and blamed the plot on vague 'evil counsellors'.

In the summer of 1678 a half-crazy clergyman, Israel Tonge, who was a genuine doctor of divinity, and a homosexual rogue, Titus Oates, who claimed to be a doctor of divinity but was not, succeeded in catching the ears of the King and Privy Council so as to outline to them a specific Jesuit plot to murder Charles II and overthrow his government. Curiously enough, Tonge's and Oates's stories were not originally precisely the same; but both agreed that Jesuits were planning to shoot, stab or poison the King and neither implicated James despite his known Catholicism. Indeed it was suggested that he as well as his brother was to be assassinated in the interest of France. Oates's revelations were set out in forty-three articles, subsequently expanded to eighty-three, and described the meeting of a Jesuit 'consult' that had been held in London on 24 August 1678 to finalize the details of the plot. In fact, as it later transpired, a consult had been held on that very day in James's own apartments in Whitehall Palace. Had that come out immediately the fat would have been in the fire for the Duke. As it was, James was not included in the widespread accusations against the alleged popish plotters. Oates's original articles were not only given to the King and handed over by him to Danby for investigation, but the truth of them was sworn to by Oates before a London magistrate, Sir Edmund Berry Godfrey, on 6 September. On 12 October Godfrey disappeared from his lodgings and when five days later his body was found transfixed with a sword on Primrose hill — apparently murdered — at least so a coroner's jury decided — it was generally considered that the 'murder' proved 'the plot' and 'the plot' proved 'the murder'.[21]

It has recently been argued that Charles II was more concerned over the reality of the plot than had formerly been supposed;[22] be that as it may, it is certain that James — even though he had not been accused of conniving at it by Oates — was from the outset profoundly disturbed by it, for he realized that he was bound to be involved. On 18 October James wrote to his son-in-law: 'I do verily believe that when this affair is thoroughly examined it will be found nothing but malice against the poor Catholics and myself in particular.'[23] James's name was soon dragged in because one of those whom Oates accused of complicity in the plot was the English Catholic, Edward Coleman, son of a clergyman and a graduate of Cambridge, who had formerly been James's secretary and later secretary to James's second wife. He had written a number of indiscreet letters to Jesuits abroad, some of which were found and some burnt. Naturally that gave rise to suspicions about James's part in the plot as soon as Parliament met on 21 October; he then thought it wise to cease attending meetings of the Privy Council and of the foreign affairs committee after 4 November.

On two points the royal brothers were agreed: the first was that Godfrey, known to be a melancholy man and a friend of Coleman, had not been murdered but had committed suicide; the second was that they had a right to be angry over Coleman's indiscretions, which, once they were made public, contributed largely to growing alarm inside and outside Parliament over the so-called plot. As soon as the majority in the House of Commons had got their teeth into the matter, however, they did not intend to let go of the Duke or his friend, Danby. They wanted not only Jesuits and others held responsible for the plot to be brought to justice but to exclude all Roman Catholics from membership of parliament, to ban James from attending the Privy Council and to prevent him from succeeding to the throne in the event of his brother's death.

Although neither James nor his brother were easily to be intimidated, both realized they were facing an extremely dangerous situation when national hysteria was being whipped up. On 12 November James wrote to William:

> As for affairs here, they do not mend but every day grow worse and worse, so that I am to prepare for a very great storm to come upon me, and I do not see it is likely to stop at me, and that their chief aim of removing me, is to come easier at the King.[24]

James also told him that they had their 'belly full of troubles' and did not see how they were likely to see an end of them, 'there being so many malicious persons in the world'. He even thought, as he added in December, that 'all things look as they did at the beginning of the late rebellion' and noted that the republicans were busy.[25] He could easily have recalled that among the causes of the civil wars had been the rising of the Catholics in Ireland against the Protestant minority there and the suspicions that his father favoured the Catholics at Court, headed by the Queen his mother.

Edward Coleman was put on trial and promptly executed on 3 December, though he swore to the end that he had no intention of trying to alter the kingdom's religion by force. This did not assuage the temper of the Commons; it was in fact heightened when Ralph Montagu, who had been the English ambassador in Paris and was now a member of parliament, revealed letters sent by Danby through him to Louis XIV asking the French King for money that was not expected to be voted to Charles II by Parliament. So Danby was impeached for treason, though he had merely obeyed his master's orders. Furthermore Oates had the impudence to accuse the Queen, because she was a Roman Catholic, of attempting to poison her husband; he let out other accusations right and left, though not against James. The Duke himself was confident that a Bill introduced into the Commons to exclude him from the succession would not be passed by the House of Lords, while he was exempted by name from the second Test Act, which was rapidly being pushed through prohibiting Roman Catholics from sitting in either House of Parliament. James himself would have been perfectly willing to remain by his brother's side and to fight in any way he could against what he regarded as the threat to the preservation of the Stuart monarchy.[26] According to Danby, when Charles told James he was unable to protect him from the fury of Parliament the Duke answered 'that his Majesty had enough of the army which was not yet disbanded to protect him if he pleased' and if he did not make use of that protection Parliament 'would not suffer him long to be King'.[27]

The King was more subtle. First, he sent the Archbishop of Canterbury and the Bishop of Winchester to try to persuade James to change his religion again. But the Duke was adamant and told them that though he was sure of their good intentions, he had no doubts at all about his faith and his conscience was absolutely clear. To prevent any further moves in the direction of exclusion Charles adjourned and then dissolved his long or 'cavalier Parliament' — it had sat for eighteen years — summoning a new one in its place. Danby thought that this was a mistake because he was more confident about controlling the old Parliament than a new one. The King also decided to send James into exile until the tempest blew over. James was not at all pleased about this; he was, however, partly consoled by a public declaration by the King that his son, Monmouth, known as 'the Protestant Duke', who was being tipped as an alternative successor to the throne, was unquestionably illegitimate and therefore ineligible. James next insisted that the King's order for his departure abroad should be put in writing. Thereupon Charles wrote to his 'most dear friend the Duke of York' that he was obliged to send him for some time across the sea, that he was sure that he would obey, and that he would not let his absence continue longer than was absolutely necessary for the good of his service.[28] On 3 March 1679 the Duke and Duchess left for The Hague where James visited his daughter Mary and his son-in-law. Then they settled in Brussels, the capital of the Spanish Netherlands, which was more congenial to their religion than Holland. There with growing dismay James puzzled over the turn of political events in England.

Three days after the Duke left England Charles opened his third Parliament, usually known to history as the first Exclusionist Parliament because the Commons were to concentrate on denying James the succession to the Crown. It was estimated after the general election that the Court party was in a clear minority of one to two in the Lower House, thus realizing Danby's forebodings. The King however was optimistic. After all, he had agreed to the second Test Act, he had demobilized most of the army which had been raised to fight the French (and, it had been feared, might be used for autocratic purposes) and he had sent his avowedly Roman Catholic brother into exile. He assumed that the thirst for revenge upon the alleged popish plotters had been assuaged by Coleman's execution as well as that of two Jesuit priests who had been named as conspirators by Titus Oates. But the Commons had their knife into Danby, whom they accused of giving the King evil advice, and although the King had already asked him to resign they demanded his impeachment for high treason. His period of office formally ended on 25 March; on 16 April he was committed to the Tower, even though Charles had assured the two Houses that he was innocent of any crime.

The Commons now turned their attention to the Duke of York. On 27 April they voted unanimously that the fact that James was a papist encouraged conspiracies against the King and the Protestant religion. Charles retorted by announcing a scheme whereby if a Roman Catholic were to succeed him on the throne, he would be subjected to constitutional limitations especially in regard to the Church of England. At first the proposal was welcomed, but within a fortnight the leaders of the Commons changed their minds, thinking that paper guarantees would be ineffective against a Catholic monarch, and debated whether they should impeach the Duke for high treason. Though that was not agreed to, on 15 May an Exclusion Bill received its first reading in the House and on 21 May its second reading was carried by 207 votes to 128. Thus what has been called the Triumvirate of the King, the Duke and Danby, who had been governing the country came to an ignominious end.

Before these events took place Charles had thought up another scheme to quieten the opposition to the Stuart dynasty: this was to invite a number of his critics to join an enlarged Privy Council, while the Earl of Shaftesbury, recognized as the leader of the opposition, was invited to become Lord President of the Council. Shaftesbury accepted the offer; his latest biographer remarks that 'few politicians in the seventeenth century refused office'.[29] It did not, however, modify his views; he announced that he 'neither could live with or under a papist'. The new Council first met on 22 April.

In Brussels James's reactions were naturally belated. Moreover his daughter Mary went down with an 'ague', possibly malaria, and James, being a good father, left the Spanish Netherlands by sea in order to visit her. After he got back, though pleased that his daughter was better and that her husband had been kind to him, he expressed his growing concern about the setting up of the new Council. The news of it surprised him exceedingly; he could not understand why the King had laid aside 'his truest servants' and he dreaded the consequences, though he hoped that his fears were mistaken.[30] He even tried to get in touch with Shaftesbury, hoping that now the Earl was on good terms with the King, he might be allowed to return home, even if he could not conscientiously change his religion.[31] That hope proved false.

By the middle of May James had learnt of the pending introduction of the Exclusion Bill, but he does not appear yet to have heard about the policy of limitations. He was more alarmed over an incipient movement to appoint by statute his nephew, the Duke of Monmouth, as the heir presumptive to the throne instead of himself. He disclosed his feelings to his other nephew, William of Orange. He said that he believed there was more danger to the King from 'the Commonwealth party' than from the papists; that those who had lately been added to the membership of the Privy Council were trying to 'make a property of Monmouth' in order to ruin the Stuart family. James trembled to think what might happen; for if the King and the House of Lords stuck by him 'then one may expect great disorders — nay a rebellion', while should exclusion be agreed to, the King would become as impotent as a Duke of Venice.[32] Three days after he wrote in this sense to William, John Churchill, his Master of the Wardrobe and Gentleman of the Bedchamber, arrived from England with 'a very kind letter' from the King. Churchill himself was against exclusion, as were James's other servants and friends. But James himself was extremely worried. Even though, as he told his brother-in-law, Henry Hyde, it was a great consolation to him that the King continued to be so kind and, as he told Prince William, was indeed resolute for him and dissatisfied with his rival Monmouth, he was genuinely afraid that if the King did not agree to exclusion Monmouth and the dissenters would 'fly out into an open rebellion'.[33] After he had learned of the first two readings of the Exclusion Bill in the House of Commons, he told William in agitation that 'except his Majesty began to behave himself as a King ought to do, not only I, but himself and our whole family are gone'.[34]

James's concern over his own future was not easily to be alleviated. Although he had been assured that the Exclusion Bill would be rejected in the House of Lords, he went on writing about his fears of a republican revolution headed by the Duke of Monmouth. He wanted the King to make use of his fleet, his garrisons and his Guards and with Scotland and Ireland loyal to him, to stand by himself and 'yet be a king'. Now or never, he exclaimed, was the time to save the monarchy.[35] But it is not clear how far these mutterings were passed on to Charles II whose courage he was invoking. It is odd that the only letter addressed by the Duke to his brother, of which the full text has survived, was about his former lady love, Susan Bellasyse, who was now one of the Duchess of York's Maids of Honour. Susan's father-in-law (the father of her first husband), a prominent Roman Catholic, had been put in the Tower as one of the alleged conspirators in the Popish Plot; James asked the King, in the event of Bellasyse being condemned to death, to fulfil his promise that Susan's son, a Protestant, should neither lose his estate nor his title. That, James concluded, was the only subject of his letter, which he ended by saying 'I shall always be the loyalest of your subjects'.[36] Such was one of the marginalia of history and of the human heart.

Apart from writing letters, James passed away his time hunting, though he complained that his hounds were 'neither staunch nor in wind', while his Duchess took the spa waters, which agreed with her but did not assist her to become pregnant.[37] They were joined by James's daughter by his first wife, the Princess Anne, who found the streets of Brussels smelly. No wonder the Duke was restless.

He should have had more confidence in the political acumen of his brother. Instead he wrote to him insisting that he could 'bear any misfortune with patience so long as you are kind' and adding that he had 'but one life to lose and I shall always be ready to lay it down in your service . . .'[38] But Charles knew perfectly well what he was doing; and on 27 May, without consulting his new Privy Council, he adjourned Parliament until August, after doubling the guards at Whitehall. He also refused to be alarmed when the extreme Covenanters rose in rebellion in Scotland — an action which might have seemed to underline James's worst fears. Charles sent his son the Duke of Monmouth to Scotland who on 22 June managed to defeat the rebels without difficulty and wanted to show them mercy. Fortified by this victory the King, again without consulting his Privy Council, determined to dissolve the first Exclusionist Parliament, saying that he would call another one in October. James was delighted with the King's resolution. Both he and his Duchess were optimistic that they would soon be recalled from their exile. Mary of Modena wrote to Susan Bellasyse to say that she had no need to join them in Brussels because she hoped to see her shortly in England; James told William that he need not worry about the suspension of Parliament, as the enactment of an Exclusion Bill would have destroyed the very basis of monarchy which depended on God alone and he expressed the hope (on 6 July) that the King would never let the existing House of Commons sit again, for if he did so, he 'would be ruined for ever'.[39]

Charles remained resilient.[40] He accepted the fact that his new Privy Council had proved useless to him; for it had neither been able to prevent the passage of the Exclusion Bill through the Commons nor had it obtained money for him to strengthen the navy. Moreover though Charles had thought that Coleman had deserved to be executed for his indiscretions, he was unhappy about the fate of the Roman Catholic peers, who had been lodged in the Tower of London because of Oates's accusations, and about the hanging of Jesuit priests. He was, however, cheered by the acquittal on 18 July of the Queen's physician, Sir George Wakeman, accused of high treason by Titus Oates; for that exonerated the Queen from participation in a plot against her husband. Still hoping — or again hoping — that the King of France would help him out of his difficulties with his own subjects Charles retired to his favourite residence, Windsor Castle, where he was suddenly taken ill on 20 August, his illness being aggravated by the attentions of his doctors. James was at once sent for from Brussels. Now everyone was anxious about what was going to happen next since the Exclusion Bill was not yet in the statute book. Should Charles die and James attempt to succeed would it mean the outbreak of another civil war?

10.

Exile in Scotland

The sudden illness of King Charles II shocked the whole political world. 'Good God, what a change would such an accident make!' wrote the English ambassador in Paris, 'The very thought of it frightens me out of my wits.'[1] Were the King to die, there would be three candidates for the succession: James, the heir presumptive; the Duke of Monmouth, who was sponsored by the Earl of Shaftesbury once he had realised that the acquittal of Sir George Wakeman, the Queen's physician, put paid to the idea of compelling Charles to divorce his wife for complicity and remarry; and Prince William of Orange, who some of Charles's Ministers preferred as a Protestant successor, especially as he was married to James's daughter. The danger of a civil war over the succession seemed very real to many informed people. A hasty meeting of members of Charles's Cabinet Council, convened in the Duchess of Portsmouth's apartments in Whitehall, agreed unanimously that James must be called home. As soon as James received this advice on 28 August by express letter, a letter which asked him not to reveal that he was being sent for, but to say he was coming of his own accord, the Duke disguised himself with a black perruque and a plain suit and took ship for Dover.[2] He arrived in London on 1 September at seven in the evening; by three o'clock next morning he was on his way by coach to Windsor. By the time he arrived at seven a.m. Charles was already on the road to recovery. James took full responsibility for his return to England, while the Ministers who called him over were eager to get rid of him again as soon as possible.

James had definite views about what his brother ought to do, which previously he had hinted at by letter and was now able to argue in person. He wanted Charles to take a tough line with Shaftesbury, the opposition leader; to dissolve what came to be

127

known as the second Exclusionist Parliament, which had just been elected; not to allow the London militia to be mobilized, but to use his own small professional army to enforce order; and to dismiss the Duke of Monmouth from all his official positions. Furthermore, he advised Charles to rely on Louis XIV both for money and for military aid if civil war should break out.

Charles accepted nearly all of James's counsel. On 4 September 1679 James dispatched his Master of the Wardrobe, John Churchill, a charming and courteous young man, to Paris with instructions to see the King of France and tell him of the need to renew 'the union and good correspondence' between the two kingdoms.[3] He was to stress the argument that unless a treaty of alliance were concluded before the new English Parliament met his master would be in serious difficulties and could not count on re-establishing his position at the centre of affairs. The King was told of Churchill's mission and its cost was met out of Treasury funds. The French monarch did not offer to provide any more money at this time, but promised his general support. As to Monmouth, Charles agreed to deprive him of his lieutenant-generalship and to order him to leave England. Finally, Charles prorogued the new Parliament as soon as it met and by repeating this process six times did not allow it to function at all for a full year.

Naturally James had hopes that he would be allowed to stay at the King's side. After all, he had disproved the fear that there would be a rebellion or an insurrection in the City of London were he to do so. But he was rapidly undeceived. He wrote to William of Orange from Windsor on 5 September to say 'they think it best to have me away when the Parliament sits'[4] while Charles's Ministers, conscious that the anti-papist agitation was still scalding hot, strongly advised the King to send the Duke away again. During the short time he remained in England he was shown a great deal of affability, for hardly anyone wanted to antagonize a future king. But it was generally feared that his mere presence in the country would provoke Parliament. Before his departure James had written to William to say that Monmouth was behaving badly 'and kept ill company in London' chiefly of dissenters who pressed him to disobey the King's orders and not go abroad.[5] It is pretty clear that trouble would have arisen in London if the two rivals for the succession had both stayed in Whitehall. Charles wisely banished them both at the same time. On 24 September Monmouth sailed for

Holland; next day James returned to Brussels; and the King, as was his custom, went to Newmarket to amuse himself with riding and racing.

Charles had allowed his brother to change his place of exile; whether the suggestion came from the King or the Duke is not clear, but it was decided that he should go to Edinburgh to stay in Holyrood Palace until he received fresh orders. Returning to Brussels to collect his wife and belongings, he found two friendly letters from Louis XIV awaiting him. In his reply to them he told the French King that he attributed to his influence with his brother the permission he had received to go to Scotland instead of remaining in Brussels and added that it was with the help of Louis that he expected soon 'to be again solidly settled near the King my brother'.[6]

James only took a few days to pack his luggage and bring his Duchess back across the Channel. On 14 October he sent the trusted Churchill to London to ask the King to allow him to stay there a few days before he travelled by land to Scotland. His request was granted no doubt because on that very day Shaftesbury had been dismissed from his presidency of the Privy Council and Parliament had been prorogued. Before he left the capital the Duke was entertained to dinner by the Artillery Company, in which he had many friends, at Merchant Taylors' Hall. The hall and the balconies were crowded; he delivered a speech in which he promised always to maintain the laws and liberties of the King's subjects, and he declared afterwards that the occasion went pretty well 'for a poor banished man'.[7] However, on his way back from the banquet he met with a hostile reception from the crowd that had gathered in the City.

On 27 October he started for Scotland. Travelling by coach it took over three weeks by way of Hatfield, Huntingdon, Biggleswade, Stamford, Grantham, Newark, Welbeck, Doncaster, Pontefract, York, Durham and Berwick-upon-Tweed before he entered Scotland. He and his wife rested a few days both in York and in Durham. Mary of Modena, who was still only twenty and had been extremely sick crossing the sea, insisted upon accompanying the Duke upon this rather tedious journey on which their reception from their various hosts was not all it might have been. The King had been willing to let her and James's two daughters, Anne (by his first wife) and Isabella, born on 28 August 1676, remain in London, but, according to James's biographer, she 'chose rather even with the hazard of her life to be a constant companion to the Duke her husband's misfortunes and hardships than to enjoy her ease in any part of the world without him'.[8] The price she paid as they neared the Scottish border was a heavy cold brought on by snow, frost and biting north winds.[9] They arrived at Edinburgh on 4 December where they were warmly received, largely through the efforts of the Duke of Lauderdale, a powerful and highly gifted man, who was Secretary of State for Scotland and had long been Charles II's principal counsellor on Scottish affairs, although because of his ruthlessness he was extremely unpopular with the English House of Commons and most of the Scottish nobility and gentry.

James was entirely satisfied with his welcome. The nobility were pleased that they had a royal Court again, while the shopkeepers in Edinburgh were delighted with his lavish expenditure; the Corporation reciprocated by inviting him and his Duchess to an expensive banquet which must have been a lively affair as thirty-six glass trenchers, sixteen glass plates and twelve jelly glasses were smashed. James held no official position and aimed to take no sides. Writing to his friend, George Legge, on 14 December, he said: 'I live as cautiously as I can and am very careful to give offence to none and to have no partialities and preach to them laying aside all private animosities and serving the King in his own way.'[10] However, he was Duke of Albany as well as of York; he was therefore entitled to attend meetings of the Scottish Council, as he did from 4 December after refusing to take the customary oath of allegiance which contained a declaration against the Roman Catholic faith and therefore would have been repugnant to him. In the Council his advice was generally accepted.

James and his wife attended Mass in Holyrood Palace, but, according to Dr Burnet, himself a Scot, he 'showed an impartial temper and considering how much the nation was set against his religion, he made greater progress in gaining them than was expected'. He was affable and industrious and said to be 'beloved' by all.[11] The peaceful atmosphere was very different from that which prevailed when he was in England. 'His discourses', wrote a contemporary, 'were very free especially concerning his own pretensions and the parliament of England.'[12] Privately he had two worries. The first was caused by the news that Monmouth had returned to England against the orders of Charles II — James would not have dreamed of doing such a thing himself — and the second was his discovery that after Monmouth had won the battle of Bothwell Bridge he had made himself popular by the mercy he had shown to the extreme Covenanters. Evidently James regarded his nephew as a dangerous rival for the succession to the thrones of England and Scotland. That was why he was eager for a fresh agreement with the French King, which would, he believed, be invaluable to him if his brother should suddenly die.

By the beginning of 1680 the tide had begun to turn against the sponsors of the Popish Plot headed by Shaftesbury. Lord Chief Justice Scroggs, whose summing up had contributed largely to the jury's acquittal of the Queen's doctor, even teased Shaftesbury when he met him at a dinner about 'his creature Oates' and proposed the health of the Duke of York in his presence.[13] On 28 January 1680 the King informed his Council that he intended to recall James from Scotland. James, mindful of his long and rather unhappy trip there by land, told his brother that he and the Duchess would return all the way by sea. It took them only a week to sail from Leith by yacht. At Deptford they transferred to barges on which they were carried along the Thames to Whitehall steps where they arrived on 24 February. They were congratulated on their safe return by the Lord Mayor and Aldermen of the City, who entertained James and his brother to supper on 8 March.

The spring and summer of 1680 passed pretty peacefully. James accompanied the King on his biennial trips to Newmarket and together they inspected new ships which had been built at Blackwall. Parliament was not sitting. Although the Earl of Shaftesbury was still active in stirring up trouble first by trying to invent a fresh Popish Plot centered on Ireland and, secondly, by attempting to indict the Duke of York as a popish 'recusant', his zeal went unrewarded. James's main concern was over foreign policy. Charles, like his brother, wanted a fresh alliance with France, but had awaited James's return before opening negotiations.[14] The French monarchy was now occupied in expanding its territorial possessions by legal ingenuity backed by threats of violence and terror. Chambers of Reunion under French influence were created to discover territories which by feudal law had once been dependent on districts handed over to the French in the treaties of Westphalia and Nijmegen. To enforce these claims Louis XIV devoted all his military and diplomatic resources. Seeing that the kingdom of England was paralysed by the aftermath of the Popish Plot he felt no need to bribe its King to stay neutral while Charles II freely admitted to the French ambassador that at this particular time he had no means of being useful.[15] Instead therefore Charles entered into negotiations with the Dutch and the Spanish to demonstrate to the French the value of his alliance. But Spain, now ruled by a regency on behalf of a minor, was militarily weak, while the Dutch were naturally suspicious of the English King's real intentions. Charles's last hope was to allow Parliament to meet and to persuade it to vote him money to enable him to make his weight felt in European affairs.

As soon as that was decided in mid-August the King realized he dared no longer keep James at his side. For he knew that the House of Commons, elected nearly a year earlier, was likely to be as ferociously exclusionist as its predecessor and might attempt to impeach the Duke. The King's mistress, the Duchess of Portsmouth, whom the Earl of Shaftesbury had vainly tried to get indicted as 'a common nuisance', had cast her influence against James. The King's ablest Ministers all pressed that James should be banished into exile again. James tried hard to prevent this by appealing for French help. Just before Parliament met he sent for the French ambassador and told him that he did not yet despair of being able to save himself.[16] He said that the King had not yet abandoned him and that opinions in the King's Council were divided. If he were attacked in Parliament, he would still have time to retire from London. He asserted that he had been betrayed and cheated by those in whom he had confided particularly Sir William Temple, Henry Sidney and the Earl of Sunderland, who had negotiated the treaty with Spain. The ambassador was warned that Louis XIV's great enemy, Prince William of Orange, would be the gainer by his downfall.[17] That was why he sought the protection of the French King which alone 'can save the King of Great Britain from utter ruin'; for, as his brother-in-law, Laurence Hyde, had assured Charles, he could not forsake his brother without being ruined himself. But everything James tried to do to avert another exile was in vain. According to his biographer, who relied on the Duke's own memoirs

> Notwithstanding all the Duke could say to show from what spring all these troubles flowed, still the cry went against him, as the Jonas for whose sake these storms were raised; and therefore the King had no sooner decided in Council on the 18th of August that the Parliament should sit on the 21st of October, but all the world cast about to save themselves; and the Duke, like that Prophet, must be sacrificed for the public peace.[18]

The King was adamant that James must leave the capital before

Parliament assembled. But he gave him several promises. He had already that year for the second time published a declaration 'on the word of a king and the faith of a Christian' that he had never married the Duke of Monmouth's mother or anyone but the Queen. He announced that this time James was to go to Scotland as his representative with full powers to govern the country on his behalf. He also assured his brother that although he might have to grant concessions to satisfy Anglican prejudices, he would not allow the Duke to be attacked on account of his religion. When James asked if he could be provided with a royal pardon in case the attempt to impeach him was renewed, the King answered that to do so would merely encourage tumults and disorder and that he conceived it would be better, if it came to an impeachment, to break the Parliament altogether. James was deeply disappointed with his brother's attitude; he thought he was unsteady in his resolution of standing by him and that he accepted advice from weak and treacherous men. The Duke pointedly reminded the King of what had happened to their father and argued that compliance with the wishes of the House of Commons was as dangerous now as it was then. Charles, however, persuaded James to go away and that he need not be afraid.[19]

The day before Parliament met the Duke returned to Scotland by sea. The Duke of Lauderdale, who had so long governed Scotland on Charles's behalf, had been compelled to resign his Secretaryship the month before partly on account of his health and partly as a sop to the House of Commons which disliked and distrusted him. Once again James was pleased with his reception in Edinburgh where the re-establishment of a royal Court was extremely welcome. But his mind was concentrated on what was happening in London. He knew that he had some good friends there including his two brothers-in-law by his first marriage, Henry Hyde, second Earl of Clarendon, and Laurence Hyde, later Earl of Rochester, while seven members of the King's Council had favoured his being allowed to stay in England, though they had been overruled by the King. He blamed his exile on Arthur Capel, Earl of Essex, a Lord of the Treasury, and on the Earl of Sunderland, Secretary of State for the South, both of whom were avowed Exclusionists, on the Earl of Halifax. whom he called an atheist, and on the feline Duchess of Portsmouth, who, he said, 'was never to be trusted'.

When Parliament at last met it was in a fiery mood because it had been in abeyance for over a year since it was elected during which time the King had been pressed by petitioners — to be known as Whigs — for it to be called together at once. Charles II calmly told the two Houses that the long interval without a meeting of parliament had enabled him to take measures for the safety of England and the repose of Christendom, referring specifically to the alliance with Spain. He promised the Commons that if it voted him money for the purposes of defence, he would agree to any remedies consistent with the preservation of the succession to the Crown 'in its due and legal course of descent'. All his pleas and promises were in vain. For the Commons were dead set on Exclusion. After they had listened to an ex-criminal named Dangerfield accusing the Duke of York of having given him money to invent a sham plot, they proceeded to read the Exclusion Bill three times and sent it up to the House of Lords. Under pressure from the King the Lords threw out the Bill by sixty-three votes to thirty; the Earl of Halifax, who had spoken against it, then proposed that if a Roman Catholic monarch came to the throne, his rights, especially over the Church of England, should be limited by statute. Disappointed at the rebuff to Exclusion, the Commons demanded that the King should dismiss Halifax from his office of Lord Privy Seal, which Charles refused to do, condemned his other Ministers and some of the judges, and then turned to the impeachment of Lord Stafford, an elderly and infirm Roman Catholic, who had been confined to the Tower of London for his alleged part in the Popish Plot. In the course of his trial it was pointed out by the prosecution that it was James's conversion that 'gave life and encouragement to the designs of destroying the Government and introducing Popery'. Stafford was duly found guilty, condemned to death and executed on 29 December. All this news made James feel extremely dismal, although naturally he was pleased that the Exclusion Bill had been rejected by the Lords at its first hearing; he asked his brother-in-law, Clarendon, to thank all his friends,[20] while he himself wrote to express his gratitude to Halifax. But he did not care for Halifax's proposed Bill of Limitations, which he thought would be dangerous to the monarchy and the fact that, as he learned, Shaftesbury was opposed to it, he knew was not out of good will. He told his friends that he hoped the King would stand up for himself and continue to deal firmly with Parliament. Finally, he again reminded his brother of what had happened to their father when he sacrificed the life of the Earl of Strafford; was not the fate of Stafford a similar case?

James continued to rely for his own personal security on the support of France. He wrote to the French ambassador in London expressing his satisfaction about Louis XIV's goodness to him.[21] He also told him he could count on the loyalty of the Scottish nobility and gentry, but emphasized that his return to England was essential if he were to promote a closer relationship between his brother and the French King, for while he was away from the capital he could do very little. Meanwhile Charles, seeing no prospect of any agreement with the Commons, prorogued Parliament on 10 January 1681. Before the House of Commons dispersed it voted that whosoever advised the King against the passing of the Exclusion Bill was a betrayer of his Majesty and the Protestant religion and a pensioner of France.

As soon as James heard of the prorogation he dispatched Churchill to ask the King for permission for him to return to London. Churchill was also to press the King not to allow Parliament to sit again, to dissuade him from allying himself with Spain and the United Netherlands against France, and to rely on Louis XIV to preserve the Stuart monarchy. Although Churchill's arguments for allowing James to return made no impression on Charles, while he was in London the King dissolved the existing Parliament and dismissed the Exclusionist Ministers including Sunderland and Essex. Churchill also saw Barrillon who assured him that Louis wished for James's recall to his brother's side and had decided to ensure his succession to the throne. Somewhat gratuitously Churchill told the ambassador that 'the Prince was not in a condition to maintain himself in Scotland if the King his brother did not support him there'.[22] James also wrote a letter to Barrillon in which he urged the conclusion of a new Anglo-French treaty and warned him that otherwise Charles would be obliged to put himself in the hands of another parliament and rely on the assistance of Prince William of Orange. He added that he thought it was time that Louis should openly show his support for him; for, he concluded 'it would be a glorious action if he re-established the King of England in full power and saved the poor Catholics'.[23] Evidently Barrillon was not notably impressed by James's worries and appeals. He informed his master that he did not think it opportune to advocate the Duke's return from Scotland and the ambassador took care to conceal from Churchill the fact that Charles had already opened negotiations for a verbal agreement with France.

Why did Charles refuse to let James come back from Scotland once Parliament was dissolved? The reason was that he was determined to see what yet another Parliament would do and arranged for it to meet in Oxford where it would not be under pressure from the London rabble (as once his father had been) and he felt convinced that James's presence in England while a general election was in progress would be highly provocative. Another reason why he did not want to recall his brother was that he was anxious for the Duke to summon and preside over a parliament in Scotland; and he even had hopes that when the English Parliament gathered in Oxford he might be able to persuade it to accept some compromise about the succession either through the policy of limitations or even through the establishment of a Protestant regency, making James simply a figurehead. He did not, however, give up the sanguine expectation that James would get him out of his political difficulties by reverting to at least outward conformity with the Church of England. Both Halifax and Laurence Hyde urged this course on the Duke. James merely answered that he was extremely mortified by such a suggestion, to which he could not possible accede, 'for', he added, 'indeed I see nothing but ruin, when such measures are taken as produced such a message to me, when there was no reason to believe I would comply.'[24] In any case James thought very little of the idea of calling yet another parliament so soon as he felt sure it would be in no better humour than the previous one.[25]

James was a great letter-writer; not only did he correspond with his brother, with Barrillon, with William of Orange, with Laurence Hyde and George Legge about political matters but he wrote to Susan Bellasyse and to his niece, Charlotte Fitzroy Countess of Litchfield, a daughter of Charles II and the Duchess of Cleveland; Charlotte had married Sir Edward Henry Lee in 1677, a marriage that lasted forty-two years and yielded eighteen children. James's letters to this niece reveal the boredom he felt in Scotland.[26] He played golf frequently on the links at Leith, went riding and sometimes made trips out of Edinburgh, for example to Stirling. In June 1681 he described to her the 'very long days and no hot weather'. The town (he wrote) was already empty of company; clearly he felt jealous of his niece, who was going to Windsor, but he had to tell her that he had no hope of seeing her that summer. In the late autumn he wrote:

I assure you that we do not pass our time here so ill as you in England think we do, for we have plays, ride abroad when it is good weather, play at bassett [a gambling card game] and have a great deal of good company, but for all that one wishes oneself with one's friends in England.

He had two personal misfortunes; his daughter, Isabella, whom he had left behind at St James's Palace, died at the age of five and his wife had a riding accident in which she was nearly killed. As the winter of 1680-1 set in there was, as he told his niece, 'no stirring abroad, a great mortification for me that loves best diversions without doors'. The Duchess went on playing bassett and Princess Anne, who was fourteen when she joined them in July 1681, danced country dances, which her stepmother could not do as her legs still hurt her after her fall. In February 1682 bassett was still 'the chief diversion', for Lent put an end to plays. However, James was cheered to find his wife was again with child, though it proved to be another daughter, born in August, who died in October of convulsions. When the weather improved in the spring he went fox-hunting and took his wife and daughter to see cock-fights.

Gilbert Burnet recorded in his *History* 'how the Duke behaved himself upon his first going to Scotland in so obliging manner that the nobility and gentry, who had been so long trodden on by the Duke of Lauderdale and his party, found a very sensible change.'[27] He proved himself to be impartial in matters of justice, encouraged the development of trade and promoted religious toleration. He advised the bishops to take no notice of conventicles, that is to say dissenters' meetings when held in private houses, and was only hard on field conventicles where he believed the extreme Covenanters, known as Cargillites or Cameronians, who gathered in them, were fanatics and rebels. In fact they were pretty harmless republicans, but they were tortured and some of them hanged as martyrs for their beliefs. Burnet noted that 'the Duke stopped their prosecution for treason, which carried the death penalty, and ordered them to be imprisoned with hard labour.'[28] On one occasion at least he watched tortures aimed at exacting confessions, but the evidence that he actually enjoyed such a spectacle is slight.

On 28 July 1681 James as Royal Commissioner opened the Scottish Parliament, which had not met for nine years. It was very different from the English Parliament, for it was carefully packed with members friendly to the Government and could not initiate legislation. In his speech the Duke promised to redress grievances, to

maintain the Protestant religion and to suppress extremist Covenanters and schismatics. He also declared that the right of the Crown
must be upheld in 'its natural and legal course of descent'.[29] Laws, in
effect promoted by the Royal Commissioner, were then enacted.
Landowners were prohibited under pain of severe penalties from
allowing field conventicles to be held on their territories. Another
Act laid it down that the right of succession to the throne of
Scotland was unaffected by the religion of the heir. Lastly an oath
was imposed on all officials of any kind to adhere to the established
religion and to be loyal to the King and his lawful successors. James
was also industrious over administrative questions; he reorganized
the militia and the kingdom's modest finances and secured peace in
the unruly highlands.

James was delighted at the ease with which he was able to handle
Scottish affairs. He discovered that there was no chance of a Titus
Oates or a Dangerfield achieving any success in the northern kingdom. As he wrote to the Countess of Litchfield in June 1681:
'Things are very quiet and like to remain so, for here false witnesses
dare not come, perjury meaning death.' 'If it had been so in
England', he added, 'innocent people would not have suffered' [that
is to say, himself and his fellow Catholics].[30] When the Parliament
assembled in Edinburgh he told her its sitting was far less troublesome than it was in England; that money had been voted for the
upkeep of troops; and that peaceful conditions were likely to
continue.[31] He thought, as he told William of Orange, that what had
been done there would not only secure the Government in Scotland
but have good effects in England also.[32] Charles wrote to thank
James for his zeal in his service and approved of the new oath of
allegiance, saying that those who refused it should be treated as
persons disaffected to the Protestant religion, a curious remark to
find in the correspondence between two Roman Catholic brothers.
However the Catholics in Scotland — and many were to be found in
the highlands — were perfectly happy so long as they were left alone.
They praised James for his good temper, impartiality and mercy
towards offenders.[33]

One powerful figure, nevertheless, was not placated; that was
Archibald Campbell ninth Earl of Argyll. Both he and his father have
been called uncrowned kings of the highlands. The father, who had
fought against royalists and had been an ally of Oliver Cromwell, was
executed for high treason after the Restoration, but his son was

released from prison in 1663 and was allowed to keep his earldom and most but not all of his family estates. He had become a member of the Scottish Council, but his sympathies were Whiggish and his feelings anti-papist and he had not approved of Lauderdale's policies. He had insisted on 'explaining' the new oath of loyalty to the Crown saying that he took it 'as far as it is consistent with itself and the Protestant religion'. James was persuaded that this devious explanation amounted to a refusal to take the oath; it was the deviousness to which James objected, for he told William of Orange that if he had positively refused the oath 'nothing would have been said to him'.[34] So Argyll was charged with treason and perjury, put under arrest and imprisoned in Edinburgh Castle. At his trial he was condemned to death for treason, though acquitted of perjury. Neither James nor Charles, who approved of the trial, intended that Argyll should be put to death nor even lose his estates, but only to deprive him of the political authority he exercised as an over-mighty subject and to frighten him into obedience. The Earl managed to escape from the castle before the sentence of death was pronounced and his property was thereupon forfeited to the Crown. He was to reappear later in James's life as an armed rebel.

Meanwhile what had been happening in England? On 21 March 1681 the King had opened the Parliament which he had summoned to meet in Oxford and it was found to be much of the same complexion as the two previous parliaments, that is to say Whiggish. Charles failed to come to terms with Shaftesbury on any 'expedient' about the succession for he now wanted the Duke of Monmouth to be the next king; the Exclusion Bill was again introduced in the Commons; the two Houses quarrelled with one another; and that gave Charles an excellent excuse for dissolving them after they had met for only a week. Furthermore while the Oxford Parliament was in session a verbal agreement between Charles and Louis XIV was at last reached. The English King promised to disentangle himself from any alliance against France, particularly from his recent treaty with Spain, and to call no more parliaments unless obliged to do so by French acts of aggression; in return the French King undertook to uphold the royal authority in England, if need be, and granted Charles a subsidy amounting to some £700,000 spread over three years. But Charles was by no means subservient. He warned the French King against again invading the Spanish Netherlands or attacking the Dutch, while he extended an invitation to his nephew,

William of Orange, to visit England that July. He also prevented another informer, an Irishman named Edward Fitzharris, who promised revelations about a plot to assassinate him with the connivance of the Duke of York, from being inflated into another Titus Oates; he foiled an attempt by Shaftesbury and his friends to provide Fitzharris with an opportunity publicly to implicate the Queen and the Duke in the Popish Plot; and he made sure, in defiance of the Oxford Parliament, that this new perjurer was safely hanged.

In the light of these events and the quiet that prevailed in Scotland, James naturally counted on being allowed to return to London. He wrote to the Countess of Litchfield on 18 July 1681 saying that he hoped to see her again soon as the King's affairs were going so well, though he 'must be governed and submit to his pleasure as I always have done'.[35] The difficulty was that Charles had now determined to screw up his courage to order the arrest of Shaftesbury himself, charge him with treason, and have him executed. The Earl, who was over sixty and a sick man, was seized on 2 July and imprisoned in the Tower of London, but he had to wait nearly five months before he was put on trial before a Grand Jury. None of the Cabinet Council was enthusiastic at this stage for James's recall. Eventually it was decided that the Duke's brother-in-law, Laurence Hyde, now Viscount Hyde, should go up to Scotland and tell him that 'his religion was still an invincible obstacle' to his return and that unless he would conform and go to church he must expect no leave to return to Court.[36] The Duke was astonished at this demand. How could Charles, himself a confessed Catholic, impose such a condition? Presumably he still had not realized what a consummate dissembler his brother was. James himself would not and could not deceive the world about his religion. Possibly Charles himself expected that Hyde's mission would be a failure, but he made it absolutely plain to his brother that if he returned to London before Shaftesbury's trial had taken place he would be asking for trouble. James understood that well enough and had to hope that he would be sent for as soon as the trial was over. But he was bored, telling his niece that Edinburgh was now empty and afforded little news; bassett was still the rage; and some actors had arrived from Ireland to perform in plays which were 'pretty tolerable'.[37]

On 24 November Shaftesbury's trial at last opened in the Old Bailey. The evidence for his treasonable activities was weak in the extreme; nothing incriminating had been found among his papers when he was arrested; the witnesses who were brought against him were exposed as liars or rogues. A Grand Jury justifiably acquitted him, the verdict being rapturously received in London where a crowd cried out: 'No Popish successor! No York! A Monmouth! . . . and God bless the Earl of Shaftesbury!'[38] James thought the behaviour of the Grand Jury was 'strange' and the demonstration by the rabble 'insolent and seditious'. It was no wonder that under the circumstances the Earl of Halifax (who was Shaftesbury's nephew) said that he was against the Duke of York's return, since when he was near the King everybody believed that Charles was guided by him and that popish counsels prevailed, whereas he was doing a great deal of good in Scotland by his influence and watchfulness.[39] But by January 1682 the King at length relented. According to James himself, his recall was engineered by the Duchess of Portsmouth, who had ended a flirtation with the Exclusionists and wanted to safeguard her own fortune should Charles die or be overthrown. The scheme was that the Duke should settle upon her part of the funds obtained from the rent of the Post Office which had been voted to him by statute for life and in return that the King should bestow on the Duke an equivalent amount from the excise. James knew in fact that the revenue from the Post Office voted to him by Parliament could not be alienated, but he kept quiet about that and argued that this complicated financial arrangement required his presence in London. However, it is highly doubtful that James was ingenious enough himself to concoct such a means to obtain his recall and in fact he admitted in his memoirs that 'the King's good nature went farther than the Duchess of Portsmouth's avarice, and he resolved with himself the Duke should come for good and all.'[40] James set sail from Leith on 4 March 1682 and after landing at Yarmouth went by way of Norwich to join his brother at Newmarket. He was received graciously and promised Charles that he would be as obedient in the future as he had been in the past.

II.

'Old Jimmy's Come Again'

James was delighted at being allowed to return to England in the spring of 1682. It had been an exceptionally boring winter for him with the weather compelling him to stay indoors and play cards.[1] His Duchess, however, was again with child. The Duke's friend, George Legge, had been sent by Charles to fetch him with orders that he was to join the King at Newmarket and that he was to come alone, but he was also instructed to tell James that the King would permit him to come to London when the Duchess of York arrived there to lie in. After animated conversations at Newmarket, where James gave the King his advice about the situation in Scotland the Duke accompanied Charles to London. When they arrived there on the evening of 8 April they were welcomed with the ringing of bells and the lighting of bonfires. The newsheets commended the King's victory over the Exclusionists and even hailed the return of James:

> The glory of the British line,
> Old Jimmy's come again.[2]

The French ambassador took note of the fact that the people of London were quite calm over the reappearance of the Duke and showed no signs of bad will.[3] Louis XIV himself was pleased to hear of his recall and wrote to him to say that his 'counsels and firmness will henceforward be very necessary to strengthen the King of Great Britain in the resolution to avail himself of the means I have offered to confirm the peace and render immovable the ties of friendship between them.'[4] What Louis had done was to lift the blockade of Luxembourg, which belonged to Spain, an event which had caused much anxiety in English political circles, and to organize the regular payment to Charles of small sums of money in accordance with the terms of the secret verbal agreement of the previous year.

On 3 May James left Windsor Castle and boarded a frigate, the *Gloucester,* which, accompanied by a squadron of small yachts, was to carry him back to Leith. Owing to a mistake by the pilot the *Gloucester* struck a sandbank known as the Lemon and Ore near Yarmouth and when it got into deep water it began to sink. Various accounts of the wreck, not easily reconcilable with one another, have survived. James evidently hoped to save the vessel and feared that if he at once left it by the long boat or lifeboat nobody would remain on board with sufficient authority to take charge of the salvage operations. Eventually George Legge, who was with the Duke on the frigate, insisted that James must abandon the ship, even if he had to force him to do so. Before James agreed he gave orders that his strong-box, which is assumed to have contained his precious memoirs, must be lowered into the long boat. Legge complained afterwards that the box was extremely heavy and that it took some time to lift it down. He asked James if it contained anything worth a man's life. The Duke replied that 'there were things of such consequence, both to the King and himself, that he would hazard his own life rather than it should be lost'. Once James and his strong-box were safely in the boat, Legge and Churchill, who was armed with the Duke's own sword, were commanded by James to prevent too many persons being crowded into the long boat lest it capsized. The result was that about 150 of the Duke's servants and seamen were drowned, though only a few gentlemen, including James's youngest brother-in-law, Lieutenant James Hyde, were lost.

Both Legge and Churchill were of the opinion, as they related in confidence afterwards, that if the Duke had abandoned ship promptly all the passengers and crew might have been saved. Churchill's wife, who was to become the first Duchess of Marlborough, recollected in her old age that her husband told her that if it had not been for the Duke's obstinacy and false courage so many lives would not have been sacrificed. On the other hand, Legge denied the ridiculous story enshrined in Burnet's *History* that James had given first preference to the safety of his dogs and priests.[5] James of course blamed it all on the pilot who managed to get away by swimming to one of the yachts, for the sea was perfectly calm. The Duke told his nephew, William of Orange, that had he known this he would have ordered the pilot to be hanged forthwith instead of being tried later, as he was, and sentenced to life imprisonment. By contrast he consoled his niece, the Countess of Litchfield, by writing: 'God be thanked I and most of the people of quality got off.'[6] James had shown bad judgment but not callousness.

On reaching Edinburgh on 7 May James expeditiously wound up his affairs in Scotland. He chose George Gordon, Earl of Aberdeen, to be Chancellor and the Marquis of Queensberry as Treasurer. Both were Protestants and were dubbed by Burnet 'proud and covetous men'.[7] Later in 1684 when the Earl of Middleton on James's advice was promoted to be Secretary of State for the North, his previous office of Secretary for Scotland was conferred on John Drummond, afterwards Earl of Melfort. John Drummond's elder brother, the Earl of Perth, was made Lord Justice General while Alexander Stewart, Earl of Moray, was also a Secretary of State for Scotland. It was on James's suggestion that two Secretaries for Scotland were appointed, one to reside in London and the other in Edinburgh. These noblemen were mostly jealous of one another and Perth and Melfort were soon to become Roman Catholics. Largely through Queensberry's intrigues Aberdeen was eased out of the high office of Chancellor, on the ground that he was too merciful to the extreme Covenanters, and was replaced by Perth. James was never to show himself notably wise in the selection of ministers as his brother was; while everything seemed peaceable enough in Scotland when he left it, he had sown the seeds of future troubles. His last administrative act was to arrange for the magistrates of Edinburgh to raise a company for police work whose officers he chose himself. He believed (wrongly) that the affairs of the highlands would soon be settled and that he had succeeded in completely suppressing the field conventicles.[8]

In spite of the wreck of the *Gloucester* and the fact that she was *enceinte*, Mary of Modena was not discouraged from travelling back with her husband by sea on another frigate appropriately named the *Happy Return*. They left Scotland on 15 May 1682 and twelve days later were with the King at Windsor where he was still on holiday. Afterwards they set up house again in St James's Palace.

More than a year had passed since Charles II had rid himself of his Oxford Parliament and had received a verbal promise from Louis XIV of support should the Whigs attempt to enforce Exclusion by an armed uprising. He had played his cards skilfully; taking advantage of the Corporation Act of 1661, which authorized royal commissioners, among other things, to remove local officials at their discretion, the Crown was able to remodel several boroughs, while writs of *quo warranto* could be issued by the law courts requiring the forfeiture of charters, though that was a longer process. What the King wanted, above all, was to obtain political control of the City of London. At the Michaelmas election of 1682 a Tory Lord Mayor and two Tory sheriffs were chosen — the Tories being those who had abhorred the Whig petitioners when they demanded the recall of Parliament. Now no parliament was sitting, for owing to the expansion of customs and excise receipts and abstention from war the King was in no need of supplies and could do without parliament; thus the Whigs lost their forum. And after his release from prison on bail Shaftesbury had gone into hiding and then fled to Amsterdam where he died on 21 January 1683.

Shaftesbury's place as Whig leader was occupied by the Duke of Monmouth, Shaftesbury's choice as Charles II's successor instead of James, but he was a weak man who easily succumbed to flattery. He had a fair number of supporters, particularly in the west of England, where he had made a triumphal 'progress' or tour during the summer of 1680 after his victory at Bothwell Bridge. But when he tried to repeat this success by touring the north during the autumn of 1682 he was put under arrest and taken to London, though subsequently discharged by the Court of King's Bench. A progress in the south during February 1683 was even more of a fiasco and he turned, as he afterwards admitted, to discussing vague plans for rebellion. The death of Shaftesbury, the foolish antics of Monmouth, the absence of a parliament, the overthrow of the Whig supremacy in London and the secret agreement with Louis XIV all contributed to the comparative domestic peace which prevailed when James returned, a period which has been described alike as that of 'the Tory reaction' and of 'Stuart revenge'.[9] In the second half of 1682 James was able to write delightedly to William of Orange about the mortification of the Whigs while warning him seriously to have nothing to do with Shaftesbury, 'a great enemy to our family', or with the fanatics who were flocking to join him in Amsterdam.[10]

During 1682 and 1683 James was invariably at the King's side whether he was in Whitehall, Newmarket, Windsor or Winchester where Charles was planning to build a new palace. In the summer of 1682 James accompanied the King to Chatham to inspect a new warship, the *Britannia,* that had been built at the cost of £62,000. They saw this first-rate launched much to Charles's pride and pleasure and he was also extremely pleased with a new yacht named the *Fubbs,* which was the nickname of the Duchess of Portsmouth, his principal mistress.[11] At Windsor James and his wife (her child, a daughter, had been born in August) enjoyed hunting in the daytime and playing bassett or crimp at night. At Newmarket cock-fighting was to be seen as well as horse racing and fox-hunting. From Winchester in Hampshire, which James thought 'a proper place for women to ride in', the Duke went hunting stags while his wife hunted hares with beagles.[12] It was also a convenient centre from which to visit Portsmouth (by sailing there from Southampton), for James had not lost his interest in the navy since he ceased to be Lord High Admiral. On 28 July 1683 he attended his daughter Anne's wedding to Prince George of Denmark, a marriage which – despite the fact that his new son-in-law was a Protestant – pleased James because for some reason or other it annoyed the Whigs.[13]

In March 1683 when James was with the King at Newmarket some stables caught fire and half the small town was burnt to the ground. Three months later an informer, Josiah Keeling, came forward with the story of a plot to murder the two brothers when they were *en route* in their coach from Newmarket to London; owing to the fire, he explained, they luckily escaped assassination because the conspirators were caught unprepared.[14] The existence of the plot was confirmed by one of the alleged conspirators, a shady barrister named Robert West, the *alter ego* of Titus Oates. The headquarters of the would-be murderers, he said, was a house named the Rye, which belonged to a former Cromwellian colonel. The news of this horrid plot was well calculated to enhance the Tory reaction against the Whigs. But what was even more satisfactory from James's point of view was that under examination West proceeded to implicate most of the Whig leaders, including the Duke of Monmouth, in a widespread conspiracy aiming at a national insurrection. One of the Whig aristocracy, Lord Howard of Escrick, turned King's evidence. Undoubtedly since and possibly before Shaftesbury's death there had been indiscreet talk about a possible rebellion, which, when disclosed and exaggerated, enabled arrests to be ordered. In no time at all, according to James (writing on 26 June), they 'got to the bottom of this damnable conspiracy'.[15] Monmouth went into hiding, staying for weeks in a country house belonging to the mother of his mistress; the Earl of Essex, as James wrote in July, 'cut his own throat to prevent the stroke of justice';[16] and Lord Russell, who admitted that he had 'heard many things and some things contrary

to my duty',[17] together with three others, were speedily executed.
At the end of the year Algernon Sidney, a son of the second Earl of
Leicester, who had been a member of the Commonwealth Council of
State, was beheaded, the delay being due to the fact that two
witnesses had not been found to testify against him. Instead of one
witness the prosecution produced what James described as 'a
treasonable and insolent paper, printed to show the world what his
principles were':[18] it was to be published posthumously under the
title of *Discourses concerning Government* advocating constitutional monarchy and attacking absolute government. James thought
that Sidney's execution did justice on 'so ill a man' and gave the lie to
the Whigs who believed that he would escape the extreme penalty.[19]

The position of Monmouth, as he was the King's eldest son, was
more difficult and delicate. Both Charles II and his Lord Privy Seal,
the Marquis of Halifax as he had become, knew where Monmouth
was hiding, though they did not tell James, who thought he was in
Holland. On 13 October Halifax, acting on instructions from the
King, paid a secret visit to Monmouth late at night and told him that
if he wished to be pardoned he must write submissively and dutifully
to his father; Halifax himself drafted a letter for him disavowing any
part in the assasination plot and particularly designed to pacify
James. In it he declared that he would henceforward serve the Duke
of York to the utmost of his power and added that should his uncle
be kind to him, 'if ever I should do anything afterwards against him, I
must be thought the ungratefullest man living'. Charles was satisfied
with the letter dated 15 October 1683, but did not, after all, show it
to his brother and ordered his son to stay in hiding. In the first week
of the following month Halifax arranged a clandestine meeting
between Monmouth and Charles at a house in Stepney. Here, as
Monmouth recorded in his diary, the King 'gave me directions how
to manage my business, and what words to say to the Duke of York',
and afterwards Halifax told him 'there must be something done to
blind the Duke of York'. So a month after he had signed his first
letter of contrition, he wrote another much more grovelling letter,
again drafted by Halifax, and again intended to be shown to James.
In it Monmouth was made to say that he did not expect

> to receive your pardon otherwise than by the intercession of the Duke of
> York whom I acknowledge to have offended, and am prepared to submit
> myself in the humblest manner, and therefore beg your Majesty would
> direct how I am to apply myself to him, and I shall do it, not as an outward
> form, but with all the sincerity in the world.[20]

In reply Charles said that he must surrender himself to the Secretary of State, Sir Leoline Jenkins, which he did ten days after the second letter had been written.

It was on 25 November that Monmouth came to Whitehall and gave himself up, as he had already been indicted by a Grand Jury. Charles sent him a message to play his part as arranged and 'to seem absolutely converted to the Duke of York's interest'.[21] After reporting to Jenkins Monmouth duly waited on James, who carried him straight to the King; the King took him to the Queen, then the Duke of York brought him back to his Duchess, whose hands Monmouth kissed. In his diary Monmouth noted that the Duke and Duchess 'seemed not too ill pleased'.[22] After he expressed his sorrow about having played so large a part in the conspiracy against the throne, though he was, he said, never involved in the murder plot, he was pardoned by the King and embraced by his uncle. But there was an implicit understanding that he would write a full confession incriminating his confederates in the scheme for an armed rebellion. However, when he was asked to do so in the first week of December, he refused and he also deliberately failed to appear as a witness against another of the alleged conspirators, John Hampden, grandson and namesake of a celebrated Roundhead. Instead Monmouth fled to Holland where he was received hospitably by Prince William of Orange. James wrote acidly to the Marquis of Queensberry on 20 December 1683: ''twas a great mercy that he [Monmouth] discovered himself so soon not to be a true penitent'.[23]

The whole episode throws a flood of light on the relations between James and the King his brother. Some questions must remain unanswered. Why did Charles fail to show James the first letter, drafted by Halifax especially in order to conciliate the Duke of York? Why did the King allow Monmouth to come back to Whitehall before the trial and execution of Algernon Sidney and before the trial of John Hampden? It was hardly surprising if, as James Welwood suggested in his *Memoirs of the most material transactions in England:*

> it was the public talk about Town that all the King's former proceedings against the Duke of Monmouth were but Grimace, and that his Royal Highness [James] being made an instrument of the reconciliation was all but a trick upon him.[24]

James had protested against any acts of clemency being shown towards the conspirators. Charles, it appeared, had been willing to spare the lives both of Essex and of Russell. But his brother induced him to change his mind about Russell and his proposed mercifulness towards Essex was never put to the test. As to Monmouth, according to James's memoirs, the King and the Duke of York had interviewed him in Jenkins's office where 'he freely owned his knowledge of the whole conspiracy except what related to the intended assassination, with which, he averred, he was never acquainted'[25] and he did not contradict any of the statements of Lord Howard of Escrick, the noble informer. This story hardly squares with what Jenkins wrote himself at the time. It rather looks as if James did not like the idea that he had been made a fool of by the King, as indeed he had been. It also illustrates Charles's insouciance and James's gullibility. Finally, the welcome given to Monmouth by William of Orange soured James's relations with his son-in-law. In May 1684 James wrote sharply to say that Monmouth's refusal to sign a confession about the participants in the conspiracy meant that 'I can never trust to what he says or believe him and I think you will be to blame if you do.'[26] Later he told him very frankly 'Let the Prince flatter himself as he pleases, the Duke of Monmouth will do his part to have a push for the Crown if he outlives the King and me.'[27]

After the death of the Whig leaders and the flight of Monmouth the party, if that is the right word to use of the Exclusionists, whom Shaftesbury had led, disintegrated. Even before the forfeiture of the City of London charter and the disclosure of the so-called Rye House murder plot, James had been promised readmission into the King's official business. Charles told him after their return from Newmarket in March 1683 that he would allow him to attend the committee of foreign affairs, which was in fact the Cabinet, and that he would consult him on all matters, not merely those of Scotland, as soon as he possibly could.[28] James was able to bring an action *de scandalis magnatum* (libel against great persons) against a former Whig sheriff named Pilkington who had said that the Duke was responsible for the Great Fire of London and had returned from Scotland to cut the throats of the citizens of London; James was awarded £100,000 damages by the Court of King's Bench. He also brought a similarly successful action against Titus Oates and against two others, though whether he was able to collect the damages awarded him is doubtful, for Oates could not have had all that money.[29]

By the beginning of 1684 it was said that the Duke of York 'did now chiefly manage affairs'.[30] On 12 February the former Tory leader, the Earl of Danby, and three out of the five Roman Catholic peers incarcerated in the Tower of London because of their alleged part in the Popish Plot (one had been executed and one had died) were released with James's approval. James was able to tell his nephew that 'all things go very well and quietly'.[31] By May James had rejoined the Privy Council and in the same month he resumed in effect the post of Lord High Admiral, although the King signed all the papers to avoid an open breach of the first Test Act.

Once Charles had outwitted the Whigs his main occupation was with foreign policy. Louis XIV was vigorously pursuing his strategy of annexing towns and territories on the borders of Germany. The English King, as has already been noticed, was relieved to learn that the French army had lifted the blockade of Luxembourg; but when in the summer of 1683 a huge Turkish army, which had swept across Hungary, was threatening to capture Vienna Louis could not resist the opportunity for further aggression while German eyes were turned towards the east. As his leading Minister, Colbert, wrote: 'We expect the siege of Vienna to be the fatal stroke, giving us all Germany.'[32] Louis ordered his army to resume the siege of Luxembourg and invaded the Spanish Netherlands a few days before the Turkish host was thrust back from the walls of Vienna. Luxembourg finally surrendered towards the end of May 1683. Charles II had been asked and had attempted to mediate between the French and the Spaniards since he had made it clear that he had no intention of fulfilling his obligation to defend Spain in accordance with the treaty of June 1680. James's excuse for not doing so was that 'we have great devils to deal with here so we must look to ourselves and not engage in any war beyond sea.'[33] In any case unless he called a parliament Charles II did not possess the means to do so. Clearly James agreed with his brother that they must make the best of a bad job by pressing the Spanish to cede Luxembourg and hope that this would bring the war to an end. For the Germans were in no position to intervene, while the ruling Dutch oligarchy had no wish to embark on another war, whatever their Stadholder, William of Orange, might feel about it.

On 7 April 1684 James wrote to William:

> We are troubled that none of the proposals made by the French have been hearkened unto nor none made to them, which might probably be

accepted by them, there being nothing more desired here than that all Christendom might be at peace, which I fear, will hardly be brought about, now that the King of France sets out so soon for the army.[34]

Satisfied by their success the French proposed a twenty-year truce, which would enable them to keep both Strasbourg and Luxembourg and thus exert a stranglehold on the Holy Roman Empire of the German nation. James, in evident agreement with his brother, was glad to learn that the Spaniards were willing to consent to the truce and hoped that the Dutch and Germans would do so as well; for he believed that unless the French conquest of Luxembourg was generally accepted the Spaniards would lose the rest of Flanders which would constitute a dangerous military threat to the United Netherlands as well as to England. Although the secret verbal treaty between Louis XIV and Charles II had expired the month before the fall of Luxembourg, the two Stuart brothers were still satisfied that the security of the throne against a Whig rebellion ultimately depended on the friendship of France. So they were both relieved when the truce was accepted by the German Diet meeting at Ratisbon in August 1684 and France and Spain concluded peace. Besides betraying the cause of the Spaniards Charles had abandoned Tangier, which he had acquired as part of his wife's dowry, thus further cutting down his military commitments. So peace reigned abroad as well as at home.

During 1684 a Cabinet reshuffle took place. Before James resumed his duties as Lord High Admiral Jenkins had resigned his office as senior Secretary of State and was replaced by Sidney Godolphin, an able and honest Minister whose only hobby was horses and horse-racing, of whom the King said he was never in the way and never out of it. But he did not hold this post for long. Laurence Hyde, Earl of Rochester, who was First Commissioner of the Treasury, had proved himself an indifferent financier; his competence was strongly criticized by the Lord Privy Seal, the Marquis of Halifax. In August the King announced his intention of appointing Rochester Lord President of the Council for the time being and later sending him to Ireland as Lord Lieutenant. Godolphin then took over as First Lord of the Treasury. Godolphin was succeeded as Secretary of State by the Earl of Middleton, formerly Secretary of State for Scotland. James had vainly tried to persuade the King to appoint his brother-in-law, the second Earl of Clarendon, to this post, but Charles had insisted that he must have someone he 'could live with'.[35] The Earl of Sunderland, another capable Minister, though far less honest than Godolphin, continued in office as Secretary of State and was one of the King's chief advisers on foreign policy. Altogether this was a team of distinction though its members were sometimes at cross-purposes and often intrigued against one another.

Where did James stand? Rochester was his brother-in-law; Godolphin and Sunderland he disliked as former Exclusionists, but he recognized their administrative abilities; he did not much care for Halifax, who was more a constitutionalist than the other Ministers, but he had reason to be grateful to him for defeating Shaftesbury over Exclusion. According to Barrillon, 'he [James] let the King know how inconvenient it was to allow Halifax, who is opposed to the interests of royalty, to be let into the secrets of his affairs.'[36] What he was referring to here was Halifax's criticism of a scheme to unite the New England colonies including New York into a single dominion under the absolute control of the Crown with no local assemblies to vote taxes and debate policies.

It has been asserted that James particularly relied on the Duchess of Portsmouth, who had become more like a morganatic wife to Charles than a chief mistress, to influence his brother's decisions; that she had been responsible both for his recall to England and his resumption of office as Lord High Admiral; and that she, James and Sunderland formed a kind of triumvirate; on the other hand, it has also been claimed that some of Charles's appointments were deliberately made in order to show that he was not entirely under James's influence and that of James's brother-in-law, Rochester.[37] The truth would appear to be that, though admittedly Charles II was taking things easily during the last year of his life and James was never far from his side, whether at Winchester hawking, hare-hunting and stag-hunting, at Newmarket horse-racing and fox-hunting or at Windsor where he found the King very accessible, he was still the master of his own affairs.

One matter that Charles was concerned about was to ensure the safety of James's succession. In Ireland the plan was that when Rochester took over as Lord Lieutenant, military power was to be placed in the hands of a lieutenant-general subject to the senior Secretary of State in London (Sunderland) while Catholics were to be given commissions in the army there. This was a policy of which James approved, for it was to be one he adopted himself during his reign. In Scotland the aim was to call another parliament, over which James himself was again to preside as Royal Commissioner with a view to ensuring the restraint of any who (like Argyll) were opposed to the succession of a Roman Catholic king. James told Queensberry of this decision in November 1684 and a month later disclosed it to Barrillon, stressing the fact that his projected absence in Scotland for three months was no disgrace, but a mark of the King's confidence in him.[38] In the same month — December 1684 — General Drummond, who was the military commander in Scotland, was ordered to exercise martial law and hang, draw and quarter all who refused to obey the King's authority.

In England Charles had built up a sizeable army which was encamped on Putney Heath and had been inspected by Charles and James during the previous October. Although the secret treaty with France had not been renewed the two brothers felt sure that it was Louis XIV's intention to help safeguard, by active means if necessary, the continuation of a strong Stuart monarchy in England. James's only personal worry was over the Duke of Monmouth, still in exile in Holland, where he was being ostentatiously patronized by William of Orange, though exactly why was a matter for speculation. James would have been even more worried had he known that Monmouth had come over to England in November to pay another secret visit to his father with the intention of obtaining permission to resume his life in England. In the previous month James had written an acid letter to Prince William telling him of his disappointment that he had shown 'so little consideration for things I have said to you of concern in our family'.[39] William had no real wish to offend his two uncles and after Arnoud van Citters, the Dutch ambassador in England, returned to London from a visit home, he tried to defend William's conduct to the Duke of York, but James was too cross to listen to him.[40]

By the end of 1684 then the royalist reaction was complete; the leading Whigs were dead or in exile or ruined by heavy fines; the only statesman tinged with Whig principles, the Marquis of Halifax, trimmed between both sides and was usually overruled by the King and Cabinet. Whatever the differences that prevailed between Charles and James at the time of Danby's supremacy and the Popish Plot, they had, after the King's victory over his domestic enemies, discovered a means of living and working together. As James's biographer wrote:

The King saw his enemies at his feet and the Duke his brother at his side, whose indefatigableness in business took a great share of the burden off his shoulders, which his indolent temper made uneasy to him, and that his Royal Highness performed with such a perfect conformity to his Majesty's inclinations and obedience to his will as made his services free from jealousy ... as they were affectionate and useful both to confirm his happiness at home and establish his reputation abroad.[41]

On Monday 2 February 1685 Charles had a stroke; he was at once lanced by a physician who happened to be waiting in his antechamber and the Duke of York was sent for. Next day hopes of recovery circulated, but on 4 and 5 February the King had further convulsions and it was plain he was dying. Anglican bishops read the prayers for the dying and absolved him from his sins, but he refused to accept the last sacrament at their hands. James, well knowing that his brother was a Catholic, asked him if he wished to receive extreme unction administered by a Roman Catholic priest. According to Barrillon, who was present in the antechamber (he was reporting to the French King), the pressure on James to ask his brother this question originated with the Duchess of Portsmouth.[42] It may have been so, but the intervention of the Duchess and the French ambassador was hardly necessary. James whispered the question in the crowded bedroom and the King at once replied 'For God's sake brother do, and please lose no time'; but then the King asked James if he would not expose himself too much to vituperation by looking for a priest. James said he did not care. He realized that neither the Queen's chaplains, who were Portuguese, nor the Duchess of York's, who were Italians, were suitable. Instead he sent for Father Huddlestone, a Benedictine monk, who thirty-four years earlier had helped Charles during his escape to France after the battle of Worcester, and happened then to be in Whitehall Palace. The Duke arranged for him to be smuggled into the King's bedchamber during the early evening of Thursday 5 February. James himself never left the King's side, but took the precaution of having two Court officials with him in the room while Huddlestone performed his religious duties. Charles then whispered his last instructions to his brother and thanked him for his affection shown during the whole course of his life including his last action in summoning the priest. King Charles II died between ten and eleven on the morning of Friday 6 February. Almost immediately afterwards James convened a meeting of the members of the Privy Council to whom he announced his intentions now that his reign was about to begin.

12.

James, by the Grace of God, King

James was in his fifty-second year when he came to the throne. His character was distinct; his policies were resolved upon. In contrasting him with his late brother one can see how each of them inherited different characteristics from their father. James was as determined openly to stick to his Roman Catholic faith as Charles I had been publicly to uphold the supremacy of the Church of England; Charles II, like Charles I, was ready to tell any lies and make any promises if they would help him to underpin his position. James had constantly urged his brother to stand up for himself, to deal firmly with Parliament and to remember the fate of their father. Charles II, however, did not rely on firmness so much as suppleness except in the last resort as, for example, when he had insisted on Parliament meeting in Oxford, protecting himself from any threats of violence by using his army, and dismissing that assembly in a week when he found its leaders refused to come to terms with him. Recognizing how after his conversion his brother's obstinacy was unshakeable, Charles was concerned with the way in which the Duke might behave if he let him do as he wished. That was why in the later part of his reign Charles often concealed things from James and required him to go into exile while he himself was confronting the Exclusionists.

There is almost universal testimony that James was a hard worker whether he was Lord High Admiral or the King's Commissioner in Scotland. Gilbert Burnet's view as expressed in 1683 was that he 'had not the King's wit and quickness' but that was made up by 'great application and industry'.[1] Admittedly Charles was often indolent; but he had a livelier and sharper mind than James and was willing to delegate duties. Thus by comparison James's assiduity was heightened and, to some extent, exaggerated. James was perfectly satisfied with the powers that the monarchy enjoyed. He did not intend to be a ruthless autocrat; when he told the Artillery Company that he would always maintain the laws and liberties of the King's subjects he meant it. He was no dissembler. Finally, largely because he was provoked and disgusted by the way in which Charles's parliaments had treated his fellow religionists, excluding them from offices of State and seats in the two Houses, James became an advocate of toleration for all Christians. Burnet — no great admirer of the Duke — recorded his view that although he was firm in his religion and devoted to his priests 'yet when I knew him' [before he he became King] 'he seemed very positive in his opinion against all persecution for conscience sake.'[2] He put his belief into effect when he was Royal Commissioner in Scotland, only showing intolerance towards the extreme Covenanters who were prepared to coerce the Government. The Duke was disappointed that Charles II had twice tamely withdrawn Declarations of Indulgence at the behest of his parliaments. As David Hume (himself a Scot) wrote later: James as King was to become 'a great patron of toleration and an enemy to those persecuting laws which, from the influence of the Church [of England], had been enacted both against the dissenters and the Catholics.'[3] Whereas Oliver Cromwell and George Monck had each imprisoned Quakers as a disruptive force in society, James soon after he became King was to order the release of 1,200 Quakers from prison.

During his brother's reign James had acquiesced in the pro-French foreign policy which dated from the mid-1660s, although it should be remembered that he was quite willing to fight against the French in 1678. But once the Exclusionist agitation got under way James recognized that a close alliance with the King of France was an essential insurance against another civil war. That did not mean, however, that James was sychophantic towards Louis XIV nor that he envied him his absolutist powers. Once his own accession to the throne passed off peacefully he felt that he did not need any outside help to rule his kingdom. As he told the Privy Council on the day when his brother died, 'I know . . . that the laws of England are sufficient to make the King as great a monarch as I can wish.'[4] His stiff pride or truculence, as some of his previous biographers have called it, would not have allowed him to kowtow to anyone.

Naturally in view of what he had gone through at the height of the Exclusionist crisis James was somewhat nervous about how peacefully his succession to the throne would be greeted by his subjects, and he made certain that all the proper precautions were taken. As was noted in the last chapter, Charles II had planned what measures he could in the last year of his life to ensure that his brother would be safe from trouble when he took his place. The principal Secretary of State, the Earl of Sunderland, who had written obsequiously four days after James's accession that 'nothing could recompense the loss of our great and good master but our present King's succeeding who receives universal applause and submission of his subjects,'[5] had in fact himself contributed largely to this submission: he had at once circulated instructions to the mayors of the main seaport towns to stop for the time being passengers from going overseas or entering the kingdom from the sea;[6] he had written to all the Lords Lieutenant confirming them in their offices and commanding them to proclaim James's succession;[7] he had instructed the Earl Marshal to see that all persons of quality wore the deepest mourning possible;[8] he had ordered one of the King's messengers to search for Richard Goodenough and any other conspirators who had managed to survive from the arrests and trials following the discovery of the Rye House plot of two years earlier;[9] finally, he told the Stationers Company that to prevent libels and better to regulate the press it must refer all publications to the Surveyor of the Press, Roger L'Estrange, a tough servant of the monarchy.[10] Furthermore James himself, while his brother was dying, begged the French ambassador to tell his master that he would always be his faithful and grateful servant because of the full support he had given him in the past,[11] and, once he became King, he warned his Protestant son-in-law, William of Orange, that he must stop showing favours to his other nephew, the Duke of Monmouth, and must cashier any officers in his English regiments who held Whiggish views.[12] All these precautions hardly proved necessary, for the Whigs in England were cowed. As Sir John Reresby wrote after the new King had been proclaimed at York:

> It was a strange effect of power from above that so strong a party as had not long before appeared in Parliament to exclude the Duke of York from the Crown of his ancestors should submit to his now coming to it with so great deference and submission.[13]

In the impromptu speech which James had delivered before his Privy Council on the day his brother died James had not only assured it that he was not a man for arbitrary power but would govern according to the laws, he had also announced that he knew the

principles of the Church of England were for monarchy and therefore he would 'always take care to defend and support it'.[14] His
audience were so relieved at this speech that they asked his permission to have it at once printed and circulated. The King had then
replied that he had nothing in writing, but had spoken 'from the
abundance of his heart'. Heneage Finch, the Solicitor-General, said
that he could repeat the very words used, could write them down
and submit them for his approval, which he did.[15] News of the
speech caused general satisfaction. But possibly the Privy Councillors took the words to mean more than they in fact did. James had
not renounced the idea of autocracy — for, in theory at least, the
prerogatives of the Crown in, for example, giving the monarch the
right to call, hold and dismiss parliaments whenever he chose,
bestowed on him a position of dominance; and when he said that he
would support and defend the Church of England he did not mean
that he would prevent any other forms of the Christian religion,
including his own, from being practised. As his biographer wrote:

> No one can wonder that Mr Finch should word the speech as strong as he
> could in favour of the Established Church nor that the King in such a hurry
> should pass it over without reflection, for although His Majesty intended
> to promise both security to their religion and protection for their persons,
> he was afterwards convinced it had been better expressed by assuring them
> he never would endeavour to alter the established religion rather than that
> he would endeavour to preserve it, and that he would rather support and
> defend the professors of it than the religion itself.[16]

When later James came to address his Parliament he was careful to
avoid saying that he would defend and support the Church of
England, but simply observed that he approved of the fact that the
members of that Church 'had showed themselves so eminently loyal
in the worst of times' and implied that he expected them to continue
to uphold the monarchy whatever the monarch might do.[17] And
James made no attempt to hide or minimize the importance of his
own religion to himself.

On the first Sunday of his reign James openly attended Mass in the
Queen's chapel in St James's Palace. He was rather admired for that
so long as he did not take advantage of his position to try to alter the
national religion. But he arranged that his brother's funeral should
take place privately — 'very obscurely' John Evelyn, a staunch
Anglican, called it[18] — after dark (on 14 February) so that it did not
have to be conducted in accordance with the rites of the Church of
England. Then he let it be known that when he was crowned he

would not allow any ceremonies to be used that were contrary to his own religion and in fact there was no sacrament taken at the coronation on St George's Day 23 April and the King and Queen were believed to have been anointed and crowned privately by the King's confessor beforehand.[19] By March James was instructing the Judges of Assize to release popish priests from gaol and to set free all loyal subjects who had been convicted for refusing to take the oaths of allegiance and supremacy or had been fined £20 a month for not going to church.[20] In Scotland the Duke of Hamilton, the King's Commissioner there, was told to obtain a positive answer from Parliament about the abolition of the Test Acts and penal laws, as the King was 'driving at an entire liberty of conscience'.[21] Early in May Sir John Reresby heard that James would expect the penal laws in England also to be abolished and the practice of the Roman Catholic religion in private to be generally permitted but that 'he would not admit the power of the Pope here'.[22] Finally James could not refrain from spontaneously praising a pamphlet written under the name of the second Duke of Buckingham advocating liberty of conscience for all nonconformists.[23]

So far as morals were concerned, as distinct from religion, the impression given at James's accession was that the Court would set a better example than it had done in Charles II's reign. John Evelyn noted straightaway that 'the face of the Court' was 'exceedingly changed into a more solemn and moral behaviour, the new King affecting neither profaneness nor buffoonery'.[24] In any case he had no sense of humour and, unlike his brother, would not demean himself by allowing any of his subjects to treat him with familiarity. Catherine Sedley, who had been his acknowledged mistress for four years, was banished from Whitehall, though James undoubtedly continued to meet her secretly.[25] Queen Mary played her part with dignity, but she was still childless and evidently jealous of Catherine. James himself had always disapproved of drunkenness; he ordered his attendants to take care that no one was drunk in the presence of the Queen.[26] He was also opposed to duelling and swearing; and he condemned bad behaviour in the London theatres. He laid it down that everyone must buy tickets and not sit or stand on the stage or make any noise outside calculated to distract the audience.[27]

One of the first decisions resolved upon by King James was to call a parliament to meet in May. He explained to the French ambassador that if he did not announce this at once there would be no merit in it.

He also said: 'I know the English; one must not show any fear at the beginning.' The more practical reason for summoning a parliament promptly was that James needed a money vote as the revenues bestowed on Charles II all expired with his death and he had left debts amounting to £1,700,000.[28] The Lord Keeper of the Great Seal was ordered to issue writs for an election on 14 February, the same day on which the late King was obscurely buried. The indefatigable Earl of Sunderland at once got busy ordering the Lords Lieutenant to appear at the county elections while he trusted that the mayors in the boroughs would do all they could to secure candidates faithful to the new King.[29] The forfeitures of many borough charters during the later part of Charles II's reign facilitated the choice of reliable members since the amended or regulated charters usually conferred the right to elect on the Corporations instead of on the freemen. The Earl of Bath was said to have carried with him to the west of England so many new charters that he was called the Prince Elector; the forty-four members for the Cornish boroughs were hand-picked for their devotion to James.[30] The diarist, Narcissus Luttrell, noted that 'great tricks and practices were used to bring in men well affected to the King'. He stressed that not only had boroughs, like St Albans, been made secure by the regulation of charters, but in the counties the polls were moved from one place to another 'to weary the freeholders'.[31] As early as 13 April James was able to tell his son-in-law William that 'most of the parliament men are chosen and not many Exclusionists among them so [that] I have good reason to believe things are very like to go very well there.'[32] The Earl of Rochester had previously written to him to say

> the elections for Parliament are generally so good that there is all the reason in the world to believe it will be a very happy meeting between the King and them, which is the best thing that can happen to both.[33]

Barrillon, however, sounded a wise note of warning, for he wrote to his master well before Parliament met:

> It is true that the old opposition has not been elected, but the members of the new Parliament will easily become fractious. They have an unsurmountable hostility to the Catholic religion and the greater part are hostile to France.[34]

Before the general election was completed the King reshuffled his Ministers. He retained all of Charles II's Ministers because, as he explained, he did not want to make the new Parliament intractable.

James at the age of four (*second from the left*) with his brothers and sisters, Princess Mary (*left*), Prince Charles (*centre*), Princess Elizabeth and Princess Anne (who died in 1641). The portrait after Sir Anthony Van Dyck hung over Charles I's breakfast table in Whitehall Palace

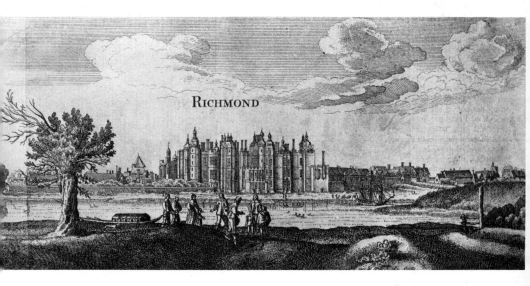

RICHMOND

Richmond Palace where James spent much of his childhood

Westminster and St James's Palace where James was imprisoned 1646-8. A pen-and-ink drawing by Wenceslaus Hollar showing (*left to right*) Westminster Abbey, Westminster Hall, Pall Mall and St James's Palace. Reproduced by Gracious Permission of Her Majesty The Queen

Left: James at the age of six by Cornelius Johnson

Marshall Turenne under whom James served in the French army 1652-5. Engraving by
Robert Manteuil

Right: James at about the age of twenty-five when he was serving in the Spanish army at
the battle of the Dunes. The portrait is attributed to Charles Wautier. Reproduced by
Gracious Permission of Her Majesty The Queen

Above: James, Duke of York, with his first wife, Anne Hyde. Portrait by Sir Peter Lely

Above right: The battle of Lowestoft, 3 June 1665. Painting by Hendrik van Minderhout. The climax of the action: the duel between the English flagship, the *Royal Charles* (*left*), commanded by James, Duke of York, and by Admiral Sir William Penn, and the Dutch *Eendracht* (*right*) under Jacob van Wassenaer, lord of Obdam. The 'bloody flag' signalling the general order to engage flies on the stern of the *Eendracht*

Right: The battle of Southwold Bay, May 1672, where James was in command. Painting by Van de Velde

Charles II by an unknown artist. Reproduced by Gracious Permission of Her Majesty The Queen

Mary of Modena, James's second wife and Queen. Portrait by Simon Verelst. Reproduced by Gracious Permission of Her Majesty The Queen

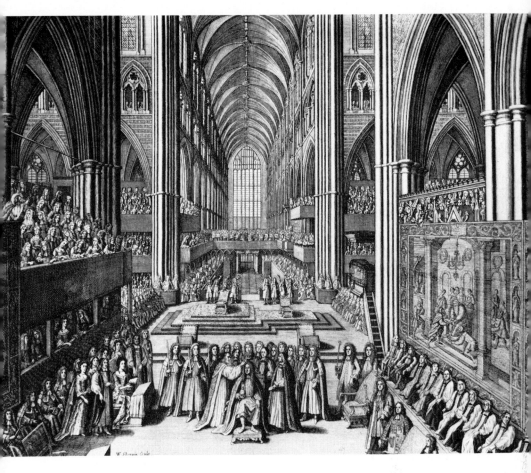

The coronation of James II in Westminster Abbey. Engraving by W. Sherwin

James as King of England about 1688 by an unknown artist

Mary of Modena at her prime in
her twenties. School of Lely *c.* 1680

Catherine Sedley, Countess of
Dorchester, one of James II's mistresses

James II (*left*) being greeted by King Louis XIV of France at St Germain in 1689.

Left: The first Baron Dartmouth. James's friend, who commanded the fleet in 1688

James Edward at the age of thirteen. He was the elder son of James II and was to be known as 'the Old Pretender'. Portrait by François de Troy, 1701

James's illegitimate son, the Duke of Berwick. His mother was Arabella Churchill. Portrait by Niccolo Cassana

The battle of the Boyne, 1 July 1690, with King William III in command. Engraving by Goldar after Wyke

The palace of St Germain en Laye where James spent his exile and died

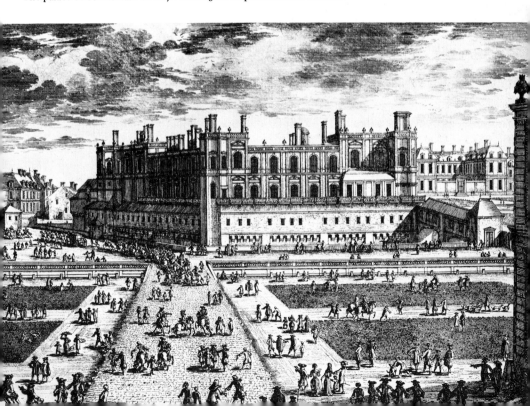

Bronze statue of James II in Roman dress sculptured by Grinling Gibbons in 1686 for which £300 was paid by the philanthropist Tobias Rustat. Originally set up in Pebble Court behind the Banqueting House in Whitehall, it was later moved to St James's park and in 1949 was placed in Trafalgar Square in front of the National Gallery

Therefore even though he did not approve of his views, he kept Halifax in office, but appointed him President of the Council instead of Lord Privy Seal on the ground that in his new post he could do no harm. He told Halifax that he would forget everything he had done in the past and remember only that he had been responsible for securing the defeat of the Exclusionists in the House of Lords. The second Earl of Clarendon became Lord Privy Seal, having been refused any office by Charles II who did not think highly of his brightness. His younger brother, the Earl of Rochester, became Lord Treasurer, an appointment he had always hankered after, though, as has been noticed, Halifax thought very little of his financial acumen. Sunderland and Middleton stayed on as Secretaries of State, while Arlington, despite James's dislike of him when he was his secretary, continued as Lord Chamberlain. The only Minister to be demoted was Lord Godolphin who, after being a Secretary of State and a Lord of the Treasury, received the modest appointment of Chamberlain to the Queen. But perhaps the Queen, who now had considerable influence over her husband, had asked for this as, according to the first Earl of Dartmouth, he 'was more esteemed and trusted by her than any man in England'.[35] And in fact Rochester, Sunderland and Godolphin came to form an inner circle of confidential political advisers. On the other hand, Court posts were given to personal friends of the King, such as Henry Mordaunt, Earl of Peterborough, who became the Groom of the Stole, and was later to declare himself a Roman Catholic, George Legge, now the first Baron Dartmouth, who was appointed Master of the Horse, and Admiral Arthur Herbert, who was made Master of the Robes.

The first problem the King and his Ministers had to face was finance.[36] The Privy Council published a proclamation that the customs should continue to be collected at the ports, for otherwise revenue would be lost and cheap imports flood in. The farm of the excise, which had been contracted for only the day before Charles died, was also continued by order of the Council. Other taxes to pay for James's needs and to meet his brother's debts awaited the meeting of Parliament. In theory these arrangements conflicted with the King's promises to uphold the laws and (as he said to the Privy Council) never to invade any man's property. But a majority of the judges ruled that the continuation of the excise farm was legitimate while it was reasonable to assume that Parliament would retrospectively vote for the customs' receipts to be put at the disposal of the

King's Government, for, after all, it was traditionally the fund which paid for the upkeep of the navy.

A good deal of nonsense was written by historians in the past about James's relations with Louis XIV at the outset of the reign. In his best-selling *History of England* Lord Macaulay wrote that 'he became the slave of France', that he 'begged hard for a French subsidy' and, basing himself on Barrillon's report to his master on 16 February, that when the ambassador told James that he had received bills of exchange for 500,000 livres (about £40,000) he exclaimed with tears in his eyes how noble and full of kindness the French King was.[37] But the truth of the matter was that when James came to the throne he was justifiably anxious over what his reception would be, while he had to await the meeting of his Parliament before he could discover how much money would be made available for his immediate purposes. However, once his accession had passed off without any trouble and the Privy Council decided to continue levying the customs and excise his difficulties vanished; each of these sources yielded in a year over ten times as much as the sum allocated to the French ambassador. Naturally Barrillon, who was both sycophantic and self-important, would have liked to have provided the same subsidies to the new King as had been bestowed on the previous King and he probably exaggerated James's gratitude. But James was a proud man; whatever his original intentions may have been, when he sent over his confidential servant, John Churchill (now Lord Churchill) to notify the King of France of his brother's death, he was told not to ask for any money, but to observe the ceremonies at the Court of Versailles so that any special French envoy could be treated in exactly the same way when he came to the Court of Whitehall. The only money that was asked for was the residue of the sum promised to Charles II as a subsidy in the verbal treaty of 1681. When Rochester asked for that to be paid, it was denied that anything was owing. Barrillon, whose reserve fund had been increased to 2,000,000 livres, was extremely disappointed at being deprived of his role as paymaster, for, as he wrote to Louis XIV on 20 April, he believed that the best way of strengthening James's position was a strict *liaison* (understanding) with him so that the King of England and his Ministers realized that Louis would do his utmost to contribute to James's greatness and security.[38] Even after Parliament met and voted the King his revenue the French ambassador urged that he would need further financial assistance to do all that he wanted to do, that is to say to promote Roman Catholicism in his kingdoms, and repeated his request to be allowed to dole out money.[39]

But Louis XIV refused to do anything in the way of bribing James to be his ally. Once bit, twice shy. He told Barrillon that he had supported Charles with large sums of money without any conditions being attached to it and had got very little in return. He was pleased that James was publicly attending Mass and that (as he had confided to the French ambassador) his ultimate aim as king was to obtain liberty of conscience for all Roman Catholics. The French monarch added that if it came to a crisis and James needed his help, he would not abandon him, but he imagined that the new Parliament would provide him with adequate means to uphold his dignity.[40] Louis also suspected that James might ally himself with the Dutch; after all, William of Orange was both his nephew and his son-in-law. On both these questions Louis XIV was to be proved right and his ambassador to be proved wrong. And if any of the argument between Louis and Barrillon percolated through to James, he was the last man to welcome the thought that he was being patronized.

The character of the House of Commons which assembled on 19 May exceeded the King's and the Earl of Rochester's wildest expectations. Sunderland (as Professor Kenyon has written) 'could point with pride to the election of a veritable parliament of courtiers, more loyally monarchist than any since the sixteenth century.'[41] Only about a hundred out of the 513 members had sat in the previous Parliament. Few former Exclusionists were elected and Parliament was visibly reminded that the days of the anti-papist frenzy had passed by because on the day that it met Titus Oates was put in the pillory at Westminster and on the next day was whipped from Aldgate to Newgate as punishment for perjury.[42] Burnet in his *History of his own Times* alleged that many of the new members 'were neither men of parts nor estates' while John Evelyn, who was present at the opening of Parliament, thought that 'the persons chosen . . . had no interest in the county and places for which they served'.[43] Sir Edward Seymour, a politician of outspoken views who was later to become an eminent Tory, wanted those he thought were obnoxious members (chiefly members he disapproved of from the west country) to withdraw from the House until it was ascertained whether they had been legally returned, but his speech was hissed and nobody seconded him. In James's opening speech on 22 May, not impromptu this time but read from a carefully prepared text, after his reference to the loyalty of the members of the Church of England and a reiteration of his promises not to exceed his prerogatives or invade any man's property, he went on to ask that the Commons should vote him a revenue for life, adding that

> there is one popular argument which I foresee may be used against what I ask of you, from the inclinations men have to frequent parliaments, which some men think would be best secured by feeding me from time to time with such proportions as they shall think convenient; and this argument ... I will answer once for all, that this would be a very improper method to take with me, and that the best way to engage me to meet you often is always to use me well. I expect you will comply with me in what I have desired, and that you will do it speedily, that this may be a short session and that we may soon meet again to all our satisfactions.[44]

He ended by informing Parliament that the ninth Earl of Argyll, whom James had been instrumental in getting condemned to death for treason when he was Royal Commissioner in Scotland, had landed from Holland in the western highlands as a rebel charging him with being a usurper and a tyrant. This news aroused the ardour of the loyal parliamentarians who had greeted the earlier part of the speech with loud shouts and they cried out 'Vive le Roi' as the king retired.[45] The Lord Keeper of the Great Seal, Francis North, Lord Guildford, delivered no speech, as the custom had been in previous reigns, although he had prepared one. James was the star turn.[46]

The Commons immediately set about passing a Bill to grant James the same revenues as his brother had enjoyed for life. It had been estimated at the beginning of the reign that his and his wife's ordinary expenditure would amount to about £1,300,000 a year;[47] the amount that had been voted to Charles II in 1660, consisting chiefly of the receipts from customs and excise and a hearth tax, then yielded less than £1,200,000 a year. However, when James succeeded trade was extremely buoyant so that both the customs and excise had substantially increased in value (the hearth tax had been abolished in 1681.) Some members of parliament, meeting in private before the King's bullying inaugural speech had been delivered, had resolved to limit James's revenue to a term of three years only because they feared dangers to the Church of England and wanted to have available a weapon they could wield against him if necessary. But this move came to nothing first, because a countermove was organized on the King's behalf by the Earl of Ailesbury and, second, because the new House did not wish at once to alienate the King. Even Seymour said he would not oppose such a grant of the revenue, though he did not understand why there was such a hurry about it.

In fact it was pretty obvious that the leaders of the Commons wanted to sweeten the royal temper, for after the revenue Bill had been dispatched to the Lords a Grand Committee on religion asked James to publish a proclamation putting into effect the laws 'against all dissenters whatsoever from the Church of England'. The King was furious; he browbeat the Commons so successfully that the House unanimously rejected the recommendation from its own committee. Furthermore when on 30 May James again asked Parliament for additional revenues to pay off his brother's debts, to buy supplies for the army and navy and to pay the cost of suppressing Argyll's rebellion, assuring them incidentally that he had 'a true English heart', it voted him duties on wine and vinegar, tobacco and sugar for eight years worth £400,000 a year.[48] Later in the second week of June when Parliament learned that the Duke of Monmouth had landed in Dorset, having failed successfully to co-ordinate his own invasion with that headed by Argyll, the two Houses of Parliament rushed through a Bill of Attainder against Monmouth and the Commons voted the King another £400,000 a year for five years to be raised by new duties on linen, silks and spirits. The Scottish Parliament, which had also been summoned at the start of the reign, settled £260,000 a year on James for life by the time that Argyll had landed.[49]

Thus altogether the King had been given a revenue of well over £2,000,000 a year, which proved sufficient both to pay off Charles II's debts and to meet the cost of strengthening the naval and military forces. As the yield from customs and excise continued to expand and as he himself was much less extravagant than his brother had been on personal indulgences (he now had only one principal mistress, Catherine Sedley) he was comfortably off, was careful with his money and incurred no debts. His position was unique in that while most previous sovereigns had been in constant debt he was affluent, while at the same time he was the last monarch in British history to be invested with a permanent ordinary revenue and thus enjoyed executive independence. It is a measure of how loyal Parliament was to the King at the beginning of his reign that it granted him enough money not only to cover his existing commitments but also to allow him to increase the size of his army, which at the cost of about £300,000 a year he was able to raise from a force of 7,000 to over 40,000 men by the end of his reign. Encamped, as it was to be, on Hounslow heath, it was in a position to overawe London. To that extent the Anglicans in the House of Commons were digging a pit for themselves. James did not again need to ask them for money nor to beg subsidies from Louis XIV, as his brother had done. If the rebellions planned by Argyll and Monmouth could be put down, James would, if he wished, be able to rule without the help of Parliament and in fact govern his kingdoms autocratically, as he believed his royal prerogatives allowed him to do.

But what James failed to realize was that since the civil wars the House of Commons had become a national forum which it was risky to dispense with and had to be cajoled rather than bullied. Yet it was understandable why James found it difficult to handle even an initially loyal House of Commons. After all, neither Charles I nor Oliver Cromwell had been able to get along with their parliaments. Queen Elizabeth had, on the whole, done so, but she was extremely astute and a woman who knew how to exploit her sex. James I had coped to some extent because he appreciated when he needed to yield. Charles II by using the prerogative powers of prorogation and dissolution had succeeded in checkmating the Exclusionists, but in his last years was content to manage without a parliament. James had learned very little from his predecessors' conduct and mistakes. After starting coolly he had become arrogant. His brother had at least kept his first House of Commons in being for eighteen years. James's similarly loyal Parliament would last for only ten months.

13.
Monmouth's Rebellion and its Aftermath

The Duke of Monmouth,[1] whose rebellion constituted a landmark in James's short reign, was not a strong character. All his life he had been spoilt and flattered because he was known to be Charles II's illegitimate son. Born of a Welsh girl, Lucy Walter, in April 1649, he had received very little education, though he was given first a Catholic and then a Protestant tutor. He adopted the name of his governor, Lord Crofts, and was brought over to England in 1662 by his grandmother, Henrietta Maria, and was at once adjudged a handsome and charming boy. His father arranged his marriage to an heiress, Anne Scott, Countess of Buccleuch in her own right, when she was twelve and he fourteen. On their wedding day they were created Duke and Duchess of Buccleuch and he took his wife's name of Scott. Before his marriage Charles II had given him the title of Duke of Monmouth. By the time he reached the age of sixteen he was an athletic extrovert. Samuel Pepys wrote that he was then 'the most leaping gallant I ever saw'. Monmouth was made a Knight of the Garter, Captain of the first troop of Life Guards, member of the Privy Council and Master of the Horse, the last office being a profitable sinecure bestowed on him by his father. He distinguished himself first as a volunteer in the French army, fighting alongside the future Lord Churchill and Colonel Percy Kirke, whose sister Mary was to be one of his mistresses as well as a mistress of the Duke of York.

Monmouth and his Duchess had little in common except their love of dancing. He had several mistresses ending up with Henrietta Wentworth, who accompanied him into exile towards the end of Charles II's reign and whom he regarded as his real wife in the eyes of God. His good manners and amiability had made him extremely popular, for, like his father, he knew instinctively how to behave when he mingled with ordinary people. Yet he was also a weakling, easily influenced by others. The Earl of Ailesbury, who knew him well, wrote in his memoirs that the Duke was 'most charming both in his person and his engaging behaviour, a fine courtier, but of a most poor understanding as to cabinet and politics and given wholly up to flatterers and knaves by consequence.'[2] It was because of his weakness of character that the Earl of Shaftesbury, when he was running his campaign to exclude James from the succession was reluctant to put Monmouth forward as the new heir to the throne instead of the Duke of York. However, in an attempt to reach agreement with the King on the exclusion of James from the succession, during the meeting of the Oxford Parliament Shaftesbury had suggested that Charles should legitimize him, which would have been tantamount to confessing that he had been married to Monmouth's mother, a fact he had always denied.[3]

With such possibilities opening up Monmouth managed to make himself a general favourite. After his victory over the Scottish Covenanters in 1680 the clemency that he showed to the defeated earned him credit in Scotland; when he returned to London he was greeted by bonfires and his health drunk as that of a hero. In the following year he had carried out the first of his semi-royal 'progresses', being hailed everywhere in the west of England as 'the Protestant Duke' in contrast with James Stuart, 'the papist Duke'. But he played his cards badly. He later allowed himself to become involved in plotting a rebellion; then with typical ineptitude he first promised to betray his fellow conspirators and afterwards changed his mind, fleeing abroad. Though in exile he was confident that he would be restored to favour, his father's death left him marooned in Holland.

In the United and Spanish Netherlands were gathered many Whiggish expatriates whose sole hope of a safe return home lay in the overthrow of James II.[4] At first Monmouth was reluctant to plan a rebellion against his uncle; he wrote: 'I am now so much in love with a retired life that I am never like to be fond of making a bustle in the world again.'[5] Later, however, after a secret meeting with the Earl of Argyll in Rotterdam they agreed that something must be done before King James 'settle in anti-christianism and tyranny at his pleasure'.[6] The ideal scheme, as Monmouth realized, was for Argyll and himself to sail simultaneously with such ships and weapons as they could muster (he actually offered to accompany Argyll to the western highlands) while sympathizers in London, south-west England and Cheshire rose to their support. In fact after prolonged discussions Argyll left Holland for Scotland on 2 May when he, his clan, the Campbells, and the lowlanders who were with him were dispersed, swiftly rounded up and crushed, while Monmouth did not sail from the Texel until 30 May in a hired frigate with a force of eighty-three men, including the soldier-philosopher, Andrew Fletcher of Saltoun, who was a kind of liaison officer between him and Argyll. His aim was to disembark in the west of England where he had been so warmly received five years earlier.

Not only were Argyll and Monmouth unable or unwilling to co-ordinate their invasions of Scotland and England, but they had not agreed on their objectives. The Earl of Argyll apparently wanted a sort of republican régime in which his own position would be secured, while most of the English exiles envisaged Monmouth as a Protestant king. Two manifestos which they published both spoke of James as a tyrant and usurper, even though he could only have been a usurper if Monmouth were clearly legitimate. In a lengthy declaration drawn up by a compulsive plotter, Robert Ferguson — signed by Monmouth but which he may not have fully read — James was accused of every conceivable crime from starting the great fire of London to poisoning his elder brother. How far such nonsense impressed anyone is hard to say.[7] The main reason why Monmouth, after safely landing at Lyme in Dorset on 11 June, was able to collect a fair-sized army of merchant seamen, skilled labourers, textile workers, peasants and other simple men was that they were for the most part nonconformists who feared their fate at the hands of a popish monarch.[8] By the time the Duke reached Taunton in Somerset with his half-trained force of about 4,000 men, he was persuaded to assume the title of king because it was hoped that the local gentry as well as the common people would rally to the cause of a *de facto* monarch, since doing so was not reckoned a treasonable offence.

The news of Monmouth's landing reached London on 13 June. The Mayor of Lyme had got away to Honiton and from there had been able to dispatch a messenger carrying exaggerated stories of the forces at the disposal of the Protestant Duke. The Lords Lieutenant of the neighbouring counties sprang into action. The second Duke of Albemarle, son of the celebrated George Monck, was Lord Lieutenant of Devonshire, the Duke of Somerset Lord Lieutenant of the county of his name, and the Duke of Beaufort Lord Lieutenant of Gloucestershire. On King James's orders the Earl of Sunderland informed them that Monmouth certainly did not have an army of 10,000, as the Mayor of Lyme had imagined; he instructed them to arrest all suspected persons and to use their own discretion about how they employed the militia whom they commanded.[9] An obvious danger was that some of the militia might go over to the enemy. So James hastily gathered together such professional soldiers as he had available and wrote to Prince William of Orange asking him to send over at once the three English regiments and three Scottish regiments which were on loan to the Dutch Republic.

What part William played or perhaps did not play in the invasions by Argyll and Monmouth was then and still is controversial. Until pressed by King James at the outset of his reign to order Monmouth out of the United Netherlands both William and his wife Mary, James's elder daughter, had been on extremely friendly terms with the Protestant Duke; for William was convinced that Charles II, whatever he had against him, would like his favourite son to be kindly treated in exile. But after Charles's death he was obliged to acquiesce in his father-in-law's demand that the Duke must be ordered to leave The Hague. So William, who was about the same age as Monmouth, gave him some money and told him to be gone. As soon as William learned of Argyll's expedition to the western highlands he notified James and offered to come over himself with the three Scottish regiments to help suppress the invaders.[10] Similarly he informed his father-in-law of Monmouth's departure from Holland the day after he sailed, though he had previously asserted that he had no idea where the Duke was. In answer to James's request for the six regiments in Dutch service he again volunteered to come over with them himself. But what nobody was able to understand then or since was how both Argyll and Monmouth had been able to hire ships and collect munitions in Holland even when the English ambassador knew what they were up to and had delivered protests to the admiralty authorities in Amsterdam.

William was a pretty ruthless man. Clearly if Monmouth succeeded in his aims, England would be less likely to keep to the alliance with Louis XIV, William's greatest foe. That alliance had been the cornerstone of Charles II's foreign policy and would, it had to be assumed, still be prized by James II. On the other hand, if Monmouth were defeated, William's wife would have no rival as heiress presumptive to the throne of England, and Mary was devoted to her husband. Fletcher of Saltoun, a man of outstanding integrity, told the first Earl of Dartmouth later, that 'he had good grounds to suspect that the Prince of Orange underhand encouraged the expedition with design to ruin the Duke of Monmouth.'[11] James had treated William extremely coldly after he came to the throne because of his patronage of Monmouth. The promptitude with which the regiments were now sent over in response to James's request and William's two offers to come over himself with them to fight for his father-in-law restored him to the King's good books and contributed to a renewal of treaties with the Dutch, as Louis XIV had feared.

As an experienced general himself James organized the resistance to Monmouth's makeshift army judiciously. He soon realized the inadequacy of the militia or 'trained bands' which, he had hoped, would hang on to Monmouth until the professionals arrived in the west. As he informed William on 17 June, he had at first thought that the militia from Devonshire and Somerset would have been able to contain Monmouth in Lyme, but in fact the rebel Duke had soon been allowed to open up his way towards Taunton, 'which is a very factious town'.[12] So James gave instructions that the militia should not attempt anything against Monmouth except 'upon great advantages', but that 'straggling people' should be prevented from going over to the Duke.[13]

On the evening of 13 June Lord Churchill, who was appointed a brigadier and commander of the King's forces in the west, rode to Salisbury with four troops of cavalry and two of dragoons, followed by five companies of infantry under the command of Colonel Kirke. On 17 June Churchill reached Bridport, having covered 120 miles in four days. There he discovered that the militia had been defeated by the rebels, even though Monmouth's cavalry under the command of his friend, Lord Grey of Warke, had at first run away; Monmouth's men were then able to seize a number of horses and, according to Churchill, half of the Somersetshire militia had gone over to the enemy: the last statement was a gross exaggeration.[14] On 21 June Monmouth left Taunton and marching by way of Bridgwater, Wells and Shepton Mallet aimed, after advancing over the Mendip hills, to cross the river Severn at Keynsham and attack Bristol, five miles away. Churchill followed close on his heels while Albemarle, with whom the

Brigadier had made contact, reoccupied Lyme and Taunton.

Meanwhile in London James had changed his mind about the command. On the very day after the Earl of Sunderland had written to the Duke of Somerset announcing Churchill's appointment (19 June) he wrote to Churchill himself to inform him that the Earl of Feversham, a Frenchman, who was a nephew of the great Turenne, was to supersede him with the rank of lieutenant-general and had been given authority over the various Lords Lieutenant involved.[15] By way of consolation Churchill was later to be made major-general and was ordered by James, who thought (rightly) that 'the principal design of the rebels was upon Bristol', to cling on to Monmouth's forces and, if possible, put himself between them and Bristol.[16] Furthermore the Duke of Somerset with his militia and the Duke of Beaufort with the Gloucestershire militia were ordered into Bristol and told to break the bridge at Keynsham, by which Monmouth was intending to cross the Severn.[17] Feversham reached Bristol on 23 June and after inspecting its fortifications in company with the Dukes of Somerset and Beaufort reported that all was in good order. The next three days were to be the most critical in the story of Monmouth's rebellion.

On Wednesday 24 June Monmouth had resolved to assault Bristol from the east: that was the side of the town which had been attacked both by Prince Rupert and Thomas Fairfax during the civil war some forty years earlier. The rebels discovered that the bridge at Keynsham had not been destroyed, as James had ordered, but was only damaged and could quickly be repaired. Their leader (now their self-declared King) determined therefore to storm Bristol that night. But first they were blinded by torrential rain and had to retire; then Feversham returned to Bristol from Bath with reinforcements; finally a reconnaissance party of royal horse inflicted a check on Monmouth's men at Keynsham bridge. Next day Monmouth, whose hopes, never high, were now dashed to the ground, abandoned all thought of capturing Bristol and turned his men back south in the vague expectation of collecting fresh recruits from Wiltshire.

James was following these events closely. Learning that Churchill had joined Feversham in Bath on 26 June, he gave instructions that he and the commander-in-chief were not to separate;[18] as it was clear by then that Monmouth was no longer going to attack Bristol, it was left to Feversham's discretion what to do next. He was also informed that reinforcements were available if necessary; for the three Scots regiments had arrived from Holland while the English infantry regiments were on their way.[19] James thus had ample reserves of foot regiments but was hesitant about employing the regiments from Holland in the western campaign, for he had always been doubtful of the loyalty of their officers. The Duke of Albemarle was told that he could, if he thought it necessary, raise a troop of horse and another of dragoons, but James believed that sufficient infantry were now available in the west.[20] He was right; for although Monmouth's army, now consisting of about 5,000 men, outnumbered the regulars under Feversham's command, the latter were fully capable of more than holding their own against the rebels, as had been demonstrated by the skirmish at Keynsham.

An encounter between the two armies could not be postponed. Feversham set out from Bath on 27 June while Monmouth, after changing his mind once or twice, rejoined the route by which he had advanced towards Bristol. After spending two days in Frome he made for Shepton Mallet and Wells because he had been told that reinforcements were awaiting him near Bridgwater. But 'King Monmouth' was now reduced to indecision and despair and even contemplated deserting his volunteer army and fleeing back across the sea to Holland; for he was being dogged by the royal army while his hopes of insurrections in London or other parts of England had evaporated. King James added to Monmouth's difficulties by publishing a proclamation that all those who had taken up arms on the Duke's behalf, with a few exceptions, would be pardoned if they surrendered within eight days.[21] At the same time Feversham was told that he had done well in hanging such stragglers as he had found and James instructed him to pay for any supplies he needed to obtain locally.[22] Once the regulars reached the west and concentrated, it could only be a question of time before the rebellion was crushed. But whatever disappointments they had suffered, the bulk of Monmouth's army — some 5-6,000 men all recruited in the west — remained loyal to their hero to the last.

So Monmouth decided on one last desperate move. Learning that the King's army was encamped on Sedgemoor, two miles south-east of Bridgwater, he prepared to surprise it by assaulting its camp at night. The battle of Sedgemoor was fought in the early hours of 6 July. In the dark Monmouth's cavalry got entangled with his infantry and once James's men were aroused, they mowed down the rebels with cannon and muskets. About 1,500 of them were killed and 1,200 taken prisoner, the losses of Feversham's army being infinitely smaller. A hundred of the prisoners were hanged after a drumhead court martial.[23] On 8 July Monmouth himself was captured ignominiously lying in a dry ditch eating peas from a neighbouring field.[24]

The campaign illustrated excellently James's strengths and weaknesses. Once he had obtained accurate information about Monmouth's army, consisting, as it did, almost entirely of volunteers, who, however enthusiastic for his cause, could hardly be trained as competent soldiers in a matter of days, and once he knew that Monmouth had only a few cannon and a small number of cavalry under the command of his inexperienced friend, Lord Grey of Warke, James realized that it was only a question of time before all the rebels could be rounded up. Nevertheless he had to take the obvious precautions, including calling over the regiments from Holland, because his own professional army was not large and might not arrive at the area of operations before Monmouth struck at Bristol, the second biggest port in the kingdom, which, if captured, might rally the local Protestant gentry to his side. The King quickly understood that the county militias were even less formidable soldiers than Monmouth's volunteers, whose morale, to start with at least, had been high. By offering pardons and forbidding his officers to impound supplies without paying for them he aimed to encourage desertions and to prevent the civil population from being alienated by the conduct of his regulars.

On the other hand, James was a poor judge of men. He ought to have known that Lord Churchill, who had been one of his most dependable servants for the past ten years, was extremely ambitious, and had seen at least as much fighting on the European mainland as himself, was a highly proficient officer. The supersession of Churchill by Feversham was therefore bound to upset him and in fact did so. It was no use consoling him with the rank of major-general later in the campaign. Similarly James offended the Duke of Albemarle, who after his father's death had been appointed commander-in-chief. Angered by being ordered to obey Feversham, Albemarle protested to the King who told him that his patent had expired on Charles II's death. Albemarle thereupon resigned as colonel of the King's Life Guards and as Lord Lieutenant of Devonshire; after all, he was the man on the spot. Nor could William of Orange have been pleased that in spite of all the efforts he had made to send over so promptly the six regiments in Dutch service they were not dispatched to the front. He himself could not but appreciate that he had been snubbed when he twice offered his own help and twice had it refused; after all, he was an experienced general who had successfully resisted the French armies for seven years. While knowing Monmouth as well as he did, must have been aware of his limitations.

The rebellions of Argyll and Monmouth enabled James, as it proved, to fortify his own position. Charles II had never possessed more than a tiny army. James could remember that when in 1678 his brother had raised new regiments for service against the French, which he himself as Duke of York had been anxious to command, the House of Commons had compelled the King to disband them by threatening to withhold supplies for their upkeep. But in James's case two other factors were of importance. The first was the inadequacy of the militia which had been forcibly demonstrated, even though the number of desertions to Monmouth had been exaggerated, particularly by Churchill; secondly, the House of Commons in its initial reaction to the news of the invasions had granted him not a lump sum to pay for his immediate needs but an additional income spread over five years. In view of the expansion of receipts from import duties and the excise owing to the increasing prosperity of England James had no cause to worry about how to pay for an army. As Barrillon had reported to Louis XIV as early as 25 June:

> It seems to me that the King of England is very glad to have a pretence for raising [regular] troops and he believes that the Duke of Monmouth's enterprise will serve only to make him still more master of his country.[25]

Monmouth and Argyll had in fact erred in thinking that because of the fear of Protestants in both countries of what a Roman Catholic monarch might do they needed to strike immediately at the outset of the reign while the iron was hot. In this it has usually been argued that they were gravely mistaken. For to begin with, in his speeches to the Privy Council and at the opening of Parliament James had succeeded in pacifying his leading subjects, while, as he told Barrillon, even in procuring liberty of conscience for his fellow religionists he was bound to go carefully. It was in fact the very defeat of his rival for the Crown that egged him on to achieve this end more rapidly than he had intended while the co-operation of William of Orange in suppressing the rebellions suggested to him that he had little or nothing to fear from his Protestant son-in-law, whose wife was in any case his heiress presumptive.

Unquestionably James was a hard man who has been blamed for the way he behaved towards the conquered. Monmouth, against whom an Act of Attainder had been passed, wrote abject letters begging that his life should be spared. In the one he wrote to James he said:

> For my taking up arms, it never was in my thoughts since the King died. The Prince and Princess of Orange will be witness for me of the assurance I gave them that I would never stir against you. But my misfortune was such as to meet with some horrid people that made me believe things of your Majesty and gave me so many false arguments that I was fully led away to believe that it was a sin and a shame before God not to do it.[26]

In the same letter he promised that henceforward he would be zealous for James's service and 'could he say but one word in this letter you would be convinced of it'. What that one word was has been the subject of speculation; it has been suggested that it referred either to the Earl of Sunderland or William of Orange. At any rate when King James, against his better judgment, agreed to see Monmouth all that happened was that the pathetic young man went on his knees to beg for his life. He had in fact no revelations to make, and was therefore beheaded two days later. The executioner mangled his job horribly. The King permitted the scaffold to be covered with mourning cloth and the Duke's body to be given to his friends to dispose of as they thought fit.

It was reasonable in the light of the time to punish Monmouth by death. Had he been imprisoned in the Tower he might have escaped, as other prisoners had done before; if he was again sent into exile, he would in effect have been a free man. In either case he could have organized another rebellion. His grovelling letters and his plan to desert his men before the battle of Sedgemoor left black marks on his career that could not be erased. His second-in-command, Lord Grey of Warke, whom Dryden called 'Cold Caleb', was more skilful in his approach to James.[27] After he wrote a full, if inaccurate confession and paid a large fine, the King spared his life but sent him to the Tower from which he was released after a few months. Major Nathaniel Wade, another of Monmouth's officers, also wrote a confession, was released from prison and was granted a pardon later. Finally Charles Viscount Brandon, who had promised together with Lord Delamere to head a rising in Cheshire on Monmouth's behalf, had been accused of complicity by Lord Grey and sentenced by the Court of King's Bench to be hanged, was spared by King James on the intercession of the Queen and Brandon's wife.[28] Lord Delamere was acquitted by his fellow peers: 'The King', wrote Lord Macaulay, 'was unable to complain of a decision evidently just'; in fact James had foreseen his acquittal.[29]

The rank-and-file of the deluded men, who had volunteered to fight for Monmouth, suffered cruelly. It is true that on the day following Monmouth's execution the King ordered the release of and the restoration of horses to persons arrested on suspicion only; but of the total of some 5,000 of Monmouth's followers 1,500 were killed at Sedgemoor, about 100 were hanged immediately after the battle, over 300 were tried for treason, found guilty, hanged, drawn and quartered, and 1,000 more were transported as indentured servants to the West Indies. After the battle the prisoners were crowded into gaols where many of them contracted fever. It was not until the beginning of September that a special commission, consisting of five judges and a public prosecutor under the chairmanship of Chief Justice George Jeffreys which had been especially appointed by King James, set out from London to take part in what were later to be known as the Bloody Assizes and James called Jeffreys' 'campaign'.

Jeffreys was a bold and able man who had had a meteoric career.[30] He was more noted for the power of his advocacy than the depth of his learning. By the time he was thirty-six he combined the Chief Justiceship of Chester, the Recordership of London and a prosperous practice as a barrister; three years later he became Chief Justice of the King's Bench. He and his colleagues began their work at Dorchester where an elderly lady named Alice Lisle, who had the misfortune to be the widow of one of the regicides of Charles I, was charged with sheltering two rebels escaped from Sedgemoor. The jury found her guilty and she was sentenced to be burnt.[31] Jeffreys allowed her a respite of two days during which time she could write to the King seeking a reprieve. The King upheld the sentence, but permitted her to be beheaded instead of burned. Jeffreys was in a hurry to get back to London because he knew that the Lord Keeper Guildford was about to retire and he had reason to hope that he would cap his judicial career by being appointed Lord Chancellor. To shorten the proceedings prisoners were told that if they pleaded guilty they would not be executed, but if they pleaded not guilty

and were found guilty they would be hanged. None of the condemned were given sufficient time to plead for mercy from the King.
In fact about 1,000 of those convicted escaped the death sentence.
Many of them were assigned to courtiers who either sold them to
West Indian planters at about £15 a head or purchased their reprieves
for much larger sums. Jeffreys himself received a plum: a Whig
landowner, who lived near Axminster, had given help to the rebels,
though he had not fought with them, and had been arrested and
imprisoned for complicity. Jeffreys was able to secure his pardon in
return for the sum of £15,000 paid by the victim.

In his memoirs the Earl of Ailesbury stated that James protested
to him that he had abhorred what had happened at the Bloody
Assizes.[32] In retrospect he may well have done so. But Jeffreys sent
regular and full reports about his conduct of the trials and the King
could have stopped the hangings and quarterings had he wished to do
so. It is pretty clear that he approved of them and of the quarters of
the men hanged being distributed for exhibition throughout the
west country because he hoped that such displays would frighten
people from rebelling against him again. He also ordered that the
quarters of Richard Rumbold, who had been accused of being
concerned in the Rye House plot of 1683 and had been taken a
prisoner in Scotland, should be scattered in four different places,
including one quarter at the Rye.[33] In fact these nauseating displays
did not achieve their end; for when in 1688 William of Orange
arrived at Exeter it was once again the common people, not the
gentry, who rallied to his standard. It does, however, appear that it
was on James's initiative that the selling of prisoners for trans-
poration to the West Indies began. Whether that was more merciful
than death can be disputed; at any rate Oliver Cromwell had earlier
followed the same procedure. But Cromwell's treatment of rebels
was fundamentally different from that of James. If Cromwell
acquiesced in the execution of ringleaders, he spared the rank-and-
file; James, as the cases of Lord Grey and Colonel Wade showed,
followed the opposite course. Furthermore, James embroidered on
the punishment of transportation by ordering that if any of the
convicted prisoners sent to the West Indies refused to acknowledge
his royal authority they should have one of their ears cut off.[34] Both
Jeffreys and James were later to blame each other for the ruthlessness of this judicial campaign. As James duly appointed Jeffreys to
be Lord Chancellor after it, obviously he had no qualms about what

the judge had done. For his part Jeffreys bullied and browbeat everyone during his rushed itinerary, which left the west of England a shambles. It was not until March 1686 that James issued a general pardon which brought the holocaust to an end.

James recalled Parliament to meet on 9 November. Meanwhile he started reorganizing the army. Convinced that the militia had proved itself to be valueless, he preferred to rely for the security of his throne on a well-drilled professional army. On 16 July he gave instructions to the colonels of his regiments that the number of men in each cavalry troop was to be reduced from sixty to fifty except for the horse guards and the royal regiment of horse.[35] The two officers who had been victorious over Monmouth, Feversham and Churchill, were respectively commissioned as colonels of the first and third troop of horse guards. The two regiments of foot guards, the Grenadiers and Coldstreamers, were, he ordered, to have eighty privates in each company instead of the usual hundred while other regiments were to have sixty in each company. Thus he acquired more compact units. James also planned to abolish the militia altogether and to ask Parliament to apply the funds set aside for its upkeep towards the pay of the regular army. The total strength of his whole army was estimated to be about 16,000 men, many of whom were stationed on Hounslow heath.[36] After he had inspected them on 23 July he expressed satisfaction with their bearing. There were then 6,000 of them, but about four weeks later he wrote to tell William of Orange that it was his intention to organize a rendezvous of most of his new cavalry and infantry on the heath, being well pleased with those he had already seen.[37] To ensure their sobriety he gave orders that none of the troops were to buy ale without the permission of their officers.

Gratified by the defeats of Argyll and Monmouth — even though, as he had told William on 30 October, some rebels were still lurking on the edge of Somerset and Devon[38] — and proud of his reorganized army, James felt his position was impregnable and was confident enough to dismiss the Marquis of Halifax, whose advanced views he had never cared for, from his post of Lord President of the Council. Before he did so, he asked the Marquis whether he would agree to vote in favour of the repeal of the two Test Acts passed in the previous reign imposing political disabilities on Roman Catholics, adding that he was determined 'he would be served by none but those that would be for the repeal of the Tests.' Halifax's answer was that he would never consent to this as he thought the laws were necessary for the King's service 'since the nation trusted so much to them that the public quiet was chiefly preserved by that means'.[39] The two men parted on amicable terms, James assuring Halifax that he would never forget what he had done for him in the past. He told the French ambassador in confidence that his aim was not only to secure the repeal of the Test Acts but also the Habeas Corpus Acts which were destructive of the royal authority.[40] He had no intention of retaining Halifax in his Council, he explained, because he thought that the Marquis would set a bad example to his other Ministers and cause divisions both in his Cabinet and in the Houses of Parliament. Through the influence of Father Petre, a Jesuit adviser much trusted by James, who had been responsible for the upbringing of his illegitimate children, Halifax was, after a short interval, replaced by the industrious, ambitious and cynical Earl of Sunderland, who had created the impression at Court that he was no longer an Anglican, though he had not yet in fact become a Roman Catholic; he also retained his office as first Secretary of State. The French ambassador was convinced that Sunderland was the coming man and suggested to his master that he should offer him a pension, which in due course he did; it was not refused.[41]

In opening the new session of Parliament James delivered a lengthy speech. He began by thanking God Almighty for the suppression of Monmouth's rebellion, but he drew the moral that the militia was insufficient for such occasions and that there was

> nothing but a good force of well disciplined troops in constant pay that can defend us from such as either at home or abroad are disposed to disturb us.[42]

He went on to defend his appointment of Roman Catholic officers, as he had done during the rebellion, because they had always proved the loyalty of their opinions by their practices. He implied that he would tolerate no criticism of their employment and asked for a supply of money sufficient to pay for the upkeep of the new army. The tone of his speech was distinctly arrogant, for he concluded by saying that it would be 'wicked' for anyone to ruin the good understanding that existed between him and his Parliament.

The House of Commons had no wish to quarrel with the King; although a good few of the members, recalling the political influence of the army during the Interregnum when it had expelled three parliaments, were reluctant to agree to the setting up of a standing army, they none the less voted in favour of giving the King a supply of £700,000 for the purpose, but they did not want the militia to be abolished and instead aimed to introduce a Bill to make it more efficient. After that an address was drawn up pointing out that it was illegal to employ Roman Catholics as army officers, though the House was prepared to pass a Bill indemnifying them from the penalties they had incurred by accepting such employment. The address was moderately worded, but emphasized that the Test Acts had been put on the statute book to ensure the security of the Church of England; the King was therefore asked that 'no apprehensions or jealousies may remain in the hearts of your Majesty's most loyal subjects'.[43] An attempt was made to induce the Lords to join in the address, but the King's Ministers succeeded in frustrating the presentation of a joint address.

When the Commons presented the address alone, James did not attempt to conceal his anger, telling them that he had hoped that the reputation God had blessed him with in the world 'would have sealed and confirmed a good confidence' of them in him. After the King left, the Commons were silent until it was moved that the House should take the King's answer into consideration. The seconder of the motion, Captain John Coke, a member for Derby, added defiantly: 'we are all Englishmen and ought not to be frightened out of our duty by a few high words'. The rest of the House were shocked and sent Coke to the Tower of London. After an adjournment the House returned to the consideration of the generous supply that it had already voted to the King. Meanwhile James was listening to a debate in the House of Lords in which leading members asserted that the establishment of a standing army officered by Roman Catholics were in effect a threat to the Church of England. Earlier, in the Commons Sir Thomas Clarges, brother-in-law to the late General Monck, had recalled that the danger of a popish King with a popish army had been foreseen during the Exclusion Bill debates. Thus the spirit of Whiggism arose from its ashes. The new Lord Chancellor Jeffreys had vainly tried to browbeat the Upper House as he had so often done witnesses in the law courts. The King could stand no more. On 20 November he ordered Jeffreys to prorogue Parliament until the following February; but at the end of the year James informed William that he did not intend to let it meet again until the next winter unless there were some great occasion for allowing it to do so.[44] In fact this Parliament was never recalled; it was finally and formally dissolved on 2 July 1687.

14.
James and Toleration

The crushing of the two rebellions against him, the dismissal of Halifax, the only open critic of his policies, and the prorogation of Parliament after it had questioned his authority all combined to give James a sense of freedom from restraint and a growing confidence in himself. The fact that he could afford to do without the £700,000 promised to him by the House of Commons showed that he was in no financial difficulties, for he was altogether more careful with his money than his elder brother had been. His aim was now to press ahead with giving the Roman Catholics throughout his three kingdoms not only liberty to worship as they wished but if possible to confer on them equality of opportunity in the services of the State and in the professions. He was also determined to stifle any condemnations or public criticisms of the faith in which he so heartedly believed. He gave orders that no bonfires would be lit or fireworks let off on Guy Fawkes night, 5 November 1685,[1] to remind people how Parliament had been preserved from the murderous intentions of papist plotters. By way of an alternative celebration he required that the day on which his reign had begun (6 February) should be commemorated with prayers and thanksgivings in all the churches and chapels throughout his realm,[2] reviving the custom by which the accession of Queen Elizabeth I had been annually remembered, although of course in her case the purpose had been to solemnize gratefully the passing away of another Catholic monarch, Bloody Mary.

Historians have differed about how precipitate James was in setting about easing the lot of his fellow Roman Catholics and whether or not he aimed from the first to do so within the framework of a general liberty of conscience for all nonconformists from the State religion.[3] Lord Acton thought that he was an old man in a hurry; other commentators, relying on what James had told the

183

French ambassador at the beginning of his reign, considered that he proceeded cautiously at the start. If so, he accelerated his rate of progress during 1686. With regard to his overall religious programme, it is obviously simple to say that so long as Catholics were burdened with disabilities they naturally accepted the idea of general toleration for all sorts of Christians in Great Britain, even though in other European kingdoms, where Catholicism was the national religion, the trend was towards enforced uniformity. In the same way during the reigns of Elizabeth I and James I the Puritans, being persecuted within the Church of England, advocated freedom of thought for all Christians so that they should be embraced in it themselves. Both Oliver Cromwell and Charles II had openly supported liberty of conscience, which they attempted to establish by law.

In James's younger days he certainly paid lip service, to say the very least, to the idea of general toleration. In 1669 he had told Dr John Owen, who had been Oliver Cromwell's chief ecclesiastical adviser, that he 'had no bitterness against the nonconformists; he was all against all persecution for conscience sake, looking upon it as an unchristian thing and absolutely against his conscience',[4] while William Penn, the Quaker son of a Cromwellian admiral, was to recall how 'on all occasions when Duke [of York] he never refused me . . . when I had any poor sufferers for conscience sake to solicit his help for.' As has already been noticed, he told Dr Gilbert Burnet that he was against persecution for conscience sake, who added in his *History* that once Monmouth had been defeated the dissenters were 'in high favour with the Court'.[5] It has to be remembered that in James's mind the Puritan nonconformists were responsible for the defeat and execution of his father; he believed that some of them were dyed-in-the-wool republicans and had been mixed up in conspiring against the throne during Charles II's reign, for example in the so-called Rye House murder plot. Furthermore many of the volunteers who had enlisted under Monmouth had been dissenters. Even the Quakers had been a disruptive element, as George Monck discovered when they tried to seduce officers and soldiers in his army from their obedience. But before James's reign was over he had ordered the release of most of the Quakers in prison and had established a close friendship with William Penn. As early as mid-July after the defeat of Argyll he had recommended to the Duke of Queensberry the release of Robert Barclay, a Quaker whom he knew to be well affected to him and said that he should not have to suffer for the faults of others of his persuasion.[6] Barclay was to testify that both before and after James became King he 'then and always since to me professed to be for liberty of conscience'. Later under the influence of Barclay and Penn James came to realize the harmlessness of the Quakers, who earlier had been confused in the public mind with the fanatical Fifth Monarchists, and he instructed Justices of the Peace to protect them from the rigours of the penal laws.

Generally speaking, however, to begin with James worried about whether the nonconformists were loyal to the Stuart line. This was exemplified by an instruction from the Earl of Sunderland to the Deputy Lieutenants of Warwickshire, sent after Monmouth's invasion had taken place, to arrest 'disaffected and suspicious persons, particularly all nonconformist ministers and such as served against Charles I and the late King'.[7] It is perfectly clear that James hesitated at first to extend toleration to all Puritans for purely political reasons. For, as he was to tell the Spanish ambassador in the summer of 1686 'he thought it contrary to Holy Writ to force consciences'.[8] English Protestant historians have always been reluctant to concede that James was a genuine believer in liberty of conscience and that the toleration he was in the end to offer to all nonconformists was other than a 'bait' to induce them to support a policy predominantly favourable to the Catholics against the resistance of the leaders of the Church of England. As an instance of how James's behaviour to the nonconformists has been misinterpreted a succession of historians from White Kennett Bishop of Peterborough, who wrote a *Complete History of England* in 1705, to Lord Macaulay, who embarked on the denigration of James nearly a century and a quarter later, drew attention to the way in which Richard Baxter, the venerable Presbyterian preacher and theologian whose health was failing, was put on trial for including a seditious libel in one of his many books during the first months of the reign. In fact, however, there is no evidence that James was consulted about the matter; Baxter was fined 500 marks and bound over with permission to live in London. Before the year was out James granted Baxter a full pardon and the fine was remitted.[9] So far as James's general attitude to the treatment of nonconformists is concerned, the episode is not illustrative but irrelevant.

In fact not long after Jeffreys' 'campaign' was finished, when his successor as Lord Chief Justice, Sir Edward Herbert, went on the western circuit, he showed grace, favour and pity to the dissenters.

They were allowed to hold their chapel services undisturbed and, according to Burnet, 'the maxim that the King set up and about which he entertained all that were about him' at the outset of 1686 'was the great happiness of an universal toleration'.[10] Barrillon reported at the same time that rumours were rife that the King was aiming to introduce liberty of conscience for all nonconformists; and by the early spring he wrote positively: 'the liberty for the exercise of their religion will be extended [from the Catholics] also to nonconformists and all Scottish sectaries so long as it is confined to their houses and they do not assemble in too large numbers'.[11]

Unfortunately for James, he began his policy of securing liberty of conscience for and equality of opportunity to all nonconformists in a year which, as Burnet wrote, 'must ever be remembered as the most fateful to the Protestant religion'.[12] This was clearly exemplified in France. After Louis XIV had consolidated his conquests by concluding the truce of Ratisbon and after he had married morganatically the pious Madame de Maintenon he turned his attention to extirpating 'heresy' from his kingdom for the good of his own soul. The French Protestants or Huguenots — there were about a million of them — had hitherto been protected by the Edict of Nantes promulgated in 1598. Now after a wholesale offensive aimed at converting the Huguenots had been launched, in which pressure was complemented by persuasion and bribery, the French King came to believe that it was proving so successful that the Edict was superfluous and could be revoked. The revocation of the Edict of Nantes in October 1685 ordered the demolition of Protestant churches, the closing of Protestant schools and the forcible conversion of newly-born children of Huguenot parents. French dragoons were deliberately billeted on the richest Huguenot households to make them as uncomfortable as possible, a procedure begun before the revocation and extended after it. The torture of men and the whipping of women were even employed to gain yet more converts. The whole campaign sent a thrill of horror through Protestant Europe, which was keenly felt in England.

The French ambassador showed James a copy of the decree revoking the Edict of Nantes soon after it had been published in France. According to Barrillon in his first report to Louis XIV: 'it would be impossible to show more delight than this Prince has shown at the measure . . . to complete the extirpation of heresy from your kingdom.'[13] But was that what James really said or did

Barrillon exaggerate? Obviously what James at first understood to have happened was that a campaign of conversion had been so persuasive that many Huguenots had voluntarily changed their beliefs. However as Huguenots fleeing from the dragonnades flooded into England — some 50,000 escaped altogether — James became perturbed over what he learned about the brutality of the methods of conversion. A special French envoy, François Bonrepaus, who arrived in England at the beginning of 1686 and was less of a flatterer than Barrillon, reported home that James was shocked by what he had heard; and when he saw the King he tried to convince him that the refugees had been exaggerating or describing the work of sub-ordinate French officials who had exceeded their instructions.[14] James told the Dutch ambassador when he explained his own religious outlook to him that 'he detested Louis XIV's conduct as not being politic, much less Christian.'[15] Barrillon also admitted that after James had discovered the truth, he disapproved of the revocation of the Edicts of Nantes[16] and the Spanish ambassador reported how 'his Britannic Majesty . . . declared that he abhorred the employment of jack-booted missionaries both as unpolitic and unchristian; that though he wished to see his own religion embraced, he thought it contrary to the Holy Writ to force consciences.'[17] Finally, James in writing to his son-in-law Prince William of Orange early in 1686 spoke of 'the very hard usage the Huguenots had and still have in France.'[18]

In March 1686 the King launched a fund to help the French Protestant refugees in England, contributing himself the sum of £500 out of his privy purse. He ordered that appeals for the fund should be read out in the churches. It is true that the exiles were expected to join the Church of England, but, after all, even in James's reign the Church was still largely Calvinist, as it had been since the sixteenth century, so there was no reason why the Huguenots should have any difficulty in accepting the Thirty-Nine Articles which enshrined the Anglican creed. Nothing has been more completely misrepresented in James's life than his attitude to the Huguenots and his relations with the King of France. The only thing that he did which seemed to suggest that he approved of Louis XIV's actions was to order the translation of a book by a French Protestant minister named Claude condemning them, an order of which his Lord Chancellor Jeffreys disapproved. James's reason for doing so he explained was that 'dogs defend each other when attacked; so do kings'. So Barrillon wrote to his master to say that though James disapproved of libellous tracts against reigning monarchs being circulated, the burning of the book did not imply that James endorsed the revocation of the Edict of Nantes.[19]

Although, therefore, James wanted his Roman Catholic subjects to be treated on an equal basis with all other Christians in his realms, the strengthening of his authority by his defeats of Argyll and Monmouth merely encouraged him to proceed more rapidly than had been his original intention and in fact rich and well-established Roman Catholic families were nervous lest he was going too fast and if the recall of Parliament was forced upon him they would be ruined. As early as March 1686 Sir John Reresby, himself a staunch Anglican, had noticed that 'there was not as yet any remarkable invasion of the rights of the Church of England', yet, he added:

> the King gave all encouragement he could to the increase of his own [Church] by putting more papists into office here (but especially in Ireland); by causing or allowing popish books to be printed and sold and cried publicly; by publishing some popish papers found in the late King's closet, and the declaration of his dying a papist and the manner of it, with that of the conversion of the late [or first] Duchess of York and her reasons for it, as written by herself, by a letter or order to the Archbishop of Canterbury to direct the ministers of his diocese to preach a good life, but not to meddle with controversies in their sermons; by sending Lord Castlemaine upon a solemn embassy to the Pope, and many other such things.[20]

That summed up pretty accurately what James was doing in the first half of 1686. In Ireland Clarendon was told after his arrival there as Lord Lieutenant that he must see to it that sermons were not preached against Popery and it was explained to him that the employment of Roman Catholics in offices in Ireland did not 'prejudice the true English interest there' so long as the Act of Settlement was left untouched.[21] In fact James was extremely anxious that the Act of Settlement, which had arranged the distribution of lands in Ireland after Charles II's restoration, should not be thought to be in the process of being undermined.[22] What he was worried about was not redressing economic grievances, but assuring the Irish Roman Catholics, who outside Ulster constituted the vast majority of his subjects there, that they would be allowed the utmost freedom to worship as they wished; for example, he wrote personally to the Protestant Archbishop of Armagh asking him to give his protection to the Capuchins in Ireland;[23] at that time James's own confessor was a Capuchin.

In Scotland, where Catholics were not numerous outside the highlands, James tried to pursue the same policy of ensuring the complete freedom of worship for them. The Drummond brothers, the Earl of Perth and Lord Melfort, both Roman Catholic converts, were the principal agents of James's policy. The Duke of Queensberry, the King's Treasurer and Commissioner there, a Protestant related to the Earl of Rochester, who had refused to be converted, was removed from office and replaced by Melfort. Parliament, after it met in April, was asked to repeal the penal laws against 'innocent subjects, those of the Roman Catholic religion'. The Scottish bishops were pressed to agree to the removal of disabilities on Roman Catholics; those who refused to do so were turned out of their sees on the express orders of the King. But James's most influential subjects in Scotland represented to him that it was impossible to allow only the Roman Catholics to have freedom to practise their religion unmolested. So in the end James agreed that this liberty must be extended to all Scottish nonconformists — and there were many Protestants who did not belong to the episcopal Church — so long as their worship was confined to private houses and they did not assemble in too large numbers. None the less Parliament was recalcitrant and for a time James was frustrated.[24]

It was much easier for the King to obtain equality of treatment for Roman Catholics in Ireland, where they formed the majority of the population and, so he had hoped, in Scotland, where the Parliament was more subservient than it was in England. Here James relied on the royal prerogative to absolve individuals from their obligation to comply with specific statutes or even to suspend penal statutes altogether by virtue of his power as Supreme Governor of the Church. In the reign of Charles II the validity of the dispensing power had not been seriously questioned though both parliament and the judicature had raised doubts about the suspending power.[25] But James had deliberately made wider use of it than his brother had done. Not only had he applied it initially to army officers who were Roman Catholics; he was also aiming to extend it to other professions and the holders of government offices. That was why he first sounded the judges; four of them, headed by William Jones, the Chief Justice of the Common Pleas, maintained that the King had no right to dispense with the laws, and they were dismissed. Neither the Solicitor-General nor the Attorney-General was prepared to implement the royal policy. However, when a collusive case was arranged at which Sir Edward Hales, a Roman Catholic, who had been appointed a colonel, was sued by his own coachman for holding his commission contrary to the Test Act of 1673, eleven out of twelve carefully chosen judges, presided over by Jeffreys' successor, Sir Edward Herbert, ruled that there was no law whatsoever but might not be dispensed with by the supreme law-giver, i.e. the King. Thus fortified, James moved forward quickly. Obadiah Walker, a Roman Catholic, was appointed Master of University College, Oxford and told that as his oratory in the Master's lodgings was too small, he could make use of any chamber in the College for that purpose;[26] another Roman Catholic, John Massey, was promoted to be Dean of Christ Church and told that he need not attend any church or college chapel where the Book of Common Prayer was in use;[27] at Cambridge James obliged Sidney Sussex College to accept in March 1687 as their Master Joshua Basset, a bachelor of divinity from Caius, who was described by one of his successors as 'a mongrel papist' and certainly celebrated Mass in his Lodge; and two other Catholics or crypto-Catholics were given bishoprics. In August four prominent Roman Catholic peers were admitted to the Privy Council, although the Jesuit Father Petre refused the invitation. Earlier James had received a nuncio from the Pope and had dispatched the Earl of Castlemaine, the Roman Catholic husband of Charles II's first *maîtresse-en-titre*, as his representative at the Vatican, where he rapidly earned the dislike of Innocent XI. But when James recommended that the Roman Catholic Earl of Carlingford should be appointed commander of the English regiments serving in the United Netherlands William of Orange would not hear of it.[28]

In order that Roman Catholicism should be given full opportunity to flourish in England James relied upon the Church of England's traditional loyalty to the Crown, to which he had referred in the first speech of his reign, when he addressed the Privy Council on the day his brother died. On 5 March 1686 he wrote to the Archbishops of Canterbury and York telling them that no preachers must meddle in matters of State; that they were not to engage in 'abstruse and speculative notions' especially concerning election and reprobation or in any other theological controversies; and that they were to take care in issuing licences to preach that the Thirty-Nine Articles were read out twice a year and see that the Lord's Day was observed.[29] When two months later Dr John Sharp, a distinguished clergyman, preached a sermon at his church of St Giles in the Fields explaining why a Protestant should resist Catholic arguments, James was furious and instructed the Bishop of London, Henry Compton, to suspend Dr Sharp from his ecclesiastical functions on the ground that he had defied his orders in the letter to the two Archbishops and had used 'unbecoming reflections and improper expressions calculated to beget an evil opinion of the King and thus encourage disobedience, schism and rebellion'.[30] On the same day James wrote a similar letter to the Dean and Chapter of York cathedral about a sermon preached by George Tully, Sub-Dean of York and a Canon of Ripon.[31] Compton refused to do what he was told; whereupon James decided to set up an Ecclesiastical Commission, to which he delegated his visitorial rights over both the Church and the universities, with the power to nominate clergy to offices and to suspend clergy for misdemeanours.[32]

The new Commissioners included the Lord Chancellor, the Lord Chief Justice, the Lord President of the Council, the Lord Treasurer and three bishops. The Commission proceeded to suspend the Bishop of London for disobeying the King, although he had in fact advised, though not ordered, Dr Sharp to stop preaching. Ironically enough, both Sharp and Tully in due course had their suspension removed, but Compton's suspension was not lifted for two years. Undoubtedly James was within his rights both in giving orders to the two Archbishops and in delegating his powers to the Ecclesiastical Commission: the delegation of ecclesiastical authority by statute had been sanctioned during the reign of Queen Elizabeth I. But it was remarked upon as odd and very likely to alienate the wisest leaders of the Church of England that a Roman Catholic monarch should use his capacity of Supreme Governor to discipline Anglican clergy on behalf of his own co-religionists. Compton was a strong character; by his rash behaviour James had made an enemy who was to contribute to his ultimate overthrow.

In resisting James's effort to proselytize, granted that they could only resist passively, the Anglicans believed that they had one valuable ally, the King's current mistress, Catherine Sedley, who had borne him two children during Charles II's reign. Whether she was an enthusiastic Protestant may be doubted, but she had a pew in St Ann's, Soho and was certainly caustic about the Catholics. How far the Earl of Rochester, the stoutest Anglican still left in the Privy Council, relied upon her to counterbalance James's Catholic advisers is not clear. At any rate neutral observers followed the lady's movements with the closest attention. At the beginning of the reign she had been dismissed from the Court, but in January 1686 she regained favour and was created Countess of Dorchester, a fact which caused the Queen to refuse to eat her dinner or speak to her husband. It was then thought that the new Countess might become as influential over James as the Duchess of Portsmouth had been with Charles II. The Queen continued to be upset; James's Catholic Ministers, supported by the Earl of Sunderland, represented to him how disadvantageous it would be if he retained a Protestant mistress; and James's priestly counsellors reminded him of the sinfulness of his liaison. So James with difficulty persuaded Catherine to depart for Ireland. In no time at all, however, she said that the climate of Dublin did not agree with her and asked permission to take the waters at Tunbridge Wells. James promised his Queen, who was still beautiful and a year younger than Catherine, that he would not see her again. Whether he kept his word or not is veiled in secrecy; probably he did not.[33] If, as is likely, leading Protestants at Court counted on her help they had been outmanoeuvred.

During 1686 James was by no means wholly occupied with religious questions, although, as his biographer observed, 'the forward disposition of the clergy and people . . . began . . . to take up a great deal of his Majesty's time',[34] for he also concerned himself with military and foreign affairs. In his camp at Hounslow he was gradually building up a highly trained and regularly paid army. By midsummer it consisted of twelve infantry regiments and thirty-five cavalry squadrons, a total of about 14,000 men. He visited the camp frequently from Windsor (it was on the route between Windsor and Whitehall); he had his own chapel there where he attended services every day. He also had a tent where were set up a kitchen and tables at which he could entertain. The Queen, the Queen Dowager (Catherine of Braganza) and Princess Anne dined there and the King arranged a review for their benefit on 30 June. The infantry were drawn up in a line, said to be three miles long, and cannon were fired. The cavalry and dragoons were well mounted and drilled. Thus the camp became quite a social centre; John Evelyn remarked on 'the great feasting' there.[35] In July James was worried because torrential rains bogged down the camp, but, as he wrote to William of Orange, the cutting of small trenches carried the water away and the ground was soon dry again. The soldiers' health was not unduly affected and James was able to note in his letter dated 16 July that it was over a month since one man had died and that very few sick were in hospital. James also paid personal attention to the needs of the navy. He commissioned the building of new warships and visited Chatham and Portsmouth almost as frequently as Hounslow. He was pleased with the state of the fleet, but appointed new Navy Commissioners with instructions to punish severely anyone who neglected their duties.

What was the purpose of these forces? Louis XIV was informed that they were not intended for use in a war. According to Barrillon, writing at the end of 1686, James was 'persuaded that he would much sooner gain what he desires from his people when they see he has an army and navy ready to make himself obeyed at home and prevent factions from receiving help from abroad'.[36] On the basis of that kind of evidence historians have often written that the object of the camp at Hounslow (which in fact was dispersed during the winter) was to overawe London. But it is doubtful if that was its chief purpose. Hounslow was a convenient place for the King to visit. As a former soldier himself, he was proud of an army which Parliament had given him the means to pay for. He realized how Charles II's dependence on Louis XIV had been largely owing to the fact that he had such a small army, small even for policing duties. Nor was James's army Catholicized. Its commanders were the Earl of Feversham and the Earl of Dumbarton, who were both Protestants. Roman Catholic officers were not allowed to attend Mass there, but were required to go up to London for such services.[37]

What James in fact did, being confident in his army and navy, was to adopt an independent foreign policy. Only at the beginning of his reign did he feel anxious for French support; but when his accession passed off peacefully he wanted to be recognized as the ruler of a Great Power, just as Oliver Cromwell had been when he commanded a considerable army and a victorious navy. James renewed the treaty of 1678 with the United Netherlands, which had been concluded for defensive purposes in case the French Government had made too high demands before agreeing to a peace. But James did not include in the treaty any guarantee for the security of the Spanish Netherlands; he told the French ambassador in September 1685 that Louis could rely on the firmness of his friendship — that was a different tone to the one used by Charles II — and he added that he did not intend to renew the treaty of 1680 with Spain, which had been a dead letter anyway.[38] What James sought was peaceful settlements.

He reached an agreement with the French about the borders between Canada and the North American colonies, which was to be adhered to even if a war were to break out in Europe. The truce of Ratisbon, which had been accepted both by the Dutch and the Germans, appeared to promise peace in Europe while the Holy Roman Emperor was contending with the Turks. When James learned of a quarrel between Denmark, which was the ally of France, and the Free City of Hamburg, he expressed his anxiety but was relieved to discover the French were not involved and was convinced that it was now Louis XIV's intention to maintain peace in Europe.[39] As it happened, peace was not secured for long because the French *Roi Soleil*, still aggressive, was soon to take advantage of the Emperor's war in the east, to put forward claims to further territorial aggrandizement and to sustain them launch a *Blitz* in the Rhineland.

Though to Louis' annoyance James had concluded the defensive treaty with the Dutch, his relations with his son-in-law were frigid. He could not forget William's past friendship with the Exclusionists and he suspected him of conniving at Monmouth's invasion. William's prompt aggreement to sending over the English and Scottish regiments from Holland temporarily soothed James, but the thaw did not last long. William was annoyed because the British ambassador to the United Netherlands chosen by James at the beginning of his reign, Sir Bevil Skelton, was generally thought to be an untrustworthy intriguer, while he had to ask for the removal of his wife's English almoner on the ground that he was selling intelligence to Skelton. For his part James could not shake off his old suspicions of his son-in-law and, according to Bonrepaus, a more reliable reporter on English affairs than Barrillon, James regarded William as his enemy and could 'scarcely hide his hatred for, and jealousy of, the Prince of Orange'.[40] Though James kept up a regular correspondence with William it became extremely perfunctory. He usually wrote that he was too tired after hunting or was going to bed early before hunting or was just off to Mass so that he could not let him have a long letter.[41]

For a time the foreign situation was quiescent, so James was able to intensify his campaign to help his fellow religionists. The Earl of Sunderland, although he had two important posts, was eager to be James's unchallenged First Minister; to reach that end he played on James's devotion to his Catholic subjects.[42] He set up a *camarilla* (or cabal) of prominent Catholics, including Father Petre, which met every Friday in the lodgings of the Keeper of the King's Closet. Sunderland's objective was to destroy the authority of the King's brother-in-law, the Earl of Rochester, whose influence with the King alone rivalled his own. Rochester was a time-server, but loyal to the Church of England. He had at first opposed and then agreed to sit on the Ecclesiastical Commission; he had at first refused and then agreed to the suspension of the Bishop of London. It was he who resisted the demotion of the Duke of Queensberry in Scotland; and it was he who hoped that the Countess of Dorchester would temper James's Catholic zeal. But Sunderland was too cunning for him; in the end James was induced to believe that he ought not to retain any Ministers except those who were fully committed to his long-term aims. On 19 December the King asked Rochester to come to see him after supper. He then told him that he 'found it absolutely necessary for the good of his affairs that no man must be at the head of his affairs that was not of his own opinion'. James then pressed the Earl to read Charles II's reasons for his belief that the Roman Church was the only true Church. According to Rochester himself, James wept almost the whole time he spoke to him, but would not allow him to get a word in edgeways.[43] Rochester was duly dismissed with a solatium of £5,000 a year. The Treasury was put in the hands of a Commission.

Rochester's dismissal was promptly followed by that of his elder brother, the second Earl of Clarendon, from his valuable office of Lord Lieutenant of Ireland. It was never likely that Clarendon, who, like his brother, was faithful to the Church of England, would be useful as an instrument of James's catholicizing policy in Ireland. In fact James had relied far more for that purpose on Richard Talbot Earl of Tyrconnel, who was himself a Roman Catholic and was commander-in-chief in Ireland. Tyrconnel scampered ahead; for example, he removed all the Protestant officers from one of his regiments; and when his right to do so was questioned, he came over to England complaining about Clarendon's behaviour and demanding to replace him in his post. With Sunderland's help James was persuaded to agree. Clarendon, who was weak and rather incompetent, was naturally distressed by his abrupt dismissal in the middle of the winter. He could not understand what he had done to earn the King's displeasure. He noted in his diary that 'sometimes I think it may be possible that the King may have altered his measures as to bring Roman Catholics into all employments' after the judges' decision in the Godden v. Hales case that no limit need be placed on the dispensing power.[44] Undoubtedly the dismissal of his two Protestant brothers-in-law from their respective offices was another milestone in James's short reign.

It was not until the first half of 1687 that James decided on his final step towards complete toleration. He had asked the Scottish Parliament in the course of May 1686 to repeal the penal laws 'against his innocent subjects, those of the Roman Catholic religion', holding out as a bait the introduction of free trade between his two kingdoms. Parliament replied evasively by promising to give his recommendation serious consideration, but insisted that the King must be careful to secure the Protestant religion as established by law. James was displeased and prorogued it. In August James ordered his Privy Council in Scotland to rescind the penal laws, to allow Catholics the free practice of their religion and to open the Chapel Royal in Holyrood Palace for their benefit. But the Council was also reluctant to do as he wished, so to obtain what he wanted James had to remove most of the Protestant members and replace them with Catholics, such as the Duke of Gordon.[45] Finally in February 1687 James, employing his dispensing power, published a Letter of Indulgence granting concessions to Catholic and Protestant dissenters alike but still maintaining the ban on field conventicles.

Once he had acted decisively in Scotland, James resolved to follow up his Letter of Indulgence there by issuing a similar general dispensation in England. He had long contemplated doing so, but had first seriously considered recalling his English Parliament and inviting it to suspend all the laws against Catholics and, as in Scotland, other nonconformists with the State Church. For he remembered how when Charles, relying on his prerogative, had attempted to publish comprehensive Declarations of Indulgence in 1662 and 1672 both the judges and the House of Commons had expressed doubts about the legality of the monarch's power to suspend statute laws. Though James had been stimulated by the verdict of the judges in the Godden v. Hales case, he hesitated to suspend the Test Act of 1673 which had excluded Roman Catholics from office as such, preferring to rely on his recognized right to dispense with the law in specific instances. However, he did aim to suspend the penal laws, which had, after all, often fallen into disuse in the past.

On 18 March 1687 James wrote to William of Orange to tell him that he had resolved to prorogue his Parliament once again for eight months and that he was determined to give liberty of conscience to all dissenters whatsoever 'having been ever against persecuting any for conscience sake'.[46] In his gracious declaration to all his loving subjects published on 4 April 1687 he granted to them the free exercise of their religion, though he added 'We cannot but heartily wish, as it will easily be believed, that all people of our dominions were members of the Catholic Church.'[47] He stated that it had always been his inclination that the consciences of people should not be constrained and thought that intolerance was against the interest of the Government as it destroyed trade, depopulated countries (was he thinking of France?) and discouraged strangers. He asserted that he had no doubt that the two Houses of Parliament would concur in what he was doing when he should think it convenient for them to meet again. James went on to insist, as he had done at the beginning of his reign, that he would protect and maintain the members of the Church of England in 'the free exercise of their religion as by law established' and would ensure that their property rights were not molested. All penal laws, such as those which prescribed a fine for not attending church or taking the sacraments, were immediately to be suspended while the King reserved to himself the right to grant from time to time dispensations under the Great Seal to his subjects, permitting them to accept State offices without swearing oaths or undergoing tests.

The declaration received a mixed reception, for it was widely thought that although the King only claimed the right to suspend laws, that really amounted to their repeal since the laws were suspended indefinitely. Furthermore, it was felt that James's condemnation of persecution sounded strange from a popish King when the whole of Europe knew how Louis XIV had not only permitted the harrying of the Protestants in France, but had exerted his influence to persuade the Duke of Savoy to resume the persecution of the Protestants in his dominions. Still James received a number of grateful addresses from nonconformists, including the Baptists and Quakers, while Sunderland succeeded in bringing pressure to bear on the weaker bishops to convey their thanks to their ruler. No doubt James was as easily deceived by such addresses as he had been about the conversion of the Huguenots. At any rate he began to drive forward more furiously. With the dismissal of the two Hydes and the purge of his Council in Scotland he appeared to have a loyal and undivided government. The only fear that assailed him was: what would happen when he died? Would toleration then be abandoned? He could grant dispensations and suspend laws; but he came to feel that only the enactment of repeal by a congenial Parliament of both the penal laws and the two Test Acts could guarantee that his life's work would not be in vain.

15.
The Dedicated Convert

James's policy of toleration, which culminated in his first Declaration of Indulgence, was mainly attacked and defended not on religious grounds — after all, Christians were supposed to love their neighbours — but for political and constitutional reasons. The tradition was that papists were prepared to use any weapon, even of a criminal character, to win over England to the service of the Whore of Babylon. Memories stretched back to the plots engineered against Good Queen Bess, the Gunpowder Plot and the Popish Plot; the twenty-four or more penal laws and the two Test Acts were therefore precautions simply designed to protect the Government from infiltration by treasonable conspirators, thus ensuring the peace of the public. The constitutional objections were concerned with the way in which liberty of conscience and equality of opportunity were being introduced. Oliver Cromwell had been wise enough to have a guarantee of liberty of worship (except for Popery and Prelacy) inserted into both the Protectoral constitutions, while Charles and James had provided for it only in self-determined declarations based on their prerogative powers. Parliaments had therefore questioned their right to do so.

What James's critics objected to was not so much the principle of liberty of conscience in itself but the use of the dispensing and suspending powers to attain his ends. Though in the case of Godden *v.* Hales the judges had upheld the King's right to dispense with the laws in particular cases, his widespread employment of that right had appeared to make a mockery of the Test Act of 1673. As to the suspending power, it was thought to be equivalent to the abrogation of that act altogether. It has been stated that 'during 1687 the Anglican clergy in general reserved their position. Few openly supported the Declaration, but the majority did nothing to oppose it or

199

hamper toleration.'[1] As to the Anglican laymen, since newspapers did not yet exist and a censorship of books did, when Parliament was not sitting no forum was available to them where criticism could be formulated and expressed. It was exactly the same situation that prevailed five or six years earlier when the Whig campaign to push through the exclusion of James from the succession had been frustrated by Charles II's refusal to call another Parliament.[2] James had deliberately prorogued the Anglican Parliament elected in 1685 because, remembering how the Commons had refused to allow him to recruit Roman Catholic officers for his army, he felt sure that were this Parliament to meet again his right to issue the Declaration of Indulgence would at once be called into question.

Nevertheless James first tried the effect of 'closeting' members of parliament, that is to say meeting them individually in his private apartments at Whitehall Palace and using his authority to persuade them to agree to the abolition of the penal laws and the Test Acts if and when he summoned Parliament to sit again after its numerous prorogations. In these closetings James argued strongly the case for complete liberty of conscience, which implied the relief of all nonconformists from their legal disabilities. He pointed out that the number of Catholics was too small to endanger the power of the Church of England; he argued that once the dissenters were saved from the threat of the penal laws they would live in harmony with their Christian neighbours. He urged that he could not retain in office men like the Hydes and Halifax who took advantage of their prestige to influence members of the two Houses to reject measures which he judged it his moral duty to promote.[3] He also told his privy councillors that during the last four reigns the penal code had signally failed to secure uniformity.[4] Consciences, he insisted, could not be forced and persecution was incompatible with the doctrines of Christianity. But James's reasoning, though obviously sensible, except when it was blatantly autocratic, made very little impact. Many members of the Church of England were persuaded that James's real intentions were to bring pressure to bear on his subjects and compel them to join his own Church, just as Louis XIV had done, with the backing of a standing army. So James was reluctantly driven to the conclusion that his present Parliament would give him no help. He had no wish to create new peers to obtain a majority for his policy in the House of Lords; and he was convinced that the House of Commons as then constituted would not commit itself to fulfilling his wishes. Indeed it might be dangerous to let it sit again and air the grievances of bigoted Anglicans.

Looked at from his own particular point of view James was certain that the Test Acts and the Habeas Corpus Acts were a violation of the traditional rights of the monarchy because they circumscribed his ability to confer blessings on all his subjects equally and to prevent the plotting of evil men. From the beginning of his reign he had stressed that he was not 'a man for arbitrary power', that he did not seek to be an absolutist or a despot, but felt certain that the laws of England were sufficient to make him as great a monarch as he wished to be.[5] Yet somewhat illogically he resented Acts passed during his brother's reign. Nevertheless he had not yet come to doubt the willingness of the Church of England to accept, if passively, the policy on which he had decided ever since he became King. As his official biographer wrote:

> The King imagined that since the Church of England and his Catholic subjects had once suffered together under a prevailing party, when the liturgy was as obnoxious as the Mass book, and they fought together in the same just cause, they would not be difficult to unite in affection and interest though they could not in faith.[6]

Thus it was first, because he was confident in the validity of his prerogative powers and second, because he trusted in the obedience of the Church of England to his orders that he went forward with his twofold programme of promoting Catholics to offices of State and at the same time paving the way for the complete abolition of the penal laws and Test Acts. His ultimate desire was to make so sure of the emancipation of Roman Catholics that nothing would be altered after his own death. That was why he became anxious to persuade his heirs to go along with him; if they would not do so, then he would aim to create a House of Commons committed to his support in achieving liberty and equality for all his subjects by statute, a state of affairs which was not in fact to be attained until the nineteenth century.

In 1687, therefore, may be followed the development both of a short-term and a long-term policy by James and his intimate advisers. In the short term the King wanted to demonstrate that the acquisition of authoritative positions by Roman Catholics and dissenters would do no harm to the peace of the kingdom; in the long term he aimed to persuade his leading subjects to underwrite the equality in law of all practising Christians. So it was that while he did not attempt to hide his inclination to bestow favours on Catholics, he tried hard not to provoke the Anglicans into believing that he was invading their rights. He wanted his co-religionists to use the benefits that toleration gave them with prudence and moderation and to show brotherly love and meekness even to those who had persecuted them in the past.[7] He began somewhat unfortunately the very day after the Declaration of Indulgence had been published by requiring the Vice-President and Fellows of Magdalen College Oxford to fill the vacancy brought about through the death of their President by appointing a Roman Catholic named Anthony Farmer, who had never been a Fellow of the College and whose morals were thought to be dubious; he was described as a cleric of troublesome humour and unquiet temper, who drank to excess for days and nights together in Abingdon and visited bawdy houses in London; he himself admitted that he behaved very unlike a Christian at the Oxford Dancing School[8] His selection was deliberate, though probably ignorant on the King's part, for he had informed the Bishop of Oxford, who was himself considered to be a crypto-Catholic, that he expected 'the person he recommended should be favourable to his religion'.[9] But the Vice-President and Fellows defied the King and proceeded to elect one of their own number, John Hough, Bachelor of Divinity, to be their new President. There the matter rested for the time being; but James was outraged and what happened afterwards was to constitute a *cause célèbre* in his reign.

The next sensation related to Ferdinand Count d'Adda, who arrived in England as the Pope's unofficial envoy in November 1685 and in May 1687 was appointed Archbishop of Amasia *in partibus infidelium* [heretical countries]. James not only allowed d'Adda's elevation to be celebrated in the Chapel Royal, where the King knelt humbly before him, but he also received him at Windsor during July as the official Nuncio from the Pope, an action which was unquestionably illegal and provocative to the Anglicans. When the Duke of Somerset, the Lord of the Bedchamber in Waiting, was ordered to conduct the Nuncio to his reception by the King, he refused on the ground that all commerce with the Holy See was high treason. James then claimed that as King he was above the law, to which Somerset retorted that though the King might be so, he himself was not, whereupon he was dismissed and a more compliant Duke (one of Charles II's illegitimate sons) was found to take his place at the ceremony.[10] D'Adda in fact was a man of good sense who felt that James was behaving rashly. But James's Catholic *camarilla,* manipulated by Sunderland, egged him on.

In July 1687 King James ordered the Attorney-General to prepare an edict under the Great Seal to dispense the aged Lord Arundel of Wardour and the rest of the Catholic peers who had been admitted to the Privy Council from taking the usual oaths of allegiance, which required them to be faithful to the Church of England.[11] But these peers, who belonged to old-established Catholic families, were, like d'Adda, not enthusiasts for the King pressing forward too blatantly – in the way that Tyrconnel was doing in Ireland – in showing favour to his Catholic subjects. The King therefore relied more on Father Petre, whom he tried to have created a cardinal, and on his Jesuit confessor, Father John Warner, whom Petre had recommended to him in place of the Capuchin Mansuete and who, like d'Adda, was moderate in his advice. The Earl of Sunderland, outstandingly James's most capable Minister, walked a tight-rope, determined not to offend the King but well aware that his open defiance of Anglican opinion by his reception of the Nuncio and his attempt to thrust a Roman Catholic President down the throats of the Fellows of Magdalen was asking for trouble. It has even been suggested that Sunderland came to regret driving the Earl of Rochester away from the King's counsels, where he had been a balancing and moderating force, because James had not then turned to Sunderland himself for advice but to the Jesuit Father Petre.[12]

To look now at James's long-term aims. He still had no son; if he were to die, his daughter Mary would succeed to the throne by hereditary right. She was devoted to her Calvinist husband, who, as the grandson of King Charles I of England, also belonged to the royal line of Stuarts. What James most desired was to persuade Mary and William to give their approval openly to the repeal of the penal laws and Tests. If that failed to work, then he would have to rely either on his existing Parliament being converted to his wishes or would have to summon a new parliament hoping that it would enact the repeal. Then, he thought, it would be extremely difficult for his successors to reverse what it did. Finally, James was anxious that Europe should remain at peace, for if a war broke out again between the French and the Dutch England might be dragged into it. Then it would be impossible to say whether James's domestic policy could be implemented.

The relations between James's Government and that of the Dutch Republic had deteriorated during the past months. James had never forgiven William altogether for failing to warn him of the plans of the conspirators to invade Scotland and England which were concocted in Holland. In 1687 colonies of former Whigs and republicans were still scattered in Amsterdam, Rotterdam and elsewhere. Although the English ambassador Skelton, stationed at The Hague, tried hard to obtain the arrest and extradition of plotters who had been exempted from James's general pardon published in 1686, the Dutch were unco-operative. For, after all, they were republicans themselves and sympathized with the point of view of the exiles; also because many of them were strict Calvinists they were not attracted to the policies, however tolerant they were intended to be, of an autocratic Roman Catholic King. Next there had been squabbles between the two countries over trading rights, which had been endemic throughout the seventeenth century. In particular rivalries persisted between the East India Companies of the two nations. English merchants and shippers were set upon breaking the monopoly of the Dutch which they had achieved in the export of pepper after they had in 1684 subjugated the Sultan of Bantam, an island lying between Sumatra and Java.[13] Finally, the Dutch Government wanted to discover what the purpose of James's rearmament was: did he contemplate a war? If so, against whom? Because of these doubts and differences between the two countries an exchange of ambassadors was arranged at the beginning of 1687.

The ambassador James selected to replace Skelton, who had not been a success, was a Roman Catholic, Ignatius White, who boasted the title of Marquis d'Albeville bestowed on him by the Holy Roman Emperor. He delighted in intrigue and was susceptible to bribery; the Dutch ambassador was Everard van Weede, Lord of Dijkvelt, a trusted friend of William of Orange and devoted to his master.[14] Dijkvelt arrived in England on 11 February but did not see James until a fortnight later because he refused to meet the Dutch envoy until d'Albeville had been officially received in Holland. Thus it came about that Dijkvelt was in the country at the very time when James published his first Declaration of Indulgence. James had already given Prince William notice of his intention; and afterwards he wrote to him on 20 May saying that 'all here is very quiet and my declaration has put people's minds at ease and I have great reason to be well pleased with having put it over.'[15] James's chief desire was to induce Dijkvelt to persuade William and Mary to lend their open approval to his decisions about abolishing the penal laws and Test Acts. During the previous autumn James had already sent William Penn to Holland to put the case for instituting full liberty of conscience; d'Albeville had received instructions about his resolve to confer liberty of conscience on all nonconformists. Dijkvelt kept his own counsel, but realizing how adamant James was, confined himself largely to solving the other problems outstanding between the two governments, such as the position at Bantam; James, for his part, insisted that the recent strengthening of his army and navy was not carried out for the purpose of taking part in a European war. On the contrary, he tried to pacify William about Louis XIV's aggressive intentions and told him how he had received memorials both from the Austrian and Spanish ambassadors asking him to guarantee the truce of Ratisbon which, concluded in 1684, was due to hold good for twenty years,[16] and of course a guarantee needed to be backed by force. But what was basically feared by William and what Dijkvelt was asked to investigate was the possibility that James's policy of openly favouring Catholics might so split England asunder that another civil war would break out and reduce Great Britain to a nullity in European affairs. Then the Anglo-Dutch treaty of 1685 would be valueless and Louis XIV might be tempted to attack the United Netherlands once again.

Dijkvelt soon realized how stubborn James was; he therefore sought assurances from James's leading Protestant subjects that they would not agree to any scheme aimed at converting England into a Catholic kingdom if James's religious mania drove him so far as that. Thus while Dijkvelt carried back to Holland the King's undertakings that his aims were purely liberal and tolerant — 'I have not', James told him, 'made one step but which is for the good of the kingdom in general as well as for the monarchy' — he also took back with him a batch of letters or verbal messages that influential persons, who were as near to the King as his daughter Princess Anne and his confidential servant, Lord Churchill, that they would on no account change their religion and if pressure to do so became unbearable, they would call upon William for help.[17]

James was deeply concerned that the position in England should not be misrepresented to William by Dijkvelt. But in fact all the information that William received from there during the early summer of 1687 was to the effect that James's determination to repeal the Test Acts, thereby allowing Roman Catholics to be put into important public offices in the United Kingdom (as men like Tyrconnel, the Drummond brothers and Lord Arundel, Lord Bellasyse and Lord Dover had already been) was likely to cause repercussions which would paralyse the monarchy. For that reason William and Mary positively refused to lend their support to the repeal of the Tests. D'Albeville reported home this news after Dijkvelt had had his first interview with William since his return to Holland; furthermore both husband and wife said they would be steadfast on this point even if it meant they sacrificed their chance of succeeding James as rulers of the United Kingdom. James was indignant and his instrument, Sunderland, was furious. On 16 June James wrote to William in reply to a letter from him dated 7 June:

> I am sorry to find by it [William's letter] that you say you are against persecuting for conscience sake, and yet you cannot be for taking off all those laws and Tests which are so very severe and hard upon all dissenters from the Church of England; and since what Mr Dijkvelt said to you from me could not alter your mind as to that I cannot expect a letter should prevail with you, so I shall say no more on that subject now.

He ended by observing that Djkvelt had misunderstood the situation in England and been misled by Protestants who 'continue their old methods of creating fears and jealousies'.[18] From then on James confined the topics of his letters to his son-in-law to the weather and hunting.

After Dijkvelt's mission which, as James and Sunderland must surely have suspected, had stirred up a hornet's nest, and the flat refusal of William and Mary to consent to the repeal of the Test Acts and even of the penal laws — though they were willing that these should continue suspended — James turned to the idea of packing a new parliament ready to endorse the repeals, having finally dissolved the old one at the beginning of July. Clearly on the face of it this was no insuperable task. Sunderland had shown himself extremely adept at fashioning a House of Commons which welcomed James's accession with enthusiasm and voted him large sums of money. The way to set about it was to get the Lords Lieutenant of the counties to exert their local influence in the election of suitable knights of the shire, while the manipulation of the borough charters by the Government either issuing a *quo warranto* writ, which involved instituting proceedings in the Court of King's Bench, or by ordering the Attorney-General to dispatch royal warrants to corporations instructing them how to draw up a new charter or by employing a writ of mandamus compelling boroughs to choose candidates acceptable to the King.[19] The obtaining of a *quo warranto* writ was rather a cumbersome business, although it had been used successfully, notably against the City of London, by Charles II; royal warrants and writs of mandamus were easier to put through. James optimistically thought that he could secure a submissive parliament within six months; Sunderland, who had to do most of the actual work, was far more pessimistic. One reason for this was a paradoxical one. What Charles II had done through his forfeiture or regulation of borough charters was to ensure that Tories, that is to say Anglicans, were put into local offices in order to 'dish' the Whigs. What James wanted was if not exactly to have the Whigs back in power, at least to enlist a sufficient number of nonconformists and sympathizers with the ideal of universal liberty of conscience — they might be called liberals — so as to prevent too many bigoted Tories being returned to the House of Commons.

The first step that was taken in August 1687 was to make changes in the Lords Lieutenant; for example, two Catholics, Lord Waldegrave and the Earl of Huntingdon, replaced Protestants in Somerset and Leicestershire respectively. In other counties noblemen, who though not Catholics were entirely loyal to the King, were substituted for the existing office-holders such as Jeffreys in Shropshire and Lord Preston in Cumberland and Westmorland. Some Lords Lieutenant were changed and changed again; altogether thirteen alterations were made in 1687 and by the beginning of 1688 hardly a single Lord Lieutenant was neither a loyalist nor a Roman Catholic. Among their names were Ailesbury (Bedfordshire), Dover (Cambridgeshire), Molyneux (Lancashire), Lord Petre (Herefordshire), Feversham (Kent), Craven (Middlesex), Litchfield (Oxfordshire), Powis (Sussex) and Sunderland (Warwickshire). Thirteen of them were Catholics.[20] James then decided not merely to ask the Lords Lieutenant to influence the choice of the county members when a new parliament was called, but to gather together in the areas over which they presided their Deputy Lieutenants, Sheriffs and Justices of the Peace, and ask them individually whether they would, if elected to parliament, favour abolishing the penal laws and the Test Acts; secondly, whether they would vote for members so committed; and lastly, if they would support the King's Declaration of Indulgence by living on friendly terms with Christians of all denominations. While these investigations were set in motion James continued to demonstrate that his indulgences were not merely for the benefit of Roman Catholics. For example, he wrote giving permission to those who did not conform to the Church of England at Blackburn in Lancashire 'of the persuasion commonly called Congregational to meet and assemble in order to their public worship and devotion' and to occupy a chapel which belonged to the local church; this caused the vicar to protest, which he did success-fully.[21] Again, James ordered the mayor and aldermen of Leeds to restore goods forfeited from Quakers there so that they might receive full benefit from the Declaration of Indulgence.[22] He also granted letters of denization not only to Huguenots but to Jews, who had been given liberty to worship freely in England since the start of the reign.[23] The King learned with pleasure that the dissenters in Scotland had cheerfully embraced the liberty given to them.[24] To discover for himself how people outside London might react to his calling a new parliament, which, he hoped, would confer complete equality of opportunity on all Christians he set out in the third week of August from Windsor, accompanied by the Earl of Sunderland, on a royal progress which extended as far north as Chester and ended with four days in Oxford.

After visiting Portsmouth, Southampton and Salisbury James joined the Queen at Bath; her mother, the Duchess of Modena, had just died; one of her doctors had advised her to try the hot spring waters there to soothe her nerves and perhaps facilitate a pregnancy. She and the King attended a service in Bath abbey where one of James's Roman Catholic chaplains preached the sermon much to the surprise of Dr Thomas Ken, the Bishop of Bath and Wells who was present.[25] The King and Queen then visited Bristol together and after the Queen had returned to Bath, James travelled to Gloucester, Worcester, Ludlow, Shrewsbury, Chester, Newport (in South Wales), Lichfield, Coventry, Banbury and Oxford. When he was in Flintshire he prayed at the well erected by the mother of King Henry VII in honour of the holy St Winifred who had been martyred there. It was a pretty rapid journey, the object of which was, as it were, to show the royal flag and thereby promote the election of men devoted to him when he decided to let parliamentary writs be issued. Three days were spent in Chester where the Earl of Tyrconnel had been ordered to meet him. Since superseding Clarendon as Lord Lieutenant Tyrconnel had adopted an extremely rash and brash policy in Ireland — building up a large army with the help of officers trained in France and replacing Protestant officials by Catholics throughout his administration. James had been expected to reprimand him for his going too quickly and too far. In fact he commended Tyrconnel for what he had done, possibly on the advice of Sunderland, who was already thinking of Ireland as a country to which he might escape if James's policies alienated the majority of the English people or if he himself was unable to fashion another loyal parliament.[26]

Everywhere the King went he courted the dissenters, even former adherents of Monmouth, telling them that he desired to take away the penal laws for their ease and security as well as that of Roman Catholics. He stressed the point that liberty of conscience was beneficial to trade and that it was the secret of Dutch prosperity. How far the tour was an electioneering success is hard to gauge. Certainly not all the local nobility were to be found in their estates during the royal visits, but James did not remark on that. William of Orange was informed in a letter written to him from Coventry on 1 September:

> I hear in all the King's progress very few of the gentry waited on his Majesty and yet the King still is assured that by his powers in the corporations he shall have a House of Commons to his liking and doubts not of getting such a party in the House of Lords as will do what he seems to desire.[27]

Two days later Halifax also wrote to William to tell him

> We do not hear that his [James's] observations on his journey can give any great encouragement to build any hopes upon as to carrying some things which every day appear to be more against the grain.

He added that although rumours of a new parliament being called were prevalent he himself did not believe one would be elected in the near future unless 'by some sudden accident it shall become necessary and unavoidable'.[28]

On 3 September the King arrived in Oxford; at three o'clock on the following day the Fellows of Magdalen were summoned to meet the King at Christ Church.[29] Since they had defiantly elected Hough to be their President the College Visitor, the Bishop of Winchester, had confirmed his appointment and Hough after taking the customary oaths (which were not required by the Declaration of Indulgence) was installed in the College chapel on 17 April. The King had retorted by referring the matter to the newly constituted Commission for Ecclesiastical Causes, which declared Hough's election invalid and suspended the Vice-President from his duties. By now the King had dropped the idea of insisting upon the appointment of Farmer, so clearly an unsuitable candidate — even Jeffreys thought him a very bad man[30] — and a week before the King had set out on his progress he had issued a mandate commanding that the Bishop of Oxford, Samuel Parker, whom he believed to be a crypto-Catholic, should be chosen as the new President. The Fellows replied that the vacancy had already been filled — by Hough. So it was that when James received the Fellows on 4 September he was furious. He said:

> Ye have been a stubborn, turbulent College . . . Is this your Church of England loyalty? One would wonder to find so many Church of England men in such a business. Go home and show yourselves good members of the Church of England . . . I will be obeyed . . . Go and admit the Bishop of Oxford . . . President of the College.[31]

The Fellows went and then came back to say that they refused to do what they were ordered as it was contrary to the College statutes. The King was speechless with rage. He determined that Parker should be elected even if all the Fellows of the College had to be expelled. The sequel was that twenty-five of them were dismissed, but the Ecclesiastical Commission only carried by one vote a resolution that they should be refused all Church appointments and thus would be compelled to live on charity. Possibly it would not even have done that had it not been for direct pressure by James, and obviously it was done reluctantly. The Lord Chief Justice Herbert (who had replaced Jeffreys) even stated that Dr Hough's election was regular. New Fellows, mostly Roman Catholics were appointed. In March 1688 Parker died, to the general surprise, an avowed Protestant. He was promptly replaced by a genuine Catholic, Bonaventura Gifford. Thus a Catholic college had been established in Oxford. But James had been openly defied while his Ecclesiastical Commission was split in two. It was an omen of events to come.

The King did not confine his attentions to Oxford. He thought that he would demonstrate the value of liberty of conscience to the University of Cambridge as well. He therefore instructed the Vice-Chancellor, Dr Peachell, to admit a Benedictine monk,[32] who lived in Cambridge, to the degree of Master of Arts without requiring him to take the customary oaths or the necessary examinations. The Vice-Chancellor refused after consulting the Senate, and a deputation was sent to King James explaining why the University could not comply with his order: they could only confer honorary degrees. The King then dispatched a second mandate and when this was also disobeyed invoked once again the aid of the Ecclesiastical Commission which summoned Dr Peachell to appear before it. The Vice-Chancellor then claimed that the taking of a degree was not an ecclesiastical matter, but the Commissioners ruled that it was; they considered that the King's right to dispense with statutes in particular cases was undeniable; and they deprived Peachell of his office for contumacy and disobedience. A new Vice-Chancellor was chosen, but the question of the monk's degree was quietly dropped.

As James had personally complained to the Vice-Chancellor of Oxford about the behaviour of the Fellows of Magdalen and had engineered the suspension of the Vice-Chancellor of Cambridge, it looked as if he were attacking the independence of both universities, hitherto regarded as pillars of the Church of England. Moreover the authority of the Ecclesiastical Commission was called into question on the ground that it was a revival of the Court of High Commission abolished with the consent of Charles I — though in fact that was not the case.[33] In retrospect even James's official biographer was to write that the King might have acted more prudently, but added that few princes 'are of a temper to receive a baffle patiently in a thing they heartily espouse'.[34] Still it was a bad time to alienate such influential gentlemen as vice-chancellors when James and Sunderland were opening their campaign to pack a parliament which would acquiesce in royal policies.[35] The admission to the Privy Council that November of the hitherto bashful Father Petre, regarded in informed circles as the King's *eminence grise,* also exacerbated Anglican opinion. They might have been even more concerned had they known that James was using every ounce of persuasion at his disposal to induce the Pope to make Petre a cardinal.

16.
Seeking a New Parliament

The year 1687 was crucial in James's life. It had begun well enough for him with the publication of the Declaration of Indulgence which was sensibly and honestly worded and was greeted gratefully by many nonconformists. But it was clear to everyone that it was part of a steadily mounting drive to free his Roman Catholic subjects from the bondage imposed on them in the recent past, an aim which had become an obsession with him, and also a matter or urgency. Why was that so? He was aware that he was mortal and he wanted to achieve his ideals before he died. He was now fifty-three; on the other hand, he was more abstemious than his brother had been (who died when he was fifty-five) and he hunted regularly in all weathers. He was in fact to live until the age of sixty-seven. The speculation by one of his biographers that he was already suffering from some kind of mental disease scarcely warrants examination. On the other hand, he had no Catholic heir; and the refusal of William and Mary to give him any help in what he wanted to do merely made him more determined and dense.

In seeking to achieve his ultimate purposes rapidly James suffered from three delusions or at any rate highly dubious assumptions. The first was that because, since the Restoration, the Anglicans had been loyal to the monarchy as long as their privileges were not taken away from them they would possibly obey him and acquiesce in the toleration of other faiths. The second was that the Whigs or former Whigs would be so enthusiastic for liberty of thought and conscience that they would troop into Westminster committed to vote for the repeal of all political restraints on Catholics and other dissenters. Lastly because he had received 200 addresses of congratulation[1] for his Declaration he did not sufficiently realize that the employment of his prerogative powers to confer general as well as particular exemptions from the statute laws amounted to a defiance of parliamentary government in defence of which the first civil war had been fought. One says that he did not realize it sufficiently because he did in fact recognize that unless the Declaration were to be underwritten by a friendly parliament his work could be destroyed by Protestant successors.

It was for this last reason that from the autumn of 1687 until the autumn of 1688 he masterminded a campaign, of which the Earl of Sunderland was the chief executive, to pack a House of Commons that would accede to his wishes. The campaign opened on 25 October when Sunderland wrote to all the Lords Lieutenant asking them to canvass their Deputy Lieutenants and the rest of the influential people throughout their counties on the basis of the three questions;[2] persuasion was buttressed by threats, for during the next few months some of the less trustworthy Lords Lieutenant (from the King's point of view) were replaced while it was made known that the lists of Deputy Lieutenants and Justices of the Peace were liable to be revised in the light of the answers to the questions. But in any case the questions could not be answered in a hurry. One of the Lords Lieutenant (the Duke of Newcastle) did not summon any kind of meeting, but wrote letters and waited for the replies. Moreover in days when public transport was virtually non-existent meetings required a great deal of organizing: some of those due to be questioned were ill or away or did not feel well enough to ride long distances. As John Carswell observed in his book on the revolution of 1688, 'the answers could not be collected quickly. For several months that autumn messages must have been passing from one country house to another. Quiet shoots among the stubble-fields, serious evenings after the fox-hunt, gradually worked out for groups and clans and interests formulae of evasion or defiance. The King had started a national debate.'[3]

The stumbling block was the first two questions which were aimed at eliciting promises that those interrogated, whether they were chosen members of parliament themselves or whether they were concerned in choosing candidates, would agree to the repeal of the penal laws and the Test Acts. As to the third question about whether they would support the King's Declaration of Indulgence (published on 4 April 1687) 'by living friendly with those of all persuasions as subjects of the same prince as all Christians ought to do', none of those interrogated objected to giving an affirmative answer; but, by and large, the response to the first two questions was disappointing to the King.

In these days when quantitative history has become the fashion, an effort has been made to analyse the answers in such a way as to suggest that in at least a dozen counties there had been a substantial minority in favour of repeal and that in Kent an actual majority (54 per cent of those asked) said they agreed to the repeal.[4] But are the answers really susceptible to statistical analysis? Only in a fairly small number of cases did those questioned reply with a straight yes or a straight no. Some answered the first question by saying that they would await the debates in the Commons before they decided how they would vote in this matter — that was tantamount to saying no; some said they did not aspire to membership; some promised to 'endeavour to perform their duty to God and his Majesty as becomes a good Christian and a loyal subject'; some said they would consent to repeal if a provision were made 'for the security of the Protestant religion'. A large number of Justices of the Peace absented themselves from the meetings called by the Lords Lieutenant; a few refused to answer the questions at all.

The impressions not only of Van Citters, the Dutch ambassador in London, but of the special French envoy, Bonrepaus, and of James's most trusted Ministers, such as Jeffreys and Sunderland, were that the campaign in the counties had, on the whole, been a failure. James's brother-in-law, the Earl of Clarendon, wrote to William of Orange in mid-December 1687 that 'while the general discourse now is that a Parliament will speedily be called', 'if one may judge by the answers which the majority of people have given to the questions which were asked of them' the King was likely to have little success.[5] Throughout the whole of Wales and the adjoining English counties only a minority and sometimes a tiny minority consented to repeal. In Cumberland and Westmorland, where there were supposed to be a fair number of Roman Catholics, only thirteen of those questioned consented and the Lord Lieutenant, Lord Preston, was gloomy, while in Lancashire, the county generally accepted as being the most Catholic in England, the Lord Lieutenant, Viscount Molyneux, himself a Roman Catholic, could not provide many affirmative answers. As to Kent, reputedly on statistical analysis the county most favourable to repeal — a county where Canterbury cathedral symbolized the dominance of Anglicanism — it was reported in September 1688 that 'the county will choose Sir John Knatchbull and Sir William Twisden; they are moderate but reserved as to the Tests'.[6] Furthermore much earlier on 15 January, it was reported that Sir William Twisden had stated that 'until he hears the debates in parliament, he cannot give a resolution'.[7]

In the counties of course the King possessed no means of exerting pressure except by depriving men of local influence and importance of their offices. The knights of the shire had for many years shown their independence of the Crown. It was typical that both Knatchbull and Twisden had sat in King James's only Parliament during 1685, that Parliament which had shown itself anxious to uphold the penal laws and stop the infiltration of the army by Roman Catholic officers; Twisden himself had actually spoken in debate, denouncing the staffing of the army by such officers.

At the same time as the Lords Lieutenant were being changed and preparing to ask the questions, the reorganization of the boroughs, which returned the majority of the members of the House of Commons, was being undertaken. It was an imposing task and required a thorough mechanism. At the top was a Commission of Regulators, consisting of Sunderland and Jeffreys, the King's most trusted advisers, and four Roman Catholics, Castlemaine (returned from his unhappy mission to Rome), Powis, Nicholas Butler and Father Petre. A committee of the Privy Council was also set up to issue orders, based on the reports of the regulating commission. The committee began purging the boroughs by one means or another at the end of November. Later at the beginning of 1688 local regulators or agents were appointed with the specific duty of visiting borough constituencies to ensure that the members who were likely to be chosen were favourable to the Court. The chief of these agents was Robert Brent, a Roman Catholic lawyer, who carried out his work of regulating or purging the boroughs under the supervision of Sunderland and Jeffreys who served on both of the higher committees. It was to Brent that the local agents reported and once their reports became available the Crown possessed many means of exerting pressure on any recalcitrant boroughs by altering their charters in such a way as to produce a local electorate, usually reduced in size, susceptible to James's wishes. The main difficulty that they faced was that although it was fairly easy to judge who should be removed from the borough council, it was much harder to make certain that the men appointed in their places were reliable.

It has recently been argued that if a general election had been held in November 1688, the campaign by the regulators would have secured a working majority favourable to the repeal of the penal laws and the Test Acts.[8] It has also been asserted that the regulators were in no position to deceive their masters, that is to say the King's Ministers, as their labours would soon have been put to the trial of electoral success or failure.[9]

A fair number of these returns have survived. Nearly half of the regulators' reports expressed doubts or reservations about the likely behaviour of borough candidates who were expected to be chosen for parliamentary seats. Out of a sample of 129 returns by regulators now in the Bodleian library[10] at Oxford thirty-six candidates were said to have been positively in favour of repeal; thirty-four were positively against repeal; and fifty-nine were doubtful. In some cases the report was that if the borough charters were regulated — which was pretty simple to do in cases where a proviso in the charter empowered the King to remove officers and approve the choice of others in their stead — then the election of pro-repeal members of parliament could be ensured. In other cases borough members were unlikely to be chosen without the approval of a patron such as the Earl of Bath and the Duke of Beaufort. Bath possessed considerable patronage in Cornwall and Devon and resented the way in which a regulator, Edward Nosworthy, was poaching upon his preserves. He complained to the Earl of Sunderland on 28 September 1688 about 'the late impudent management of affairs by Mr Nosworthy and others of the regulators' and added that 'as the case now stands if they proceed immediately to the election of parliament men there will be disputes in most places. Scarcely a corporation knows its own magistrates.'[11] Eleven days later, writing from Plymouth, Bath told Sunderland that Exeter, 'our London', was bitterly divided because the regulators had turned out the most substantial rich and loyal citizens and replaced them by 'a packed chamber of dissenters'. He then advised Sunderland to restore the borough charter as otherwise a garrison would be needed to defend the mayor and aldermen. Although in April 1688 the regulators had reported that the two candidates for Exeter were both 'right' (that is pro-repeal) and would certainly carry the election, two months later they admitted that 'the chief interest' in the City was in the bishop, dean-and-chapter and their tenants and other Church of England stalwarts, notwithstanding the regulation effected there.[12] The election in fact was 'popular' and, as William of Orange discovered when he reached

Exeter, the 'common people' were all in his favour as against King James II.

Like Exeter, the city of York, which returned two members, was said to be pro-repeal. In September 1688 the agents in the county wrote: 'they will choose Sir John Reresby and Sir Metcalfe Robinson. The first is undoubtedly right, and the last has given a good assurance that he will be so.'[13] Yet in his memoirs Reresby makes it perfectly clear that he would not have voted for the repeal of the Test Acts had parliament met in 1688 and that he would have expected that if liberty of conscience were allowed, it would have been 'with due regard to the rights and privileges of the Church of England'.[14] Sir Metcalfe Robinson had represented York in the first Exclusionist Parliament and was to sit for the Convention that voted William and Mary the Crown. So it is unlikely in the extreme that either of them would have voted for the repeal of the Test Acts.

Thus it is plain that both in the cases of Exeter and of York the regulators got it wrong, while the wide claims of success in Cornwall and Devon evidently had little basis of truth in the opinion of the Earl of Bath, who was one of the first to go over to William when he landed in Devonshire. As to the argument that the regulators were in no position to deceive their masters, that did not mean that they were restrained from putting an optimistic gloss on their conclusions, which undoubtedly they did. King James II's view that in his first House of Commons 'there were not above forty members but such as he himself wished for' has often been quoted; yet that very House of Commons soon showed itself to be anti-Catholic. The Earl of Sunderland had then manipulated the charters so as to ensure a loyal House; he tried to do so again upon an elaborate scale, basing his work on the reports of the regulators, in the early autumn of 1688, but the precedent of 1685 did not suggest that a parliament consisting entirely of Anglicans (since the second Test Act did not allow dissenters to be members of the House of Commons and the King was not prepared to force them into it) had it met in November 1688 would have behaved in a way strikingly different from its predecessor. It is doubtful if any knight of the shire would have voted in favour of complete repeal and it is obviously probable that their friends among the landed gentry representing boroughs would have been influenced by their example rather than such promises as they may have made to the regulators. The Marquis of Halifax, who was an extremely shrewd observer of the political scene and who sometime in 1688 wrote a pamphlet called *The Anatomy of an Equivalent* (the equivalent being a statutory guarantee of the rights and privileges of the Church of England in return for the repeal of the Test Acts) exposing this device, had told the Prince of Orange in July 1688 when the regulators' campaign was at its height:

> I still remain persuaded that there is no effectual progress towards the grand design [i.e. repeal] . . . the thing that party relies upon [is] subject to so many accidents and uncertainties and according to all human probability we are all secure.[15]

There is no really convincing evidence to show that he was mistaken.

Whatever Roman Catholics like Brent or Nicholas Butler, who is said to have been especially active around London, may have believed, neither Sunderland nor Jeffreys had much confidence that a House of Commons ready to do the King's will was likely to be elected in the course of 1688. According to a report by Bonrepaus, Sunderland had gone too far to draw back, but accepted no responsibility for the results of the regulating campaign. Jeffreys also was neither hopeful nor much interested. Indeed some of the extreme Catholics, headed by the Earl of Melfort, Secretary of State for Scotland, tried hard to get rid of them both on the ground that they were insufficiently energetic in the regulation of the boroughs. Their position was momentarily precarious, but Sunderland was a favourite of the Queen, while his knowledge both of foreign affairs and of how to manage the electorate made him almost indispensable.

Another factor entered into the political account in the autumn of 1687: by mid-November it was generally known that the Queen's visit to Bath and the King's prayers at St Winifred's well had achieved their ends: Mary of Modena was pregnant. How exactly did this affect the effort to pack a parliament? From the King's point of view, it made an election less urgent; for if the Queen were to give birth to a healthy son a Catholic dynasty was assured (assuming that the Anglicans displayed their customary loyalty, as they had done when James himself succeeded to the throne in 1685). Therefore to ensure continued liberty for those Christians who did not belong to the Established Church a new parliament, though highly desirable, was not essential. On the other hand, it was possible that those who were against a liberal policy and hitherto had relied on the fact that James's heir presumptive was a Protestant princess might despair of the future and resist a Catholic succession by force. The imperial envoy reported home in March 1688 that 'judicious people think if a prince is born, an effort will be made to prevent the Catholic succession'.[16] Equally it was observed that 'if the Great Belly should in any way fail, the Court will take much warmer measures'.[17] In other words, informed opinion feared that the Queen's pregnancy might be a prelude to civil war.

From the autumn of 1687 then the division of political thoughts about the future began to make itself felt. Prince William had already made his position about the repeal of the penal laws and the Test Acts absolutely plain to his father-in-law; but now, taking advantage of a propaganda opportunity, William's friend, Caspar Fagel, who was the Pensionary or leading official in Holland, published an open letter (which was translated into English by Gilbert Burnet, then living in the United Netherlands) setting out clearly the point of view of William and Mary on the question of toleration. It was explained that

> they freely consented to the covering papists from the severities of the laws against them on account of their religion and also that they might have the free exercise of it in private. They also consented to grant a full liberty to dissenters. But [and this was the crux] they could not consent to the repeal of those laws that tended only to the security of the Protestant religion.[18]

The argument was that these laws were essential to secure the public peace and the established religion. The *Letter* caused a sensation. James arranged that replies to it should be published pointing out, among other things, that in Holland itself Catholics were not excluded from public appointments. A war of words was waged. Pamphlets printed in the United Netherlands flooded into England and copies of Fagel's *Letter* were in big demand. Earlier the Marquis of Halifax had published an anonymous pamphlet entitled *A Letter to a Dissenter upon Occasion of His Majesty's late gracious Declaration of Indulgence* in which he asserted that the liberty of conscience promised to Protestant nonconformists was simply a bribe to induce them to acquiesce in opening the floodgates to Popery. 'The alliance between Liberty and Infallibility', Halifax wrote, 'is bringing together the most contrary things that are in the world. The Church of Rome doth not only dislike the allowing liberty, but by its principles it cannot do it.' 'Let us', he concluded, 'be still and quiet and undivided, firm at the same time in our religion, our loyalty and our laws.'[19] The argument in Halifax's brilliantly written pamphlet that James's attitude to liberty of conscience for all was a deception, merely intended to restore the supremacy of the Pope over the British people entered into the mainstream of the Whig interpretation of history and was repeated again and again by eighteenth-century authors. But it is not true. However obsessed he was with his own religion and with the treatment of his fellow Roman Catholics, James had always been (like his brother) a believer in liberty of conscience for all.

During the autumn of 1687 and the following winter events began to move rapidly. James was pleased with the results of his royal progress; he was hopeful of good results from the canvassing by his Lords Lieutenant and the work of the regulators in the boroughs; and he was delighted with the prospect that after so many disappointments his wife might bear him a son. He realized, however, that many important and knowledgeable people were critical of his plans or were doubtful about their likelihood of success. He tried to stop the flow of pamphlets from Holland to England by publishing on 13 February 1688 a proclamation prohibiting the circulation of unlicensed literature.[20] He took a growing interest in the training of his army, dispatching an officer to Hungary to study the methods and weapons employed by the imperial armies fighting victoriously there.[21] And he ordered the Lord Chancellor to make arrangements for the addition of Catholics and dissenters to be Justices of the Peace.[22]

What most worried James and Sunderland, who was in effect his foreign secretary, was the danger of renewed war in Europe. The King's relations with the Dutch had deteriorated ever since Dijkvelt's mission and the publication of Fagel's *Letter*; he also continued to be annoyed that English and Scottish republicans in exile in the United Netherlands had not been rounded up despite frequent representations by his ambassadors. James had refused to guarantee the truce of Ratisbon because he did not want to provoke the French by sitting in judgment on them nor in fact had he sufficient resources to do so. He was extremely concerned over a prolonged quarrel between Louis XIV and Pope Innocent XI which arose out of half a dozen causes and threatened to split Roman Catholic Europe asunder.[23] If in the last resort his plans to secure a friendly parliament collapsed or invited rebellion he recognized that he might become dependent on the French for assistance, as his brother had been before him. Furthermore if the Holy Roman Emperor as the official leader of the Germans was able to finish with the Turks (they were decisively defeated at the battle of Mohács that autumn) and were to turn his attention back to the west he might well tear up the truce of Ratisbon and aim to stop any further French penetration across the Rhine. Should a war begin James felt he might be dragged into it; it was mainly for this reason that he decided to recall the six English and Scottish regiments in the service of the United Netherlands as he did not want them to be employed in fighting the French.[24] If he could add some or all of them to his existing army, that would strengthen his position at home as well as abroad.

According to Sunderland's biographer, it was he who originally put forward the proposal to withdraw these regiments in order to fortify the situation of Catholics and Catholic sympathizers in the event of James's death, though naturally he did not tell his master that.[25] At any rate, whoever suggested it, James took up the idea with enthusiasm. He had told the French ambassador about it in October 1687, but he did not ask for the recall of the troops until January 1688.[26] To his intense surprise the Dutch States-General refused to release them, although by a convention concluded in 1678 his request was entirely legitimate.[27] From the point of view of the Dutch the refusal was understandable; they did not want the size of their army to be reduced at a time when war might be approaching. The most they were prepared to do was to let the officers leave if they wished. Eventually on 14 March 1688 King James published a proclamation ordering all British soldiers in Dutch service or serving elsewhere abroad to return home. All that happened was that about a quarter of the officers came away, while the enlisted men, who were well and punctually paid, stayed where they were.

James could not in any case have afforded to pay for the upkeep of six regiments, even though his revenue in 1687 showed only a small deficit.[28] Sunderland had tried to persuade the French Government to subsidize the cost of their withdrawal on the ground that it would weaken the Dutch and strengthen James when his relations with them had become delicate; certainly the move was generally interpreted as being anti-Dutch. It was a crackpot idea; all that Louis XIV offered to do after lengthy negotiations was to contribute to the cost of James raising three fresh infantry regiments in England with the help of such officers who had come back from Holland. The first small payment was made in May.[29]

May was the month when James had wanted his new parliament to be elected. Its meeting might happily coincide with the birth of a son. But the belief that a House of Commons packed with royal supporters could be built up in six months was entirely unrealistic. It had become obvious early in 1688 that the campaign by the Lords Lieutenant had succeeded only in uniting Anglican opinion to resist the repeal that James wanted. There was, writes a modern historian who has examined the evidence carefully, an 'overwhelmingly unfavourable response to the three questions from the gentry'.[30] As to the work of the regulators, it was impossible for them to finish it satisfactorily in the time. The temper of existing corporations had to be examined; the nomination of new members in place of refractory ones had to be arranged; lastly, the selection of candidates had to be carefully organized. So well before May came James had to postpone any idea of obtaining a House of Commons ready to fulfil his wishes until October or November. In April he was encouraged by optimistic preliminary reports from the regulators. To demonstrate to his subjects that he was not to be shaken from his determination to secure the repeal of the penal laws and the Test Acts he reissued on 27 April 1688 his Declaration of Indulgence, first promulgated a year earlier, together with the promise that a new parliament would definitely be summoned in November.[31] Particular stress was laid on the fact that the King's chief purpose in seeking general religious toleration was to improve trade.[32] Next he commanded that the Declaration should be read out from every church pulpit in the land during the following four weeks. From then on can be traced clearly enough the reasons why King James lost his throne.

17.
Nearing Revolution

In the spring of 1688 James was feeling optimistic. He was delighted by the victories won by the Emperor's armies in Hungary and their advance on Belgrade and equally with the Venetians' capture of Athens from the Turks; apart from the war in the east Europe was at peace and he hoped it would remain so. After three months of hard work by the Earl of Sunderland Louis XIV had agreed to open negotiations for a settlement of his quarrels with the Pope and London had been chosen as the venue for preliminary negotiations;[1] the French King had also promised to contribute to the cost of James's new regiments — not much, but it was at least an earnest of goodwill; and the idea of an Anglo-French naval alliance had been adumbrated.

There was only one fly in the ointment; that was the deterioration in Anglo-Dutch relations since the States-General had snubbed James when he demanded the return of the six regiments. However, he still corresponded politely with his son-in-law; on 15 May he wrote to William to say that he was anxious to help to ensure the peace of Christendom so that the Emperor and the Venetians could continue to prosecute the war against the Infidels. He also told the Prince of Orange that he did not expect that his navy would find much to do that summer, while his army would, as usual, be encamped at Hounslow as an agreeable social centre. 'You shall find me', he concluded, 'as kind to you as you can expect.'[2]

Indeed James was more concerned with maintaining and extending his policy of toleration at home, with particular care for his fellow Roman Catholics, than he was with foreign affairs. Although the date of the general election had been postponed, an intensive campaign had begun with the dispatch of agents to discover candidates for membership of parliament who would support the

King's policies after the efforts of his Lords Lieutenant had failed. Meanwhile he was determined to enforce full toleration by means of his prerogative powers of suspending or dispensing with the laws until such time as a carefully prepared House of Commons could be summoned that was committed to the repeal of the penal laws and the Test Acts.

To make known his wishes throughout his kingdoms an order in council was published on 4 May requiring that his second Declaration of Indulgence should be read out in London churches on Sundays 20 and 27 May and elsewhere on the following two Sundays during June. Precedents for giving such an order were unquestionable; it had been done during the previous reign; but the established clergy did not relish the idea of publishing a declaration slanted in favour of Roman Catholicism and indeed encouraging their own congregations to cease attending church. On 12 May a dinner party was held at Lambeth Palace, the London house of the venerable Archbishop of Canterbury, William Sancroft, at which a number of bishops in his province were present: after two of them, the Bishop of Chester, a friend of Father Petre, and the newly appointed Bishop of St David's, who was later to be deprived of his see and excluded from the Act of Grace of 1689, had withdrawn, the rest earnestly debated what should be done.[3] Some argued that a refusal to broadcast the royal declaration might be interpreted by the King and his Catholic advisers as a failure in the great principle of loyalty to the Crown, to which the Church of England adhered and further that the Protestant dissenters would regard it as showing a lack of tenderness towards them. But in the end it was resolved to petition the King to withdraw his order in council and to summon as many bishops as possible to London to lend their countenance to such a petition.

On 16 May the Bishops of St Asaph and Ely arrived; after visiting the City, they reported at Lambeth that the London clergy as a whole were resolved not to read the declaration.[4] On 18 May at ten o'clock in the evening six of the most distinguished bishops but not the Archbishop of Canterbury himself nor the Bishop of London, who had been suspended from his functions by the Ecclesiastical Commission, saw the King by appointment and presented him with the petition written by the Archbishop in his own handwriting and signed by all of them. Their point was that the royal declaration was based on the King's dispensing power, which had twice been condemned as illegal by Parliament in the reign of Charles II and once during James's own reign. They took care to explain that they did not put forward their petition 'from any want of tenderness to dissenters' but because it was contrary to their honour and consciences to proclaim in the house of God an endorsement of so dubious a constitutional construction of the relations between Church and State.[5]

When James read the petition — he had received no warning of its contents because his two Secretaries of State had taken care not to get involved — he blenched and four times asserted that it was a standard of rebellion. The Bishop of Chichester exclaimed: 'Sir, we have quelled one rebellion, and will not raise another', while the Bishop of Ely said: 'We rebels! Sir, we are ready to die at your feet!' James insisted that he must be obeyed in the publishing of his declaration. The bishops were adamant; they replied: 'God's will be done' and respectfully withdrew.[6] According to James's official biographer, the King thought it was the sounding of Sheba's trumpet* and considered that 'the seditious preachings of the Puritans in the year 1640 were not of so ill consequence as this was': they raised 'a devil they could not lay'.[7] Afterwards other bishops subscribed to the petition and on the last Sundays in May very few London clergy read the declaration from their pulpits. The King retained the petition until three weeks later when the six offending bishops, now accompanied by the Archbishop, who earlier had insisted that he was a dying old man, ever sinking under the double burden of age and sorrow,[8] were ushered before a meeting of the Privy Council. There they were told that they would be charged with seditious libel at the Court of King's Bench in Westminster hall. The Lord Chancellor Jeffreys demanded recognizances from them. As members of the House of Lords they refused to provide these. Thereupon they were dispatched along the Thames as prisoners to the Tower of London. 'Wonderful was the concern of the people for them', noted John Evelyn, 'infinite crowds of people on their knees, begging their blessing and praying for them as they passed out of the barge [and] along the Tower wharf.'[9] A week later they were

---

* 'And there happened to be a man of Belial, a Benjamite: and he blew the trumpet, and said, We have no portion in David, neither have we inheritance in the son of Jesse: every man to his tents, O Israel.'

— II Samuel 20 1-2.

brought before the Court of King's Bench where they agreed to offer small sureties and were allowed to return to their own homes.

What had been happening at the royal Court and in the Privy Council during the fateful month is by no means clear. Not only the Earl of Sunderland and Lord Jeffreys but even Father Petre were anxious to wash their hands of the whole business because they felt that it was a bad issue on which to encourage the King to fight the Church of England. Nor did the King's other Catholic advisers like Arundel and Dover want charges to be pressed against the bishops. Lord Huntingdon, another Roman Catholic member of the Privy Council, told Sir John Reresby the day after the bishops were committed to the Tower that 'if the King had known how far the matter would have gone, he would not have enjoined the reading of the declaration in the churches'.[10] According to Jeffreys, James had at one stage been persuaded to drop all proceedings against the bishops, but

> that he was grieved to find that he [James] had changed his mind, that he knew not how it came to pass, but said there was no remedy; some men would hurry the King to his destruction.[11]

Three alternatives were presented to the King. The bishops might be tried for misdemeanour on the ground that since their petition had been printed (possibly with the connivance of the Bishop of London) they were inciting people to sedition by claiming that James had committed an unlawful act. They might be brought before the Commission for Ecclesiastical Causes, which could suspend them from their duties; but as this Commission was manned by Protestants like Rochester and Jeffreys and included three bishops it was scarcely a practical proposition. Alternatively, the King might severely admonish the seven in the hope that having been once warned they would mend their ways and back his plans for toleration if and when the House of Lords met in the autumn.[12] The suggestion has been made that James was finally swayed by the Jesuits, in which case presumably Father Petre, who was their leader, must have changed his mind.[13] At any rate the ultimate decision of James to have the bishops tried for seditious libel was an extreme step that he was later to regret. For the wide publicity given to the bishops' petition merely stimulated the clergy to refuse to read the royal declaration in their pulpits during the first fortnight of June. A contemporary chronicler noted that it had 'met with a cold reception in the country, having been read in very few places'.[14] What had happened therefore was that James had succeeded in antagonizing the entire Church of England except for a few sycophants or crypto-Catholics.

It has sometimes been argued that the Church had already been alienated from the King before the bishops were imprisoned in the Tower and brought to trial, for example, by the treatment of the Vice-Chancellors of Oxford and Cambridge, by the transmogrification of University College and Magdalen College at Oxford and Sidney Sussex at Cambridge, by James's saying that he would only employ as his Ministers in England, Scotland and Ireland men who were either Roman Catholics or favoured a programme of equal opportunity for Catholics and Protestant dissenters, and by the favouritism he showed to the Jesuits, and so on. But this was a much larger matter. James's official biographer (this part of James's *Life* was not based on his memoirs) wrote that 'his Majesty had done better in not forcing some wheels, when he found the whole machine stop' and he (wrongly) blamed the affair on Jeffreys and even more on Sunderland who gave James 'pernicious advice', deliberately intending to widen the breach between the King and the majority of his subjects.[15] Of course it had always been easy and even commonplace to blame a monarch's 'evil counsellors' for his own errors of judgment. But James was no puppet. He had acquired the fixed idea not only from the beginning of his own reign but during the last years of his brother's reign that the Church of England had always preached obedience to their sovereign's will and always would. That was why James was shocked and angry and spoke of the standard of rebellion.

In fact the whole foundation of what he thought was his strength had been undermined. James no doubt was a stupid man or at any rate a stubborn man, but he could hardly fail to perceive that the majority of his subjects were still loyal to the Church of England and were accustomed to obeying laws passed by parliament. At the beginning of his reign James had stated confidently that his aim was to establish 'liberty of conscience' for Roman Catholics, but that he did not expect to be able to do so immediately and would certainly wait until he saw how his Parliament behaved. It was ten days after he succeeded to the throne that he had told Barrillon that to achieve his ends he would have to 'rely on the support of the episcopal party, which he regarded as the loyalist party'.[16] After Monmouth's rebellion was suppressed and James found himself with enough money to manage without a parliament, he pressed forward rapidly, putting Roman Catholics into all sorts of offices in defiance of the Test Act of 1673, publishing his two declarations of Indulgence and counting on peace abroad and manipulation of the parliamentary constituencies at home to attain all his objectives within the space of three years. Now suddenly, and to him entirely unexpectedly, the 'episcopal party', on which he had so much relied, defied him almost to a man. He found it hard to grasp what had happened; the shock was delayed; but, in the end, he lost his nerve. Temporarily, however, he was cheered by the birth of a healthy son on 10 June, the very day after the seven bishops had been brought before the Privy Council.

The King had spent the night of 9 June with his wife in her apartment in St James's Palace to which she had just returned from Whitehall. First thing next morning he went across to his own part of the Palace, where around about eight o'clock he received a message from the Queen asking him to summon witnesses. It was Trinity Sunday so that some important people such as the Countess of Sunderland and the Earl of Clarendon were in church. A Woman of the Bedchamber, Mrs Dawson, who was the first to arrive, had also been at church. She arranged for the Queen to return to her bed, which was prepared for her with a warming pan.[17] Round the bed clustered and jostled a crowd of witnesses many of whom followed the nurse when she carried the child into the ante-chamber. The child was a boy. He was named James Francis Edward — Edward after the Black Prince, who was also born on Trinity Sunday — and was to be known to history as 'the Old Pretender'. The proud father was so delighted that he gave the midwife a purse of 500 guineas.

To announce the event to the common people the guns at the Tower of London were fired and the church bells rung. The King told the Earl of Clarendon when he came to congratulate him after dinner and found James shaving that 'the Queen was so quick in her labour and he had so much company that he had not time to dress himself till then'.[18] An order in council instructed Lord Dartmouth, Master-General of the Ordnance, 'to cause suitable public demonstrations of joy within their respective garrisons for the birth of a son';[19] two days later the ever resourceful Earl of Sunderland, who was Lord Lieutenant of Warwickshire, communicated the news to his Deputy Lieutenants and Justices of the Peace, ordering them to arrange public rejoicings.[20] But the truth was that the rejoicings were largely manufactured to order by the Court. As James's biographer wrote:

> The birth of the Prince of Wales as it was an argument of the greatest joy to the King and Queen and to all those who wished them well, so it gave the greatest agonies imaginable to the generality of the kingdom.[21]

For now, provided the child survived his early years safely, a Catholic succession to the throne seemed sure. It did not help matters when it was made known that the Pope had consented to be one of the godfathers.

The fact was that the news of the royal birth had been over-shadowed by the dispatch to the Tower of the Archbishop of Canterbury (who for that reason was not present at the birth) and the six other bishops who were imprisoned there. Even the loyal Sir John Reresby noted in his memoirs briefly that the Prince of Wales was born at four minutes to ten, then went on to write that all the time the bishops remained in the Tower crowds visited them to ask their blessing and lament their confinement. After the Earl of Clarendon, the King's brother-in-law by his first wife, had been conducted by James to see the child asleep in his cradle, he then proceeded to pay a visit to the bishops in the Tower and confided to his diary the next day that he had heard a strong rumour that the young prince was already dead.[22] The child in fact overcame a dangerous period a few weeks later because the death of his mother's other offspring was blamed on their foster mothers and it had therefore been decided that he should not be suckled. However, he was removed from St James's to Richmond Palace where he was suckled by a carefully selected nursing mother and recovered sufficiently to be in perfect health.[23]

Five days later the bishops were brought from the Tower of London by river to Westminster hall to be greeted with a fabulous reception by the crowds who were awaiting their arrival. They pleaded not guilty and were released on bail. The birth of the Prince of Wales had enhanced the fears of those who imagined that the King was bulldozing his way towards a fully Catholicized state, as in France. Sunderland realized this; he tried to persuade the King to celebrate the safe arrival of his son and heir by publishing a general pardon embracing the errant bishops. But James still held to his conviction that he had to be tough in the way that his father and brother had failed to be. On the morning the trial was resumed, 29 June, he inspected some of his troops in Hyde park stationed there in case of trouble. It is doubtful if he could in fact have relied upon the obedience of his army had the bishops been condemned. While they were still in the Tower the soldiers on guard there drank the healths of the bishops and declared that they would drink no other healths while they remained incarcerated. When the Archbishop of Canterbury reached Lambeth Palace after he had been bailed, soldiers stood outside to ask for his blessing.

The trial lasted all day. The counsel for the defence argued convincingly that all that was really at stake was whether the bishops had or had not the right humbly to petition their King; all other questions, as, for example, whether James's use of the dispensing power was legal or not, were irrelevant. Out of four judges two summed up for the King and two for the bishops. The jury sat up all night without food, drink or light; next morning they returned a verdict of not guilty.

James was taken aback by the acquittal. He went for comfort to the camp at Hounslow where the soldiers had greeted the news with cheers. Everybody could see how disturbed he was. In due course he dismissed the two judges who had summed up against the Crown; he contemplated asking the Ecclesiastical Commission to punish all the clergy who had refused to read the declaration under the guidance of the acquitted bishops, but that would have been impossible and absurd. He recognized that he had made a wrong decision in allowing the trial to take place. Sunderland, who had done his best to dissuade the King from letting it be carried on, had even gone so far as to declare himself a Roman Catholic in the hope that James would take more notice of his advice than that of the Jesuits.[24] James expressed joy at the conversion of his leading Minister, but nobody else regarded it very seriously.[25] What Sunderland hoped to do was to induce James to follow a moderate line as, for example, by insisting on the repeal of the penal laws but not of the Test Acts. That was also advocated by the King's nonconformist adviser, William Penn.

Shaken by the bishops' acquittal James realized that he had only one resource left: that was to push forward even more energetically towards packing a House of Commons to meet, as he had promised, in November and with the help of the Protestant dissenters to obtain the enactment of complete religious toleration. On 5 July he added three of them to the membership of the Privy Council including a son of the famous republican leader, Sir Henry Vane the Younger.[26] A fortnight later regulating agents were sent out from London looking in particular for small towns in such counties as Dorset, where Protestant dissenters were numerous, so that they could be introduced into corporations to promote the election of candidates committed to repeal.[27] But James's behaviour towards the bishops had diminished the enthusiasm of such nonconformists for the King's policies. While the seven bishops were in the Tower they had been visited by ten leading nonconformist ministers to express their sympathy with their plight; when James sent for four of these ministers to reprimand them, they told him that they could not fail to adhere to the bishops 'as men constant to the Protestant faith'.[28] In any case the idea that the Protestant dissenters could be played off against the Anglicans was only practical in limited parts of the kingdom. Even in the west of England where they were fairly numerous they were not likely to forget how they had been treated by the King's judges and officers after Monmouth's invasion three years earlier.

While preparations for a general election were continuing James hoped that Europe would remain at peace. The prospects, however, were ominous. On 24 May the Elector of Cologne had died; his coadjutor (or ecclesiastical assistant), Cardinal Wilhelm von Fürstenberg, had long been a French agent. If he were chosen to succeed the late Archbishop, as Louis XIV wished and Pope Innocent XI did not, the French hold on the Middle Rhine would be strengthened, Germany weakened and divided, and the independence of the United Netherlands again threatened. Furthermore Louis XIV put forward property claims in the name of his brother's wife, Elizabeth Charlotte Duchess of Orleans, sister to the Elector Palatine, who died a little earlier; as Gilbert Burnet wrote caustically, 'the Duchess of Orleans's pretensions to old furniture was a strange rise to a war'.[29] Yet they were to serve as a pretext for a French army to cross the Rhine 150 miles south of Cologne and attack Phillipsburg, a fortified city which, it was alleged, was a menace to the security of France. At about this time too the French Government embarked on a tariff war against the Dutch: the import of textiles was prohibited and also of herrings unless they were cured with French salt. Moreover William's patrimony of Orange in the south of France was seized by dragoons and its walls destroyed, while nearby Avignon, the ancient home of the Popes, was also occupied. No one who studied European affairs could doubt that Louis XIV was contemplating further aggression against Germany while the Emperor was still fighting in the Balkans or that he was ready to outflank and defy the Dutch Republic which had aroused the Germans against him during the previous war that ended in 1678. The French King had hoped to distract the Dutch by involving them in a naval war against the Swedes who were at odds with the Danes over the possession of Schleswig-Holstein. That was why he tried to induce James II to agree to a naval treaty that would have enabled him to retain most of the French navy in the Mediterranean, leaving it to the English fleet to ward off any danger of Dutch involvement in the quarrel between the two Baltic Powers, the Danes being French allies.

James was far too absorbed in his domestic problems to wish to be embroiled in a war at sea, even though he was offered financial help and the assistance of a French naval squadron stationed at Brest. He wanted to be neutral. He remained on polite, if somewhat frigid terms with his Dutch son-in-law. He expressed his gratitude that a Dutch nobleman, related to William, Count William Henry Zuylestein, had been sent over to congratulate him on the birth of his son; earlier he had confided to William his anxiety over the consequences of the death of the Elector of Cologne; on 13 July he wrote to say how sorry he was that the campaign against the Turks was now going more slowly in Hungary; as late as the end of August he remarked on his hopes that the imperial troops would soon take Belgrade.[30] It is true that during July James carried out inspections of his fleet lying at the mouth of the Thames and had reminded William that his soldiers were still encamped at Hounslow,[31] but he was not trying to intimidate the Dutch or even impress them. The reason why James visited the fleet was that the sailors had become restless when Masses were openly celebrated on board their vessels. The King went from ship to ship explaining that he had granted liberty of conscience to all while appeasing them by ordering Roman Catholic priests to be sent ashore.[32] Just as at Hounslow heath Roman Catholic officers were expected to go into London for their religious services so naval sea captains were instructed not to provoke their crews. Until August James was as innocent of the thought that the Dutch had any hostile intentions against him personally as he had been in his belief that whatever he chose to do, the Church of England would accept. He had been shocked by the petition of the bishops, the defiance of the clergy and the verdict of the jury in Westminster hall; now a new and bigger shock awaited him. Hitherto he had been convinced that William of Orange, whatever his peccadillos as, for instance, his patronage of the dead Monmouth, his failure to secure the release of the six regiments, and his refusal to approve of the Declaration of Indulgence, was still his amicable relative; he continued to give him the avuncular assurance: 'I shall always be as kind to you as you can with reason expect.'[33]

What James did not know was that ever since April and probably earlier Prince William had considered invading England.[34] The idea of doing so had stemmed from the reports and letters which Dijkvelt had brought back after his diplomatic mission to England in the spring of 1687. A number of the most distinguished and politically-minded noblemen had then made it clear to William that they were, in the words of the Earl of Nottingham, his 'votaries';[35] and it became remarked upon by foreign ambassadors in London that the Prince of Orange already had 'a party' there. These men — they could hardly be called Whigs — were disgusted by James's favouritism for his co-religionists who now occupied a number of key posts; they regarded James's dispensation of many individuals from the prohibition embodied in the Test Act of 1673 against their holding offices or commissions as stretching his prerogatives too far; they feared the fastening upon England of a Roman Catholic dynasty that might well involve the recognition of the authority of the Pope. William was less concerned with all this — he was no constitutionalist himself — except that he did not want his wife to be defrauded of her right to succeed to the throne. James's heavy-handed attempts to convert her had back-fired, while the unexpected birth of a healthy half-brother meant that her succession to her father was no longer likely — hence William's conversion to the idea that the baby was an imposter. What worried William above all was either that James would ally himself with Louis XIV or that his continued provocations of his leading Protestant subjects, culminating in the trial of the bishops, would lead to another civil war, leaving the kingdom impotent to intervene on his side in European affairs. Ideally William would have liked the English Government to join him in resisting the threats to European peace and stability offered by the French King's demands on Germany; if not, he wanted to be absolutely sure that England would remain a neutral. For these reasons William established a first-class intelligence service in England; and he twice sent over his half-brother, Zuylestein, once in 1687 on the pretext of commiserating with Queen Mary of Modena on the death of her mother and again in 1688 to congratulate her and her husband on the birth of their son. James's own intelligence service was infinitely poorer, almost non-existent otherwise he would have refrained from antagonizing not only his nephew but the States-General by demanding the return of the six regiments in January 1688.

This in fact was the event, if any single event can be picked out, that paved the way for Dutch intervention in his kingdom. When Edward Russell, brother of the William Russell, whom Charles II with James's approval had allowed to die on the scaffold, saw William in The Hague in April, the Prince told him that if he were invited by men of standing in England 'to come and rescue the nation', he thought he would be ready to do so by September. The birth of the Prince of Wales acted as a catalyst, while the trial of the bishops showed that James had estranged the bulk of the Anglicans. The letter which William required, signed by six noblemen and the Bishop of London, was carried over to Holland by Arthur Herbert, who, like Russell, had been an admiral and now disguised himself as a common sailor. The letter was dated 30 June, the day on which the bishops were acquitted by the Court of King's Bench.

Although the letter to William was signed only by seven men, others, such as Halifax, Nottingham, the Earl of Bath and Henry Sidney, who had been ambassador at The Hague and was on most friendly terms with William, knew about the letter in which the signatories promised to rise in rebellion against James as soon as William landed. How was it that James had no suspicions of this conspiracy against him? Presumably he relied for his intelligence service primarily on the Earl of Sunderland, who had the whole thread of affairs in his hands. Sunderland had written polite letters to William, while Sunderland's wife, unlike her husband, an enthusiastic Protestant, had actually begged William not to support the repeal of the Test Acts. Henry Sidney, known as 'handsome Sidney', was Sunderland's uncle and, some thought, the lover of Sunderland's wife. It is almost incredible that the Earl had no idea of what was afoot. Later King James came to believe that Sunderland had deliberately egged him on to make mistakes so that he in fact helped to bring about William's invasion. But that was far too complicated an idea. Nevertheless Sunderland, who was a man ever greedy for power and money, may well have insured himself both ways. His announced conversion to the Roman Catholic Church after the birth of the Prince of Wales was meant to keep him in James's good books, while he could have hoped that Henry Sidney and his wife would be able to get him out of trouble if James were overthrown.

James received the first hint that an expedition was being planned against him in Holland from the French.[36] D'Avaux, Louis XIV's representative at The Hague, was an extremely skilful and well-informed diplomatist, whereas D'Albeville was not, and although a Roman Catholic, was distrusted by James. Moreover D'Albeville was a scaremonger; D'Avaux was not. It was not until the middle of August that James began to believe that William had hostile intentions and even then he quickly changed his mind.[37] His view was that the naval preparations in Holland were being undertaken for fear of French aggression, especially in view of the attitude taken by Louis XIV over the deaths of the Elector Palatine and the Elector of Cologne. James therefore pertinently asked Barrillon what Louis's forces were doing and told him that in his opinion 'the Prince of Orange did not dare to undertake anything against England in the present conjunction'. For he could not engage the States-General in a war against the French King and James himself at the same time.[38]

Ten days before James made these remarks D'Avaux, on instructions from his master and at the instigation of the English ambassador in Paris, Skelton, presented a memorial on 30 August to the States-General warning them that if an attack were made on England, such an action would involve them in an open rupture with France. James was furious, for he realized that one thing that was certain to provoke the Dutch would be the suggestion that a secret treaty of alliance between himself and Louis XIV was in existence. Skelton, on whom the *démarche* was blamed (Louis XIV thought that he should have been praised for it)[39] was summoned home and put into the Tower of London. After Van Citters, the Dutch ambassador in London, who had been on leave, returned to England, James received him at Windsor to tell him that great naval preparations were unnecessary for defence at that season of the year and he would not make war on the Dutch unless they began it. Moreover he took pains to explain that he was in no need of protection from the French — 'his spirit as well as his dignity was too high to place himself on the level of Cardinal von Fürstenberg', the avowed agent of France.[40]

Nevertheless James was at last sufficiently concerned to take precautions. After all, the French might know something. He pointed out in a letter he wrote to William on 17 September that he was going to Chatham to examine the condition of the warships there and to inspect new batteries that he had ordered to be erected in the Medway, a hint that he had not forgotten the events of 1667. He also told his son-in-law that he was sorry to hear of the likelihood of there being a war on the Rhine — Louis XIV had in fact declared war on the Emperor three days earlier — thus impressing upon him that the Dutch had their hands too full on the mainland of Europe to permit them to interfere in England.[41] On 21 September, acting on a suggestion from his Lord Chancellor Jeffreys, James published a proclamation to quieten the minds of his own people and to ensure their loyalty, reminding them that he was calling a parliament to meet in November and that although he wanted to secure universal liberty of conscience, he would guarantee the privileges of the Church of England, admit no Catholics into the House of Commons and do nothing inimical to the Church of England.[42] But a few days later intelligence from Holland left him in no doubt that an amphibious expedition was being made ready to cross the North sea. He knew that Dutch warships were not needed to help stem French aggression at that time of the year, while he learned that the main French army was attacking Phillippsburg in the Palatinate, nearly 200 miles from the nearest Dutch frontier, so that William could move against him if he liked to face the risks. Once James felt sure that his own position was imperilled, he lost his nerve.

18.

Awaiting Invasion

James's loss of nerve and retreat from the policies that he had outlined at the beginning of his reign dated from the second half of September 1688. During the first half of that month the Earl of Sunderland, acting on his master's orders, was busily signing dozens of letters aimed at securing the kind of House of Commons that the King wanted. Some of these letters were warrants for new charters giving the King the right to dismiss and replace members of borough corporations, thus obtaining, so it was hoped, a small and servile electorate; other letters simply nominated candidates for borough constituencies in the forthcoming election who had been recommended by the regulators. Lastly, believing that all the Lords Lieutenant in office were now devoted to the royal wishes, they were invited to apply pressure in order to produce friendly knights of the shire. The proclamation agreed to by the Privy Council on 21 September was not intended to quieten the minds of people about the preparations for war known to be in progress in Holland, but to rally as many as possible behind the drive for a parliament which would enact universal liberty of conscience. Two days before the proclamation was agreed to, writs had been sealed and sent out to the sheriffs to set in motion a general election for a new parliament to meet in November.

But at this very moment James was at last and reluctantly being convinced that William of Orange was getting ready to invade England, though with what objects in mind nobody yet knew. John Evelyn paid a visit to London on 18 September where he 'found the Court in the utmost consternation upon a report of the Prince of Orange's landing [already] which put Whitehall in a panic of fear'.[1] The Lord Chancellor told the Earl of Clarendon, after explaining to him how the proclamation of 21 September had been drawn up, that

237

the King meant to send for the two Hydes and the Archbishop of Canterbury to discourse with them on the whole state of his affairs.[2] James obviously wanted not only to persuade the leaders of the Church of England that the new parliament would not seriously endanger Anglican privileges, but to unite the whole of the political nation behind him in the event of a Dutch invasion, though he still regarded its chances of success as problematical. So far as the coming election was concerned, James hoped to satisfy or stifle all opposition. As Sunderland explained to James's illegitimate son, the Duke of Berwick, who was not only Governor of Portsmouth but Lord Lieutenant of Hampshire:

> The King, having upon the issuing of writs for the meeting of Parliament, published the declaration [of 21 September] enclosed, hopes it will induce deputy lieutenants and justices of the peace lately removed to serve the King.[3]

If so, Berwick was empowered to reinstate them. In fact the King let it be known to all Lords Lieutenant that they could put back in office deputies earlier turned out and that the Lord Chancellor could reinstate Justices of the Peace.[4] No doubt James hoped that if he were able to reconcile the Church of England and thus be sure of a friendly parliament, that would discourage William from his projected invasion because when he arrived, he would find no one willing to support him.

That James was worried to death during the second half of September is clear enough. Princess Anne confided to her uncle, the Earl of Clarendon, on 23 September that she had found the King 'much disordered about the preparations which were making in Holland' while when Clarendon saw James himself on the following day the King told him that 'the Dutch were now coming to invade England in good earnest'.[5] On that same day Sunderland wrote to the Archbishop of Canterbury saying that the King wanted to see him and the Bishop of London on Friday 28 September.[6] The Archbishop, ever since he refused to serve on the Ecclesiastical Commission, had been forbidden to come to Court, while the Bishop of London was still suspended from his duties, so an olive branch had been conspicuously held out. Indeed James now wanted to induce the Established Church to give him the utmost help it could to prevent his subjects from lending their support to William of Orange. James then transferred all his attention from holding a general election to concentrating on repelling invasion. When he saw the

Archbishop he was able to tell him that the writs had been cancelled.

Anyone could see that it was an inappropriate time for election-eering. In fact after 21 September Sunderland stopped writing letters about who ought to be chosen for parliament and turned his mind to strengthening the army. On 24 September he wrote to George Legge, Master General of the Ordnance, informing him that the King wanted all his own regiments to be increased in size, that he was to see that every cavalry colonel had sufficient new and 'best-proof' armour for his troopers, and that he was to provide special suits of armour to be worn by the Earl of Feversham and Lord Churchill, who were destined to be appointed commander-in-chief and second-in-command of a large army mobilized to stop William and his cohorts from landing anywhere in the island.[7] The Lord Deputy of Ireland was commanded to dispatch two regiments of foot, one of dragoons and a battalion of guards to Chester or Liverpool.[8] Later other troops were summoned from Scotland. The Lords Lieutenant were instructed to call out the militia. The Duke of Newcastle, only son of the peer who had fought for Charles I on Marston Moor, was put in charge of all the Ridings of Yorkshire (having previously been cold-shouldered as too much of a Protestant) and commanded to raise a new regiment there.[9] Lord Dartmouth, as one of the most trusted of James's Protestant friends, was sent away from the Ordnance office at the beginning of October (though he retained the title of Master-General) to assume command of the fleet with instructions to restore order among the sailors who had been restless because their previous admiral, Sir Roger Strickland, was a Roman Catholic and intensely disliked.

During the next four or five weeks James was able to build up an army of about 40,000 men, of whom 5,000 were brought over from Ireland and 4,000 from Scotland, while fresh regiments were being raised in England. All these were professional or pressed soldiers. The militia or so-called trained bands were useless. That was James's own fault since, after their failure to stem the earlier invasion by the Duke of Monmouth, he had come to distrust them. Moreover the constant changes-about of the Lords Lieutenant and Deputy Lieu-tenants, whose main responsibility it was to look after and organize the militia, had caused it to be neglected. The Earl of Lindsey, Lord Lieutenant of Lincolnshire, wrote to the King personally on 27 September to explain that the militia was in great disorder because of the removal of the chief gentry from their offices in the county, while 'hearing musters were not pleasing to your Majesty they had met only once since your coronation'.[10] The Earl of Bristol, who was Lord Lieutenant of Dorset, wrote two days later to say that most of the Deputy Lieutenants who had been dismissed were also officers of the militia and in consequence there were no Deputy Lieutenants nor militia officers in the county.[11] Lord Aston, Lord Lieutenant of Staffordshire, wrote more tartly to Sunderland, stating that no militia was in existence there, but 'presumed that several besides Roman Catholics will be glad to sell their lives as dear as they can in defence of his Majesty'.[12]

While the mobilization of the army and navy was going forward as rapidly as possible, James tried by two other means to prevent an invasion. The first was to persuade the States-General that he had no intention of attacking them, but only of defending himself, if attacked. As early as 4 September he had instructed D'Albeville at The Hague to remind the Dutch Government that since the start of his reign a defensive alliance between them had been in existence. Unfortunately their 'great and surprising preparations of war' had alarmed Europe and compelled him to reinforce his own fleet to maintain the peace of Christendom.[13] The trouble was, however, that D'Avaux's memorial to the Dutch submitted a week earlier, inspired by Sir Bevil Skelton in Paris, made it seem as if a secret Anglo-French treaty had actually been signed. Though James had recalled Skelton and imprisoned him in the Tower, the States-General were able to reply to D'Albeville's representations by stating that the reason they were arming was that the English and French were doing so and might be intending to attack them. Vainly D'Albeville was ordered on 2 October to point out that it was the true interest of both nations to live in strict friendship together by which means their trade might flourish.[14] James had rightly recognized that D'Avaux's memorial was fatal. Indeed it was because of their fear of another Anglo-French assault (as in 1672) that the States-General gave their consent to William's expedition, which was regarded as a personal venture, on condition that he left behind sufficient forces at home under the command of his friend, the Prince of Waldeck, to guard all the frontiers and, if necessary, give active support to William's ally, the Elector of Brandenburg in preventing the French from occupying the city of Cologne.

Secondly, James aimed to induce the Archbishop of Canterbury and other bishops of the Church of England, publicly to express their abhorrence of William's aggression by persuading them to forget their grievances over his favouritism towards the Roman Catholics in the universities and elsewhere. It was here that the King deceived himself. As the Earl of Clarendon remarked, when the King observed to him after the news of the coming invasion had been confirmed, 'And now, my lord, I shall see what the Church of England men will do', 'Your Majesty will see that they will behave themselves like honest men, though they have been somewhat severely used of late.'[15] This was said on 24 September, the day on which the King was reinforcing his regiments and ordering suits of armour for his troopers.

The fact was that during the whole of his short reign James had convinced himself that whatever he did and however outrageously he behaved, whether it was transforming an Oxford College into a Catholic seminary, introducing a Jesuit Father into his Privy Council, or sending his Archbishop of Canterbury to prison, he could still count upon the unquestioning loyalty of the Church of England to the Stuart monarchy. Even though he had accused the Anglican bishops of raising the standard of rebellion against him after he had been shaken to the core by their humble petition, he was unable to realize how much he had done to alienate those who were normally loyal to the Crown. And so now, when confronted with invasion, he thought he could undo everything he had done by abandoning the methods — legitimate though he had believed them to be — of abrupt dismissals and open intimidation. He even imagined that mere soothing generalities would satisfy the bishops that he was going to mend his ways.

In the last week of September and the first of October James put his whole machinery of government into reverse. Knowing that at this very time William of Orange was embarking his troops and was to be accompanied on his expedition by a number of leading Englishmen, including Arthur Herbert, who was put in supreme command of the Dutch fleet, James was compelled desperately to rally his subjects, redistribute his regiments and station his warships at the mouth of the Thames to watch out for and impede the movements of his enemy.

On 28 September James published a proclamation about the coming invasion; he told his subjects that though the pretence that he had threatened their liberties, property and religion was being used as 'a colour', what was about to happen was an attempt at the absolute conquest of his kingdom by a foreign power.[16] They would find, he delcared later, that William was a worse tyrant than Oliver Cromwell.[17] So everything had to be subordinated to defence against a ruthless foe. That was why he had been compelled to withdraw the writs for a general election since he could not meet a new parliament while his place was at the head of his army. On Thursday 27 September a general pardon had been proclaimed for political offences and three days later, after the King had a private interview with the Archbishop of Canterbury at which he said that he hoped the Primate was satisfied with the assurances he had already given to some of the other bishops, that this was not the time to enter into detailed disputes, but that all must gather together in unity beneath the royal standard. He ended by saying that he was now going to church, but that the Archbishop or any of the other bishops could come to see him whenever they liked and he would listen to what they had to say.[18]

James attempted not only to pacify the clergy but to gratify the laity. The City of London's charter was restored; the popish Lords Lieutenant were replaced; the regulators were rebuked; and finally, all the borough charters which had been forfeited or amended since the year 1679 during his brother's reign were restored. Even Henry Compton, the Bishop of London, was allowed to resume his duties.

The Archbishop and other bishops had made it perfectly plain to the King after they had seen him again on 3 October that unless specific concessions were granted, they would not be able to help him. They were not to be satisfied by affable generalities; not only must he make good the wrongs he had done to the Church of England, but he must stop the issue of *quo warranto* writs, he must abandon the use of the dispensing power until a parliament met, and he must restore the nobility and gentry to their traditional positions of authority in the towns and counties, ridding local government of dissidents and time-servers. They required the abolition of the Ecclesiastical Commission, the reinstatement of the President and Fellows of Magdalen College, a ban on Roman Catholics teaching in schools, the deprivation of foreign bishops wielding ecclesiastical jurisdiction and the filling up of vacant bishoprics.[19] In return for all that the bishops agreed to draw up collects (or short prayers) for the King and the kingdom's safety, but they refused to sign a document expressing their abhorrence of William's conduct; after all, it was obvious to the meanest intelligence that although during the first fortnight of October James gave way to all their demands, he would not have done so had it not been for the pressure exerted on him by the expected invasion. Even then people were naturally aware that if William were to be defeated and a packed parliament, as planned by the regulators, be called, James might cancel everything he had then done or promised to do.

What has also to be remembered is that James did not altogether abandon his reliance on his fellow religionists. He kept Father Petre and his other Catholic advisers at his side; he did not dismiss Roman Catholic officers from his army — in fact two regiments consisting largely of Roman Catholics were raised; most of the soldiers whom Tyconnel sent over from Ireland were Roman Catholics; and some of the Roman Catholics from Ireland were employed to strengthen existing regiments in England. Those Irishmen who were dispatched to Portsmouth, where the Roman Catholic Duke of Berwick was in command, so upset some of the garrison officers that five of them protested and asked permission to resign their commissions. James ordered that these officers should be brought under escort to Windsor where they were court-martialled and dismissed.[20] That was certainly an error of judgment; the King made another such error later on when he removed Berwick from Portsmouth, which he had intended to be an escape hatch for the Queen and himself if the worst came to the worst, ordering him to join his high command at Salisbury where he arrived too late to do any good.

In fact most of the things that James did during October when William was known to be embarking his troops were panic measures. As a former general and admiral himself James naturally had his own ideas about what he thought his enemy was going to do. He was aware that the autumn was a treacherous time for naval operations. Only third-rate warships and light vessels could be risked at sea. But the dangers from gales and fogs cut both ways: while they would be hazards for the invading fleet, they might equally prevent English frigates from venturing out across the North sea and would make it extremely difficult for them to detect the movements of Prince William's armada. Furthermore it was impossible for James to guess where his enemy would attempt to land. It might be, as rumours from Holland suggested, somewhere on the east or north-east coasts at one of the nearest harbours facing the Netherlands. But the mouth of the Thames or the Downs were also places likely to attract the Dutch. James's warships could hardly protect the whole of the vulnerable coasts where landing places were numerous and harbours deep. On the other hand, dared William risk landing anywhere so long as the English fleet was in being capable of wrecking his troopships and drowning his soldiers?

James therefore made up his mind that William would first send forward his warships under the command of the renegade Admiral Herbert to fight Lord Dartmouth and perhaps persuade some of Dartmouth's men to desert him — for Herbert had been a very popular admiral; then the troopships would be able to dock safely. On 5 October James wrote to Dartmouth from Whitehall to tell him that he thought that what D'Albeville's latest dispatches from Holland reported about the Dutch navy's intentions to come out and engage his fleet was highly probable.[21] James added that he considered it was likely that at the same time William would bring over his land forces, protected by a few men-of-war. There was talk of their being landed on the isle of Thanet; if that was so, then they might be aiming to attack Chatham. 'We must expect them', he concluded, 'with the first snatch of wind.' That was not wise reasoning and in the event proved entirely wrong. For everyone knew that the defences of Chatham had been immensely improved since the disaster of 1667: why should the Dutch direct their thrust against the most formidable point in the English defences? Anyhow changing weather conditions and dubious rumours induced James to believe that Dartmouth must at all costs keep his fleet together at anchorage until he could be absolutely certain of his enemy's movements and intentions.

A week later James had not altered his opinions about likely Dutch strategy. He deprecated the proposal put to him by Dartmouth that he should show himself on the coast of Holland, coming out from the Buoy of the Nore, where the bulk of his ships were concentrated and, reinforced by the vessels stationed at Portsmouth, attempt to find out what the Dutch were doing and even to frighten them from setting out at all. James warned the Admiral to consider such an operation very carefully before risking it at that season of the year.[22] He felt sure that Admiral Herbert would seek Dartmouth out while the Prince of Orange with his troopships and escort squadron would look for somewhere to land. Dartmouth was not a particularly bold commander and needed little persuasion to avoid being over-adventurous. For his part James, having been an admiral himself, fighting twice against the Dutch, was reluctant to give any precise orders to the man on the spot. 'I make no doubt', he wrote on 14 October, 'that God must protect me . . . He [Dartmouth] must govern himself according to the enemy's motions and as wind and weather will permit.'[23]

The Dutch fleet outnumbered the English; though the English vessels carried more guns, the Dutch men-of-war, built so as to sail easily in the creeks and harbours which dotted their coasts, were more manoeuvrable. Dartmouth was a less experienced officer than Herbert and the loyalty of his sailors was more dubious. From the beginning, therefore, James realized that although the risks accepted by William were grave, the English fleet might be defeated or at any rate bottled up; that was why he hoped that Dartmouth would move away from the mouth of the Thames to an anchorage from which he could watch out for the movements of the Dutch and fight them if a favourable opportunity presented itself, especially when the wind was westerly. But James really relied more on his army than on his navy to repel the invasion. On paper, by bringing troops from Scotland and Ireland and recruiting fresh regiments in England, he had an army of over 53,000 men, whereas even D'Albeville's liberal estimates of those of William's command did not stretch higher than 20,000 mixed fighting men.[24]

James dispersed his land forces widely. On 23 October Sunderland told the Earl of Bath that the King had received information that William would probably land small parties at different places along the coasts so as to raise false alarms.[25] Bath was therefore instructed to arrange for watching the coasts in his lieutenancy of Devon and Cornwall and to prevent 'evilly disposed persons' from going over to the enemy, should they appear in those counties. Orders also went out that horses were to be commandeered for the use of the army.[26] Evidently James was under the same impression as Lord Arlington had been under twenty-one years earlier — that the operations of the Dutch navy could be successfully impeded by the presence of cavalry on or near the beaches. At the end of the month the Lords Lieutenant were informed by the Earl of Middleton that

> The King having by proclamation directed that all coasts should be carefully watched and upon the first approach of the enemy all horse, oxen and cattle were to be removed twenty miles inland, they should instruct their deputy lieutenants and justices of the peace accordingly.[27]

So James's army was distributed along the coasts and in the ports and garrison towns, but he retained a central reserve no longer in London but on Salisbury plain.

The chief question, however, remained whether the Dutch would be able to cross the North sea at all so late in the year and whether, if they did, William's troops could be disembarked safely. James personally visited the fleet twice; he studied the weather reports closely; and he was delighted to learn that although the winds had been easterly in the middle of October, as soon as William had ordered his warships and transports to put out to sea, the wind changed westerly and stormy compelling the armada to return to port after hundreds of horses, shipped to mount the Prince's cavalry, had been swept overboard and drowned. That was on 19 October. Next day James wrote to Dartmouth to suggest that the change in the winds gave him an opportunity to get out and hinder the enemy from coming over.[28] Dartmouth did not attempt as much as that, but by 24 October he did manage to anchor his ships at the Gunfleet, south of Harwich, where he could await the next move of the enemy with more confidence, having put out to sea before they had done.

Though James carefully supervised the order of battle of his army, trusting it to repel the invaders if it came to the crunch, he did not neglect propaganda. William's declaration, dated 30 September, in which he claimed he was coming over to secure the religion, laws and liberties of the realms ruled by James, which had been overturned by the advice of evil counsellors, had also asserted that the same evil men had, to fulfil their wicked designs, 'published that the Queen hath brought forth a son'; yet — the declaration continued — the suspicion that the pretended Prince of Wales was not borne by the Queen was shared not only by William and Mary but by 'all good subjects of those kingdoms'.[29] James got hold of a copy of the declaration and later had it read out to the bishops; but before that, on 22 October, he held a meeting of his Privy Council in Whitehall in the presence of the judges, the Lord Mayor and Aldermen of London and other prominent people where the midwives, nurses and nobility who had been present at the lying-in-state all solemnly swore on oath that the Queen's delivery was genuine. Everything was taken down in writing after the witnesses had been examined by the King's counsel. Ten days later members of the Privy Council carried a copy of these testimonies to Princess Anne, but she, who with her women had laughed and jested about the meeting, now merely said sarcastically that she had so much duty to her father that 'his word must be more to her than these depositions'.[30] The King may have realized that he had acted far too late to quash scandal while the elaborate and secretly arranged performance before the Privy Council merely conveyed the impression that there was something to hush up or to camouflage.

At about the same time that all this was going on in London James had been pleased by the news that the Dutch ships had been damaged by storms while Dartmouth's ships had at length reached the Gunfleet safely. James now took a dramatic step: he dismissed his leading Minister, the Earl of Sunderland, from his posts of President of the Council and senior Secretary of State. The Earl of Middleton replaced him as Secretary of State and Lord Preston, previously Secretary of State for Scotland, stepped into Middleton's shoes. These two Scotsmen were both Protestants and competent administrators, but neither possessed nor exercised any political influence over the King. Sunderland had undoubtedly done so.[31] But when he found that his various schemes had foundered, beginning with the humiliation which was inflicted on his master when the Dutch States-General refused to release the six regiments, his nerve cracked. He had tried to make his personal position safe by declaring himself to be a Roman Catholic, but he left it too late. No one at the time knew exactly why he had been dismissed: his successor, Middleton, said he did not know, while the Earl of Clarendon was also mystified, though he heard a rumour that it was because the late Secretary had held a private correspondence with the Prince of Orange.[32] James's biographer was to write that 'the King was convinced that My Lord Sunderland was not the man he took him for, nor any longer to be trusted' and added that 'this artful dissembler thought it too early to pull off the mask and own to the world his treachery.'[33] Certainly the letters that the Countess of Sunderland had written to William and to William's friend, Henry Sidney, were rather remarkable if done without her husband's knowledge. But at the time James did not know about them and exonerated his former Minister from disloyalty. Still James had discovered rather too late in his reign that Sunderland was 'not the man he took him for', while his sudden departure at the time of supreme crisis showed that James had lost his own grip, for, after all, Sunderland had offered him some pretty sensible advice, particularly about not prosecuting the seven bishops, which he neglected.

In fact James had never recovered from the shock given him by the bishops' petition and the jury's verdict at their trial. On 2 November he tried to assure himself that none of the bishops were mixed up in William's invasion plans — for William in his declaration definitely asserted that he had been 'most earnestly solicited [to come over] by a great many lords both spiritual and temporal' — and again and again the King begged the Archbishop of Canterbury and the rest to deny their complicity and to publish a statement of their abhorrence of William's conduct. All of them, including the Bishop of London, who had indeed signed the invitation to the Prince, disclaimed responsibility, but refused their abhorrence; they would only pray for James. The King gave up. 'If you will not assist me as I desire', he exclaimed, 'I must stand upon my own legs and trust myself and my own arms.'[34] It was therefore no treachery by Sunderland, but James's own delusions about the loyalty of the Church of England to the monarchy, at last shattered, which caused his world to topple about him.

19.
Defeat and Departure

At his second attempt on the evening of 1 November 1688 William of Orange with his fleet and transport ships set sail for England, carried forward by a fierce easterly wind. On the Prince's flagship a banner fluttering on the mast-head proclaimed his motto: *Pro Religione et Libertate — Je Maintiendrai*. Next day the expeditionary force turned south-west, thus evading Lord Dartmouth and the English navy which still lay anchored in the Gunfleet. On 3 and 4 November 5-600 vessels of all shapes and sizes passed slowly through the Straits of Dover, watched by crowds lining the white cliffs. But it was not until some time on 6 November that James knew for certain that his enemy was aiming to land upon the south-west coast. Orders were then sent to the Earl of Bristol, who was Lord Lieutenant of Dorset, to impede William's progress until regular forces could arrive from the east; the Duke of Beaufort, Lord Lieutenant of Gloucestershire, had earlier been dispatched to take charge at Bristol and the Earl of Bath, Lord Lieutenant of Devon and Cornwall, was warned to see to the safety of Exeter.[1] Realizing that there was no longer any danger upon the east coast, where it had been pretty generally expected that the Dutch would try to disembark, the King ordered the Duke of Norfolk not to fire any beacons without express permission from Whitehall and to come up himself to help settle matters in Berkshire and Surrey, leaving his Deputy Lieutenants to take care of Norfolk.[2] Two fascinating sidelights on the working of James's mind are the order he gave that same day to a local alderman to make sure that 'no indignities' were commited at the Roman Catholic chapel in Gloucester and the dispatch of a letter to the Duke of Beaufort to break down the bridge at Keynsham, which was the place where over three years earlier the Duke of Monmouth had attempted to cross the Severn to attack Bristol

249

from the east.[3] Thus his thoughts dwelt on the problems of the past.

On 6 November James was still trying to extract a paper of abhorrence from the Anglican bishops, but they remained adamant. The Archbishop of Canterbury said that they had been 'severely smarted for meddling with matters of state and government that it may well make us exceeding cautious as how we do so any more' and added for good measure that after their acquittal in the King's Bench trial they had still been reviled by the circuit judges. The King replied that the matter was 'quite out of the way'; everything had been forgiven and forgotten; but it was all no use.[4] James was hoist with his own petard. The bishops said they would assist him only with their prayers.

Exactly when James knew for certain that William had landed, as he did, in Torbay on 5 November is not clear. The Earl of Clarendon recorded in his memoirs that the King learned it on the sixth; he was absolutely sure on the eighth; for on that day the Duke of Beaufort was informed that regular troops were already on their way to Somerset, while three battalions of the Guards, the King's own regiment of dragoons, and a hundred grenadiers on horseback were instructed to make a forced march to Portsmouth, though if the enemy were found to be moving westward they were commanded to ride to Salisbury where the bulk of the royal forces were being concentrated.[5]

James's army, encamped on Salisbury plain, was divided into three groups, one stationed at Warminster, twenty miles north-west of Salisbury on the road to Bath, one at Marlborough, twenty-five miles north of Salisbury on the road that ran from Reading to Bath via Newbury, and the main body at Salisbury itself. Lord Feversham went to Salisbury to assume charge as commander-in-chief under the King, while on 7 November Lord Churchill had been appointed to command both the cavalry and the infantry immediately under Feversham.[6] To safeguard the north-west of England James wrote to Lord Tyrconnel urging him to send an infantry regiment by forced marches so that it could be embarked at once for Chester or Liverpool.[7] Then on the next day James wrote to Lord Dartmouth to assure him that he did not blame the Admiral for failing to intercept William's fleet, but hinted that he might take advantage of the continuing easterly wind to enter the Channel and attack the Dutch fleet at anchor in Torbay.[8] Three days later James, having learned that the wind had changed westerly, proposed to Dartmouth that he should attempt to intercept reinforcements which William was thought to be expecting. Yet the King still refrained from giving precise orders to his Admiral: 'You must know your own strength', he wrote, 'whether you are in a condition to make use of this westerly wind to attempt anything upon them.'[9]

When James was writing the first of these letters to Dartmouth he knew that William had reached Exeter, which the Earl of Bath had not attempted to hold and whence the Bishop and most of the local gentry had fled. Three days earlier Bath had written to the Earl of Middleton to tell him that while the gentlemen of Devon were eager to serve his Majesty 'yet the common people are so prejudiced with the late regulators and so much corrupted that there can be no dependence at present on the militia but only upon his Majesty's standing forces'.[10] In fact for nearly a fortnight after William's unhampered disembarkation at Torbay, the two sides eyed each other uneasily wondering what the other was going to do. William, James thought, might make either for Bristol or for Portsmouth or even march up the Welsh border to Cheshire, the other part of England where, again three years earlier, Monmouth had found supporters. Alternatively, William could, if he chose to take the risks involved, head straight for London. Broadly, James resolved that it was wisest to concentrate his army along the Portsmouth-Salisbury-Warminster line. Before taking any offensive action himself he needed to reinforce his cavalry at Salisbury with the slow-moving footguards and artillery train; and he had also to ensure that his capital was securely guarded lest his main force was menaced from the rear. On 12 November the King's printer, Henry Hills, whose offices were at Blackfriars and had been responsible for producing Roman Catholic literature, including the order of thanksgiving and prayer when the Queen was big with the Prince of Wales, had his offices assaulted by a mob who broke their windows; and the Lord Mayor had to be instructed to set a guard on the printing office provided from the London trained bands.[11] It was not until James was satisfied that all was well in London that he himself left it on 17 November going by way of Windsor and Basingstoke to Salisbury which he reached on 19 November. According to Lord Middleton, the Secretary of State who accompanied the King there, he arrived 'in perfect health' and on the next day rode out on horseback to inspect the terrain.[12]

Up till then James had been in a highly optimistic mood; he

fancied that time was on his side. William, he had been told, was hanging about in Exeter vainly hoping that the local bigwigs would join him. This James heard at first hand from the Bishop, who had come up to London and was promptly rewarded for his loyalty by being appointed Archbishop of York. (In fact this cleric was soon to throw in his lot with William.) The King counted on his army being swollen by troops arriving from Scotland and Ireland. Lord Tyrconnel had been commanded to send over every man he could possibly spare.[13] James hoped that all sources of unrest had been stifled. Lord Delamere, the most powerful figure in Cheshire, who had lit the fire of a northern rebellion by inciting his tenants to support the Prince of Orange, would, the King trusted, be dealt with satisfactorily by the troops coming over from Ireland. At the other end of the kingdom Portsmouth, though Berwick had been called away from its governorship, was believed to be quite safe in the care of the King's Roman Catholic friend, Lord Dover, who had been sent there in Berwick's place. On 11 November Lord Lovelace, who was the first peer to attempt to go over to Prince William with a party of soldiers, was captured by the Gloucestershire militia at Cirencester and escorted as a prisoner to London. The Duke of Beaufort was relied upon not only to safeguard Bristol but to prevent any trouble arising on the Welsh border. It is true that on the day James left London for Windsor the peers spiritual and temporal who were still in the capital, led by the inconveniently unco-operative Archbishop of Canterbury, had presented him with a petition asking him to call a parliament; the King then, though displeased, indeed angry, had the sense to answer that although a parliament could hardly be summoned while he was faced with invasion and rebellion, he would do so as soon as the crisis was over so as to prevent the shedding of blood.[14] James then set out for Salisbury.

It is fascinating that during James's absence from London his Queen told the second Earl of Clarendon that the King was misunderstood by his people; that he intended nothing but a general liberty of conscience and that he had always meant to support the Established Church because he was satisfied with its loyalty.[15] Unquestionably James had shared his views with his wife and both of them were genuinely puzzled about why his excellent resolutions should have caused such dreadful consequences. Surely righteousness should triumph in the end?

Before James got to Salisbury he was informed that the first

effective desertion from his army had already taken place. Lord
Cornbury, the eldest son of Clarendon, who had reached Salisbury
with his own regiment of dragoons during the second week of
November, found two cavalry regiments stationed there but without
their colonels. He persuaded these regiments to join his dragoons and
march with him via Blandford and Dorchester as far as Honiton in
Devon and thence to Axminster, claiming that his mission was to
beat up the enemy's quarters in the area, it being some fifteen miles
from Exeter where William was still encamped. However, the
officers in the two other regiments became suspicious of Cornbury
and asked to see his orders. Thereupon Cornbury went off with sixty
of his dragoons to link up with the Prince of Orange. When his father
learned of his son's desertion he uttered a prayer: 'O God, that my
son should be a rebel! The Lord in his mercy look upon me and
enable me to support myself under this great calamity.' Next day he
saw the King, who was pleased to perceive such anguish in a stalwart
of the Church of England and graciously told the Earl that he pitied
him with all his heart and that he would still be kind to his family.[16]
No doubt James felt that the arrest of Lord Lovelace and the escape
of Lord Cornbury cancelled one another out; that was why he still
seemed cheerful enough when he arrived at Salisbury and collected
the details.

But by then other desertions and defections were taking place. On
20 November, his second day at his army headquarters his nose
started bleeding. The faithful Lord Middleton begged his master to
avoid exposing himself to danger and not to prejudice his health by
overwork and worry; he should leave the detail to others.[17] Unquestionably the cause of James's fit of nose-bleeding was psycho-
logical. For the physicians, who were sent for, said after they had
packed him off to bed, that 'it was only a ferment in his blood
occasioned by too constant and anxious application to business'.[18]
But it was more than that. His visit unnerved him. He had always
counted on his large army at the last resort to protect him against
any rebellion or invasion. As it was, not only did he find his army
demoralized by the desertions but he received intelligence that
William was at last on the move. On 21 November, his son-in-law
passed through Chard and Yeovil in Somerset while thrusting advance guards as far as Sherborne in Dorset, thirty-seven miles from
Salisbury. No wonder James was upset. Confrontation was near. The
doctors let more blood out of him, then gave him opiates which

enabled him to have a good night's sleep.[19] Though the news percolated through from the west to James's headquarters, the intelligence about the enemy's moves and intentions was wholly inadequate, for, as Middleton wrote to his fellow Secretary of State, Lord Preston, 'none of the gentry in the neighbouring counties to Wiltshire came near the Court' and the commoners were spies for the enemy.[20] On the following day James's nose still bled so he had to cancel a projected visit of inspection to Warminster.

Now what was to be done? Next day James was well enough to summon and attend a council of war. His commander-in-chief, Lord Feversham, advised the withdrawal of the army towards London because he believed it was too late to face William's army along a wide-flung front in Dorset and Wiltshire. James therefore gave orders that the whole army should be withdrawn eastward and encamp along the banks of the Thames as far south-east as Marlow, thirty-three miles from London, and linking together garrisons at Windsor, Staines, Egham, Chertsey and Colbrook. Feversham's second-in-command, Lord Churchill had argued against such a retreat, but had been overruled. Whatever his motives were for doing so, he undoubtedly was right. James might have recalled his days under Turenne when he had recorded in his memoirs that rivers, unlike mountains, rarely offer good defensive positions.

The King believed, as he wrote later, that Churchill had all along intended to betray him to William, even planning to kidnap him if he had gone to Warminster. At any rate that very night John Churchill, who had been one of James's most trusted servants ever since he had first appeared at Court as a page-boy and whom he had twice appointed second-in-command of his army, went over to the enemy, as did also the Duke of Grafton, James's nephew, who too had been favourably treated by him. Churchill together with Grafton reached William at Axminster with 400 cavalrymen, while other officers followed in his wake. Shaken and ill, James left Salisbury for Andover. It was from here that he dispatched Lord Dover to take over the command at Portsmouth, giving him a letter for Lord Dartmouth, who had at last ventured as far west as Spithead, to tell the Admiral that the Prince of Wales (not yet six months old) was being brought there so that if the worst came to the worst he could be carried over in safety to France.[21]

From Andover James returned to London on 26 November only to learn to his consternation that the desertions from his army had been transformed from a trickle into a flood. Besides Churchill and Grafton Prince George of Denmark, the Duke of Ormonde, the Earl of Northumberland, Colonel Trelawney and 5,000 other officers and men were going over to the Prince of Orange. Vainly James started replacing the noble deserters: Dover took over from Churchill as colonel of the third troop of horse guards, Lord Peterborough filled the vacancy as Gentleman of the Bedchamber, the Duke of Berwick was appointed second-in-command under Feversham. Sir Edward Hales, who had been Governor of the Tower of London ever since the bishops were sent there as prisoners, was removed from his office and relieved by Sir Bevil Skelton, whom James had only recently imprisoned there. Perhaps he considered that to retain a Roman Catholic in this important post would be provocative or maybe he thought he would be too rash, for James had already countermanded an order by Hales to employ a mortar to frighten the Londoners.[22] The truth was James no longer knew on whom he could rely. Though he made light of his son-in-law, Prince George's desertion, he was shaken to the core after he heard on his arrival back in London that his second daughter, Princess Anne, accompanied by Lady Churchill and the Bishop of London, had fled from the Cockpit, her home in Whitehall, with the ultimate intention of joining her husband in William's camp. All of them claimed that the reason for their disloyalty was that the Church of England was in peril; they did so in spite of the fact that James had reversed every act of his from the establishment of the Ecclesiastical Commission to the Catholicizing of Magdalen College which had aroused Anglican fears. When after reaching Whitehall in the afternoon of 26 November James had digested all the bad news awaiting him there he exclaimed 'with holy David . . . O if my enemies only cursed me, I could have borne it,'[23] but the way in which he was betrayed by his two daughters, Mary and Anne, his two sons-in-law, William and George, and his two closest servants, Churchill and Grafton, shocked him by its malice and ingratitude. 'God help me!' he exclaimed, 'even my children have forsaken me.' His first thoughts then turned to ensuring the safety of his wife and son, before considering whether or not he could somehow come to terms with Prince William now advancing slowly but steadily towards London.

As has been noticed, before James left Andover for London he sent Lord Dover to Portsmouth with secret instructions to Lord Dartmouth to make ready to put the Prince of Wales on a ship to carry him to France. The King had a most pathetic faith in his Admiral, who had long been a favourite of his and with whom he had corresponded confidentially when he had been exiled in Brussels. Dartmouth was now at the prime of his life, but had hardly distinguished himself during William's invasion when he had allowed the Prince to enter the Channel and land unmolested in Devonshire. As late as 29 November James was writing sympathetically to his friend to say how sorry he was that he had 'been roughly used by winds and the sea' and agreed that it was 'a bad time of year for any action in that inconstant element'.[24] Four days later Lord Berkeley, Master of Trinity House, was telling Dartmouth that though many loyalists railed at him for his failure to stop William, the King continually justified him.[25] It was on Dartmouth that James depended for the safety of his son and heir. For James had decided, not unnaturally in view of the ribaldry with which the child's birth had been greeted by his enemies that "'tis my son I must endeavour to preserve, whatever becomes of me.'[26]

The Prince of Wales had been conveyed to Portsmouth under the charge of Dover and in the care of two other Roman Catholics the septuagenarians, Lord and Lady Powis: the latter had been appointed the child's official governess. When James realized how precarious his position had become he resolved to put into effect his scheme to send the Prince to France. Indeed the Modenese envoy in London, an Italian abbot devoted to the Queen whose marriage he had promoted, begged James with tears in his eyes to dispatch the child to safety and his mother as well.[27] But now Dartmouth played him false. In a long letter he refused point-blank to send James Edward to France on the ground that if he did so, he would be accused of high treason.[28] The King immediately hurried a special messenger to Portsmouth to tell Lady Powis that he thought his son was no longer safe there and ordered her to bring him back to London. Lord Dover had anticipated the King's wishes. After many adventures Lady Powis and her charge, who left Portsmouth in the early morning of 8 December, succeeded in reaching London the next day, a remarkable feat considering the chaos in the country at large. The Queen was with difficulty persuaded that she must herself carry her son away because she did not want to leave her husband. Though the royal pair parted in anguish and sorrow, in the end the Queen felt she had chosen her duty rightly. Disguised as an Italian laundress, she left Whitehall in the early hours of 10 December.

Elaborate plans for her journey, concocted by her friends and admirers, worked out satisfactorily. She and her party reached Gravesend in the middle of a cold and rainy night whence they were rowed out to a packet-boat which carried them to France. She landed with her baby at Calais on 11 December.[29]

A fortnight earlier on 27 November James had resumed his discussions with his spiritual and temporal peers where they had left off before he went to Salisbury. He met about forty of them; an animated discussion took place in which the two Hydes were prominent. The Earl of Rochester told James that the calling of a parliament was now 'the only remedy in our present circumstances', though whether it would have the desired effect of reuniting the kingdom no one could tell. His elder brother, Clarendon, whose only son had already joined William, spoke much more roughly and frankly. He said:

> Sir, it is a maxim in our law that the King can do no wrong, but his Ministers may, and be called to account for it too. Now in the present juncture of affairs, what would you have us do to appease the nation since the people have been so provoked by the papists? . . . when your Majesty was at Salisbury, you might have had some remedy, but the people do now say that the King is run away with [?from] his army — we are left defenceless and must therefore side with the prevailing party.[30]

The Lord Chancellor Jeffreys and the Queen's Chamberlain, Lord Godolphin, favoured the calling of a parliament; the Marquis of Halifax, the Earl of Nottingham and the Earl of Rochester, who spoke more respectfully than Clarendon, all advocated dispatching commissioners to treat with William of Orange. But they also went so far as to urge that James should issue a general pardon to all who had gone over to William, including the rebels in the north, and that Roman Catholics (none of whom were present at this meeting) should be dismissed from their appointments, civil or military. In winding up the debate, James announced that he would at once call a parliament and would offer a general pardon, but said he must have time to think about the other proposals put to him; he would have to sleep on them. (He was still having to take opium at nights to guarantee proper sleep.)[31] Nottingham received the impression that despite desertions the King still had confidence in the fidelity of the bulk of his army.[32]

On the next day (28 November) the King duly published a proclamation calling a parliament to meet at Westminster on 15 January 1689; it could not assemble any sooner since it took time to issue writs and forty days had to be allowed to gather in the returns. Clarendon was pleased by the decision; he recorded in his diary that it had given 'infinite satisfaction'; and as to himself, he resolved after arranging for his son's election in Wiltshire to join William of Orange at his headquarters.[33] The King was understandably angry with the tone that Clarendon had adopted at the conference; but Halifax and Nottingham, who saw James privately on the 29th, persuaded him to negotiate with William; the King chose them, together with Lord Godolphin, to act as his commissioners after obtaining passports to cross the lines. Their instructions were to inform the Prince that James was summoning a parliament at which all matters and differences could be settled and to propose, if they thought fit, an armistice with both sides holding their forces at equal distances from London while the Commons were being elected and meeting. The commissioners did not in fact reach William's headquarters, which were now at Hungerford, sixty-five miles from London, until 8 December.

During those first ten days of December the King was mainly concerned about the safety of his son and the dispatch of his commissioners. He demonstrated his meekness by writing to the Senior Fellow of Sidney Sussex College Cambridge to say that they could elect any Master and Fellows they liked (a Roman Catholic had earlier been foisted upon them); he also recommended his Protestant friend, Dartmouth, as new Chancellor of the University instead of the second Duke of Albemarle, who had died in Jamaica.[34] On 6 December James reviewed some of his remaining troops in Hyde Park, but it was generally thought that there would be no fighting between the two sides, that 'all will go with the invaders' side without blows',[35] James appreciated that three courses were open to him: the first that he should await the meeting of Parliament and hope for some compromise with his son-in-law; the second that he should fight it out, trusting the Virgin Mary to procure his victory; the last — and this was the advice of his Catholic friends like Lord Melfort — was that he should temporarily go into exile in France, relying on the ensuing chaos in England to require his return.[36] In the end the King himself became pessimistic and chose the third course of action. Writing to Dartmouth on 10 December, he informed him that it was because his affairs were in such a desperate condition that he had been obliged to send away his wife and son, and that, as he had been basely deserted by many officers and soldiers of his army and as 'the same poison has got among my fleet', he had resolved 'to withdraw till this violent storm was over'.[37] In other words when he parted from his Queen after supper on the same day he had written to Dartmouth he had already decided to follow her.

It is pretty clear that when James sent his commissioners to William he was unhopeful and was merely playing for time to effect his and his family's escape from London. Even if he had not finally made up his mind at that moment, as soon as he learned of William's terms for an armistice, sent to him by his commissioners on the afternoon of 11 December, terms which though moderate in tone were drastic in fact, he felt he had no choice but to join his Queen in France, once he knew that she had reached there safely. His official biographer, basing himself on the ninth volume of James's memoirs, wrote:

> As soon as the Queen set sail from Gravesend . . . a French gentleman . . . came back to acquaint the King that he had seen them on board the yacht . . . so the King prepared to follow them, seeing no security where he was, and well remembering how the King his father and several of his predecessors had been used on like occasions; he was resolved never to consent to those mean things which would have been imposed upon him and saw plainly by the Prince of Orange's answer, which he received that night [11 December] that nothing but the Crown would satisfy his ambitious nephew and son-in-law.[38]

But it is practically certain that James had more or less determined to flee before he received the report from his commissioners at nine o'clock in the evening because earlier on this very day the Earl of Feversham, James's commander-in-chief, wrote to William of Orange from Uxbridge stating that he had had a letter from James that morning containing the 'unfortunate news' of his resolution to go out of England and ordering him to make no opposition to anybody so as to prevent the effusion of blood.[39]

The King left Whitehall in the early hours of 12 December, taking with him the Great Seal, the patents to the new sheriffs and the writs for calling a parliament. A cry of *'sauve qui peut'* had already gone up among James's former intimates. The Catholic Secretary for Scotland, Lord Melfort, and Father Petre had gone off first; Sunderland and his wife managed to find a ship to carry them to Rotterdam; Lord Chancellor Jeffreys tried to get away disguised as a sailor, but was caught at Wapping; Sir Edward Hales, the recently relieved Governor of the Tower, joined his master soon after mid-

night on the 11th in a hackney coach in which they drove to
Vauxhall and having crossed the river, rode on horseback as far as
Sheerness in the Isle of Sheppey where they planned to board a hoy
or small sailing boat bound for France.

But now their luck deserted them. Parties were out and about
hunting for fleeing papists; one of these parties soon discovered that
Hales, who was a local man, was around, so went out searching for
him. At eleven in the morning of 12 December three boatloads of
rough men boarded the hoy and carried off Hales and James, whom
they did not recognize, for questioning by the Mayor of Faversham,
some fifteen miles away. Their failure to spot the King was understandable as he wore an old cloak, an odd pair of boots, a short black
wig and a patch on the left side of his mouth. A vain attempt was
made by Hales to bribe the leader of the search party to release them,
while James was obliged to hand over some, but not all, of his
valuables to his captors. They even undid his breeches, examining
him 'for secret treasure so indecently as even to the discovery of his
nudity'.[40] The coach that was to carry the prisoners to the Mayor
drew up at an inn, 'The Queen's Arms' in Faversham, where the King
himself was first identified. He then managed to send a message to
Lord Winchelsea, the Lord Lieutenant of Kent, who came there
from Canterbury, but did no more than arrange for the King to be
placed in the custody of the Mayor at his house, where, despite all
sorts of efforts to get away to France, he was compelled to stay for
four days.[41] Eventually he was rescued by Lord Feversham, who
arrived with a military detachment, disentangled him from the local
rabble, and carried him to Rochester *en route* to London. Before he
left he was given back his watch, sword and pistols, but not his
money: he was upset by the loss of a crucifix. Once out of the hands
of the mob, James's spirits revived; he became a new man with new
hopes and was convinced that his troubles would be ended if only he
could reach an agreement with his son-in-law from Holland.

Prince William was in Windsor Castle when he heard of his
father-in-laws's adventures and whereabouts. When James arrived at
Rochester he sent a letter to the Prince which was carried to Windsor
by Lord Feversham, angling for some kind of understanding. William
was extremely annoyed that James had been allowed to leave
Faversham at all and placed Lord Feversham under arrest. Then he
sent back a message by his trusted friend and relative, Count
Zuylestein, to tell James to stay at Rochester. But before he could

arrive James had determined to return to Whitehall; he had had enough of roughing it and being jeered at by the uncouth mob. After dining in Deptford, he got into a coach which took him through Blackheath and Southwark and thence across London Bridge into the City and on to Westminster. He arrived at night to an unexpected welcome; the bells rang; bonfires blazed; and the crowd, assuming naturally enough that all was settled and well again, cheered. It looked as if he had come into his own once more. On the night of 17 December he retired to bed in his usual room and was soon fast asleep.

When James had written to William he had suggested that the Prince should come to St James's Palace so that they might confer together about the future of the kingdom. He was somewhat perturbed when he heard that Lord Feversham had been put under arrest by the Prince; but, on the other hand, he was buoyed up by the reception he met with at his arrival. Woken in the middle of the night by the Earl of Middleton, who was sleeping in the same room and had been told by emissaries who had come from William at Windsor — the Marquis of Halifax, the Earl of Shrewsbury and Lord Delamere — that they must speak to the King immediately, they at once dealt with him firmly. They told him that three battalions of Dutch foot guards had been posted around Whitehall and that the King's First Foot guards (the Grenadiers) had declared for the Prince of Orange. To avoid disturbances in the capital, which had already been subjected to two nights of riot and terror during which the houses of Roman Catholics had been attacked and foreign ambassadors' chapels sacked, James was commanded to leave London at once for his own as well as the City's safety. It was suggested that he should take up his residence at a house belonging to the Duchess of Lauderdale known as Ham in Surrey. Halifax said 'he might take what servants he pleased with him, but must be gone before ten'. James replied that he would rather return to Rochester, whereupon the three peers said they must first consult William, who had now arrived at Syon house, where James's younger brother and sister had been imprisoned when they were children. This conversation took place about midnight, but the emissaries assured James that he should have William's answer by nine next morning. They were as good as their word. His son-in-law raised no objection to his going to Rochester. Accompanied by two boat-loads of Dutch guards James set sail on a river barge at eleven in the morning; by four the same afternoon William himself arrived at St James's Palace. So the King was not allowed to meet his conqueror; and he never saw London again.

Owing to the time it took to embark James only got as far as Gravesend that night.[43] The next day he reached Rochester where he stayed for four days and was joined there by several officers who had resigned their commissions. Among them was James Graham of Claverhouse, Viscount Dundee, who said to the King: 'Sir, the question is whether you shall stay in England or go to France. My opinion is you should stay in England. 'Tis true your army is disbanded by your own authority. I will undertake to get 10,000 of them together and march through England with your standard at their head.' The King said he believed it might be done, but it would cause a civil war; he would not do such mischief to the English nation, which he loved 'and would soon come to their senses again'.[44]

It was ironical that while James was in Rochester he heard that the aged Sancroft, who had taken charge in London after the King left Whitehall for the first time, had now refused to serve William at all so long as James was under restraint. The Primate realized, so James's official biographer remarked

> that the Church of England, which had only been the Prince of Orange's stalking horse in this expedition, was like to reap no other benefit by it than the confusion of having deserted her celebrated doctrine of non-resistance and adherence to her Prince, and to be despised by those he had ruined her reputation to assist.[45]

Unquestionably this sentence reflected very precisely what James himself thought first and foremost about the causes of his own fall, but he failed to perceive that he himself was to blame for alienating the Anglican leaders who had welcomed back his brother in 1660 and had declared their loyalty to him during Monmouth's rebellion of 1685. Nevertheless James was right in thinking that William had not come to England primarily to protect the Church or peoples' liberties and properties, as he declared, but to ensure that the kingdom did not become the ally of the French King, who had so recently launched his third attack upon the peace of Europe. By sending his wife and child to France James had merely underlined William's impression — wrong though it was — that he was Louis XIV's obedient ally.

The house at Rochester backed on the river Medway. Evidently it was William's intention to allow his father-in-law to escape to France, for no guards were placed on duty at the back of the house while the captain in charge of the guard was a Roman Catholic. On 23 December James, accompanied by his son, the Duke of Berwick, was rowed down the Medway; they transferred to a pinnace near the mouth of the West Swale river and finally boarded a yacht that was waiting for them not far away. The wind was easterly and the voyage slow and difficult. On Monday 24 December the weather improved following the customary Christmas snow. At three o'clock next morning, after James had lapped up a midnight meal of fried bacon, the yacht anchored at Ambleteuse near Calais.[46] The news of her husband's safe arrival delighted Mary of Modena. It was Christmas Day in England, but Christmas was ten days over in France. Nevertheless his coming so soon presaged a happy new year for the Queen who welcomed James at the palace of St Germain put at their disposal by the King of France. Did James recall his youth? It was nearly forty years earlier that as a young, handsome and promising prince he had set off from St Germain to serve under Marshal Turenne in the French army.

20.

Retreat from Ireland

The self-exiled King and Queen were courteously and generously welcomed in France. James was granted an income of about 200,000 francs a month, though he said he only needed half of that.[1] At the French Court he was given the precedence allowed to a reigning monarch. But the impression conveyed by the gossips at Versailles was that James was a tired old man more or less resigned to his fate and a bit of a bore with his escape stories. The Queen, on the other hand, at the age of thirty, was till thought to be lovely and animated enough to attract Louis XIV himself. He said of her: 'she was always a queen in her prosperity: in adversity she is an angel'. But to the general surprise she was faithful to her husband, who was twenty-six years older than herself.[2]

James appeared to accept the loss of his throne with dignity and without resentment against those of his servants who had not accompanied him into exile. He told his Secretaries of State, Middleton and Preston, that they need not follow him to France[3] and he remained friendly towards Dartmouth despite his comprehensive failure as a naval commander. If it is true that James was obstinate and proud when he ruled his three kingdoms, he was tempered by adversity. He was recognized in France as a good man, but it was thought improper that he should be contented with his lot, as indeed he was. He admired the many beautiful things to be seen in the palace of Versailles, such as the paintings, the porcelain china and the crystal glass.[4] Like all the Stuarts, he enjoyed hunting anywhere. One of the first letters he wrote from St Germain to Lord Dartmouth was to ask him to discover whether William of Orange would be willing to let him have his coaches and horses sent over to him. These were promptly dispatched together with all his hunting equipment and plate.[5] So James was able to show himself as a

264

sportsman, a connoisseur and a devout Catholic; when he visited Paris it was either to meet Jesuits or to pay his respects to Mère Agnes of the Carmelites, who had played a major part in his conversion. It is pretty certain that after the traumatic experiences he had been through he would have been willing to pass his time in honoured retirement unless anything unexpected turned up. But neither Louis XIV nor Mary of Modena wanted him to lay down his arms.

Of the three kingdoms that James had abandoned Ireland was the only one where the population was still largely loyal to him. James, however, showed no urge to go there to raise his battle standard once more. On 12 January 1689 he wrote to Lord Tyrconnel to say that he hoped his Lord Deputy would be able to defend himself against William and to support his interest there at least until the summer; meanwhile he would try to persuade the French King to provide him with muskets. Tyrconnel, however, begged James to consider whether he could with honour stay in France when he might possess a kingdom of his own 'plentiful in all things for human life'.[6] To that view Louis XIV gave his assent.

The French were by then absorbed in yet another campaign against the Habsburg Emperor and were fighting their way into Germany, although it was not until May that they were officially at war with the United Netherlands and Great Britain. Naturally Louis wanted James to create a diversion in his favour. Ireland was obviously a suitable terrain, lying on the western flank of Europe, where trouble could be created for William of Orange which might even prevent him from interfering with Louis's still unsatiated ambitions. On 20 January 1689 James was invited to supper at Louis XIV's palace of Marly, which was much nearer to St Germain than was Versailles. There Louis XIV persuaded him to go to Ireland as Tyrconnel wished.[7] Tyrconnel had not asked for French soldiers to fight there; he knew he would have little difficulty in enlisting Irishmen; what he wanted was money and arms: he specified 500,000 crowns, 16,000 muskets and 12,000 swords.[8] These requests tuned in with Louis's own plans. He therefore provided James with money and arms and a number of military advisers, headed by Marshal Rosen, a professional officer from the Baltic. Little had James anticipated when he arrived in France that he would have to leave it again so soon. After a tearful parting from his wife he set out for Brest and landed safely at Kinsale on 12 March. Louis XIV's last words to him were: 'I witness your departure with sorrow; however I desire never to see you again; but if you do return, be assured that you will find me just the same as when you leave me now.'[9]

James was accompanied to Ireland by Count D'Avaux, who had previously distinguished himself as the French diplomatic representative at The Hague, and was now attached as special ambassador to the King of England. To his dispatches we owe a clear, if somewhat jaundiced, picture of James's behaviour. From the outset D'Avaux was convinced that James was by no means enthusiastic about conquering the whole of Ireland so as to secure a base there for further operations: what he wanted to do was to invade Scotland, the home of his ancestors, where the Duke of Gordon still held Edinburgh Castle in his name and Lord Dundee was arousing the highlanders for him in the spirit of Montrose; after that, he hoped to move back into England as soon as possible. There although William and Mary had been named as monarchs on 13 February, as if James were already dead, a great deal of opposition to this step had been shown by the ruling classes and the new sovereigns were required to give their assent to a Declaration of Rights which limited their authority. Thus for James Ireland was simply a ladder to higher things.

Tyrconnel, James's Roman Catholic Lord Deputy, who went to Cork to meet him on 14 March, where he was created a duke, did not, so D'Avaux reported, think the situation in England was as favourable as his master imagined.[10] What Tyrconnel wanted to do first was to make the King's position in Dublin, where there was a large Protestant minority, absolutely secure and afterwards to conquer Ulster where the Protestants outnumbered the Catholics. For this purpose the Duke thought a military force of about 30,000 men was necessary, but James aimed at an army of 40,000 so that he could send part of it to help Dundee in Scotland. Though the Irish for the most part made good soldiers time was needed to train them in the use of the arms provided by the French Government. But James hoped that Ulster could be quickly conquered, a rebellion against William and Mary could succeed in Scotland, and that he could then ask for a number of French regiments to join up with the Irish and Scottish regiments to invade England.

All this savoured of an old man in a hurry, which D'Avaux did not care for at all. He took the view that James should, before he did anything else, secure the whole kingdom of Ireland and then perhaps

4,000 men could be spared for Scotland where many of the high-landers at least were loyal to James's cause.[11] From the French point of view D'Avaux was undoubtedly right, for William could hardly afford to have a hostile Ireland on his flank when he left England to fight the French in the Netherlands. To Louis XIV D'Avaux expressed his anger with the conduct of King James and the support given to him by John Drummond Earl of Melfort who had accompanied him to Ireland as his Secretary of State.[12] Melfort succeeded in making himself extremely unpopular with the Irish, particularly with Tyrconnel, while as a Scot he naturally sympathized with James's urge to intervene in that kingdom, long ruled by the Stuarts.

The first thing that James did after he arrived in Dublin on 24 March was to publish a proclamation on religion. In this he insisted that his aim was, and always had been, to procure liberty of conscience in all his three kingdoms. Of that D'Avaux at least approved because his instructions had been to ensure that James did not alienate the Irish Protestants; for if he did so, he was obviously going to have a difficult time in Ulster. On the other hand, the French ambassador did not want James to risk his life by fighting in Ulster himself. But James wanted to get on as quickly as he could; so on 8 April he left Dublin for Charlemont in Ulster at the beginning of a visit of inspection. The Ulster Protestants were concentrated in two places: Londonderry in the north and Enniskillin in the south; they had evacuated Coleraine and Dungannon; their garrisons, together with those of one or two smaller towns in Ulster, went to swell the defenders of Londonderry. James hoped that if only he showed himself at Londonderry, the city would surrender.

Ten days after he left Dublin James reached the outskirts of Londonderry, accompanied by Rosen, his chief military adviser, Melfort and D'Avaux. Tyrconnel remained in Dublin where he occupied himself in training and arming a sizeable force. James spent two days outside Londonderry and four times summoned it to surrender, promising to pardon all those who gave themselves up.[13] But George Walker, a Protestant rector from Tyrone — 'a fierce minister of the Gospel, being of the true Cromwellian or Cameronian stamp' — who raised a regiment to fight for William and Mary, had inspired the garrison to stronger resistance (later he became its Governor) while a certain Captain James Hamilton had succeeded in bringing into the city money and arms and a reinforcement of 2,000 men from England. Pushed hard by Walker, Colonel Robert Lundy, who had been appointed Governor of Londonderry before James had left England, gave up all idea of surrender and swore to uphold the cause of the new monarchs against any Irish army fighting for James. He and Melfort soon realized that the garrison at Londonderry was 'very obstinate' and that the city must be subjected to a formal siege.[14] So on 6 May they returned to Dublin.

Here James was greeted by good news. He learned that a French convoy, escorted by twenty-four warships, which was bringing over more expert French officers (including engineers), money, arms, ammunition and Jacobite troops, had docked in Bantry Bay near Cork where it had been attacked by Admiral Arthur Herbert, whose duty it was to prevent French help reaching Ireland. A battle took place on 1 May; Herbert was compelled to draw off and the men and supplies in the convoy were safely landed. It is said that when the news of this defeat of the English by the French navy was reported to James, he observed patriotically: 'It is the first time then.'[15] The other cheering fact for James was a harmonious meeting of the Irish Parliament in Dublin on 7 May, to which he delivered yet another declaration in favour of liberty of conscience: he explained that he had 'always stood for liberty of conscience and for doing to others what they do for you.'[16] It was this liberty of conscience, he added, which his enemies inside and outside the kingdom of Ireland feared so much. The Earl of Melfort was able to report on the following day that the Irish Parliament would 'do all the King asks of them'.[17] James was duly voted £20,000 a month and the French were thanked for their help. But James was careful not to commit himself to the repeal of the Act of Settlement, brought in at Charles II's restoration, because he did not want to antagonize the Irish Protestants who were holding up his military plans in Ulster.

Although, therefore, James had reasons for satisfaction and hope, the French regarded him as volatile, sometimes going too quickly and sometimes too slowly. In early May D'Avaux told Louis XIV that everything was in a bad state in Ireland and James ought to be pressed to restore order. He suggested that his Queen should be persuaded to write to her husband in this sense: otherwise, unless French troops were sent over, he doubted whether the country would be able to resist an invasion by William if it came about. Furthermore, D'Avaux thought it absurd of James to harp on sending reinforcements to Scotland later in the year when most of his army was tied up trying to subdue Londonderry.[18] When D'Avaux begged James to seize the Protestants in Dublin, whom the ambassador regarded as a Trojan horse, and to confiscate the estates of rebels to pay for the upkeep of the Irish army, James merely replied that he had neglected nothing that he could do legally.[19] Louis told D'Avaux at the beginning of June that he was disappointed that Londonderry had not yet fallen and agreed that James would be unwise to move any of his troops to Scotland or England before he was absolute master of Ireland.[20] Louvois, the French Minister of War, had no wish to dispatch regiments to Ireland when they were needed on the European mainland, while he was careful to see that the arms that were provided for the Irish were surplus to his King's requirements elsewhere, the muskets and swords he sent being of particularly poor quality. Thus even though James had a friendly Parliament in Dublin and was able to recruit a fair-sized army, his material handicaps were real. It was superficial to blame his lack of military progress on the fact that he was always looking over his shoulder to see what was happening in Scotland and England.

By mid-summer James's position in Ireland had seriously deteriorated. At the end of July three provision ships succeeded in forcing their way into Loch Foyle, thus giving welcome relief to the harassed garrison of Londonderry which, owing to the blockade under the command of Marshal Rosen, had been eating dogs and cats.[21] Rosen immediately raised the siege; a more aggressive attitude earlier might well have enabled him to capture the city; Rosen's only positive plan was to compel the garrison to surrender by frightening it through slaughtering captured Protestants in front of the walls; James vetoed this. Nor were James's troops any more triumphant at Enniskillin where at about the same time his commander there, Justin MacCarthy, Lord Mountcashel, was driven off, wounded and taken prisoner. The only consolation for James was that Lord Dundee had in this same month won a victory on his behalf at Killiecrankie south of Stirling. In the letter that Dundee wrote to James describing his 'great victory', he assured him that Scotland was generally well disposed towards him, but went on to say 'For God's sake assist us with Irish troops, especially horse and dragoons.'[22] That was impossible; Dundee died of the wounds he had sustained during the battle; and just over three weeks later the highlanders fighting gallantly for James were defeated by a Presbyterian army at Dunkeld. Disappointed of his hopes

269

from Scotland, James had to turn his mind back to Ireland.

Soon after the relief of Londonderry the septuagenarian general, the Duke of Schomberg, sent over from England by King William III, landed with 10,000 men, largely raw recruits but stiffened by a few Dutch soldiers, at Bangor near Belfast. By now James's situation was considered by some of his military advisers to have become so desperate that they counselled him to withdraw to Athlone and the line of the river Shannon, which would have meant surrendering three-quarters of Ireland to his enemies. James was made of sterner stuff. He determined to get rid of Marshal Rosen, who, as he wrote in the ninth volume of his memoirs, 'would never give any advice but retire and avoid fighting';[23] he also recognized that the Earl of Melfort had aroused the animosity of everyone in Ireland, so he sent him back to France. At the same time he dispatched Lord Dover to ask Louis XIV to recall Rosen 'as one, after having done what he did at Londonderry, was incapable of serving us usefully'; and the French King was also to be asked not only for more and better muskets and firelocks, swords and barrels of gunpowder, but also for money and 6,000 French infantrymen.[24] James himself resolved to confront Schomberg on the borders of Ulster.

Schomberg, after leaving Belfast, had advanced south by way of Carrickfergus, Newry, which had been burned to the ground by the young Duke of Berwick, and Dundalk. But he was in some difficulty because his supply ships had not yet arrived there owing to storms and he possessed little artillery. He therefore decided to encamp a mile north of Dundalk, which he fortified and where he was protected by the river Fane. At the beginning of September James reached Drogheda, twenty miles south of Dundalk, with one cavalry regiment and proceeded to build up an army capable of fighting Schomberg. He then moved to Ardee, a town roughly half way between Drogheda and Dundalk, and tried to provoke the Marshal to battle. According to D'Avaux, James's forces outnumbered those of Schomberg, but even when James's army moved forward to within three miles of Dundalk Schomberg refused to be tempted into fighting;[25] for he knew that many of his troops were ill trained and that his supplies were inadequate. His intention was to stay where he was until the winter, counting on William of Orange to bring over a better army in the following year.

In letters that James wrote to his ambassador in France, Lord Waldegrave, he expressed optimism. It was, he wrote, 'of great consequence that this war should be speedily ended'.[26] He thought he had a fine army with which he wanted urgently to subdue Ireland and then transport it directly to England where he heard that his friends were in good heart. Unhappily for him, however, Schomberg was determined to protract the war. Without assistance from France James felt that he was being bogged down as autumn lengthened. He therefore did everything he could to press Louis XIV into aiding him immediately: not only did he send over Lord Dover to the French Court, but both Waldegrave and Melfort joined in putting his case there. Even D'Avaux, who was habitually critical of James, sounded a note of cheerfulness, saying that provided the King had sufficient supplies for his army and enforced discipline upon it, he should be able to maintain himself in Ireland.[27]

Feeling then that this side-show was worth keeping on, Louis agreed to send over French troops either that November or in the early spring to strengthen James, provided that they were exchanged for a similar number of Irish soldiers. The decision was also taken to replace Rosen by the Count of Lauzun, a self-made man with little military experience but plenty of ambition, disliked both by the French Minister of War, Louvois, who was glad to get rid of him, and by the Duke of Tyrconnel, so hardly a good choice. It was Tyrconnel, who, since the departure of Melfort and the defeat of Rosen at Londonderry, had become James's principal adviser and had induced him to confront Schomberg instead of retiring behind the Shannon.[28] But the campaigning season was then nearly over. Heavy medical casualties weakened both the opposing armies. D'Avaux began carping at James again; he told Louvois that 'the King of England does not behave with the nobility of heart that one expects not from a king but from a simple gentleman'.[29] He added that James disputed and quibbled over the officers and men that were to be sent to France. Clearly James was frustrated, first by his failure to bring Schomberg to battle, secondly by the limitations on the help that he had hitherto been given by the French, particularly in poor weapons. On 8 November he returned to Dublin, feeling tired of trying to defend Ireland and still nursing the dream that if only he could invade England, his subjects would be found disillusioned by the Dutch tyrant, now absorbed in making war upon France (a Grand Alliance of the Emperor, the Dutch and the English had been concluded the previous May) and would welcome back their old peaceful master.

During the winter of 1689-90 James made arrangements for the next campaign. He was in a fairly cheerful mood because towards the end of the previous campaign Patrick Sarsfield, an experienced Anglo-Irish officer from the Pale, had inflicted a considerable defeat on William's allies at Sligo, which was the gateway to Connaught; Schomberg had evacuated Dundalk and it was occupied by two battalions sent there by James; Charlemont, a key town in Ulster, was still held by the Jacobites; and the promise of French troops arriving in Ireland in the spring was firm. In January 1690 D'Avaux informed Louis XIV that it was hoped to begin the next campaign early and that supply dumps were being established with a view to attacking Schomberg in north-east Ulster.[30] It was not believed at that time that William would send large reinforcements to Ireland; he was thought to be too occupied with English affairs and with the war on the mainland of Europe to come there himself. The English navy had not been notably successful in cutting off Ireland from France; Sir Cloudsley Shovell, who had replaced Herbert in charge of these operations, informed King William's Secretary of State, the Earl of Nottingham, that King James was 'very well and vaunt mightiley of his suckers coming from France', while people were bringing olive branches of good-will, saying that his (Shovell's) fleet had sustained 'incredible losses', partly through the weather and partly at the hands of the French.[31]

But the truth was that James was over-optimistic. He spent part of his time in Dublin, where his courtiers were said to have engaged in debaucheries, and partly in Kilkenny in southern Ireland to which he retreated to avoid the infectious diseases which had spread through his army at the end of the previous campaign. Furthermore, each side was delayed in taking the field by the need to build up their forces. D'Avaux, who was recalled to France after Lauzun had been appointed James's leading military adviser in Rosen's place, because he was not expected to get along with the newcomer, expressed great anxiety about the quality of the Irish soldiers who were going to be swapped for 6,000 French infantrymen.[32] In fact the Irish made excellent soldiers when properly equipped and trained and were to serve Louis XIV admirably in his wars first against King William III and later against Queen Anne's commander-in-chief, the Duke of Marlborough. Five regiments from France landed at Cork during March, of which three were French and the other two hired mercenaries, most of them Protestants, which was rumoured not to be to

James's taste, although that hardly accorded with his pronounce-
ments in the Irish Parliament on liberty of conscience. In the same
month Schomberg was strengthened by the arrival of 7,000 Danes —
this was a polyglot war if ever there was one. The new French
general, although he was appointed ambassador as well as chief
military adviser to James, did not speak a word of English and had to
leave the training of his troops for warfare in Ireland to the Duke of
Tyrconnel.

By now William had reached the conclusion that he himself must
go to Ireland, for the aged Schomberg had not distinguished himself
and he wanted to remove this thorn from his side. He was unhappy
about leaving Queen Mary in charge in London because he did not
altogether trust the Lords Justices he left there to advise her, while
he wrote to his friend, the Prince of Waldeck, another ageing general,
saying 'I am in despair when I think I can be of no use to the common
cause [i.e. the Grand Alliance] while I am in Ireland. During that
time you must count me as one dead and do the best you can.'[33] He
was determined, however, not to handicap himself by lack of resources; he obtained large sums of money with which to pay his
troops, brought over artillery which James lacked and collected an
army (including Schomberg's men) estimated to number 45,000. His
enemy is generally said to have had only 25,000 men, though a list is
in existence which suggests that James had almost as many as
William, but some of these troops were garrisoning other parts of the
kingdom, while King William drew nearly all his soldiers together
under his command.[34] In any case, apart from numbers, James's
army was less well supplied and equipped than William's.

On 12 June 1690 William left Hoylake near Chester and arrived in
Ireland with some 15,000 men and guns, carried over by a fleet of
300 vessels, which were disembarked at Carrickfergus on the 14th.
On the 16th James set off for Dundalk from Dublin, still feeling
reasonably hopeful. After all, there might be an insurrection in
England during William's absence or his army might be cut off by the
French fleet. Lauzun, for his part, was not confident and disagree-
ments arose over what was best to be done. The Governor of
Charlemont, the Jacobites' last foothold in Ulster, had surrendered
on 12 May, while James's son, the Duke of Berwick, had suffered a
setback when he had attempted an incursion into Schomberg's
winter-quarters. James's own plan was to devastate the country
south of Ulster with a view to depriving William's men and horses of

food and forage.[35] But the plan was not of much value since William
had made such elaborate preparations that he did not need to live off
the country, while according to James, Irish Catholics who had fled
from Ulster 'brought such prodigious flocks of cattle with them as to
eat up the grass and meadows of other provinces and destroyed even
a great share of the corn too'.[36] So James's army also had its supply
difficulties. The King then decided to withdraw from Dundalk to
Drogheda, thirty miles farther south, and man the line of the river
Boyne which flows west and then south-west from the Irish Sea and
was arguably the only feasible defensive position between Ulster and
Dublin. The Jacobite army crossed the river without difficulty and
concentrated chiefly on the hills south of the village of Oldbridge
(three miles west of Drogheda) where the river could be forded at
low tide and therefore was reckoned to be the place where William
was most likely to attack. But to cross a deep river in the face of
enemy fire was always dangerous and dips in the ground made it hard
to discover how James's army was distributed. William had waited a
few days to collect his artillery; then he sent his army forward in two
columns, one directly south through Dundalk, the other making a
detour south-westwards through Armagh so that it could outflank
James's army if it tried to retreat to Dublin.[37]

James stationed himself in the churchyard at the village of Donore
about a mile south of Oldbridge from which he watched William's
army being deployed. From there he saw a large detachment, commanded by Schomberg's son, marching upstream with the intention
of outflanking or threatening to outflank his own army; learning
that the next bridge beyond Oldbridge was broken, this force
managed to cross by a ford at a village called Rosnaree, five or six
miles up the river from Drogheda. The manoeuvre was in part at least
a feint; William's major thrust was to be against Oldbridge. It was
now that James made a grave mistake; he thought that the bulk of
William's army was being shifted to the right: he therefore ordered
most of his own troops to march to the left so as to conform with the
enemy's movement. He and Lauzun moved left too, while Tyrconnel
with part of the cavalry and two brigades of infantry, approximately
one-third of James's army, stayed at Oldbridge, where in fact the
main assault came. The best of William's infantry, led by his Dutch
Guards, forded the river, some plunged up to their waists and others
up to their necks in the water. As they reached the other side of the
Boyne they were charged by Tyrconnel's Irish cavalry who, stimu-

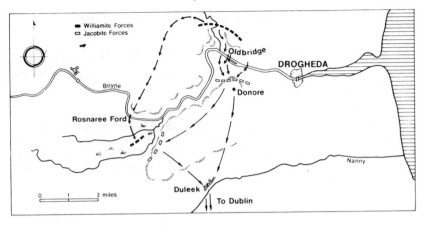

Map of the Battle of the Boyne

lated by a ration of brandy, fought bravely enough. Both Marshal Schomberg and George Walker, the hero of the defence of Londonderry, were killed in the attack, but once the Dutch Guards had succeeded in forcing their way on to the southern bank they formed up and fired by platoons, while William himself, finding a ford lower down, led his cavalry forward. After two hours or more of fierce struggle Tyrconnel's men were overwhelmed.

Meanwhile James himself, accompanied by Lauzun, who had been pessimistic from the start, were in danger of being enveloped on both sides, that is to say by the Dutch infantry on their right and the detachment under the younger Schomberg on their left, which had forded the river at Rosnaree. Except for the French, who kept good order, most of James's army retreated in panic, 'like sheep flying before the wolf', wrote one who was present,[38] the Irish on both wings converging in confusion at the narrow crossing of the river Nanny, which flowed five miles south of the Boyne, at the village of Duleek on the only road to Dublin. James himself, under pressure from Lauzun, rode as fast as he could to Dublin where he arrived at ten o'clock that evening. He was very silent and dejected and seemed to be stunned. He told Lady Tyrconnel that all was lost.[39] After consulting such members of his Privy Council as were there, he resolved to return to France. William was expected to reach the Irish capital on the following day: so early next morning James rode away to Wexford. Before he left he gave strict instructions that Dublin was not to be set on fire nor plundered. A French frigate awaited him at Kinsale. But it was not until 10 July that he landed safely at Brest.

Why did James fight and why did he lose? His official biographer says — and it is reasonable to believe that his account was based directly on James's own memoirs — that what induced him

> to hazard a battle on this inequality of forces [which, it is suggested, was about one to two] was that if he did not there, he must lose all without a stroke, and be obliged to quit Dublin and all Munster, and retire behind the Shannon, and so be reduced to the province of Connaught, where having no magazines, he could not subsist very long, it being the worst corn country in Ireland.[40]

Certainly the idea, which had been pressed on him by some of his military advisers, of converting Connaught into a defensive bastion was a counsel of despair. Historians have tended to make a mockery of James at the Boyne on the ground that he ran away so fast. Obviously it would have been more heroic to have died at the head of his loyal Irishmen. But at least he had taken a bold decision in fighting a battle at all which, had he been victorious, would surely have won back his lost thrones for him. It can be argued that he ought to have fought that battle against William at Salisbury in 1688, not at the Boyne in 1690. The actual losses at the Boyne in killed and wounded were not high in relation to the size of the two armies and the disparity between them has clearly been exaggerated by Jacobite scribes. Where James went wrong was in the selection of his military advisers — as he had been wrong with his civilian advisers like Sunderland and Petre. It was James himself who had asked for the inexperienced Lauzun to replace Rosen, chiefly, it seems, because Lauzun had been extremely helpful in getting the Queen and her son away from Whitehall to France in December 1688. James's son, the Duke of Berwick, was to live to be a famous and successful French general, but he was only nineteen at the time, though he fought gallantly in his father's cause. Tyrconnel seems to have had the right idea when he stayed at Oldbridge rather than follow the rest of the army up the river.

However the fact remains that the Boyne was too easily fordable all the way along and so did not prove a very serious military obstacle. It has also been contended that if a strong garrison had been posted at Drogheda it might have checked William's offensive.[41] Had James still been the young lieutenant-general who fought by the side of Turenne, he might have recognized all this, though once the fighting had begun it was difficult to control the battle. Few men are flexible in their middle fifties and it is always easy to be wise after the event. Those of James's courtiers who asserted, as they did, that he ought to have rallied his army, fought a delaying action and awaited better days omitted to consider one important factor, sea power. It was because the Anglo-Dutch fleets held the mastery at sea that William was able to land his large expeditionary force safely in Ireland during the middle of June, even though a fortnight later, on the day before the battle of the Boyne was fought, they suffered a humiliating defeat by the French navy off Beachy Head in Sussex. John Churchill, now Earl of Marlborough, could not have subdued southern Ireland for his new master in a campaign that lasted only six weeks during the following autumn had it not been for this command of the sea. Finally, after the French navy was crushed at the Battle of La Hogue in 1692, James's hopes, such as they were, of regaining his lost kingdoms by war were doomed.

21.

The Last Years

The campaign in Ireland did not end, as King William hoped it would, when he entered Dublin on 6 July 1690. The severe proclamation that he published before he reached the Irish capital served only to stimulate Irish resistance. Though Waterford was quickly captured, William met with defiance at Limerick upon the Shannon and for the time being most of Munster and Connaught remained unsubdued. William's absence from England with the bulk of his army left Queen Mary II and her advisers extremely nervous. In Flanders William's friend, the Prince of Waldeck, was defeated by Louis XIV's ablest general, the Duke of Luxembourg, ten days before the battle of the Boyne, while the French victory at sea off Beachy Head exposed the defences of the English Channel. After James got back to France, he argued when he saw Louis XIV for the first time, that now was the propitious moment for an invasion of England, which under the circumstances would be perfectly feasible. But the French King was uninterested; he was not a marine animal. He had, it was said, 'arranged France as if she had been a huge fortress in the heart of Europe';[1] he was accustomed to wars being fought on the fields of Flanders or on the plains of northern Italy, not in the English Channel. As to James, he had not been enthusiastic about going to Ireland in the first place; but Louis thought of that as a means for usefully distracting William's gaze from the Netherlands. Learning that Tyrconnel wanted to conclude peace and that Lauzun counselled the withdrawal of the remaining French troops from the island, Louis was content to write it off as a bad debt. To a large extent James agreed with this view: he was glad to forget the battle of the Boyne.

James thought of his fate in ideological terms. As soon as he first arrived in France at the end of December 1688 he had written to

Pope Innocent XI to say that as not only his own cause but that of religion was at stake as a result of William's usurpation of the throne — for William, he asserted, had permitted churches to be plundered and demolished and the very houses of the ambassadors of Catholic rulers to be pillaged — 'we have no small hope that divine Providence will shortly restore our fortunes' and that Catholic princes would unite in his aid.[2] Unhappily for him, after the formation of the Grand Alliance Catholic princes were fighting one another. Both the Holy Roman Emperor and the King of Spain were in conflict with Louis XIV. Thus though James repeated his appeal for help to Pope Alexander VIII,[3] who succeeded Innocent XI in 1690, he realized that he could count for certain on no other aid than that of the French whose resources were pretty fully extended in what was to be known as the Nine Years War. Furthermore the rapidity of James's retreat from Ireland, which was owing not so much to personal cowardice as to disillusionment with the Irish, lowered his prestige at the French Court. The brilliant feat by Patrick Sarsfield, the victor of Sligo, in reinforcing and provisioning Limerick so that William was compelled to abandon its siege in August merely underlined by contrast James's own ineffectiveness as a commander in Ireland.

We owe to Elizabeth Charlotte, the second wife of Louis XIV's brother, some caustic and revealing remarks about James at this time. Elizabeth Charlotte was a formidable character, a middle-aged German who generally wore a riding habit and a man's wig. She told her confidant, the Electress of Hanover (whose son was to succeed to the English throne in 1714) that 'the worthy James would not even make a good saint'; that the Duchess of Portsmouth had told her that Charles II had prophesied that his brother would lose his throne because of his religious bigotry and his soul through his 'unsightly wantons'.[4] The Duchess of Orleans is the sole source for the story that when James was in Ireland he had two 'frightful scarecrows' of mistresses with whom he was always carrying on. In another letter she wrote: 'I am sure the Queen would be glad if her husband never saw any ladies more beautiful than I am'; then, she thought, 'her mind would be at rest and not troubled with jealousy and dear King James would not get his ears boxed'.[5] She also related how her husband, 'Monsieur', had said to James: 'And has not your Majesty, who had such great wealth not built and furnished some beautiful palaces?' to which James answered that though he had had plenty of money, he spent it on 'great ships and cannons'. 'Yes', said his Queen, 'and a lot of good they did you.'[6] So, if one may trust the German princess's recollections, James must have felt as uncomfortable at home in St Germain as he did when he was in Versailles or Fontainebleau, the palace where he was invited every year as an autumn treat, aware no doubt of the courtiers sniggering at him. No wonder he turned for consolation to his religion.

Both James and his wife had their religious ports of call. Mary of Modena went to the nunnery, inhabited by the Daughters of the Visitation, at the village of Chaillot just outside Paris, which had been founded by James's mother. It was situated on a hill overlooking the Seine and had lovely gardens. Here, in rooms decorated for her by Louis XIV, Mary of Modena found peace away from her husband. Other paying guests were taken in; attached to the convent was a school, a carpet factory and farms. It must have made quite an agreeable change from St Germain. James's resort was much more severe, although Mary called it his 'Chaillot'. It was a monastery presided over by the Abbé Armand Jean du Plessis de Rancé de la Trappe, who had been a soldier and a scholar before he retired from the world to devote himself to the maximum austerities. The monastery was situated in a valley where mists gathered which bred fevers. James visited it for the first time after his return from Ireland. The Abbé was clearly a powerful and influential figure. James went to stay at the monastery whenever his wife was at Chaillot and in between his visits he corresponded regularly with the Abbé. James was told that he was right in thinking that kings had more obstacles to overcome and more temptations to fight against than ordinary Christians and, on the other hand, the Abbé agreed that holiness was entirely compatible with the exercise of power. James was also assured that one did not have to be a monk or a friar to be a true Christian. Moreover the Abbé tried to cheer him with the hope that, like other kings, such as Edward the Confessor and Louis IX, he might in the end be sanctified. Thus he could resign himself to God's purpose 'if He wills you to purchase by the loss of limited and transitory greatness a glory of infinite duration and value'.[7]

But James still had some hopes of worldly gains. William III did not endear himself to his English subjects; for this reason men like the Earl of Marlborough, Lord Godolphin, Lord Dartmouth and others thought it worth their while to insure themselves in the event of another Stuart restoration by writing friendly, if cautious, letters

to the King across the water, assuring him that should an opportunity arise they would serve him to the best of their ability. James
was not over-impressed by such double-dealing but recognized that
if these soldiers and statesmen lost William's favour they might assist
him in the end. James was also cheered by the news from Ireland
where although Galway had been lost, Limerick and Athlone still
held out along the line of the Shannon. James contributed part of his
limited funds to the Irish defence against William's new commander-
in-chief, Lieutenant-General Ginkel, a Dutch officer who had fought
at the battle of the Boyne and the siege of Limerick in 1690.
Furthermore, a new French general, Marshal St Ruth, accompanied
by lieutenant-generals, reached Limerick in May 1691 with arms,
ammunition and other supplies, though their arrival was greeted
with limited enthusiasm by the Duke of Tyrconnel. James also
started issuing letters of marque to privateers based in France or the
Netherlands to prey upon English trade.[8]

James's hopes from Ireland were soon disappointed. Ginkel defeated St Ruth and by taking the town of Athlone undermined the
whole Irish position along the Shannon. St Ruth was killed in a
battle fought at Aughrim south of Athlone; Tyrconnel died; and in
the autumn Limerick surrendered upon terms. Sarsfield, the ablest
Irish general, whom James created Earl of Lucan, realized that the
situation was hopeless, but stood out for permission to transport the
Irish troops under his command to France where they might serve
James more usefully than in their own country. It is estimated that
12,000 Irish soldiers altogether were brought over by Lucan at the
end of 1691. James went to Brittany to greet them.[9] So at least
James had an army of his own; for the French Government under-
took to pay for it. Stationed, as they were in the following year, at
Boulogne, they constituted a genuine threat to William.

During 1691 the French had successes on two fronts in their war
against the Allies. Both Mons and Nice were captured. Louis XIV
himself assumed charge of the siege of Mons (though the real work
was done by the famous Marshal Vauban) and had taken his morganatic wife, Madame de Maintenon, along with him for company
and to watch the siege. James was disappointed that he too had not
been invited on the jaunt; he had to turn to the Abbé de la Trappe for
consolation and sympathy.[10] At the end of the year Louis XIV's War
Minister, Louvois, died and in the following year his Navy Minister,
Seignelai. So Louis himself became involved in plans for the cam-

paign of 1692 more closely than ever before. The decision was taken to besiege Namur, a powerful fortress at the junction of the Meuse and the Sambre, sufficiently near to the United Netherlands to frighten the Dutch were it to fall. At the same time an army was gathered at the Cap de la Hogue, consisting of English and Irish soldiers as well as French, with a view to the invasion of England.

James felt now indeed was the right time to strike. At the beginning of the year William III had dismissed his ablest English general, the Earl of Marlborough, who, he believed, had been plotting against him. As has been noticed, during the previous campaign Marlborough had entered into correspondence with James, while, under the influence of Marlborough and his Countess, Princess Anne wrote a contrite letter to her father, a letter which took five months to reach him. On 5 May Marlborough was arrested and sent to the Tower of London; at the same time Anne and the Countess were exiled from the Court. Melfort, still James's Secretary of State, had written to the Cardinal of Norfolk at Rome from St Germain to say that 'those of England are more divided than ever . . . and we hope to fish some good in these troubled waters.'[11] At the beginning of the year James put Berwick in charge of the first troop of Guards and Patrick Sarsfield, Earl of Lucan, commanded the second troop. In the spring James himself went to the Contentin peninsula and ordered Major-General William Buchan to march to Dunkirk with such Scottish officers and soldiers as he had collected with the aim of landing in or near Aberdeenshire. The main thrust, however, was to be directed against England. James envisaged Marlborough directing an army, Russell (who had also sent pleasant messages to him) taking charge of the fleet and Princess Anne rallying the Church of England all in his cause.[12] At the Cap de la Hogue James drew up an enormous declaration dated 20 April 'in the eighth year of our reign' promising all sorts of benefits if his loving subjects would but resume their allegiance to him.[13]

His aspirations were soon blighted. The invasions of England and Scotland required command of the sea. Louis XIV had ordered the Count de Tourville, victor of Beachy Head, to seek out the enemy's navy wherever it was and fight it. De Tourville, however, was outnumbered by the combined English and Dutch fleets. Russell, who commanded the English, forgot all about the vague promises he had made to James and fought the French with gusto; though a battle off Barfleur was indecisive, on 8 May, the next day, de

Tourville lost twelve of his best ships while attempting to shelter inshore at La Hogue. James himself watched English sailors boarding and destroying the French vessels and, forgetting his own plight, exclaimed: 'Ah! none but my brave English could do so brave an action!'[14]

After this defeat of the French navy James came gradually to despair of his own fortunes, even though King William had the worst of the fighting on land in the Netherlands, losing Namur and being beaten at the battles of Steenkirk and Landen. James concentrated on issuing propaganda and encouraging privateers. In July 1692 Melfort wrote:

> The King has resolved to govern by the known laws of the kingdom, to consult with his parliament on all things relating to the establishment of peace and quiet in his kingdoms, to maintain the liberties and properties of his subjects, to protect the Protestant religion and to obtain liberty of conscience for dissenters.[15]

But James still had to spend the eighth year of his reign in exile in the kingdom of England's enemy in war; he had left his good resolutions too late. As the King told the Abbé de la Trappe: 'We have not yet suffered enough for our sins, I mean myself and my subjects.'[16]

During the next three years James devoted himself to his domestic affairs and to his religion. In April before he went to the Cap de la Hogue James rather pathetically invited the members of his Privy Council, the Speaker of the House of Commons, the Lady Mayoress of London and other notabilities to come and witness the Queen's labour and the birth of his next child, who was expected in the middle of May;[17] he had also learnt that lesson too late. A daughter, named Louise Mary, was duly born in June and was to die of smallpox when she was twenty. James conferred the knighthood of the Garter on the youthful Prince of Wales, apologizing for the fact that the ceremony could not be carried out at Windsor. He himself settled down at St Germain on an income of 600,000 francs a year, provided by the French King, eschewed extravagances and gave what help he could to his fellow exiles and retainers many of whom were poverty-striken. Mary of Modena vainly sought the help of Madame de Maintenon to obtain more money from the French King and did what she could herself by selling some of her jewels.[18] The Irish, who had originally come over to France to fight for James, were absorbed into the French army at contest with the Grand Alliance. Turning his mind away from mundane things, James started composing letters of spiritual advice for the benefit of his elder legitimate son, while his ablest but illegitimate son, Berwick, went off to fight for the French in Flanders where he thought very little of William's generalship. James was equally pleased with the loyalty and faithfulness of Berwick's younger brother, Henry Fitzjames, whom he created Baron of Romney, Earl of Rochford and Duke of Albemarle — for titles at least were cheap.

The Jacobites were now divided between Compounders and Non-Compounders. The Compounders — many of whom lived in England or Scotland, though occasionally some of them managed to pay secret visits to St Germain — favoured the King who made every attractive concession he could think of to bring his subjects back to the service of the hereditary monarchy; the Non-Compounders were against soothing promises and still aimed to reinstate James by war. It has been said that the Non-Compounders tended to be in control because they had the closest access to James and Mary.[19] But Melfort, who headed the Non-Compounders, was as much disliked in France as he had been in Scotland and Ireland and was twice dismissed (but rewarded for his past services with a dukedom), while the Earl of Middleton, a Compounder, managed to escape from England to be restored as James's principal Secretary of State. It is true that Roman Catholics held several offices in the Jacobite Court, but James also had to employ non-Catholics at St Germain as most of the eldest and most distinguished members of the old Catholic nobility had not followed him into exile. Middleton remained a Protestant and so also did Bevil Skelton, his Comptroller, and Sir Edward Herbert, his Lord Chancellor. The declarations that James published in 1692 and 1693 were obviously influenced by the Compounders.

At the end of 1694 William's wife and James's daughter, Queen Mary II, died of smallpox. This gave a fillip to the Non-Compounders, for Mary had been much more popular than her husband with the English and William's subjects were tiring of the long European war in which he personally had achieved little military glory. Now seemed the moment to resume the fight against him on behalf of the exiled King. James sent a message to his supporters in England, headed by Sir George Berkeley, giving them permission to rise and make war on William, 'the usurper of our throne', but warned them that the troops that might be spared from France would be insufficient without the active help of his own subjects.[20] Berwick then went off on a secret visit to Berkeley — which was brave of him as he had been attainted for treason by the English Parliament in the previous year. He brought back a report that the Jacobite sympathizers stood ready to raise cavalry regiments on James's behalf, while a proposal was adumbrated to kidnap or assassinate William when he was in the country. As soon as Berwick returned with this news James sent him to Louis at Marly while he himself went to Calais in February 1696 to wait on events. Here he commissioned officers with the French Marshal d'Harcourt (later to be the French ambassador in Madrid) as his Captain-General and the Irish Catholic, Richard Hamilton, a nephew of the Duke of Ormonde, as his second-in-command.[21] However the French King, who was busily occupied in the Netherlands, rejected the idea of a full-scale expedition to England — even though the Jacobites there pared down their demands from 30,000 to 10,000 men — but did allocate a small force to join James and his son at Calais in case a rebellion against William should in fact take place.

The scheme, which never looked hopeful, broke down because the conspirators refused to take part in an insurrection until James landed with troops from France, while Louis XIV would not sanction any fresh attempt at invasion unless James could guarantee that his supporters would first seize ports on his behalf where troops could disembark safely. James might well have remembered that exactly the same dilemma had occurred in 1658-9 when the King of Spain had given conditional undertakings to assist Charles II's restoration.

So James returned to his devotions, 'convinced', as his biographer wrote, 'that Providence had marked out no other way for his sanctification except suffering'.[22] Only if his subjects invited him to return would he consider taking action again and then less for his own interests than those of his son, the Prince of Wales. For himself he preferred to resume his religious reflections and pious scribblings:

> Sure there was never a more dismal prospect of affairs in Christendom than now [he wrote] to see it involved in almost universal war and the generality so insensible of the heavy hand of God that is and has been upon them for now these seven years, by war, pestilence and famine, we are now become more stiff-necked than the Jews.[23]

At this time, too, James concerned himself with the upbringing of his legitimate son who had reached the age of eight. The Earl of Perth, brother to the tiresome Duke of Melfort, was appointed as the

Prince of Wales's governor: elaborate instructions were laid down by James to ensure the boy's safety, education and religious up-bringing.[24] The Prince was to hear the Mass at nine o'clock every morning before turning to his studies and physical exercises; he was allowed an hour for play before another two hours of education in the afternoons. No one was to whisper to him or give him anything to eat or to read to him without the permission of the governor or under-governor. James also found time to warn his grown-up son, the Duke of Berwick, about the dangers of 'deceitful pleasures'. Evidently James thought that Berwick had been led astray since he left Ireland, where his behaviour had been so edifying that James used to tell the Prince of Wales that he should follow his brother's good example, for he wrote to Berwick to say he could not tell him to follow his example any more.[25] Only too clearly James re-membered his own ill-spent youth, for he wrote how he abhorred and detested himself 'for having lived so many years in almost a perpetual course of Sin' and repented that he had continued to sin not only in the heat of youth but when he reached the years of discretion.[26]

In 1696 the Nine Years War was approaching its end unsuccess-fully for the French. James fully realized that the failure to over-throw the Grand Alliance spelt the death knell of his hopes of restoration. He was not allowed to have any part in the peace negotiations which were concluded at Ryswick, though he did send an agent to Vienna and, when he learned the terms of the treaty, published a dignified protest. As Louis had in effect lost the war he refused to allow any rejoicings over its ending. In the treaty he was compelled to recognize William III as the legitimate King of England, Scotland and Ireland. The only concession that affected James was that he and his family were allowed to continue living at St Germain. A verbal promise given to the Swedish mediator that the English Parliament would pay his Queen her jointure of £50,000 a year was never carried out on the ground that she could not have it unless she recognized William as King of England.[27] Louis XIV tried to temper the wind to the shorn lambs by encouraging James to put his name forward as a candidate for the elective monarchy of Poland after the death of John Sobieski, the hero of the siege of Vienna, in 1683. At sixty-four James would have been an odd successor. However, he refused to let his name go forward to fill the vacancy as he thought that acceptance, if the throne were offered him, would damage his son, James Edward's chance of succeeding William III when he died.[28] Indeed when in the summer of 1698 Princess Anne's son, William Duke of Gloucester, died at the age of eleven, consideration was given on both sides of the Channel to the idea of James Edward being made heir to the throne, at any rate after his half-sister Anne became Queen, provided that he changed to the Protestant faith. There was never any likelihood of James agreeing to that.

Louis continued to shower kindnesses on the exiled King and Queen. They were invited to Fontainebleau as usual in the autumn of 1697 when the news of the signature of the treaty of Ryswick was received. James obtained the impression that Louis was more mortified about having to tell it to him than he was at hearing it.[29] Next year James was invited to a review of the French army held at Compiègne, a demonstration by Louis that despite his surrenders in the treaty of Ryswick he remained a dominant figure in European affairs. The visit could only induce in James the melancholy reflection 'how very few amongst this great and formidable army thinks of their duty to the King of Kings'.[30] By now he had resigned himself to his losses and began to prepare himself for the next world. He denied himself such indulgences as visits to plays, balls and operas and contemplated seriously giving up hunting. Remembering his immoral past, he resolved not to rely on the consequences of a death-bed repentance. His daily prayer was:

> I give Thee o my God most humble thanks for taking my kingdom from me; Thou didst awake me by that from the lethargy of sin. Had not Thy goodness drawn me from that wretched state, I have been forever lost. I return Thee also my most humble thanks for that out of Thy infinite bounty thou didst banish me into a foreign country where I learned my duty and how to practise it.[31]

Between 1695 and 1701 James was taken ill several times; once his wife had to be recalled from Chaillot to nurse him. He himself wanted to die, as he confided to the Abbé de la Trappe, to the Duke of Berwick and to his wife. Mary naturally protested. 'Is it possible', she asked him, 'you have so little consideration for me and your children?' to which James replied that God would take care of them.[32] By 1700 he had come to the conclusion that the sooner God called him the better: 'as long as I am in this world', he wrote, 'I am never in safety and can never be so until I am freed from the corruptible body and united to Thee.'[33] All agreed, he noted, that 'a perfect Christian is one who desires to die'. At Compiègne the poet and diplomatist, Matthew Prior, who saw James there considered that he looked lean, worn and shrivelled.[34] During April 1701 his wife persuaded him to take the waters at Bourbon, as he had fainted during Mass at the beginning of March. Although the resort was pleasant enough and everybody, including the King of France, was kind and sent him comforts, he suffered slight haemorrhages and tired easily. Soon after he and the Queen got back to St Germain he had a seizure; he again fainted while attending chapel on 22 August.

From then on James knew for certain that he was dying and he prayed to God to let him die on the same day of the week that Jesus Christ had ended his mortal life, that is to say on a Friday.[35] Louis XIV, a good and faithful friend — he himself was sixty-two that month — came to visit him for the last time two days before his death on 5 September, which was in fact a Friday. The French King bent over him during this final visit so that James could hear better what he had to say. The courtiers respectfully drew back, but Louis explained that he wanted everyone to hear him. 'I have come', he told all who were present, 'to learn about the state of his [James's] health and to assure him that if God should dispose of your Majesty, I shall recognize and treat the Prince your son as King of England and pay to him the same consideration that I have done to you.'[36] (That was a promise which two years later he was to have occasion to regret, for it helped to bring the England of Queen Anne once more into a Grand Alliance against him during the war of the Spanish Succession.) Before James's death the holy sacrament was exposed on the altar for three days. He passed away at three in the afternoon, as the Queen, who was not present, was informed. Never, wrote one of the sisters at Chaillot, 'had two married people loved each other with so much mutual tenderness, passionate and reasonable at the same time'.[37] One wonders.

James had not written his final testament until eight days before his death. In it he bequeathed all his personal estate to his elder legitimate son and named the Queen as the sole executor and the boy's guardian during his minority. He had already made provision for the Queen and Princess Louise Mary in the codicil to an earlier will.[38]

In his last will he asked that his body should be buried in the parish where he died. Twenty-four hours after his passing, once the *De Profundis* had been recited and the priests had sung the offices for the dead, the Duke of Berwick and the Earl of Middleton led the funeral procession carrying the body to the priory church of the English Benedictine monks in Paris. Before then James had been embalmed: part of the bowels were sent to the parish church at St Germain where a memorial tablet is erected to him; the rest went to the College at St Omer; his head and brains were deposited in the Scots College in Paris.[39] Two years after his death it was reported that miracles were being performed at his sepulchre in a side chapel at the Benedictine priory church.[40] But as yet he has not been officially recognized as a saint.

22.
Summary and Conclusions

James II had a profound sense of the value of history. Not only did he write nine volumes of memoirs, but he kept copies of his letters to Charles II, William of Orange, the Abbé de la Trappe and many others; he also retained his papers of devotion, the spiritual advice he furnished for his son, the Old Pretender, and even copies of his prayers. It is ironical that the original text of his memoirs was destroyed during the French Revolution, although it cannot be doubted that much of what he wrote was embodied in the official life (improved and corrected by his son) compiled after his death by William Dicconson in the Scots College at Paris, which in turn was preserved for the benefit of British readers by the Hanoverian George IV and the manuscript of which can be seen to this day in the Windsor archives.[1] Even letters to two of his lady friends have survived for the enlightenment of posterity.[2] He took all this historical evidence or material extremely seriously. That was why when he insisted that his strong-box should be removed from the frigate which ran aground off Norfolk in 1682 he told his friend Dartmouth that 'there were things of such consequence in it . . . that he would hazard his own life rather than it should be lost.'[3] It would be possible to write a not inaccurate, though no doubt superficial life of James purely out of the many letters and the quotations from his extant memoirs.

According to his lights, James was an extremely honest man, who rarely indulged in subterfuges or subtleties. Only two instances of deviousness at once spring to mind. The first was his willingness to opt out of his marriage contract with Anne Hyde, when Charles Berkeley provided him with an excuse.[4] Did he really believe that the girl who was about to bear him a child was a whore? He may have done, just as later he took notice of the untrue story that his Duchess was having an affair with handsome Henry Sidney and used it to excuse his own infidelities. The other case was when he induced Charles II's mistress, the Duchess of Portsmouth, to exert her influence to persuade him to allow James to return from his exile in Scotland to the centre of government in London on the basis of a complicated financial arrangement with the lady which he alleged would require his presence there. As he saw himself, it was not a very convincing reason and no doubt Charles would have let him come back in any case.[5] But, broadly, James believed in honourable and clear-cut methods of behaviour. He was unable to fathom why his brother did not immediately get rid of the Exclusionist parliaments or defy them to challenge the prescriptive right of hereditary succession. Remembering only too clearly their father's fate, James was willing then to face civil war, if need be, in what he regarded as an eminently just cause. He felt certain that Charles I's hesitations and tergiversations were the root cause of his defeats. That was why when James became monarch himself he set about building up a professional army with which to impress his domestic enemies as well as to enhance his kingdom's prestige in Europe. He aimed to be hard and tough and stand no nonsense from his parliaments. Though he conscientiously used all the financial resources which were placed at his disposal by his only House of Commons to buy weapons of defence rather than spend it on self-indulgence of any kind, the trouble was, as his second wife pointed out, they did not do him a lot of good.[6]

Neither from his father nor mother did James inherit characteristics of much value to a ruler of his country. Both of them were of course utterly devoted to their own religion which played a fundamental part in their lives, as at least from his early middle age it did in his. But it is clear that James's conversion to the Roman Catholic faith owed little to his mother. More likely it was a slow process, beginning perhaps when he served with Catholic officers in the French army, continuing when he was encouraged to attend High or Low Mass in France and the Spanish Netherlands and reaching its apex about the time when his first wife died. As a straightforward character James was unable to understand why his elder brother, who avowed himself a Roman Catholic in 1669, should conceal his beliefs and even repudiate the two Declarations of Indulgence he issued which would have allowed a general liberty of conscience to all Christians. As for James himself, he insisted more than once that on no account would he abandon or hide his religion not even when it caused him to be marooned in exile and threatened to deprive him of his right of succession in favour of his Protestant nephew, the Duke of Monmouth. When James did overcome all his difficulties and become King he did not drop his first Declaration of Indulgence but reiterated it. In so far as he inherited any of his mother's character it was her utter determination never to be evasive or unsure. Again and again she urged her husband either to stand up to the parliamentarians, who eventually sent him to the scaffold, or to give way to their demands to the extent that he could at least retain his monarchical position. James inherited, too, from his maternal grandfather, Henri of Navarre, that excessive and indiscriminate love of women which in the end he came to think of as a black form of immorality, a commission of sins which made God take his thrones away from him as a punishment for them.[7]

James had little education largely because of the circumstances of the civil wars; even though he dwelt for a time in Oxford it was much more of a military base than a haven of polite learning. He joined the French army when he was eighteen so that his higher education was that of a military officer. There he recognized the duty of carrying out orders unquestioningly, as he was later to expect his Ministers to do, of taking the rough with the smooth and of being loyal to his own side. It is often contended that he automatically obeyed his elder brother in the same way that a soldier obeys his general; yet there was a dualism in his relations with Charles II from the time when he became king, at any rate in name, after their father's death. For James did not invariably agree with his brother's decisions. In exile he often thought that Charles was frivolous, neglectful of business, inclined to be lazy and insufficiently resolute in attempting to win back his father's lost thrones. Certainly James's father-in-law, Edward Hyde, thought so, as we know from the letters he wrote at the time.[8] James also resented having his servants chosen for him and being obliged to leave the French for the Spanish army in 1656. Once Charles was restored James, as his heir presumptive, naturally did what he was told, though he did not always like it and did not refrain from offering his advice on many occasions.

Again, James disliked being told that he must cease to fight at sea after his victory at Lowestoft; later when the Popish Plot and the Exclusionist movement loomed up he detested being thrust into exile especially when at the beginning he had nothing to do except hunt and play cards. As Lord High Admiral he did not approve of the laying up of the main fleet in 1667 while he was disappointed when in 1678 he was deprived of the opportunity of commanding an expeditionary force in the Netherlands. In the end of course James always did assent to his brother's wishes, but it is a mistake to assume that because he did so he approved of his policies. In fact he certainly did not. He considered that Charles was irresolute. His own lack of flexibility during the middle period of his short reign is partly to be attributed to the fact that he believed that neither his father nor his brother was firm enough with their subjects and thus they dug their own graves. When he came to the throne himself he was determined to be hard and strong and to treat his official Ministers as his servants rather than as advisers. Indeed they found him a difficult taskmaster. Whether he was unduly influenced by Jesuits like Father Petre is not easy to decide, but the Earl of Sunderland, his most capable Minister, must have thought so because he preferred to work with the King through the Catholic *camarilla* rather than the Privy Council or the Cabinet.[9]

Undoubtedly James was a sincere believer in liberty of conscience for all Christians. Admittedly he was primarily concerned with the needs of his co-religionists, just as the Puritan sects during the reign of Charles I advocated liberty of conscience in order to avoid being harried by Archbishop Laud and other High Church bishops. James favoured it during his brother's reign because he wanted to put an end to that persecution of Catholics which had taken place spasmodically ever since the time of Queen Elizabeth I, had reached its highest point during the hysteria of the Popish Plot, and was remembered every Guy Fawkes' day.

The view that James desired to convert all of his subjects to Roman Catholicism by force if need be or otherwise die a martyr, that he was a sychophant of France and that it was only towards the end of his reign that he was prepared to grant genuine toleration to the Protestant nonconformists so as to counter-balance the power of the Anglicans was long accepted by historians, led by Lord Macaulay and vouched for by Leopold von Ranke.[10] That view is no longer tenable. We have the evidence of Gilbert Burnet, a future Anglican bishop, who knew James personally before he came to the throne, that though firm in his own religion and loyal to his priests he 'seemed very positive in his opinion against persecution for conscience sake'; we know how during the time he spent in Scotland he allowed the Presbyterians to worship in their own way; we know that although during the period of the Popish Plot and Exclusionist agitation James agreed with Charles that a French alliance was the best security against a renewal of civil war, yet when he became king himself he rejected the idea of being dependent on the whims of the French King and renewed a treaty of friendship with the Dutch. Again, there is not the slightest doubt that James disapproved of the forcible conversion of the Huguenots once he realized how it had been obtained and he welcomed those of them who fled to England. We know how James told the Spanish ambassador in 1686 that 'he could force no man's conscience but only aimed at the Roman Catholics [in England] being no worse treated than the rest instead of being deprived of their liberties like traitors'.[11] Finally, we have the evidence of James's release of hundreds of Quakers from prison at the outset of his reign, of his genuine friendship with William Penn the Quaker leader and of how the position of all Protestant non-conformists was eased as soon as Monmouth's rebellion was out of the way.

It is perfectly understandable in light of the fact that the majority of the people who fought for Monmouth were nonconformists that James hesitated to confer complete freedom on them. In the same way he would not permit the holding of field conventicles in Scotland because he regarded the Cameronians and Cargillites who gathered in them as enemies of the monarchy. Yet it goes against everything he said or did to argue that his policy of general toleration and the ultimate conferring of equality of opportunity on all Christians was a mere trick to induce the nonconformists to side with him against the Anglicans and thus help him on towards Catholic supremacy. James was a perfectly straightforward man. His two Declarations of Indulgence reflected his real beliefs. Furthermore, they anticipated legal equality for every citizen embracing the right to attend universities and to stand for parliament, which was not to be completely achieved until the nineteenth century.

James then was an honest man; but he was also a stupid man. He was heavy-handed and foolishly tried to bludgeon his most influential subjects, who were either aristocrats, elected members of the House of Commons or accepted leaders of the Church of England, into doing what he wanted. He had got it fixed into his head that because of the traditional loyalty of the Church to the King, who was Supreme Governor of the Church (a factor which

Danby had attempted to exploit in Charles II's reign) and because his accession had been welcomed with almost as much enthusiasm as had been shown to his brother when he was restored, the bulk of his subjects would accept his policies without question and without opposition.

It was because his brothers-in-law doubted his wisdom that he dismissed them, but he did not aim to have none but Catholics as Ministers of State or military commanders. He simply expected his Ministers to acquiesce in his indulgences. That was why he continued to employ men like Middleton and Preston, Feversham and Dartmouth, who were all Protestants, right up to the end of his reign. He also relied on the Earl of Sunderland, who did not pretend to be a Roman Catholic until the last moment in the reign when he feared he was losing the royal favour.[12] James's sudden moral collapse in 1688 was not brought about by any mental or physical illness — for he was to live in good health for almost another thirteen years — but by his shock realization after the protests and acquittals of the bishops and their refusal to abhor William's declaration that he had deluded himself in always expecting their unquestioning obedience to his commands. His subsequent, though not contemporary, conviction that he lost his Crown largely through Sunderland's unscrupulous plotting and evil advice is also evidence of his ability to deceive himself.[13]

Was James a coward (and a bully)? It has always been a mystery how and why this man who had fought so bravely on land and sea before he became king afterwards totally lost his nerve. His defeatism in the autumn of 1688, his failure to order Dartmouth to go out and fight the Dutch expeditionary force, his refusal to lead his own army forward from Salisbury and finally his two ignominious escapes from Whitehall, seeking exile in France, do strongly suggest lack of courage. He also quickly lost heart after the battle of the Boyne while it was with considerable reluctance that he allowed himself to be pressured by his wife and Louis XIV into further efforts to regain his thrones. In fairness he could justify his last rejection of opportunity by his unwillingness to fight against those whom he still regarded as his own subjects and patriotically he admired when they inflicted defeats on his French friends.[14] Yet it was his weakness in times of crisis and his habitual stupidity not his bigotry or tyranny or sycophancy which explain why he was one of the least successful or effective of English monarchs.

Appendix *The Memoirs of James II*

When Cardinal Bouillon, who was the nephew of the famous French marshal, the Vicomte de Turenne, was visiting the Palace of St Germain in 1695, he was told by James II that he had already 'written pretty exactly year by year in English the memoirs of his own life'.[1] James was particularly proud of the account he had written of his early life when he served both in the French and Spanish armies; every evening, it is said, he sat down and recorded the happenings of the day in his journal in a matter-of-fact way, which presumably was rough-and-ready and even ungrammatical. One may speculate that it was for these reasons that during his reign in England James employed Charles Dryden, son of the Poet Laureate, to rewrite this account of his early years, changing it from the first person into the third person and improving the style of the narrative. Thus when Bouillon asked the exiled King for his re-collections of Turenne James was able to arrange that everything in his memoirs relating to the French Marshal should be translated into French for Bouillon's benefit. Before the translation was begun James himself revised and corrected the English original, based on his journals as edited by Dryden. This can be assumed because the translated narrative is written in the third person throughout.[2]

After James's death in 1701 his widow, Mary of Modena, or-ganized a second translation into French of this part of her husband's memoirs to be carried out under the supervision of John Caryll, who had been created Baron Caryll by James's eldest legiti-mate son, known as 'the Old Pretender', and had served him as his Secretary of State. This second translation was completed in 1704 and given to Cardinal Bouillon, presumably to be collated with the Dryden version.[3] That translation — or most of it — was printed as an appendix to A. M. Ramsay's *Histoire du Vicomte Turenne,* pub-

296

lished in 1735; Ramsay was a nephew of Cardinal Bouillon, who did not live to write the book himself. Bouillon had died in 1715, but he had written a preface explaining how James gave him the first translation, which was entitled *Campagnes de Jacques Stuart.*

On 24 March 1701, six months before his death at St Germain, James dispatched several of his historical documents, including the so-called Dryden version of his life up to 1660, to be placed in the care of the Scots College of the University of Paris, whose principal was Lewis Innes, a scholar well known to James and who devoted himself to the preservation and arrangement of the records in the College library.[4] It was for this reason that Caryll, when supervising the second translation of James's campaigns, was obliged to go to the Scots College for the purpose.

Evidently James did not send all his papers to the Scots College before he died because on 22 January 1707 his son, the Old Pretender, signed a warrant for the removal from St Germain of part of his father's memoirs, relating to 1678 and later times, to the Scots College and commissioned William Dicconson, who had been treasurer at the Court of St Germain, to go to Paris and write a life of his father, based on all James's surviving papers. This he did apparently during the years 1710-15.[5]

The late Godfrey Davies expressed the opinion that the *Life* was written not by one author (i.e. Dicconson) but by three different authors:[6] (1) by the secretary of the Duke of York, Caryll; (2) by a different author, who supplied no marginal references and used the third person throughout: more of a formal history than a biography; (3) the rest from 1678 to 1701, probably by a third compiler who used many quotations from James's memoirs and citations from the devotional papers, letters and other last writings of James II.

However, Mr Davies was, I think, wrong about this. Thomas Innes, Principal of the Scots College, specifically stated in a letter of 17 October N.S. 1740 that Dicconson wrote the *Life* both before and after the Restoration.[7] The *Life* came into the hands of the Duchess of Albany, an illegitimate daughter of the 'Young Pretender', Charles Edward, and thus great-granddaughter of James II. She found it in her father's house in Florence after his death in 1788 and bequeathed it to the English Benedictines in Rome. This information was given to Sir John Hippesley, who was a member of parliament but had lived much of his life in Italy, by Abbé Walters, the Procurator-General of the English Benedictines in Rome.[8] The

Prince Regent (afterwards George IV) was interested in the Stuarts and instructed Hippesley to buy the *Life* on his behalf and dispatch it to Carlton House in London. As a reward the Prince Regent gave a pension to Abbé Walters, which he did not enjoy for long.[9]

There is good reason to suppose that Dicconson's *Life* was originally in five volumes because Lord Shelburne, who visited the Scots College in Paris on 23 November 1771, informed the Earl of Hardwicke that he had seen these 'five very thick folio volumes which appear to be a history of James's *Life* compiled about sixty years ago from his journal'. He stated that the fifth volume contained the correspondence between English statesmen, such as Marlborough, Shrewsbury, Godolphin, Dartmouth and Admiral Russell who 'were in constant communication' with James II.[10]

The Prince Regent instructed his historiographer royal, the Reverend J. S. Clarke, to edit and have printed the *Life* by Dicconson, which was duly done and published in two volumes in 1816. By the gracious permission of Her Majesty the Queen I examined the Dicconson *Life,* now kept in Windsor Castle. It is in four volumes, the first covering the years 1633-60, the second runs from 1660 to 1685, the third from 1685 to 1689, and the fourth from 1689 to 1701. All the four volumes are written in the same handwriting; according to a note in the first volume the transcriber was named Etienne Monnet.

J. S. Clarke faithfully reproduced all the material in these volumes including the marginal notes referring to the sources. The first volume of Dicconson is clearly based on James's own memoirs, derived from his journals, as revised by Dryden, and references are given to the first three volumes of James's memoirs. The second volume contains no references to James's memoirs until 1679 when references to tomes 7, 8 and 9 of James's original memoirs begin to occur and to some extent overlap; for that reason this volume is far and away the least valuable part of the book. Presumably the description of the battle of Lowestoft was based on papers that James had compiled about his greatest victory. But the volume clearly contains factual dubieties and inaccuracies. For example, the account of James's first marriage does not square with other accounts; it is surely curious to say that Long Island was in the West Indies; Colonel Richard Nicholls is referred to as 'Nicholas'; the claim that the second Anglo-Dutch war 'begun now under the conduct of R.H. was the first wherein fighting in a Line and a regular

Form of Battel was observ'd' is unfair and untrue. So this part of Dicconson's *Life* is untrustworthy. Dicconson's third volume, however, contains many references to 'loose sheets' and to tome 9 of the memoirs. In the fourth volume the references to James's memoirs and to his letters are sparse, but it is obviously based largely on James's papers of devotion, which were published in full by Godfrey Davies in 1925.

To sum up, the *Life* as a whole is based on volumes 1-3 and 7-9 of James's memoirs, on his letters to and from Charles II, on certain 'loose sheets', on his papers of devotion and his letters to the Abbé de la Trappe, the monastery which he visited regularly during the last years of his life.

To turn back to the 'original' or 'holograph' memoirs on which this *Life* was partly based; according to Gilbert Burnet who, in my opinion, is usually pretty reliable, James when he was Duke of York, told him that he kept 'a journal of all that passes' and showed him 'a great deal' of it. He also said that he had employed 'the late duchess [Anne Hyde] to write it out in the style of a history, for she wrote very correctly'.[11] The first Duchess of York died on 31 March 1671 so it is not at all clear what she did. Could she have written the draft which Dryden corrected? Or did she write about the first ten years of Charles II's reign, in which case what she wrote might have formed part of the material for Dicconson's second volume, which, as I have suggested, is not very accurate, or else it must have disappeared.

Did any of the visitors to the Scots College actually see the original 'journals' or 'memoirs'? David Hume, it has been suggested, might have done so, but if he did, he made no use of them. According to Charles James Fox, who visited the Scots College in 1801, when he was planning to write a life of James II, the then Principal, Alexander Gordon, told him that neither Thomas Carte, who visited the college during the first half of the eighteenth century, nor James Macpherson, who went there in the 1770s, was allowed to see the original memoirs.[12] The so-called extracts from James's memoirs, based on what Carte and Macpherson copied and published in Macpherson's *Original Papers* in 1775 are not what they claimed to be but were almost certainly summaries (not extracts) from parts of Dicconson's *Life*. There is no reason to suppose that Carte's 'extracts' were any more or less authentic than those of Macpherson.

Lord Shelburne apparently saw volume I of the memoirs, but otherwise only Dicconson's four-volume *Life* plus a fifth volume clearly derived from Sir David Nairne's papers which are now in the Bodleian library at Oxford. Shelburne said that the Principal of the College kept James's memoirs in a closet 'locked by a double key'.[13] Sir John Dalrymple told the Earl of Dartmouth on 9 October 1772 that he had read about how James had been advised to seize his ancestor, Lord Dartmouth, who commanded James's fleet in a life of James which was at the Scots College in Paris, written by Caryll in four quarto volumes.[14] This must surely have been the Dicconson *Life* that had earlier been shown to Shelburne and on which Carte and Macpherson had been allowed to graze.

In his introduction to Charles James Fox's *A History of the Early Part of the Reign of James II*, dated April 1808 and published after Fox himself was dead, Lord Holland wrote that there was a note among Fox's papers of a list of works that were placed in the Scots College soon after the death of James II. These consisted of four volumes folio and six volumes quarto of memoirs in James's own handwriting plus two thin volumes containing letters from Charles II's Ministers to the Duke of York when he was in exile in Brussels and Scotland and two thin quarto volumes of Charles II's letters to his brother.[15]

If Dicconson and Fox are to be trusted, therefore, at one time nine or ten volumes of James's memoirs were in existence (though the tenth volume was probably the Nairne papers). But Dicconson makes no reference to volumes 4, 5 or 6 of the memoirs, which might have covered the years 1660-79 and his reign from 1685 to 1688. My feeling is that these volumes may have disappeared or been destroyed before Dicconson even started writing the *Life* and he had to do what he could with the letters and loose sheets instead.

It is well established that whatever memoirs James himself wrote were finally destroyed by Madame Charpentier in St Omer in 1793 whither they had been sent for safety from the Scots College after the outbreak of the French Revolution. So when Fox reached Paris in 1802 he found nothing at all at the Scots College neither the memoirs nor Dicconson's *Life*. For by then the *Life* had been sent to Italy.

But it is curious that according to a *Short Narrative of the Scots College* in Paris mentioned by M. V. Hay in his edition of the *Blairs Papers,* pp. 8-9, the holograph MSS of James II, which were burnt at St Omer, were said to have been in five volumes not nine. What became of the four other volumes which Dicconson never saw and about which Fox was informed and which probably covered the most important years of James's life has not been discovered. That they existed at some time or another is likely enough, for, after all, James spent much of his time writing letters when he was in exile during his brother's reign and probably also scribbled in his journals and may have continued to keep some kind of records when he was king. One of these volumes, as I have already suggested, may have contained the Nairne papers; the other three volumes were either lost by the Scots College and thus not available to Dicconson, or accidentally destroyed, or will turn up somewhere one day.

Select Bibliography

MANUSCRIPT SOURCES

In the British Library Additional MSS are to be found letters from James and his Ministers to the Papacy (9341); the reports of Count Francesco Terriesi of Modena (25358-25381); letters of the Earl of Melfort when he was James's Secretary of State in exile in France (28228); material about James's adventures in 1688 (32094-32095); Mackintosh transcripts (34510-34523) many of which were not printed in Sir James Mackintosh's *History of the Revolution in 1688*; Hardwicke papers which bear on what was seen of James's memoirs in the eighteenth century (35839); and the correspondence of D'Albeville, the English ambassador in Holland (41814-41816). In the Public Record Office are Armand Baschet's transcripts of most of the correspondence to and from the French ambassadors in England (P.R.O. 31/3/106-178). The dispatches of the French ambassador, Paul Barrillon, were printed in whole or in part by Campana de Cavelli, *Les derniers Stuarts* (1871), John Dalrymple, *Memoirs of Great Britain and Ireland* (1790), Charles James Fox, *A history of the early part of the reign of James the Second* (1808) and F. A. J. Mazure, *Histoire de la révolution de 1688 en Angleterre* (Paris 1825). Also in the P.R.O. is material of various kinds from the State Papers such as Privy Council Registers, Entry books and State Papers (France and Holland). In the Bodleian library at Oxford are the Clarendon MSS. Some letters are published in the *Clarendon State Papers* (1786); the rest are summarized in the *Calendar of Clarendon State Papers* (the last of the five volumes edited by F. J. Routledge was published in 1970). In Carte MSS 181 are letters and papers about James's campaigns in Ireland in 1689-90 including 'the Journall of what has Passed since his Majesty's arrival in Ireland'; this volume also contains details about James's wills. Rawlinson MSS A 139a and 139b contain detailed information about James's campaign to pack a parliament willing to repeal the penal code and Test Acts, which were printed in G. F. Duckett, *Penal laws and the Test Act* (two vols, 1883) but the originals merit examination. In MSS Piggott d 10 are letters misleadingly indexed as from James to Susan Bellasyse; in fact most of them are from James's second wife: Susan Bellasyse was one of her Maids of Honour.

The *Life of James II* which was printed and edited with notes by J. S. Clarke (1816) is in the Round Tower at Windsor Castle together with the Stuart papers acquired by King George IV (R.A.S.P. 1/9-1/18) nearly all of which have been printed and summarized in the Historical Manuscripts Commission reports. Other Stuart MSS in exile are in the Bodleian MSS ADD C 106-107 which were edited by F. Madan for the Roxburghe Club in 1889 and in British Library Add

Select Bibliography

MSS 28224-28226 and 34638. The Portland MSS deposited in the Nottingham University library contain a little material bearing on the reign of James II, notably the letters of James Johnstone.

BIOGRAPHIES

The original of J. S. Clarke's *Life of James II* (two vols 1816) which I have discussed in the appendix above and have referred to as the 'official biography' in the text was read and notated by his son, the Old Pretender. This is a primary source which is used by all James's later biographers. A slightly different version of the first volume covering the period from 1652 to 1660 dealing mainly with his campaigns as Duke of York was discovered in France in 1954 and published as *The Memoirs of James II* (translated and edited by A. Lytton Sells in 1962). This is in fact a translation into French of parts of his memoirs given by James to the Cardinal de Bouillon, the nephew of Marshal Turenne, and now retranslated into English and expanded with extracts from Clarke; it is of minor value. Popular lives of James were written by A. Fea, *James II and his wives* (1908) and F. M. G. Higham, *King James the Second* (1934). Books on James by Hilaire Belloc, *James II* (1928) and M. V. Hay, *The Enigma of James II* (1938), the latter being an expansion of an essay on *Winston Churchill and James II of England* (1934), are apologias by Roman Catholics and not detailed biographies. A less partisan view of James II by a Roman Catholic author is to be found in J. Lingard, *A History of England to 1688* (1855). The best part of Belloc's book is his account of the battle of the Boyne. The best modern biography of James is by F. C. Turner (1948). Mr Turner had valuable advice from and assistance by Dr Esmond de Beer, the doyen of seventeenth-century historical scholars. Mr Turner, however, was not much interested in James as a soldier and sailor; he seems to me an unsympathetic biographer; and I am not convinced by his argument that James suffered from some mysterious mental disease. Jock Haswell's *James II* (1972) is admittedly a study of James as a soldier and sailor, thus supplementing Turner. It follows the account in J. S. Clarke very closely and is surprisingly brief on the Irish campaigns of 1689 and 1690. There is an entertaining essay on James in chapter V of John Kenyon, *The Stuarts*, first published in 1958 and now available as a paperback. Turner's biography appeared thirty years ago and during that time many valuable primary and secondary authorities have been published. Among the primary are the *Calendar of State Papers (Domestic)* from 1685 to 1688, admirably edited but unhappily without historical introductions by the editors (no doubt for reasons of economy) and the fifth volume of the *Calendar of Clarendon State Papers* (ed. F. J. Routledge, 1970).

JAMES'S LETTERS

These are widely scattered but mostly in print. His letters to the Earl of Queensberry are to be found in volume 1 and 2 of the Historical Manuscripts Commission's report on the Buccleuch papers; his letters to William of Orange in the H.M.C. report on the Foljambe MSS as well as in Dalrymple, the *Calendar of State Papers (Domestic)* for the relevant years, and Groen van Prinsterer, *Archives de la maison d'Orange-Nassau* 2nd series V 1584-1688 (1861). His letters to Lord Dartmouth are in the H.M.C. report on the Dartmouth papers. Other letters to Dartmouth will be found in Campana de Cavelli and in S. W.

303

Singer, *The correspondence of Henry Hyde Earl of Clarendon and of his brother, Lawrence Hyde Earl of Rochester* (two vols, 1828). James's letters to his niece, the Countess of Litchfield, are printed in full in *Archaeologia*, vol. LVIII.

JAMES AND THE REVOLUTION OF 1688

Since Mr Turner's biography appeared three books on the revolution of 1688 have been published: Maurice Ashley, *The Glorious Revolution of 1688* (1968, revised paperback 1970); John Carswell, *The Descent on England* (1969) and J. R. Jones, *The Revolution of 1688 in England* (1972). My own book contains a fairly extensive bibliography.

SECONDARY AUTHORITIES

The following is a select list of important books on the period of James II's life published since Mr Turner's book appeared in 1948:

Maurice Ashley, *Charles II* (revised paperback 1973) [*at least that is what I like to think*].
Stephen Baxter, *William III* (1968).
W. B. Braithwaite, *The Second Period of Quakerism* (York 1961).
Andrew Browning, *Thomas Osborne Earl of Danby*, vol. I (1951).
Edward Carpenter, *The Protestant Bishop* (1956).
C. D. Chandaman, *The English Public Revenue 1660-1688* (Oxford 1975).
W. R. Emerson, *Monmouth's Rebellion* (Oxford 1951).
K. H. D. Haley, *The First Earl of Shaftesbury* (Oxford 1968).
C. H. Hartmann, *The King My Brother* (1954).
Henry Horwitz, *Revolution Politics. The career of Daniel Finch second Earl of Nottingham* (1968).
G. H. Jones, *The Mainstream of Jacobitism* (Oxford 1954).
　　　　　Charles Middleton (Chicago 1967).
B. Kemp, *King and Commons 1600-1832* (1957).
John Kenyon, *Robert Spencer Earl of Sunderland 1641-1707* (1958).
　　　　　The Stuart Constitution (1966).
　　　　　The Popish Plot (1972).
Tresham Lever, *Godolphin* (1952).
John Miller, *Popery and Politics 1660-1688* (1973).
David Ogg, *England in the Reigns of James II and William III* (Oxford 1955).
Carola Oman, *Mary of Modena* (1962).
Charles Petrie, *The Marshal Duke of Berwick* (1953).
J. G. Simms, *Jacobite Ireland* (1969).
Charles Chevenix Trench, *The Western Rising* (1969).
David Underdown, *Royalist Conspiracy in England 1649-1660* (Oxford 1960).
J. R. Western, *Monarchy and Revolution* (Poole 1972).
J. B. Wolf, *Louis XIV* (1968).

ARTICLES

The following is a selection of articles bearing on James II:

Maurice Ashley, 'King James II and the Revolution of 1688: Some Reflections on the Historiography' in *Historical Essays 1600-1750 presented to David Ogg* (1963). C. D. Chandaman 'The Financial Settlement in the Parliament of 1685' in *British Government and Administration Essays presented to S. B. Chrimes* (1972). R. Durand, 'Louis XIV et Jacques II à la veille de la revolution de 1688', in *Revue d'histoire moderne et contemporaine*, X (1908). R. H. George, 'Parliamentary Elections and Electioneering in 1685', *Royal Historical Society Transactions*, XIX (1936); 'The Financial Relations of Louis XIV and James II', *Journal of Modern History*, III (1931); 'The Charters Granted to the English Parliamentary Corporations in 1688', *English Historical Review*, 55 (1940). John Kenyon, 'The Birth of the Old Pretender', *History Today* (June, 1963). John Miller 'The Militia and the Army in the reign of James II', *Historical Journal* (1973); 'Catholic Officers in the Later Stuart army', *English Historical Review*, 80 (1975). A. A. Mitchell, 'The Revolution of 1688', *History Today* July, 1965. R. Thomas, 'The seven bishops and their petition', *Journal of Ecclesiastical History*, XII (1963).

ABBREVIATIONS

The following abbreviations are used in the notes of reference:

Ailesbury: *Thomas Bruce Earl of Ailesbury Memoirs* (ed. W. E. Buckley Roxburghe Club 1890).
Baschet: Transcripts of Armand Baschet in the Public Record Office.
B.L.: British Library.
Bodley: Bodleian Library.
Burnet: Gilbert Burnet, *History of His Own Time* (ed. 1823).
Cal. Cl S.P.: *Calendar of Clarendon State Papers.*
C.S.P. (Dom): *Calendar of State Papers (Domestic).*
C.S.P. (Venetian): *Calendar of State Papers (Venetian).*
Campana: Campana de Cavelli, *Les derniers Stuarts et le château de Saint-Germain en Laye* (1871).
Clarendon: Clarendon, *The history of the rebellion and Civil Wars In England* (ed. W. D. Macray, 1888).
Clarendon S.P.: *State papers collected by Edward Earl of Clarendon* (1786).
Dalrymple: John Dalrymple, *Memoirs of Great Britain and Ireland* (1790).
D.N.B.: *Dictionary of National Biography.*
Evelyn: *The Diary of John Evelyn* (ed. Esmond de Beer, 1955).
Haswell: Jock Haswell, *James II Soldier and Sailor* (1972).
H.M.C.: Historical Manuscripts Commission's report.
Kenyon: John Kenyon, *Robert Spencer Earl of Sunderland* (1958).
Ogg: David Ogg, *England in the reigns of James II and William III* (1955).
Oman: Carola Oman, *Mary of Modena* (1962).
Pepys: Samuel Pepys *Diary* (ed. H. B. Wheatley, 1899).
Sells: *The Memoirs of James II 1652-1660* (ed and trans. by A. Lytton Sells, 1962).
Reresby: *Memoirs of Sir John Reresby* (ed. Andrew Browning, 1936).
Singer: *The correspondence of Henry Hyde, earl of Clarendon and of his brother, Laurence Hyde, earl of Rochester* (ed. S. W. Singer, 1828).
Turner: F. C. Turner, *James II* (1948).

Notes

Chapter 1
1. John Drummond Earl of Melfort to the Duke of Queensberry 10 and 14 Feb. 1685. *H.M.C. Buccleuch*, II, p. 215.
2. Ailesbury, I, p. 131.
3. Evelyn, IV, pp. 474-5.
4. Cited from *Memoirs of Mlle de Montpensier*. Carola Oman, *Henrietta Maria* (1936), p. 16.
5. Edward Hyde to John Wilmot Earl of Rochester 5 Dec. 1653. *Cal. Cl. S.P.*, II, p. 281; Edward Hyde to Edward Nicholas 4 July 1653. *Clarendon S.P.*, III, p. 176.
6. cit. Burnet, III, p. 4.
7. Earl of Bristol to Charles II 30 Aug. 1657. *Cal. Cl. S.P.*, III, p. 353.
8. Clarke, I, p. 487.
9. James to Colonel George Legge 28 May 1679. Campana, I, p. 169.
10. Note by Honoré de Courtin. ibid., I, p. 169.
11. Whytford to Lewis Innes Jan. 1680, cit. M. V. Hay, *Winston Churchill and James II* (1934), p. 29.
12. Andrew Hay to Lewis Innes 15 Oct. 1681. ibid., pp. 51-2.
13. Burnet, III, p. 5.
14. Ailesbury, I, p. 184.
15. James to Lord Feversham 10 Dec. 1688. Clarke, II, pp. 249-52.
16. *H.M.C. Ormonde*, VIII, pp. 401-2.
17. Godfrey Davies, *Papers of Devotion of James II*, (Oxford 1925), p. xxiv.
18. Clarke, II, pp. 560-1.
19. ibid., pp. 83 seq.

Chapter 2
1. cit. Oman from the *Memoirs of Mme de la Fayette*, p. 152.
2. cf. Carola Oman, *Henrietta Maria* (1951), p. 16.
3. See illustration and Oliver Millar, *The Age of Charles I: Painting in England* (1972), p. 76.
4. *S.P.* CCLI nos. 22 and 23.
5. The biography by Carola Oman is the best; a more recent biography by Quentin Bone, *Henrietta Maria* (1972) tries to minimize her political influence; there is also a biography by Elizabeth Hamilton, *Henrietta Maria* (1976) but it contains nothing new.
6. Burnet, III, p. 3.

7. Louis XIV wrote copious letters of advice just as James did.
8. Davies, *Papers of Devotion*, p. xix.
9. John Bowle, *Charles the First* (1975), is the latest biography, but it is not strong on the political side. The character of Charles I is well delineated in C. V. Wedgwood, *The King's Peace* (1954) and also in her *Trial of Charles I* (1964), pp. 11 seq.
10. *C.S.P. (Dom) 1641-1643*, pp. 308 seq.
11. Basil N. Reckitt, *Charles the First and Hull* (1952), chap. IV; Clarendon, V, pp. 88 seq.
12. Wedgwood, *King's War*, p. 88.
13. Clarke, I, pp. 15-16.
14. Peter Young, *Edgehill* (Kineton 1967) p. 118; Brigadier Young prints the Duke of York's account of this battle in full on pp. 274 seq.
15. cf. Margaret Toynbee and Peter Young, *Strangers in Oxford* (1974).
16. cf. Maurice Ashley, *Charles II* (Panther ed., 1973), pp. 20 seq.
17. John Rushworth, *Historical Collections* (1659-1701), pt. iv, vol. I, pp. 280-1.
18. B. Whitelocke, *Memorials* (1732), p. 303.
19. *D.N.B.* Evelyn, III, pp. 414-15 and note 10.
20. Haswell, pp. 29-31; Clarendon, XI, pp. 19 seq.
21. Clarendon, X, pp. 115-16.
22. *H.M.C. VII*, p. 455; Clarke, I, pp. 31 seq.; Clarendon, X, pp. 103 seq.
23. *Autobiography of Anne Lady Halkett* (1875), pp. 20 seq.
24. *Lords Journals*, X, p. 220.
25. Clarendon, *Life* (1759), III, p. 468; cf. J. R. Powell, *The Navy in the English Civil War* (Hamden, Connecticut 1962), chap. XI.
26. Clarke, I, p. 46.
27. S. E. Hoskins, *Charles II and the Channel Islands* (1854), I, p. 347 seq.; A. C. Saunders, *Jean Chevalier and his Times* (Jersey 1937), pp. 159 seq.
28. Saunders, *Chevalier*, p. 158.
29. *Memoirs de Mlle de Montpensier*, I, p. 320 seq.
30. Saunders, *Chevalier*, p. 158.
31. Sir John Berkeley to Edward Hyde 22 Mar. 1650. *Cal. Cl. S.P.*, II, pp. 50-1.
32. *Cal. Cl. S.P.*, II, pp. 90, 114, 126.
33. *Charles II's Escape from Worcester* (ed. William Matthews, 1967), pp. 38 seq.
34. Clarke, I, p. 72; Sells, pp. 57-8.
35. Sells, pp. 58-9; Clarke, I, p. 63.

Chapter 3
1. For the Frondes see E. H. Kossmann, *La Fronde* (Leiden 1954).
2. For Turenne see A. M. Ramsay, *The History of Henri de La Tour d'Auvergne Viscount of Turenne* (English trans. Paris 1735); Jules Roy, *Turenne sa vie et les institutions militaires de son temps* (1896); Turenne, *Mémoires*, vols I and II (Paris 1914).
3. Roy, *Turenne*, I, pp. 133-4.
4. Clarke, I, p. 55.
5. ibid., I, p. 56.
6. cit., Haswell, p. 76.
7. Clarke, I, p. 86.
8. ibid., pp. 114-15.
9. ibid., p. 135.

10. ibid., p. 157.
11. Sells, p. 127.
12. Clarke, I, p. 336. The summary referring to 1658 says 'The Duke's remarque upon the Spaniards' fortifying of Rivers with his opinion that works of this nature never ought to be relied upon by a General'.
13. ibid., p. 173.
14. Sells, p. 148.
15. Hyde to Nicholas 9/19 Jan. 1654. *Clarendon S.P.*, III, p. 249.
16. Roy, *Turenne*, pp. 142 seq.
17. Draft by Hyde. *Cal. Cl. S.P.* II, p. 382.
18. ibid., loc. cit.
19. Haswell, p. 63.
20. Clarke, I, p. 192.
21. ibid., p. 206.
22. ibid., p. 219.
23. ibid., p. 228.
24. Lord Jermyn to Charles II 19 Sep. 1654. *Cal. Cl. S.P.*, II, p. 391.
25. Sells, p. 202 and note 3.
26. ibid., p. 203.
27. ibid., p. 213.
28. Clarke, I, p. 264.

Chapter 4
1. Nicholas to the Earl of Norwich 3/13 Dec. 1651. *Nicholas Papers: correspondence of Sir Edward Nicholas Secretary of State* (ed. Sir G. F. Warner, 1886-1920), I, p. 281.
2. Thomas Carte, *A Collection of Original Letters and Papers* (Oxford 1739), I, p. 441.
3. Nicholas to Hatton Sep. 1650. *Nicholas Papers*, I, p. 196.
4. Charles II to James 8 July 1654. *Cal. Cl. S.P.*, II, p. 382.
5. There is a good account of this episode in Hester Chapman, *The Tragedy of Charles II* (1964), IV, chap. 2, 'The Ordeal of the Duke of Gloucester' based on the *Clarendon S.P.*
6. Charles II to Henrietta Maria Dec. 1654 (draft). *Cal. Cl. S.P.*, II, p. 435.
7. Charles's instructions to Ormonde 10 Nov. 1654. *Cal. Cl. S.P.*, II, p. 421.
8. *Nicholas Papers*, II, p. 137.
9. *Ut supra* note 7.
10. Ormonde to Charles II from Paris 27 Nov. 1654. ibid., p. 435.
11. Chapman, loc. cit.
12. Nicholas to Hyde 18/28 Dec. 1651. *Nicholas Papers*, I, p. 282.
13. *H.M.C. Bath*, II, p. 97.
14. Charles II to Henrietta Maria Dec. 1654. *Cal. Cl. S.P.*, II, p. 430.
15. W. C. Abbott (ed.), *Writings and Speeches of Oliver Cromwell* (Cambridge, Mass. 1937-47), III, p. 429 and IV, p. 152; Hyde to Henry de Vic 22 Feb. 1656 from Cologne. *Clarendon S.P.*, III, p. 287; Clarke, I, pp. 264-6.
16. James to Charles II from Paris. *Cal. Cl. S.P.*, p. 418.
17. Clarke, I, p. 266.
18. Charles to Ormonde. *Cal. Cl. S.P.*, III, p. 101.
19. Hyde to Ormonde 24 Mar. 1656 from Cologne. ibid., p. 103; Ormonde to Hyde 7 May 1656 from Bruges. ibid., p. 124.
20. Clarke, I, pp. 269-70.

Notes

21. cf. Bristol to Hyde from Brussels. *Clarendon S.P.*, III, p. 411. The pension appears to have been 10,000 livres a month.
22. *Clarendon S.P.*, III, p. 294.
23. Clarke, I, p. 282.
24. This is added in one of the versions of James's memoirs given to the Duc de Bouillon. Sells, p. 219 and note 2.
25. Clarke, I, p. 280.
26. ibid., p. 292.
27. Cromwell to Mazarin 26 Dec. 1657. Abbott, *Cromwell*, IV, p. 369.
28. Clarke, I, p. 298 cf. ibid., p. 207.
29. Bennet to Hyde 18 Apr. 1657. *Cal. Cl. S.P.*, p. 272; cf. ibid., p. 207.
30. Clarke, I, p. 299.
31. ibid., p. 304.
32. ibid., pp. 306, 311, 312.
33. ibid., pp. 321-2.
34. ibid., p. 327.

Chapter 5
1. Clarke, I, p. 323.
2. The Earl of Bristol to Charles II 30 Aug. 1657. *Cal. Cl. S.P.*, III, p. 353.
3. Clarke, I, p. 330.
4. Sells, p. 250.
5. Charles H. Firth, *Last Years of the Protectorate* (1909), II, pp. 182, 187, 188.
6. Sells, p. 255.
7. ibid., p. 256.
8. ibid., p. 259.
9. See Bernard de Gomme's battle plan reproduced in Firth, *Last Years of the Protectorate*, II, pp. 193-5.
10. Ramsay, *History of Turenne* p. 499.
11. James's account of the battle is in Sells, pp. 270 seq.
12. ibid., p. 266.
13. ibid., p. 276.
14. ibid., pp. 278-9.
15. Clarendon, VI, p. 98.
16. ibid., VI, p. 98.
17. David Underdown, *Royalist Conspiracy in England 1649-1660* (1960), chaps 5, 9 and 10.
18. J. R. Jones, 'Booth's Rising of 1659', *Bulletin of the John Rylands Library*, No. 39 (1957), pp. 413 seq.; Godfrey Davies, *The Restoration of Charles II* (Oxford 1953), pp. 131 seq.
19. *Cal. Cl. S.P.*, IV, pp. 243, 248.
20. See articles by Marjorie Hollings and David Underdown in the *English Historical Review*, 43 (1928) and 69 (1954); Underdown, *Royalist Conspiracy*, pp. 248 seq.; Davies, *Restoration*, pp. 142-3. There is little doubt that Willys was one of Thurloe's agents in 1659; the question is what his motives were.
21. Clarke, II, p. 370.
22. cf. Underdown, *Royalist Conspiracy*, p. 251.
23. Clarke, II, p. 372.
24. ibid., p. 373.
25. ibid., pp. 376-7.

26. Henshaw to Hyde 12/22 Aug. 1659 from Paris. *Cal. Cl. S.P.*, IV, pp. 321-2; Hyde to Mordaunt 9/19 Sep. 1659. ibid., IV, pp. 363-4.
27. Clarke, II, p. 378.
28. Mordaunt to Charles II 1 Sep. 1659. *Clarendon S.P.*, III, pp. 548-9.
29. Bennet to Hyde 20/30 Aug. 1659 from Fuentarrabia. *Cal. Cl. S.P.*, IV, p. 332.
30. Quoted by H. Chapman, *Tragedy of Charles II*, p. 350.
31. Ormonde to Hyde 27 Jan. 1658. *Clarendon S.P.*, III, p. 387.
32. Hyde to Ormonde 5 Aug. 1659 from Brussels. *Cal. Cl. S.P.*, IV, p. 311.
33. cf. A. Broderick to Charles II 7 May 1659. *Clarendon S.P.*, III, p. 462.
34. Mordaunt to James 27 Oct. 1659 from London. ibid., pp. 590-1.
35. Clarendon, XVI, p. 46.
36. Clarke, I, p. 379.
37. James to Mordaunt 26 Oct./5 Nov. 1659. Carte, *Original Letters*, II, pp. 237-8.
38. Clarke, I, p. 379.
39. James to Mordaunt 5/15 Nov. 1659. *Clarendon S.P.*, III, pp. 604-5.
40. Nicholas to Charles II 8 Oct. 1659. Carte, *Original Letters*, II, pp. 237-8; W. H. Dawson, *Cromwell's Understudy* (1938), pp. 342-3.
41. See note 39 above.
42. Clarke, I, p. 381.
43. Pepys 23 May 1660.
44. ibid., 25 May 1660.
45. Hyde to Ormonde 11 Oct. 1659 from Brussels. *Ormonde Letters*, II, p. 233.
46. cf. Ashley, *Charles II*, pp. 327 seq.
47. Nicholas to Hyde 18/28 Dec. 1651. *Nicholas Papers*, I, p. 382; Nicholas to Hatton 9/19 May 1652; ibid., I, p. 299; Byron to Hyde 12/22 Nov. 1651. *H.M.C. Bath*, I, p. 98.
48. Dr Morley to Hyde 14/24 April 1659. *Clarendon S.P.*, III, pp. 458-9.
49. Turner, pp. 56-7.

Chapter 6
1. cf. Violet Rowe, *Sir Henry Vane the Younger* (1970), chaps V and VII.
2. Pepys 31 July 1660 etc.
3. J. R. Tanner, 'The Administration of the Navy from the Restoration to the Revolution', *English Historical Review*, 12 (1897), p. 52.
4. A. W. Tedder, *The Navy of the Restoration* (1914), p. 46.
5. Sir William Penn, *Memorials* (1833), II, pp. 243-5.
6. Pepys 20 Jan. 1664.
7. Pepys 8 Oct. 1662.
8. Penn, *Memorials*, II, p. 268.
9. 'General Instructions to Captains', B.L., 816 m 7 (28).
10. Printed in Penn, *Memorials*, II, p. 597.
11. ibid., loc. cit.
12. ibid., p. 268.
13. Maurice Ashley, *John Wildman Plotter and Postmaster* (1947), pp. 164-5.
14. Clarke, I, p. 388.
15. ibid., I, p. 389-90.
16. ibid., I, p. 391.
17. Clarendon, *Life* (1857), II, pp. 237-8.
18. Charles Wilson, *England's Apprenticeship 1603-1773* (1965), p. 138.

19. Tedder, *Navy of the Restoration*, p. 112.
20 James from the Gunfleet 15 May 1665. ibid., p. 117.
21. Clarke, I, p. 388.
22. ibid., p. 410.
23. ibid., pp. 412-15.
24. Pepys 21 Oct. 1667.
25. Clarke, I, pp. 420-1.
26. Reresby, p. 55.
27. Clarke, I, p. 425.
28. Tanner, 'Admistration of Navy', loc. cit., pp. 38 seq.
29. Harleian MSS 7464; Tedder, *Navy of Restoration*, pp. 181 seq.
30. Davies, *Papers of Devotion*, pp. 107-8.

Chapter 7
  1. James to Charles II 12 May 1662. *Cal. Cl. S.P.*, V, pp. 215-16.
  2. cf. Burnet, III, pp. 4-5.
  3. Clarendon, *Life*, III, p. 62.
  4. ibid., p. 63.
  5. ibid., p. 64.
  6. Pepys 8 Oct. 1662.
  7. Clarendon, *Life*, p. 63.
  8. *Memoirs of the Comte de Gramont by Anthony Hamilton* (trans. Peter Quennell, 1930), p. 159.
  9. Reresby, p. 55.
 10. Clarke, I, p. 387.
 11. Clarendon, *Life*, I, pp. 337 seq.
 12. ibid., pp. 378-84.
 13. A paper about the receipts and debts of the Duke of York from 25 May 1660 to 25 May 1663 is in Clarendon MSS 79, f. 203 and an account by Thomas Povey, Receiver-General to the Duke of York, on the state of his finances from 15 Feb. 1660 to 29 Sep. 1661 is in Clarendon MSS 75, f. 228.
 14. White Kennet, *A Complete History of England* (1719), pp. 319-20.
 15. Clarke, I, p. 388.
 16. Gramont, p. 164.
 17. Pepys 9 Jan. 1666.
 18. Reresby, p. 55.
 19. Pepys 10 June 1666.
 20. Burnet, II, pp. 15-16.
 21. *H.M.C.*, VIII, p. 498.
 22. James to Lady Bellasyse from St James's. The copy is dated 28 Dec. 1688; possibly it should be 1678. Piggott MSS d 10, f. 13.
 23. Lady Bellasyse to James dated 27 April 1687 in the copy; possibly 1677. Piggott MSS d 10, f. 425.
 24. Pepys 3 Nov. 1662.
 25. ibid., 17 Nov. 1665.
 26. Gramont, p. 176.
 27. ibid., pp. 137, 141, 164, 167, 191 etc.
 28. Ailesbury, I, p. 132.
 29. ibid., p. 135.
 30. *Supplement to Burnet History of his Own Time* (ed. H. C. Foxcroft, 1902), pp. 51-2.
 31. Pepys 8 Feb. 1661.

32. Clarke, I, p. 440. James's own account of his conversion is to be found in ibid., pp. 629-30.
33. ibid., I, pp. 441-2.
34. Carola Oman's biography of Mary of Modena is excellent, but unfortunately gives few references.
35. James to Peterborough 1 Aug. 1673. Campana, I, p. 12 seq.

Chapter 8
1. Charles's second paper on religion 29 July 1670. *Stuart Papers* (ed. Cavan), p. 286.
2. Clarke, I, p. 441-2: this is the sole authority for the meeting.
3. See the argument in my book on *Charles II* (Panther edition, 1971), pp. 170-3.
4. Charles II to Henriette 6 June 1669. C. H. Hartmann, *The King My Brother* (1954), p. 263.
5. The letters are printed in full in Hartmann, op. cit.
6. ibid., p. 297.
7. ibid., p. 307.
8. Macpherson, I, pp. 54-5.
9. ibid., loc. cit.
10. The text of the treaty is in *English Historical Documents 1660-1714* (ed. A. Browning), pp. 863-7.
11. Hartmann, *The King My Brother*, p. 352.
12. Clarke, I, p. 461.
13. Charles II to James 2 May 1672. Royal Archives at Windsor S.P. Add MSS 1/18.
14. David Ogg, *England in the Reign of Charles II*, p. 358.
15. For the battle of Solebay see R. C. Anderson's introduction to *Journals and Narratives of the Third Dutch War* (1946) and the accounts of the battle in ibid., pp. 164 seq.; Clarke, I, p. 461; F. R. Harris, *Life of Sandwich* (1912); La Roncière, *Histoire de la marine francaise*, V, pp. 531 seq.; H. T. Colenbrander, *De Groote Nederlandsche Zeeoorlogen 1652-1676* (The Hague 1919), II, pp. 94 seq.
16. Macpherson, I, p. 67; Clarke, I, p. 478; Foreign Entry Book 176 22 June 1672 cit. K. H. D. Haley, *The First Earl of Shaftesbury* (Oxford 1968), p. 301.
17. Clarke, I, pp. 480-1.
18. cf. Sir Charles Lyttleton to Lord Hatton. *Hatton Correspondence*, I, p. 95.
19. James to Lord Clifford 15 July 1672. C. H. Hartmann, *Clifford of the Cabal* (1937), pp. 258-9.

Chapter 9
1. *Thomas Osborne Earl of Danby 1632-1712* (ed. Andrew Browning, 1944), II, pp. 92-3. Dr Miller says that it was 'the fact of the duke of York's Catholicism underlying all the politics of the period' that broke up the Cabal. In my view it was the failure to win the third Anglo-Dutch war that broke up the Cabal. John Miller, *Popery and Politics 1660-1688* (1973), p. 121.
2. Haley, *Shaftesbury*, p. 355.
3. ibid., p. 342.
4. Burnet, II, p. 40.
5. ibid., p. 42.

6. Macpherson, I, p. 82; Clarke, I, pp. 502-3.
7. Browning, *Danby*, I, p. 165 citing Mignet; Clarke, I, pp. 499-500. cf. Coleman's letter to the French King's confessor dated 29 June 1673: 'his Royal Highness my master is very sensible of the friendship of his Most Christian Majesty which he will endeavour to cultivate very carefully.' George Treby, *A Collection of Letters* (1681), p. 5.
8. Browning, op. cit. p. 152.
9. ibid., pp. 198-9.
10. ibid., p. 203 quoting Privy Council register 65, pp. 349, 361.
11. Reresby, pp. 120-1.
12. Browning, op. cit., I, p. 219 note 1.
13. Clarke, I, p. 504.
14. ibid., pp. 508.
15. ibid., loc. cit.
16. ibid., pp. 509-10.
17. Browning, op. cit., II, p. 348.
18. James to William 21 May 1678. Dalrymple, p. 227.
19. James to William 20 July 1678. ibid., p. 241.
20. For the background see John Kenyon, *The Popish Plot* (1972), chap. 1; Miller, *Popery and Politics in England* (1973), chaps 1-4; Bryan Magee, *The English Recusants* (1938). Dr Miller shows that the estimates of the size of the Roman Catholic minority by Professor Kenyon and Mr Magee are too high.
21. Roger L'Estrange, *A Brief History of the Times* (1688), III, p. 10 cit. Haley, *Shaftesbury*, p. 459.
22. Kenyon, *Popish Plot*, p. 53; on the other hand, Charles II usually found scoundrels amusing.
23. James to William 18 Oct. 1678. Dalrymple, I, p. 257.
24. James to William 12 Nov. 1678. *H.M.C. 15 V Foljambe MSS*, p. 123.
25. James to William 3 Dec. 1678. Dalrymple, I, p. 258.
26. James to William 8 June 1679 from Brussels. *H.M.C. Foljambe*, pp. 131-2.
27. Browning, *Danby*, II, p. 90.
28. Charles II to James 28 Feb. 1679. Dalrymple, pp. 292-3.
29. Haley, *Shaftesbury*, p. 514.
30. James to William 8 May 1679 from Brussels. *H.M.C. Foljambe*, p. 129.
31. James to Legge 28 Apr. 1679. *H.M.C. Dartmouth*, pp. 32-3.
32. James to William 14 May 1679. *H.M.C. Foljambe*, p. 330.
33. James to William 29 May 1679. ibid., p. 131.
34. James to William 1 June 1679. Dalrymple, I, pp. 300-1.
35. James to Legge 28 May 1679. Campana, I, pp. 269-70.
36. James to Charles II 30 May 1679 from Brussels. MSS Piggott d. 10, ff. 6-8.
37. James to William 21 Aug. 1679 from Brussels. *H.M.C. Foljambe*, p. 136; cf. Oman, p. 63.
38. Clarke, I, p. 551.
39. James to William 6 July 1679 from Brussels. Dalrymple, I, chap. IV, p. 305.

Chapter 10

1. cit. Haley, *Shaftesbury*, p. 545.
2. *Carte MSS 232, f. 51.*
3. Louis XIV to Barrillon 11/21 Sep. 1679. *Correspondence politique Angleterre*, t. 137, ff. 87-9.
4. James to William 5 Sep. 1679 from Windsor. *H.M.C. Foljambe*, p. 137.

5. James to William 16 Sep. 1679 from Windsor. Dalrymple, I, p. 329.
6. James to Louis XIV 18 Oct. 1679. ibid., p. 323.
7. Charles Hatton to Lord Hatton 21 Oct. 1679. *Hatton Correspondence*, I, pp. 198-9.
8. Clarke, I, p. 574.
9. James to Legge 13/23 Nov. 1679. Campana, p. 309.
10. James to Legge 14 Dec. 1679 from Edinburgh. Dalrymple I, chap. IV, p. 332.
11. Charles Whytford to Lewis Innes, cit. Hay, *Winston Churchill and James II of England*, p. 29.
12. ibid., loc. cit.
13. Kenyon, *Popish Plot*, pp. 186-7.
14. Barrillon to Louis XIV 22 Feb. 1680. Dalrymple, I, p. 335.
15. Barrillon to Louis XIV 2/12 Mar. 1680. Baschet.
16. Barrillon to Louis XIV 21/31 Oct. 1680. Dalrymple, I, pp. 346 seq.
17. Barrillon to Louis XIV 18/28 Oct. 1680. ibid., pp. 344-5.
18. Clarke, I, pp. 593-4.
19. ibid., pp. 595 seq.
20. James to Clarendon 23 Nov. 1680 Clarendon MSS 87, f. 331.
21. James to Barrillon Dec. 1680 from Edinburgh. Dalrymple, I, p. 363.
22. Barrillon to Louis XIV 24 Jan./3 Feb. 1681. ibid., 364-5.
23. James to Barrillon Feb. (?) 1681. ibid., 367-9.
24. James to Legge 2 Feb. 1681. Campana, pp. 351-2.
25. Clarke, I, pp. 699 seq.
26. These letters are printed in *Archaeologia*, vol. LVIII.
27. Burnet, II, pp. 292 seq.
28. ibid., p. 295.
29. N. Luttrell, *A Brief Relation of State Affairs from September 1678 to April 1714* (Oxford 1857), I, p. 113.
30. James to the Countess of Litchfield 6 June 1681. *H.M.C.*, 2, II, p. 32.
31. James to Countess of Litchfield 20 Aug. 1681. *Archaeologia*, LVIII, p. 161.
32. James to William 12 Sep. 1681. *Archives de la Maison d'Orange Nassau* (1861), V, p. 520.
33. Andrew Hay to Lewis Innes 15 Oct. 1681. op. cit. Hay, *Winston Churchill and James II*, pp. 51-2; Clarke, I, pp. 708-9.
34. *Archives*, V, p. 533.
35. James to Countess of Litchfield 18 July 1681. *Archaeologia*, LVIII, p. 160.
36. Clarke I, pp. 699-700.
37. James to Countess of Litchfield 18 Oct. 1681. *Archaeologia*, LVIII, p. 161.
38. Haley, *Shaftesbury*, p. 681.
39. Reresby, p. 239.
40. Clarke, I, p. 726.

Chapter 11
1. James to Countess of Litchfield 19 Feb. 1682 from Edinburgh. *Archaeologia*, LVIII, pp. 166-7.
2. op. cit. Keith Feiling, *A History of the Tory Party* (Oxford 1924), p. 198.
3. Barrillon to Louis XIV 24 April/4 May 1682. Campana, I, p. 385.
4. Louis XIV to James 10/20 March 1682. Dalrymple, pt. 1, bk. 1, p. 45.
5. Winston S. Churchill, *Marlborough: His Life and Times* (1933), I, p. 158; Burnet, II, p. 316 note y.

6. James to Countess of Litchfield 9 May 1682. *Archaeologia*, LVIII, p. 168.
7. Burnet, II, p. 317.
8. James to Lord Hyde 13 May 1682 from Edinburgh. Singer, I, p. 74.
9. Feiling, *Tory Party*, chap. VII; Ogg, *Charles II*, II, chap. XVII.
10. James to William 18 Dec. 1682 from Windsor. Dalrymple, pt. I, bk. 1, p. 114.
11. James to Countess of Litchfield 2 July, 18 Aug. and 15 Sep. 1682. *Archaeologica*, LVIII, pp. 170, 171, 173.
12. James to Countess of Litchfield 8 Sep. 1683. ibid., p 181.
13. James to Queensberry 9 May 1683. *H.M.C. Buccleuch*, II, p. 189.
14. For an account of the Rye House plot see Maurice Ashley, *John Wildman*, chap. XVIII.
15. *H.M.C. Buccleuch*, II, pp. 192-3.
16. ibid., II, p. 194.
17. *State Trials*, IX, p. 88.
18. James to William 4 Jan. 1684. Dalrymple, pt. I, bk. 1, pp. 117-18.
19. James to William 4 Dec. 1683. ibid., p. 116.
20. Allan Fea, *King Monmouth* (1902), pp. 172 seq.
21. ibid., p. 179.
22. ibid., p. 182.
23. James to Queensberry. *H.M.C. Buccleuch*, I, p. 200.
24. cit. Violet Markham, *The Protestant Duke* (1976), p. 112.
25. Clarke, I, p. 742.
26. James to William 20 May 1684. Dalrymple, pt. I, bk. 1, p. 118.
27. James to William 6 June 1684 from Windsor. Dalrymple, II, p. 57.
28. Luttrell, I, p. 738.
29. ibid., p. 745.
30. Reresby, p. 329.
31. James to William 2 Sep. 1683. Dalrymple, pt. I, bk. 1, p. 108.
32. cit. J. B. Wolf, *Louis XIV* (1968), p. 417.
33. James to William 2 Sep. 1684. Dalrymple, pt. I, bk. 1, p. 108.
34. James to William 7 April 1684. ibid., p. 110.
35. Clarke, I.
36. Barrillon to Louis XIV 7 Dec. 1684. Fox, *Early History of the Reign of James II*, Appendix pp. vii-ix.
37. Turner, p. 223.
38. James to Queensberry 8 Nov. 1684. *H.M.C. Buccleuch*, I, p. 210.
39. James to William 3 Oct. 1684. Dalrymple, pt. 1, bk. 1, p. 125.
40. Barrillon to Louis XIV 25 Dec. 1684. Fox, *Early Part*, Appendix, pp. ix-xi.
41. Clarke, I, p. 746.
42. Barrillon to Louis XIV 8/18 Feb. 1685. Dalrymple, II, p. 95.

Chapter 12
1. H. C. Foxcroft, *A Supplement*, p. 31.
2. ibid., p. 32.
3. David Hume, *A History of England* (1818), VIII, pp. 256, 258.
4. Clarke, II, p. 3.
5. Sunderland to Ormonde 10 Feb. 1685. *C.S.P. (Dom) 1685*, pp. 8-9.
6. ibid., p. 1.
7. ibid., loc. cit.
8. ibid., p. 4.
9. ibid., p. 5.

10. ibid., p. 142.
11. Barrillon to Louis XIV 8 Feb. 1685. Dalrymple, pt. I, bk. 1, p. 153.
12. Lyttleton to Hatton. *Hatton Memoirs*, II, p. 54.
13. Reresby, p. 352.
14. Clarke, II, p. 3.
15. ibid., p. 4.
16. ibid., loc. cit.
17. ibid., p. 14.
18. Evelyn, IV, p. 415. 14 Feb. 1685.
19. Barrillon to Louis XIV 23 March 1685. Baschet.
20. *C.S.P. (Dom) 1685*, pp. 52-3.
21. James to Hamilton 11 Feb. 1685. Dalrymple, II, pt. I, bk. V, pp. 99-100.
22. Reresby, pp. 363-4.
23. Barrillon to Louis XIV 11 May 1685. Fox, *Early Part*, p. lxxx.
24. Evelyn, IV, p. 415.
25. *D.N.B. sub* Catherine Sedley.
26. Oman, p. 82.
27. James to all whom it may concern 27 Apr. 1685. *C.S.P. (Dom) 1685*, p. 139.
28. C. D. Chandaman, *The English Public Revenue 1660-1688* (1975), p. 256.
29. *C.S.P. (Dom) 1685*, p. 19.
30. R. H. George, 'Parliamentary Elections and Electioneering in 1685', *Transactions of the Royal Historical Society* (1936); Kenyon, *Sunderland*, p. 114.
31. Luttrell, I, p. 341.
32. *C.S.P. (Dom) 1685*, p. 129.
33. ibid., p. 107.
34. Barrillon to Louis XIV 20/30 Apr. 1685. Baschet.
35. Burnet, III, p. 8 note c.
36. See Chandaman, *English Public Revenue* and 'The Financial Settlement in the Parliament of 1685' in *British Government and Administration* (1974).
37. Barrillon to Louis XIV 16 Feb. 1685. Fox, *Early Part*, Appendix, pp. xxviii, seq.
38. Barrillon to Louis XIV 20 Apr. 1685. Baschet.
39. Barrillon to Louis XIV 23 May 1685. Fox, *Early Part*, appendix p. lxxvi.
40. Barrillon to Louis XIV 28 Feb. 1685 and 14 Apr. 1685. Fox, *Early Part*, appendix pp. lii, liii, lx.
41. Kenyon, *Sunderland*, p. 115.
42. Luttrell, I, p. 343; Burnet, III, p. 35; Evelyn, III, p. 440 note 4 and p. 445.
43. Burnet, III, p. 16; Evelyn, III, p. 444.
44. Clarke, II, pp. 14-15.
45. Evelyn, III, p. 443.
46. ibid., p. 445.
47. Add MSS 15896, f. 56 v.
48. Chandaman, *English Public Revenue*, p. 256.
49. ibid., pp. 261-79.

Chapter 13
1. Possibly the best biography of Monmouth remains Allan Fea, *King Monmouth* (1902), but for the military side of Monmouth's career Charles Chevenix Trench, *The Western Rising* (1969) is first class.
2. Ailesbury, I, p. 131.

3. In his biography of Shaftesbury Professor Haley writes (p. 464) 'Shaftesbury never explicitly committed himself to the claims of the Duke of Monmouth and there are signs that he would have preferred a different solution if it could be arranged.' On the other hand Professor Haley admits (p. 634) that during the meeting of the Oxford Parliament Shaftesbury had advocated settling the Crown on the Duke of Monmouth.

4. For the origins of the invasion see Emerson, *Monmouth's Rebellion*, chaps I-II.

5. J. Welwood, *Memoirs of the most material transactions in England for the last hundred years* (1700), appendix XV, pp. 377-8.

6. See Patrick Hume's narrative in G. H. Rose, *A Selection from the Papers of the Earls of Marchmont* (1831), p. 7.

7. The declaration is printed in full in G. Roberts, *The Life, Progress and Rebellion of James Duke of Monmouth* (1844), I, chap. XV; for Ferguson see *Robert Ferguson the Plotter* (1887). His confession for which I searched in vain when I wrote my biography of John Wildman has been discovered among William III's state papers in the Public Record Office. According to J. Bramston, *Autobiography* (1845), p. 188 Monmouth declared that he had signed the declaration without reading it.

8. In Sir George Clark's view it was a time of industrial depression in the clothing towns in the west so that 'poverty and unemployment among the wage-earners were Monmouth's recruiting agents'; David Ogg, *England in the Reign of James II and William III* (1955), p. 149 casts doubts on this and says that Monmouth's army consisted mainly of peasants.

9. Sunderland to Albemarle 13 June 1685. *C.S.P. (Dom) 1685*, p. 195.

10. James to William 2 June 1685. Dalrymple II, pt. I, bk. II, p. 22.

11. Burnet, III, p. 25 note p. Nesca Robb, *William of Orange* (1966), rejects any suggestion that William encouraged or helped Monmouth. But it seems to have been common knowledge in Amsterdam that Argyll and Monmouth were planning expeditions. It would have been remarkable if William had not known about them. He may well have closed his eyes to what was going on. cf. Winston Churchill's ironical remarks in his *Marlborough*, chap. 12. Stephen Baxter in his life of *William III* (1966), does not discuss the question.

12. James to William 17 June 1685. Dalrymple, pt. I, bk. II, p. 23.

13. Sunderland to Albemarle 14 June 1685. *C.S.P. (Dom) 1685*, p. 196.

14. Churchill to James 17 June 1685 from Bridport. *H.M.C. Northumberland*, III, p. 99.

15. Sunderland to Somerset 18 June 1685; Sunderland to Churchill 19 June 1685. *C.S.P. (Dom) 1685*, p. 209.

16. Sunderland to Churchill 19 June 1685; James to Somerset and Beaufort 19 June 1685. ibid., p. 209.

17. Godolphin to Feversham 21 June 1685. ibid., p. 217; James to Somerset 21 June 1685. ibid., p. 218.

18. Sunderland to Feversham 29 June 1685. ibid., p. 232.

19. Sunderland to Feversham, loc. cit.; Sunderland to Albemarle *C.S.P. (Dom) 1685*, p. 234.

20. *ut supra*, loc. cit.

21. Trench, *Western Rising*, pp. 186-7.

22. *H.M.C. Stopford Sackville*, p. 18.

23. Ailesbury, I, p. 119.

24. Bramston, *Autobiography*, p. 207.

25. Barrillon to Louis XIV. Dalrymple, pt. I, bk. III, p. 102.
26. Fea, *King Monmouth*, pp. 318-19.
27. Cecil Price, *Cold Caleb* (1956), chap. 12.
28. Ailesbury, I, p. 132.
29. Macaulay, *The History of England* (1886), I, p. 348; he goes on to write [the King] 'went into a rage with Saxton, an informer who had appeared as a witness against Delamere'. Saxon, not Saxton, was later convicted of perjury, fraud and flogged. Macaulay misrepresents this trial; he says that Jeffreys 'conducted himself, as was his wont, insolently and unjustly'. But as Professor G. W. Keeton points out in his book *Lord Chancellor Jeffreys* (1965), pp. 342-7 the Lord Chancellor acted courteously and fairly and summed up impartially. Ailesbury, who was a cousin of Delamere, was told by the King that he would 'come off' and that his trial had been ordered 'to convince his subjects that he had named persons that would not find a man guilty right or wrong'. *Memoirs*, I, p. 136.
30. Professor Keeton's biography cited above is an able attempt to whitewash Jeffreys; for the opposite side of the case see David Ogg, pp. 151 seq. who contrasts him with his predecessor and successor as Lord Chief Justice.
31. Sunderland to the High Sheriff of Hampshire 1 Sep. 1685. *C.S.P. (Dom) 1685*, pp. 318, 327.
32. Ailesbury I, pp. 121-2. cf. *D'Orleans Mémoires* (1724), preface, quoted by Turner, p. 282.
33. James to High Sheriff of Hertfordshire 27 Sep. 1685. *C.S.P. (Dom) 1685*, p. 337.
34. James VII to Lords of Secret Committee of the Privy Council in Scotland. *H.M.C.* 15th report pt. VIII, p. 105.
35. James to Colonels of regiments 16 July 1685. *H.M.C. Hastings*, II, p. 179.
36. Barrillon to Louis XIV 6 Sep. 1685. Baschet; Ailesbury, I, p. 121; Luttrell, I, p. 355.
37. James to William 18 Aug. 1685. *C.S.P. (Dom) 1685*, p. 307.
38. James to William 30 Oct. 1685. ibid., p. 373.
39. H. C. Foxcroft, *A Character of the Trimmer* (1946), p. 216.
40. ibid., p. 217.
41. Kenyon, *Sunderland*, pp. 125-6.
42. Clarke, II, pp. 48-50.
43. ibid., pp. 53-4.
44. James to William 29 Dec. 1685. *C.S.P. (Dom) 1685*, p. 420.

Chapter 14
1. Luttrell, I, p. 362, Nov. 1685.
2. Order of 23 Dec. 1685. *C.S.P. (Dom) 1685*, p. 419.
3. For a detailed discussion of the historiography see Maurice Ashley, 'James II and the revolution of 1688: some reflections on the historiography' in *Historical Essays presented to David Ogg* (1963), pp. 185 seq.
4. Macpherson, I, p. 51. Mr Turner in his *James II*, p. 307 writes 'this report is unfortunately not contemporary and may only represent what James wished posterity to think of him.' But what he said was the same as he said later, e.g. to Burnet and Dom Pedro Ronquillo. I have little doubt it is authentic.
5. Burnet, III, p. 97.
6. James to Queensberry 16 July 1685. *H.M.C. Buccleuch*, I, p. 215.

Notes

7. Sunderland to deputy lieutenants of Warwickshire. *C.S.P. (Dom) 1685*, p. 226.
8. Letter of 12 Aug. 1686. J. Mackintosh, *History of the Revolution in England in 1688* (1834), p. 678.
9. Keeton, *Jeffreys*, pp. 297-9; F. J. Powicke, *The Reverend Richard Baxter under the Cross 1662-1691* (1927), pp. 136-50.
10. Burnet, II, p. 97. See note to chap. 12; Dr Owen Wynne to Sir William Trumbull 21 Dec. 1685. *H.M.C. Downshire*, I, p. 79.
11. Barrillon to Louis XIV 29 Oct. 1685. Baschet.
12. Burnet, III, p. 69.
13. Barrillon to Louis XIV 29 Oct. 1685. Baschet. For James's attitude to the revocation see Maurice Ashley, *The Glorious Revolution of 1688* (1966), pp. 63-4.
14. 28 June 1686, cit. R. Durand, 'Louis XIV et Jacques II à la veille de la révolution de 1688', *Revue d'Histoire moderne et contemporaine*, X (1908).
15. Add MSS 34512, f. 48.
16. Barrillon to Louis XIV 3 May 1686. Baschet.
17. See note 8 above.
18. James to William 26 Jan. 1686. Dalrymple, III, p. 109.
19. Barrillon to Louis XIV 3 May 1686. Baschet.
20. Reresby, pp. 416-17.
21. James to Clarendon 18 Feb. and 6 Apr. 1686. Singer, I, pp. 258, 339.
22. Sunderland to Clarendon 14 Jan. 1686. *C.S.P. (Dom) 1685-1686*, p. 172.
23. Sir John Loudon, *Decisions of the Lords of Council and Sessions 1678-1712*, pp. 415, 419; Barrillon to Louis XIV 19 Apr. 1686. Baschet.
24. Luttrell 16 June 1686: James to Parliament of Scotland 26 Aug. 1686. *Cal. Cl. S.P.* V, 666; P. Hume Brown, *History of Scotland* (1902), chap. VII; Ogg, pp. 173 seq.; Clarke, II, pp. 64 seq.
25. John Kenyon, *The Stuart Constitution 1603-1688* (1964), pp. 401 seq.
26. Sunderland to Obadiah Walker 15 Aug. 1686. *C.S.P. (Dom) 1685-1686*, p. 241.
27. Singer, II, pp. 472 seq.
28. James to William 22 Aug. 1686. *C.S.P. (Dom) 1685-1686* p. 246; William to Sunderland 12 Sep. 1686. Dalrymple, III, p. 31; Luttrell, I, p. 385.
29. James to Archbishops of Canterbury and York. *C.S.P. (Dom) 1686-1687*, pp. 57-8.
30. James to Bishop of London 14 June 1686. ibid., p. 171.
31. ibid., p. 298.
32. Ogg, pp. 175 seq. who shows that the Ecclesiastical Commission was not identical with the Court of High Commission abolished by the Long Parliament.
33. Evelyn, IV, pp. 496-7; V. de S. Pinto, *Sir Charles Sedley* (1905), pp. 352 seq.; Reresby, p. 460; P. Bertie to the Countess of Rutland 6 Feb. 1686. *H.M.C. Rutland*, II, pp. 102, 203; Luttrell, I, p. 372; *D.N.B. sub* Catherine Sedley.
34. Clarke, II, p. 93.
35. Barrillon to Louis XIV 1 July 1686. Baschet; James to William 29 June 1686. Dalrymple, II, p. 303; newsletter 1 July 1686. *C.S.P. (Dom) 1685-1686*, p.193.
36. Barrillon to Louis XIV 19 Dec. 1686. Dalrymple, II, p. 104.

37. Barrillon to Louis XIV 31 May 1686. Baschet.
38. Barrillon to Louis XIV 3 and 7 Sep. 1685. Baschet.
39. Barrillon to Louis XIV 9 Sep. 1686. Baschet.
40. Bonrepaus to Louis XIV 17 May 1686. Baschet.
41. James to William 18 Feb., 16 Feb. and 2 Apr. 1686. *C.S.P. (Dom) 1685-1686*, pp. 39, 49; *C.S.P. (Dom) 1686-1687*, p. 94.
42. Kenyon, *Sunderland*, pp. 121 seq.
43. Singer, II, pp. 116 seq.
44. ibid., loc. cit.
45. James II to Parliament of Scotland 26 Aug. 1686. *Cal. Cl. S.P.*, V, p. 666: Hume Brown, *History of Scotland*, II, p. 435.
46. James to William 18 Mar. 1678. Dalrymple, pt. I, bk. V, pp. 52-3.
47. Kenyon, *Stuart Constitution*, pp. 410-11.

Chapter 15
1. J. R. Jones, *The Revolution of 1688 in England* (1972), p. 119.
2. See the argument in Haley, *Shaftesbury*, chap. xxix.
3. The phrase 'closeting' is used by James's official biographer. Clarke, II, p. 183; Barrillon described what he was doing and said that his demand for definite undertakings was 'considered by many an encroachment on their liberty and privileges' cit. Turner, p. 322. According to Kenyon, *Sunderland*, pp. 147-8 it is doubtful if Sunderland approved of the idea which seems to have originated with James himself.
4. Clarke, p. 111.
5. See p. 157 above.
6. Clarke, II, p. 114.
7. ibid., p. 115.
8. J. R. Bloxam, *Magdalen College and King James II 1686-1688* (Oxford 1886), pp. 47, 66, 69; Farmer's defence is given on pp. 72-4.
9. ibid., p. 4.
10. Clarke, II, p. 118 and note; Burnet, III, pp. 177-9 and note on p. 178.
11. Warrant of 3 July 1687. *C.S.P. (Dom) 1687-1688*, p. 23.
12. Kenyon, *Sunderland*, p. 149.
13. For Bantam see C. R. Boxer, *The Dutch Seaborne Empire 1600-1800* (1963), pp. 188-9, 198-9.
14. For Dijkvelt's mission see Burnet, III, pp. 164 seq.; *Correspondentie van Willem III en van Hans Willem Bentinck* (ed. N. Japikse, The Hague 1927-37), II, pp. 746-51; N. Japikse, *Prins Willem III* (Amsterdam 1930), pp. 219 seq.; J. Muilenberg, 'The embassy of Dykvelt', *Nebraska University Studies*, XX (1920); Baxter, *William III*, pp. 218-20.
15. James to William 20 May 1687 from Windsor. Dalrymple, pt. I, bk. V, p. 53.
16. James to William 10 May 1687 from Whitehall. ibid., p. 52.
17. James to William 28 May 1687. ibid., p. 54. The letters carried back by Dijkvelt are in ibid., pp. 56 seq.
18. ibid., p. 55.
19. Most of these are printed in *C.S.P. (Dom) 1687-1689*. I am obliged to Mr J. D. Cantrell of the Public Record Office for distinguishing the different methods used by James. R. H. George in his article on 'The charters granted to English parliamentary corporations in 1688', *English Historical Review*, 55, pp. 47 seq. says that of thirty-five reincorporations a dozen were

forfeited as a result of *quo warranto* actions and twenty-three surrendered their charters under pressures of one kind or another.
20. Jones, *The Revolution of 1688*, p. 136.
21. *C.S.P. (Dom) 1687-1689*, pp. 34, 55, 85. The warrant of 25 July was revoked on 20 Oct.
22. Sunderland to Mayor and Aldermen of Leeds. ibid., p. 117.
23. ibid., p. 57; Cecil Roth, *A History of the Jews in England* (1964), p. 183.
24. Clarke, II, pp. 108 seq.
25. Oman, p. 104.
26. Kenyon, *Sunderland*, p. 163.
27. J. Fitzpatrick to William of Orange. *C.S.P. (Dom) 1687-1689*, p. 66.
28. Halifax to William 5 Sep. 1687. Dalrymple, II, V, p. 84, misdated 1 Sep.
29. Bloxam, *Magdalen College*, pp. 84 seq.
30. W. Sherwin to T. Turner 31 July 1687. ibid., p. 79.
31. ibid., pp. 85 seq.; Sunderland to the Commissioners visiting Magdalen College. *C.S.P. (Dom) 1687-1689*, p. 89.
32. Clarke, II, p. 124. The monk's name was Alban Francis.
33. Ogg, pp. 175 seq.
34. Clarke, II, p. 124.
35. See Sunderland's letter of 22 Dec. 1687 from Whitehall and James's letters to the Pope in Add MSS 93418, ff. 31 seq.

Chapter 16

1. Luttrell, I, pp. 401 seq.
2. Sunderland to the Duke of Newcastle, Lord Molyneux and others 25 Oct. 1687. *C.S.P. (Dom) 1687-1689*, pp. 87-8.
3. Carswell, *The Descent on England*, p. 106.
4. ibid., appendix pp. 238-43.
5. Clarendon to William 15 Dec. 1687. *C.S.P. (Dom) 1687-1689*, p. 118.
6. G. F. Duckett, *Penal Laws and Test Act* (1883), I, p. 364.
7. ibid., p. 354.
8. Jones, *The Revolution of 1688*, chap. 6.
9. ibid., p. 169.
10. Rawlinson MSS A 139 B; Duckett, *Penal Laws*, I, pp. 213 seq.
11. Earl of Bath to Sunderland *C.S.P. (Dom) 1687-1689*, p. 287. cf. Duckett, *Penal Laws*, II, pp. 217, 270, 300.
12. ibid., I, p. 102.
13. ibid., p. 102.
14. Reresby, p. 497.
15. Halifax to William 25 July 1688. Dalrymple, pt. I, bk. V, pp. 116-17.
16. Campana, II, p. 181.
17. Letter of 8 Dec. 1687. Nottingham University Library PA 21 10a.
18. Burnet, III, p. 205.
19. Halifax, *Complete Works* (ed. John Kenyon), p. 106.
20. Clarke, II, p. 133.
21. Warrant to Lord Dartmouth 24 Feb. 1688. *C.S.P. (Dom) 1687-1689*, p. 151.
22. James to Lord Jeffreys 25 Feb. 1688. ibid., p. 152.
23. Barrillon to Louis XIV 7/17 May 1688. Baschet.
24. Kenyon, *Sunderland*, p. 164.
25. ibid., p. 177.

26. Barrillon to Louis XIV 6/16 Oct. 1687. Dalrymple, II, pt. 1. bk. V, p. 138.
27. This convention was found among the papers of Thomas Butler, Lord Ossory, who in 1678 was in command of the British forces in Holland and died in 1680. Barrillon to Louis XIV, 1 Mar. 1688. Baschet.
28. According to the tables published by C. D. Chandaman, *The English Public Revenue*, the receipts from Easter 1687 to Easter 1688 were £2,133,710 and the issues £2,175,918.
29. 'The Financial Relations of Louis XIV and James II' by R. H. George. *Journal of Modern History*, 3 (1931), pp. 412-13.
30. Jones, *Revolution of 1688*, pp. 134-5.
31. Barrillon told Louis XIV on 30 Apr. that if a parliament met that summer the Dutch would have sent a fleet to stir up agitation so as to prevent the repeal of the penal laws and Tests and that this was why James postponed summoning a parliament until November. Baschet PRO 31/3/177 ff. 449v and 451. It seems to me that this was a mere speculation on Barrillon's part and highly unlikely.
32. Rawlinson MSS 139 B f. 105.

Chapter 17
1. Barrillon to Louis XIV 22 Mar., 27 Apr., 7 and 14 May 1688. Baschet.
2. James to William 15 May 1688. *C.S.P. (Dom) 1687-1689*, p. 198.
3. Singer, II, p. 171. G. D'Oyley, *William Sancroft* (1821), p. 260.
4. ibid., p. 172.
5. Kenyon, *The Stuart Constitution*, p. 126.
6. Singer, II, pp. 479-80.
7. Clarke, II, pp. 154-5.
8. D'Oyley, *Sancroft*, I, p. 224.
9. Evelyn, IV, p. 156.
10. Reresby, p. 499.
11. Singer, II, p. 177.
12. Barrillon to Louis XIV 24 May 1688. Baschet.
13. Burnet, III, p. 220; Kenyon, *Sunderland*, p. 195.
14. Luttrell, I, p. 442.
15. Clarke, II, p. 157.
16. Barrillon to Louis XIV 16 Feb. 1685. Baschet.
17. Oman, pp. 108-9.
18. Singer, p. 176.
19. *C.S.P. (Dom) 1687-1689*, p. 211.
20. ibid., p. 212.
21. Clarke, II, p. 161.
22. Singer, II, p. 176.
23. Oman, pp. 113-14; Evelyn, IV, p. 597; Luttrell, I, p. 453; Sunderland to Tyrconnel, 11 Aug. 1688. *C.S.P. (Dom) 1687-1689*, p. 249.
24. Kenyon, *Sunderland*, pp. 197 seq.
25. Luttrell, I, p. 446; Barrillon to Louis XIV 28 June 1688. Dalrymple II, pt. 1, bk. V, p. 157.
26. Clarendon to William 7 July 1688. *C.S.P. (Dom) 1687-1689*, pp. 229-30.
27. Sunderland to the Duke of Beaufort and other Lords Lieutenant. ibid., p. 239.
28. Clarke, II, pp. 165 seq.
29. Burnet, III, p. 280.

30. James to William 22 July, 24 July, 13 July, 31 Aug. 1688. Dalrymple, II, pt. 1, bk. V, pp. 162-4.
31. James to William 13 July 1688. ibid., p. 163.
32. Reresby, p. 503.
33. James to William 22 July 1688. Dalrymple, II, pt. 1, bk. V, p. 163.
34. I have discussed in some detail my view of William's conduct in *The Glorious Revolution of 1688* (1968), chaps V, VI and VIII.
35. Nottingham to William 18 May 1687. Dalrymple II, pt. 1, bk. V, p. 64.
36. *Receuil des Instructions données aux Ambassadeurs*, vol. XXV (1929), pp. 403 seq.; Dalrymple II, bk. V, pp. 152-3.
37. Barrillon to Louis XIV 16 Aug. 1688. ibid., p. 153.
38. Barrillon to Louis XIV 8 Sep. 1688. ibid., p. 155.
39. Singer, II, p. 187; Louis XIV to Barrillon 20 Sep. 1688. Dalrymple II, pt. 1, bk. V, p. 166; Sunderland to Skelton 27 Aug. 1688. cit. G. H. Jones, *Charles Middleton* (Chicago 1967), p. 213.
40. Middleton to D'Albeville 11 Sep. 1688. Add MSS 41823, f. 72.
41. James to William 17 Sep. 1688 from Windsor. Dalrymple II, bk. V, p. 164.
42. R. R. Steele, *Royal Proclamations* (Oxford 1910), I, pp. 460-2; Singer, II, p. 188. The proclamation was agreed to on 21 Sep. and published in the *London Gazette* on 24 Sep.

Chapter 18
1. Evelyn, IV, p. 597.
2. Singer, II, p. 189.
3. Sunderland to Berwick 22 Sep. 1688. *C.S.P. (Dom) 1687-1689*, p. 280.
4. Luttrell, I, p. 463.
5. Singer, II, p. 189.
6. *C.S.P. (Dom) 1687-1689*, p. 281.
7. ibid., loc. cit.
8. James to Tyrconnel 25 Sep. 1688. ibid., p. 283.
9. Sunderland to Newcastle. ibid., p. 289.
10. ibid., p. 284.
11. ibid., p. 287.
12. Aston to Sunderland. ibid., pp. 287-8.
13. Middleton to D'Albeville. Add MSS 41823, f. 71; cf. Middleton to D'Albeville 11 Sep. 1688. ibid., f. 72.
14. Middleton to D'Albeville. Add MSS 41823, f. 77.
15. Singer, II, p. 189.
16. King James II's proclamation. Ashley, *Glorious Revolution*, pp. 205-6; Clarke, II, p. 184; Luttrell, I, p. 464.
17. Singer, II, p. 194.
18. ibid., p. 192.
19. D'Oyley, *Sancroft*, pp. 339-44; James's concessions were reported to the States-General by Van Citters on 19 Oct. Add MSS 34512, f. 108.
20. Reresby, pp. 509-10.
21. James to Dartmouth from Whitehall. *H.M.C. Dartmouth*, V, p. 144.
22. ibid., p. 158.
23. Dalrymple, II, bk. VI, p. 136.
24. *C.S.P. (Dom) 1687-1689*, p. 386.
25. ibid., p. 329.
26. Sunderland to the Duke of Newcastle and the Bishop of Durham 6 Oct. 1688; Middleton to the Duke of Newcastle 30 Oct. 1688. ibid., pp. 301,

335. The hackney coachmen in London were asked by the King to provide 200 horses for war service. Luttrell *sub* 2 Oct. 1688.
27. Middleton to the Duke of Newcastle 30 Oct. 1688. *C.S.P. (Dom) 1687-1689*, p. 334. Similar letters were sent to other Lords Lieutenant. ibid., pp. 334-5.
28. *H.M.C. Dartmouth*, p. 169.
29. Ashley, *Glorious Revolution*, p. 204.
30. Singer, II, pp. 196, 199.
31. cf. Jones, *Middleton*, chap. XI.
32. Middleton to Tyrconnel 30 Oct. 1688. *C.S.P. (Dom) 1687-1689*, pp. 336-7; Clarendon's diary 26 Oct. 1688. Singer, II, p. 197.
33. Clarke, II, p. 203 and note.
34. Singer, II, p. 501.

Chapter 19
1. Middleton to Bristol 6 Nov. 1688; Sunderland to Beaufort 18 Oct. 1688; Sunderland to Bath 18 Oct. 1688. *C.S.P. (Dom) 1687-1689*, pp. 321, 322, 343.
2. Middleton to Norfolk 6 Nov. 1688. ibid., p. 342.
3. Middleton to Alderman Wagstaff 6 Nov., 1688; Middleton to Beaufort 12 Nov. 1688. ibid., pp. 342, 347.
4. Singer, II, pp. 497 seq.
5. Middleton to Beaufort 8 Nov. 1688. *C.S.P. (Dom) 1687-1689*, p. 341.
6. ibid., p. 343.
7. ibid., p. 345.
8. James to Dartmouth 9 Nov. 1688 *H.M.C. Dartmouth*, p. 190.
9. James to Dartmouth 12 Nov. 1688. ibid., pp. 194-5.
10. Bath to Middleton 6 Nov. 1688. Add MSS 41805, f. 129.
11. Middleton to Lord Mayor of London 13 Nov. 1688. *C.S.P. (Dom) 1687-1689*, p. 348.
12. Middleton to Preston 20 Nov. 1688, ibid., p. 357.
13. James to Tyrconnel from Salisbury. ibid., p. 358.
14. Singer, II, p. 205.
15. ibid., p. 206.
16. ibid., pp. 204-5.
17. Middleton to Godolphin 22 Nov. 1688. *C.S.P. (Dom) 1687-1689*, p. 319.
18. Middleton to Godolphin, loc. cit.
19. Longueville to Hatton 22 Nov. 1688; Nottingham to Hatton 25 Nov. 1688. *Hatton Correspondence*, II, pp. 110-11.
20. Middleton to Preston 23 Nov. 1688 from Salisbury. *C.S.P. (Dom) 1687-1689*, p. 360
21. James to Dartmouth 25 Nov. 1688. Dalrymple, II, pt. VI, p. 243.
22. Middleton to Hales 22 Nov. 1688 from Salisbury. *C.S.P. (Dom) 1687-1689*, p. 359.
23. Clarke, II, p. 229.
24. James to Dartmouth 29 Nov. 1688. *H.M.C. Dartmouth*, p. 219.
25. Berkeley to Dartmouth 3 Dec. 1688. ibid., p. 222.
26. Oman, p. 128.
27. ibid., loc. cit.
28. Dartmouth to James 3 Dec. 1688 from Spithead. Dalrymple, II, pt. VI, pp. 245 seq.; E. B. Powley, *The English Navy in the Revolution of 1688* (1928), pp. 134-6.

29. Oman, pp. 130 seq.
30. Singer, II, p. 211.
31. Roger Jones to Lord Hatton 28 Nov. 1688. *Hatton Correspondence*, II, p. 116.
32. ibid., loc. cit.
33. Singer, II, p. 211.
34. *C.S.P. (Dom) 1687-1689*, p. 369.
35. Longueville to Hatton. *Hatton Correspondence*, II, p. 120.
36. Add MSS 18675, f. 48.
37. *H.M.C. Dartmouth*, p. 226.
38. Clarke, II, p. 249.
39. Feversham to William 11 Dec. 1688 from Uxbridge. *C.S.P. (Dom) 1687-1689*, pp. 377-8; Middleton to the Commissioners 1 Dec. 1688 and proceedings of the Commissioners. *H.M.C. Finch*, II, pp. 193-4.
40. Add MSS 32095, ff. 303 seq.; Lady Dartmouth to Lord Dartmouth. *H.M.C. Dartmouth*, p. 234.
41. James to Winchelsea 12 Dec. 1688 from Feversham. Add MSS 32095, f. 298.
42. Sir Henry Shere to Lord Dartmouth 17 Dec. 1688 from Whitehall. *H.M.C. Dartmouth*, p. 236.
43. Newsletter from London *C.S.P. (Dom) 1687-1689*, p. 381; Clarke, II, pp. 261 seq.
44. Macpherson, *Original Papers*, I, p. 300. This story is not in Clarke, but sounds authentic.
45. Clarke, II, p. 278.
46. Clarke, II, p. 278.

Chapter 20
1. *Dangeau Mémoires* (1882), II, pp. 202-3.
2. Oman, chap. V quoting the *Memoirs of Madame de Sévigné*.
3. James to Preston 26 (?) Jan. 1689. Add MSS 34516, f. 38.
4. *Dangeau Mémoires*, II, p. 293.
5. James to Dartmouth 19 Jan. 1689. *H.M.C. Dartmouth*, p. 252; *Dangeau Mémoires*, II, p. 326.
6. James to Tyrconnel 12 Jan. 1689; Tyrconnel to James 29 Jan. 1689. cit. Bagwell, *Ireland under the Stuarts*, III, p. 198.
7. Oman, p. 153; *Dangeau Mémoires*, I, p. 336.
8. Tyrconnel to James, *ut supra*.
9. *Lettres Historiques de Madame de Sévigné* (ed. J-B. Ebeling, 1934), p. 207.
10. D'Avaux to Louvois 19 Mar. 1689 from Cork. D'Avaux, *D'Avaux Négociations de M. le Comte d'Avaux en Irelande* (Dublin 1934), I, pp. 43-4.
11. D'Avaux to Louis XIV 24 Mar. 1689. ibid., p. 49.
12. D'Avaux to Louis XIV 13 Apr. 1689. Baschet.
13. D'Avaux to Louis XIV 26 Apr. 1689. *Négotiations*, I, 109.
14. Melford to Lord Waldegrave 8 May 1969 from Dublin. Macpherson, I, p. 303.
15. Clarke, II, p. 371 note.
16. ibid., p. 355; D'Avaux *Négotiations*, I, pp. 152-3.
17. Melfort to Waldgrave, *ut supra*.
18. D'Avaux to Louis XIV 5 June 1689. *Négotiations*, I, pp. 188 seq.
19. James to D'Avaux 4 June 1689. Macpherson, I, p. 308.

20. Louis XIV to D'Avaux 29 May/8 June 1689. D'Avaux *Négotiations*, I, p. 400.
21. G. Walker, *A true account of the siege of Londonderry* (1689), pp. 32, 34, 37.
22. Dundee to James 1 Sep. 1689. Macpherson, II, pp. 372-3.
23. Clarke, II, p. 378.
24. D'Avaux to Louis XIV 25 Aug./4 Sep. 1689. D'Avaux, *Négotiations*, I, p. 433.
25. D'Avaux to Louvois 17 Sep. 1689. D'Avaux, *Négotiations*, I, p. 477.
26. James to Waldegrave, Macpherson, I, pp. 314-15.
27. D'Avaux to Louvois, *ut supra*; James to Waldegrave, *ut supra*; Melfort to James Oct. 1689. Macpherson, I, pp. 319 seq.
28. Bagwell, *Ireland under the Stuarts*, III, p. 267.
29. D'Avaux to Louvois 11 Oct. 1689 from Ardee. D'Avaux, *Négotiations*, I, p. 517.
30. D'Avaux to Louis XIV 25 Jan. 1690. ibid., I, pp. 629 seq.
31. Cloudesley Shovell to the Earl of Nottingham 15 Mar. 1690 from Milford Haven. *H.M.C. Finch*, II, p. 274.
32. D'Avaux to Louis XIV, *Négotiations*, p. 650 etc.
33. William to Waldeck 14 Feb. 1690. P. L. Müller, *Wilhelm III von Oranien und Georg Friedrich von Waldeck* (The Hague 1873), II, p. 215.
34. Singer, II, pp. 512-14.
35. Clarke, II, p. 392.
36. ibid., p. 386.
37. Good secondary accounts of the battle of the Boyne are by Hilaire Belloc in his *James II* (1928), D. C. Boulger, *The Battle of the Boyne* (1911), Sir Charles Petrie, *The Marshal Duke of Berwick* (1953) and J. G. Simms, *Jacobite Ireland 1685-91* (1969). Dr Simms has also contributed articles on the subject to the *Irish Sword*, e.g. 'Eyewitnesses of the Boyne' in vol. VI. The primary authorities on James's side include John Stevens, who however got nowhere nearer the battle than Duleek, Berwick's *Memoirs* and *A Jacobite Narrative of the War in Ireland* (ed. J. T. Gilbert, 1879). I have followed Dr Simms's account, but do not take the view that this was a 'defensive battle'. The main evidence for this appears to be that the royalists were ordered to send away their baggage before the battle, but that is by no means conclusive. All battles are in a sense defensive, but James could have withdrawn farther south or west if he wished; William gave him ample time to do so. That would have meant surrendering Dublin and demoralizing most of Catholic Ireland. James had to fight where and when he did to stand any chance of regaining his throne. To fortify himself in some corner of Ireland, e.g. Connaught or Munster would have been an open confession of failure. James himself makes this point plainly enough in his own account of the battle, clearly taken directly from the ninth volume of his memoirs in Clarke, II, pp. 393-401.
38. *The Journal of John Stevens* (ed. R. H. Murray, Oxford 1913), p. 123.
39. Simms, *Jacobite Ireland*, pp. 152-3 and note.
40. Clarke, II, pp. 393-4.
41. This point is made both by Hilaire Belloc and Sir Charles Petrie.

Chapter 21
1. *Cambridge Modern History*, V, p. 58.

2. James to Pope Innocent XI 22 Jan. 1689. *H.M.C. Stuart Papers at Windsor Castle* I, pp. 35-7.
3. James to Pope Alexander VIII 21 July 1690. ibid., p. 53.
4. *Letters of Elizabeth Charlotte Duchess of Orleans* (ed. G. Stevenson, 1924), 10/20 Aug. 1690.
5. ibid., 27 Aug./6 Sep. 1690.
6. ibid., 10/20 Aug. 1690.
7. Oman, pp. 160-2.
8. James to Edward French Nov. 1694. *H.M.C. (Stuart Papers),* I, p. 92; Clarke, II, p. 527.
9. James to Berwick 14 Jan. 1692, ibid., p. 68.
10. Abbé de la Trappe to James 24 Mar. 1691. ibid., I, p. 64.
11. Melfort to Cardinal of Norfolk 7 Mar. 1692. ibid., p. 270.
12. Dalrymple *Memoirs*, I, pp. 460-7. cit. Clarke, II, p. 478 note.
13. Clarke, II, pp. 479 seq.
14. Macpherson, I, p. 433.
15. Melfort to Abbé Leti 4 July 1692. Add MSS 37661, f. 4v.
16. *Stuart Papers,* II, p. 328.
17. Clarke, II, p. 474.
18. Mary of Modena to Mme Priolo 29 Aug. 1700. *Stuart Papers,* I, p. 41.
19. Turner, p. 496.
20. Clarke, II, p. 547.
21. See the discussion in G. H. Jones, *The Mainstream of Jacobitism* (Cambridge, Mass. 1954), pp. 49-51.
22. Macpherson, I, p. 545.
23. Clarke, II, p. 528.
24. *Papers of Devotion,* p. 57.
25. *H.M.C. Stuart Papers,* I, p. 114 seq. Entry Warrants ff. 196, 246.
26. *Papers of Devotion,* p. 139.
27. ibid., p. 61.
28. Carte MSS 181, f. 680. cf. Oman, pp. 187-8; Macpherson, I, p. 569.
29. Clarke, II, pp. 561-2.
30. ibid., pp. 575-7.
31. ibid., p. 588; *Papers of Devotion,* p. 53.
32. Clarke, II, pp. 590-1; *Papers of Devotion,* pp. 83, 96; *Stuart Papers,* II, p. 328.
33. Nov. 1696. *Papers of Devotion,* p. 99.
34. Matthew Prior to the Second Marquis of Halifax. cit. Oman, pp. 187-8.
35. Account of James's last illness by one of the Sisters of Chaillot. *Stuart Papers,* II, p. 263.
36. *Stuart Papers,* II, p. 345.
37. ibid., II, p. 263.
38. As note 36 *supra.*
39. Clarke II, pp. 602-5.
40. *Stuart Papers,* II, p. 345.

Chapter 22
1. See Appendix below.
2. That is the letters to the Countess of Litchfield and to Susan Bellasyse. The Countess of Litchfield was James II's niece; there is no suggestion that she was at any time his mistress.

3. See p. 143 above.
4. See p. 192 above.
5. See p. 141 above.
6. See p. 280 above.
7. See p. 286-7 above.
8. See Maurice Ashley, *Charles II*, chap. 4.
9. See Kenyon, *Sunderland*, chaps 4 and 5.
10. I discuss the historiography in more detail in my essay in *Historical Essays 1600-1750*, pp. 185 seq.
11. See p. 185 above.
12. See Kenyon, *Sunderland*, pp. 219-23.
13. See Clarke, II, pp. 132, 133, 187, 203.

Appendix
1. Sells, p. 52.
2. Churchill, *Marlborough*, I, pp. 356-7.
3. Sells, p. 22.
4. ibid., p. 16.
5. cf. Clarke, I, p. xxii; Lord Herries, who visited the Scots College at Paris in September 1717, wrote that he 'saw a collection of original letters, journals and many other papers in four volumes in folio finely bound all writ by the late King James'. *Herries Memoirs*, p. xxi. These presumably were the four volumes now at Windsor Castle.
6. *Papers of Devotion*, introduction.
7. *ut supra*, note 2.
8. Clarke, I, p. xiii.
9. ibid., loc. cit.
10. Add MSS 35839, f. 292 v.
11. Burnet, I, p. 291.
12. Lord Holland, preface to Fox, *Early Part*, p. xx.
13. Add MSS 35839, ff. 292-3: this is entitled 'Some Account of James's Memoirs given me [Lord Hardwicke] by Lord Shelburne'. Shelburne and Isaac Barré visited Paris in the summer of 1771.
14. Sir John Dalrymple to the first Earl of Dartmouth. *H.M.C. Dartmouth*, pp. 446-7.
15. Holland preface, p. xix note.

Index